Poland

Prague

Regensburg

Hungary

Danube

Russia

...val
...e

Black Sea

Constantinople

Jerusalem

# NIGHT TALES
# OF
# THE SHAMMAS

## Michael Jay Katz

Jason Aronson Inc.
*Northvale, New Jersey*
*London*

**Library of Congress Cataloging-in-Publication Data**


Katz, Michael Jay, 1950–
        Night tales of the Shammas / Michael Jay Katz.
            p.        cm.
        ISBN 0-87668-926-8
        1. Legends, Jewish.      2.  Jews–Germany (West)–Rhineland–
–Miscellanea.
BM530.K38   1988                                                        88-4226
296.1′9–dc19                                                                CIP


Manufactured in the United States of America.

# CONTENTS

h, good evening again, Rabbi. Yes, I know – it is always hard to sleep on the night of the full moon. Well, just put your feet up on the side bench here, and I will open the stove door. Let me push this coal back: there is nothing like that white glow; it washes away the cares of a hard day. I heard your final prayers tonight, Rabbi, and there is no use denying it – you are overworked. Oh yes, even a shammas like me can tell. I kept one eye on you even when I cleaned the dishes, and I saw that you were watching the door, hoping that Reb Elbaum would leave early. And then, Reb Anton stayed to argue about the *Shem ha-Gedolim* passage. Of course you are worn out. . . . So what is that? A story from me? Rabbi, all that I know are the children's tales, the grandmother fables. You need something new and fresh to keep your mind keen. Otherwise you will become an old man like me, and you will find yourself constantly musing and dozing and nodding off in front of the stove.

What do you mean you are already an old man, Rabbi? Old? Do you think that sixty years is old? You are still a child, Rabbi. When you reach eighty, *then* you will be old. . . . You doubt that you will live to see eighty years? If so, Rabbi, then you will never grow old. . . . All right, all right – as I have said, I know no special stories, but listening to

3

you and Reb Anton put me in mind of the last river voyage of Rabbi
Amram.

No, of course it was not the Persian Rabbi Amram, the scholar
who wrote the prayer book *Siddur Rav Amram*. He lived well before
Rashi, hundreds of years before him. No, our Rabbi Amram was
German. This Amram was a fine and pious man—in fact, he was the
chief rabbi of Cologne. Alone, he held together the tiny Jewish community of Cologne in the Dark Middle Ages—but originally he had
moved there from Mainz, where he was raised and where his parents
were buried. . . .

What? Of course there is more, Rabbi: I only closed my eyes for
a moment—can an old man not take a little rest? Now you have
interrupted my thoughts. Let me see, where was I? Yes, yes, as my
grandmother said: "A boat is only good for one voyage, my little man."
Did you ever hear her say that, Rabbi? You never knew her? That is
too bad; you missed a fine woman. Ah well—anyway, Rabbi, I first
heard about Rabbi Amram of Mainz and Cologne from my grandmother, may her soul visit happily with her parents for ever and ever,
amen.

Once upon a time, said my grandmother, there lived in Cologne
on the River Rhine a pious scholar named Rabbi Amram. Rabbi
Amram had a yeshiva; it was the only Jewish school in all of Cologne—but originally Amram had come from Mainz. As you know,
Rabbi, there were few Jews in Cologne in those days, and Rabbi
Amram was the main scholar and the founder of a fine and holy
tradition. (This was still two centuries before all the Jews were expelled
from the city by the Catholic burghers.) When Rabbi Amram reached
seventy years of age, he became very ill. He could not walk up stairs, he
had leg pains every night, he was always wheezing, and he was short
of breath. One day, the Rabbi sent for his pupils in the small back study
room of the old Cologne yeshiva, and the Rabbi said to them: "My
dear young men, I am lying ill and I am about to die. Therefore, I ask
you for this one last good deed: when I die, follow the oldest customs—
wash me and close my eyes and my mouth, dress me in my Sabbath
robes, cover me with sweet spices, curl me like an unborn baby, and
bury me next to my parents in the old Jewish cemetery in Mainz."

The pupils looked at each other. They were silent a moment, and then the senior student replied: "Our dear master, we cannot do this, for it is dangerous to take you so far. You know quite well that Jews are not welcome to travel about in these parts. And what would happen to us if we were caught with a dead body?" Then Rabbi Amram said: "Ah yes, young men, you are right. Let me pray quietly." The Rabbi closed his eyes and he prayed for one hour and for two. His pupils looked at each other, and they waited; still the Rabbi prayed. It was time for the evening prayers. No one moved. The pupils looked at one another: the evening prayer, they remembered, was not an absolute duty, but certainly it was a sacred obligation. How could they forgo it? Was the Rabbi silently reciting the *Shema*? They could not hear; they did not know. There were ten pupils, so they mumbled the evening services together. No one moved from the little back study room, and they stood all night together.

Early the next morning, the Rabbi opened his eyes; his voice was weak. "I have never been in a boat," he said. The pupils did not know what to reply. "Are you here, my sons?" asked the Rabbi. "Yes," answered the young men. "Listen, dear boys," said Rabbi Amram quietly, "when I die, wash my body, put it in an open coffin, and place it in a coffin boat on the River Rhine; then let it go to Mainz by itself. I must be buried beside my parents. Remember, my good pupils: only those who are buried side by side can remain together in Sheol forever."

The next day, Rabbi Amram died. His pupils mourned, and they washed the body; then, they dressed the body in its Sabbath robes, they put it in an open coffin, and they carried it out of the yeshiva in the dead of night. Silently, they passed the great Catholic cathedral–the Dom– in which the three kings of Cologne are buried. (Those kings–Kaspar, Melchior, and Balthazar–were the three wise men who came from the East to see the infant Jesus.) The white shrouded body of Rabbi Amram was draped in black so that it would not be seen at night, and his students gently placed him in a coffin boat on the River Rhine. The young men said a quiet prayer and they pushed the boat off from the shore. Immediately, the little boat went up the stream running directly against the current, and soon on its starboard side it had passed the town of Bruhl at the base of the Eifel range.

The boat moved on smoothly in the center of the dark river. An even wake trailed behind as it passed Bonn on the starboard side of the great River Rhine. Yes, quietly it passed Bonn, with the German academy that is built on old fortifications and with the monastic church of Kreuzberg clearly visible from the river behind and above the Poppelsdorf. You have heard of that church, Rabbi: it has a flight of twenty-eight steps, which the pilgrims ascend on their knees. Then on the port side, the little boat flowed past Konigswinter sitting in front of the Drachenfels Hill crowned by the ruins of a castle; this castle was built by the Archbishop of Cologne, and in that very hill is a cave that once hid the dragon killed by the German hero Siegfried. . . . What is that, Rabbi? No, I am not inventing this – it is exactly as my grand-mother told me.

By morning, Rabbi, the boat was drifting south past Honnef, there at the base of the Siebengebirge Hills. Honnef has the famous spring of Drachenquelle with mineral water that is good both for drinking and for bathing in order to cure all manner of heart and stomach problems. (My grandmother told me that an uncle of hers once regained the sight in his left eye after spending two days at Drachenquelle.)

A stretch of beautiful countryside came and went, and next on the starboard side was Remagen. Perhaps it was fate that old Rabbi Amram had to pass Remagen. Just before the town, on a height overlooking the River Rhine, is the Chapel of Apollinaris. Once long ago, a ship traveling from Milan to Cologne became caught on the chapel rocks in a storm. This ship was carrying the remains of three kings and of the Bishop Apollinaris, and after it ran aground it could not be moved from the spot. An old mystic Jew of Remagen was called to advise. "Captain," he said, "you will not be able to travel farther until the bones of the Bishop are buried right here in this very chapel." The chapel was called the Church of St. Martin at the time, and after Bishop Apollinaris was interred in a stone crypt in the back room of the chapel of St. Martin, the ship suddenly floated from the rocks on a surging tide. The name of the church was later changed to the Chapel of St. Apollinaris. And, Rabbi, Remagen itself has many miraculous buildings – in Remagen, there is a door on the Catholic church that was carved with grotesque animal sculptures by an itinerant angel, ages and ages ago.

All morning, the little boat slipped gently upriver. By noon, the dark and gloomy town of Andernach appeared on the starboard side of the River Rhine. An ancient basilican church loomed over the water;

behind the church, Rabbi Amram could have seen the watchtower and on its right the famous waterfront crane that sits on walls two meters thick–Rabbi Amram could have seen these had the good Rabbi been able to see at all. The trading town of Neuwied came and went on the port bank of the river. Then came Ehrenbreitstein, opposite Coblenz. Ehrenbreitstein has a vast and impregnable fortress, a citadel sitting on a rock one hundred meters above the city. This fort has never been captured by force. (Although once it was taken by siege when the attackers starved the citadel for ten weeks during a bleak and awful winter.)

Coblenz, on the opposite shore, has its own triangular fortress built where the River Mosel enters the River Rhine. The Mosel is crossed by a Gothic bridge of fourteen arches, and on the bridge road is the famous church of St. Castor with its four towers built by Louis the Pious a thousand years ago. On went the little boat, and Niederlahnstein arose on the port bank of the River Rhine where the Lahn river enters. Next, Oberlahnstein appeared with its ancient walls and towers and with the castle Schloss Martinsburg, once the home of the German king Wenceslaus. And Braubach came and went, and then on the starboard side the boat floated beyond the walled town of Boppard with its Benedictine monastery that sits on a hill overlooking the wide black monkish River Rhine, River Rhine.

The coffin boat with its two covering doors like the doors to a storm cellar drifted blindly past Kestert on the port side and then past St. Goarshausen. St. Goar was on the starboard bank, just beyond the great feudal castle, the Schloss Rheinfels, atop a cliff. And then on the port side of the River Rhine was the Lorelei Rock where, could Rabbi Amram have heard, an echo of a poor young woman calls continually to her lost love–Rabbi Amram could have heard the echo, had he been able to hear at all.

Next, Oberwesel was on the starboard bank and Caub was on the port side, with the ruins of Gutenfels standing watch. And what do they watch, those old ruined walls? They guard the rock in midstream where the small castle of Pfalzgrafenstein awaits for the young Palatinate countesses who come in childbirth. Rabbi Amram's tiny coffin boat quietly came and it quietly went, past the rocky castle mounds. The boat floated on, passing Bacharach, the vintner's town on the starboard side, and passing Lorch on the port side–Lorch lying at the edge of the vineyard-covered hills that descend right to the River Rhine. Rabbi Amram skirted the Bingerloch, the stony whirlpool, and then he drifted by the Mauseturm, an evil rock on which the Archbishop of Mainz was eaten by mice near the spot where the Nibelung treasure is hidden deep within the River Rhine.

On the starboard side appeared the town of Bingen opposite the town of Rudesheim; there, the Nahe river is crossed by an old stone bridge built by the Romans. In the distance on a hill is the ruined castle of Klopp and higher still is the Chapel of St. Roch. Then came Ingelheim, which is the birthplace of King Charlemagne, and Gonsenheim on the starboard side and Eltville on the port side – Eltville is a wine town where, I am told, a man named Johann Gutenberg later set up printing presses for the first books. And suddenly there is Biebrich, a shady, well-gardened city on the port side of the River Rhine with the palace of the dukes of Nassau directly on the river bank and with their lawns running into the water itself.

The dark River Rhine widens tremendously here, and finally opposite the River Main and the town of Castel, the little coffin boat reached the city of Mainz, which spread out along the starboard bank as far as eye could see, and the old Rabbi would have seen the end of his one river voyage had he opened his eyes, by the grace of the good Lord God, blessed be He. The Rabbi's little boat had sailed upstream by itself for two days and for three nights, and when the people of Mainz saw the strange sight of a boat floating against the current and all by itself, they came toward it in wonder. These people crowded the shores, and they saw that it was a coffin boat. Some said: "This boat is sacred, we must not touch it." Others said: "There must be a holy man inside who desires to be buried here." But whenever anyone went to lay his hands on the boat, it slipped and it slid away.

This was mysterious and profane: the watchers on the shore immediately reported the boat to the Bishop of Mainz, and the whole population came running to the River Rhine, Jews and Christians together. When the Jews approached the river bank to see the great miracle, the boat moved toward them. But when the Gentiles tried to take hold of the boat, they were not able to grasp it, for the tiny ship slipped away each time. At last it became clear that the boat wanted the Jews and that it did not want the Gentiles.

A group of men representing the Bishop said to the Jews: "Go over to the boat, open the shutter doors, and see what is in it." As the Jews approached, the little boat rocked gently in the waves. Two young men opened the shutter doors. They found the coffin, and they saw the shrouded figure of Rabbi Amram. There was a letter pinned to the shroud; it was written in Hebrew and it said: "Dear brethren and friends, good and pious Jews of the town of Mainz – I am Amram, once Rabbi of Cologne. I have come to you here, although I died in Cologne. I come alone and I come by water, and it is my last wish to be buried beside my beloved parents, who lie together in the old Jewish cemetery in Mainz, so that we three may reside hand-in-hand as souls in Sheol forever. May you have much peace and long life; may the good Lord God, blessed be He, shine His countenance down upon you and grant that you too may someday rest forever with your gentle loving families, amen."

When the Jews had read the letter, they cried aloud and mourned, and they brought the coffin onto the land at the edge of the River Rhine under a tree. The Gentiles could not understand why the Jews would bring a dead body onto the land at the edge of their city. The Jews tried to explain, but the Gentiles said that the Jewish cemeteries were too full as is, and the Gentiles drove the Jews away from the river bank. Two strong young Gentiles tried to lift the coffin and throw it back into the River Rhine, but they could not move the thin wooden box – two strong young Gentiles tried to push the boat from the edge of the shore, but it would not budge. Then the people of Mainz became afraid, and quickly they went back to the Bishop.

The Bishop of Mainz suspected witchcraft, and he ordered that the coffin and the boat be guarded day and night so that the Jews could not come and remove these things and thereby do some evil with them. But all remained at a stalemate – the Jews could not retrieve poor Rabbi Amram's body, and the Gentiles could not move the body from the spot.

As you know, Rabbi, the town of Mainz has a famous old cathedral, which was originally built in the year 1000. Many Catholic ecclesiastics are buried there, including the Archbishop Boniface. The Mainz Bishop at the time of Amram's arrival (a bishop whose name has not been preserved) wished to be remembered as an Archbishop someday; therefore, he was building his own church alongside the River Rhine, near the spot of this difficulty with the Jews. Daily, the

Bishop saw the little Jewish coffin lying under the tree; each morning the tiny Jewish boat floated gently beside the River Rhine. The Bishop could not bear to see these things, and he ordered that a small side chapel be built over the coffin and extended out over the boat: if he could not move these eyesores, then at least he could hide them. The Jews of Mainz beggged, entreated, and petitioned for permission to take the body, but all was in vain. The chapel was built and the boat and the coffin were hidden from sight, and today this little side chapel has come to be known as the Chapel of Emmeran, after Rabbi Amram – and the Bishop of Mainz has been forgotten. . . .

What? Of course there is more, Rabbi: I only closed my eyes for a moment – can an old man not take a little rest? Now you have interrupted my thoughts. Let me see, where was I? Ah yes, as my grandmother said: "A boat is only good for one voyage, my little man." Did you ever hear her say that, Rabbi? You never knew her? That is too bad – you missed a fine woman. Anyway, Rabbi, my grandmother was correct: a boat can only be used for one voyage, and this little boat was never moved again. But of course it was not the same for Rabbi Amram.

From the day that his little coffin boat came to rest at the edge of the River Rhine, alongside the great city of Mainz, Rabbi Amram appeared every night in his pupils' dreams, and he said to them: "Bury me with my parents." Finally, the pupils took courage; they disguised themselves as Gentiles, and they traveled to Mainz. When they reached Mainz, they had no trouble locating the small chapel that the Bishop had newly built. They could break in and steal the Rabbi's body – but what would happen then? The Bishop would discover that the body was missing and he would punish the local Jews. Then one of the young scholars had an idea. He said a quiet blessing, and he went out alone in the dead of the night. From the gallows in the central marketplace, he cut down an old thief and he dressed the body in a white Jewish shroud. Carefully, he carried the body to the chapel, he broke the lock on the door, he put the thief in the place of Rabbi Amram, and he removed the Rabbi's body. When the local Jews heard what the yeshiva student had done, they quickly sent a Jewish locksmith, and in the dead of the night he made the door look as good as new.

The young men from the Cologne yeshiva took the body of

Rabbi Amram and they laid it out in the back room of a little Jewish store. Following the oldest customs, they closed the eyes and the mouth of the old Rabbi, for he was now staring straight at the sky; they rewashed the body, they covered it with sweet-smelling spices, they dressed it in its best Sabbath robes, they put the Rabbi's old worn prayer book in his hands, and they gently folded his body into the position of an unborn child so that someday he might roll smoothly into the Holy Land beyond the grave. Then they secretly buried Rabbi Amram next to his parents in the Jewish cemetery at the base of one of the large Mainz bridges. They buried him beside his mother, who lay beside his father, for family who are buried together will remain together hand-in-hand in Sheol forever. And, as my grandmother said, the good Lord God (blessed be He) protected the Jews; Rabbi Amram was reunited with his parents in the Great Hereafter – and the truth remained a secret forever from all the Gentiles of the town of Mainz on the edge of the dark wide River Rhine, the dark medieval River Rhine.

ood evening, Rabbi. No sleep for the weary? That is what my grandmother said, and she said it almost nightly. If you are cold, then sit down here on the bench and I will stoke up the oven. This stoker? It is one of the iron shoe scrapers from the front hall—you probably do not recognize it because it is covered with soot. (Also, I bent it in order to make it fit through the oven door.) Of course there are still two scrapers in the anteroom for dirty shoes. But I myself am of the old school: I think that all pious men should pray barefoot. (And not just for *Yom Kippur,* Rabbi. I mean on every single day. But, then, what does a poor shammas know?) I have seen your Talmud students walking barefoot through the streets. Are they too poor to buy shoes, or is it their piety that drives them to go shoeless? Whatever the case, you know young men these days: everyone needs his own special prayer slippers. It certainly feels holy to pray in soft shoes—ah, if only we were all so rich as to have woven prayer slippers, praise the Lord.

Now that I have you here in the quiet, Rabbi, let me just review my Saturday speech with you. It is the decree on Reb Bectam. What is that, Rabbi? Certainly it *is* a shame that you have been forced into this, but it is the fifth or the sixth time that he has reneged on a business agreement. Now, at the end of the other announcements, I will use the standard form:

> Hear all you Jews who are present, Reb Bectam refuses to follow his word: he will not honor his pledges, although they were given under witness and before the sight of the good Lord God, blessed be He. Therefore, the Council of Rabbis decrees that Reb Bectam should be removed from our holy congregation of Israel—he is unworthy to attend this synagogue, and he is hereby banished.
>
> This is by order of the Rabbinical Tribunal, the *Bet Din*.

Ah yes, it does sound harsh when said aloud. Well, Rabbi, perhaps if you really wish to reconsider, then we can postpone the announcement for another week.

You are a charitable man, Rabbi, but frankly I do not know whether this procrastination is a service to the community. Reb Bectam will just go out and deceive another poor Jew. As my grandmother said: "Charity begins in the heart." She said this often—and of course how could you question that? . . . What did she mean, Rabbi? Well, let me illustrate with a story of hers. (It is always best to use my grandmother's own words.) I remember that she told of a certain Rabbi Moshe ha-Kohen, a scholar from France who was beloved as a rabbi and as a cantor, and he was famous for his ascetic piety.

Exactly, Rabbi. This was the very same Rabbi Moshe ha-Kohen who wrote the two volumes of medieval liturgical poems. You may not know this, Rabbi, but Moshe ha-Kohen refused to use any money. Oh, you knew that? Did you know that every bit of his salary was given to the poor? I see—then you must also know that his wife Belet and his children Eljakim and Ogia were forced to beg in secret: often they would go to other congregations in disguise in order to get sufficient food and clothes to survive the winters. . . .

What? Of course there is more—I was just resting my eyes, Rabbi. Let me see, where was I? Oh yes, once upon a time Rabbi Moshe ha-Kohen came from France to Cologne on the Rhine, begging alms. . . . Yes, yes—I know that I said he never accepted money, but that was for *himself*. He owned nothing and he wanted nothing. But one day his son Eljakim fell ill. The doctors said that the little boy needed food, good nutritious healthful food. Where was Rabbi Moshe to get this food? Where was he to get the necessary money? In Cologne, of course.

Now Rabbi, how can I know why Moshe ha-Kohen journeyed all the way to Cologne? This happened centuries ago, and my grandmother heard the tale from her grandmother–both are now long dead (blessed be their souls)–so we must just rest with the facts. As I was saying, Rabbi Moshe ha-Kohen came to Rabbi Amram of Cologne and asked him for help. Could the good Rabbi Amram provide some money for Reb Moshe? Rabbi Amram welcomed his holy visitor, he washed Reb Moshe's feet, and he gave him a fine chair in which to rest. Together, they said the evening prayers in the synagogue, surrounded by young talmudic scholars. (And I am certain that Rabbi Moshe said the prayers barefoot, for he was a very holy man.) Then, after prayers Rabbi Amram appointed three scholars to travel about and to collect money from the rich Jews of Cologne in order to help poor Rabbi Moshe, and when he slept that evening, on the floor of the yeshiva, Rabbi Moshe dreamt that he jumped so high that he could touch a cloud.

The appointed scholars were Eliezer ben Shimshon, Samuel ben Natronai, and Ephraim ben Jacob ben Meir. (In their later lives, each of these scholars became a famous rabbi.) At that time, individuals, whether strangers or members of the local congregation, were allowed to make special appeals for money to the benevolent members of the Jewish Quarter of Cologne. Therefore, the three scholars went around from house to house, saying to everyone: "The good Lord God, blessed be He, has brought to our town the holy Rabbi Moshe ha-Kohen from France. He is in great need of our help, and Rabbi Amram asks that you contribute as much as you can to a fund. In this way, we shall send Rabbi Moshe back home with an abundance for his suffering family." Then, because the scholars were not allowed to touch the money, a shammas like myself followed behind and collected all of the contributions.

After a long day of walking and of talking, the scholars collected seventy coins. Yes, Rabbi, seventy gold coins. But they felt that an even greater windfall was about to arrive, because now they had come to the house of Reb Tanechum, a very rich man and the president–the

Parnas – of their congregation. Reb Ephraim ben Jacob ben Meir, the head of the scholarly delegation, knocked on the rich man's door. Reb Tanechum himself answered; silently, he heard out the request for money. I am sorry to say that in his heart of hearts Reb Tanechum was a miser: the scholars asked him for a contribution, but Reb Tanechum refused. "My friends," he answered angrily, "each month I am assessed for charity three times as much as any other member of the congregation: the Gabbai is constantly at my door."

"It is true, Reb Tanechum: you are a fine and upstanding supporter of the needy," said Reb Ephraim. "You are also a rich man (by the good graces of the Lord our God, blessed be He), and a man's gifts must be proportional to his means."

"I give in proportion to my means. But for a gift to be worthwhile it truly must be a gift – it must be voluntary."

"Exactly," said Reb Samuel ben Natronai, "and we know that a pious and dedicated man such as yourself – the Parnas of our congregation – will give voluntarily a great many coins to help out the needy Rabbi Moshe ha-Kohen of France."

"I contribute endlessly to the poorbox in the synagogue," said the Parnas. "I give every week, not only on Purim. Why, I even try to give a few pennies each morning before leaving the synagogue."

"Good Reb Tanechum," said Reb Eliezer ben Shimshon, "no man has ever become poor through giving too much in charity."

And the Parnas said: "Listen, my young scholars: the Lord will provide. As Psalm 140 says":

> I know that the good Lord God
> Will maintain the cause of the poor.
> He provides for the helpless and hungry;
> He loves those whom others ignore.

"Ah, but do not forget the 'Hallelujah' Psalm, Reb Tanechum. First, it says: 'Happy is the man who fears the Lord, and well is it with him who deals graciously and who lends to the poor.' Then it says: 'Happy is the man who has scattered abroad, who has given to the needy – his righteousness shall endure forever; his horn shall be exalted in honor.'"

But Reb Tanechum replied: "If you are truly a scholar, Eliezer, then you will remember that the Talmud fixes one-fifth of his property as the upper limit that a generous man can give. I am certain that I surpass that amount many times over – and I do not wish to go against the counsel of the talmudic Sages, who are obviously wiser than me."

The scholars persisted, and in the end old Reb Tanechum bitterly took out a single penny, and he threw it on the ground in the mud. "Take that," he told the three scholars. "Pick up the penny, and take it back to your holy rabbi from France."

Now, Rabbi, picture the situation. Here were three of the most respected talmudic scholars in all of Cologne. Should they stoop to the dust and pick up the lone penny? Should even the shammas retrieve the coin? They were annoyed – no, they were more than annoyed, they were furious. The three scholars were very angry. . . .

What? Yes, yes, Rabbi, I am about to continue. I was just thinking quietly here in the glow of the stove. Now, where was I? Oh yes, the scholars were angry with Reb Tanechum, and they left the penny on the ground. "Better to give no alms at all than to give them in public," quoted Reb Eliezer from the old sayings. And then he added: "They who give publicly and with ostentation will never get farther than the outskirts of paradise in the next life." . . . No, I am not certain myself why he said this, Rabbi – anyway, the story continues:

The three scholars returned and they reported to Rabbi Amram. The Rabbi raised his eyebrows; he creased his forehead. Rabbi Amram thought a moment, and then he reminded the scholars – the good Eliezer ben Shimshon, the studious Samuel ben Natronai, and the thoughtful Ephraim ben Jacob ben Meir – that Maimonides had set out a chart ranking all charitable givers.

Maimonides said that foremost among benefactors is the donor who makes a poor man self-sufficient by giving him a loan or by taking him into business. Next comes the generous man who gives to the poor without knowing to whom he gives (and also where the recipient does not know the identity of his benefactor). Third on this list comes the man who gives anonymously, although knowing in advance who will get the charity. (Maimonides maintained that it is not as selfless to give – even though giving generously and willingly – when the poor man knows where the gift comes from.) Then there is the kind soul who gives openly before he is asked, donating from the inner goodness of his heart. And next there is the man who must be asked, but who gives freely when charity is requested.

Now, lower still is he who gives something to charity when he is asked–although he may not give anonymously, adequately, or self-lessly, still he is a man who gives with a good grace. Finally, charity is charity no matter how it is given, and last on the list is the man who gives openly, inadequately, and gracelessly.

"I am afraid," said Reb Eliezer, "that Reb Tanechum falls last on Maimonides' list of donors."

"True," said Rabbi Amram, "but remember, good friends, the great Maimonides has also said: 'In the end, we must look through the eyes of the needy–a gift that helps is better than none at all, no matter how it has been given.'"

The Rabbi and the three scholars talked in the small study room in the back of the old Cologne yeshiva. The room was crowded with books and manuscripts; it was dim and it was smoky. There were no windows. In the dimness, the shammas gave Rabbi Amram the seventy gold coins that already had been collected from the community. And Rabbi Amram said to the three scholars: "My dear brothers, go back to Reb Tanechum's house; pick up the penny and bring it to me. The good Lord God of Israel, blessed be He, has decreed that Rabbi Moshe must depend upon the gifts of others, and we cannot reject any help, small as that help may be. And, my scholars, be sure to thank Reb Tanechum for his gift."

The three scholars walked out of the dim back room. They stepped into the main prayer hall filled with wooden benches, they passed the twelve stained glass windows with their colored lions and snakes, and they walked by the Holy Ark made of stone. They passed through the synagogue and out into the bright afternoon street, fol-lowed by the shammas.

When they reached the house of the Parnas, Reb Tanechum was standing in the doorway. Reb Ephraim said to Reb Tanechum: "Rabbi Amram has said that we should bring this penny back for Rabbi Moshe–and we thank you for the gift." Then, the shammas bent down, and he picked up the coin. While this was all happening, a small boy, a little Jewish child, was in the shadows by the wall, listening. He had a penny in his hand. Was it for a treat from a store? Or was he just holding it for luck? He heard the men talking; he saw the interchange.

Suddenly, he ran to the shammas and he gave him the penny. Then the little boy was embarrassed and he turned and ran away.

The Parnas saw this. He put on his hat, he took his cane, and he walked directly to Rabbi Amram. "Will you forgive me, Rabbi?" asked Reb Tanechum. "Let me give you a large sum of money for Rabbi Moshe."

"That is kind of you," said Rabbi Amram. The Parnas took out many gold coins, and he set them on the Rabbi's table. Rabbi Amram put the money aside. Still, the Parnas stood there. "I think," said Rabbi Amram, "that you will feel better if I say something more."

"Yes," answered Reb Tanechum, "I think that I will."

"Very well," said Rabbi Amram, "here is my decree: You are fond of a good dinner and an extra glass of wine, are you not?"

"I am."

"Then whenever you purchase a pot of butter, a pound of meat, or a bottle of wine for yourself, you must also buy a second pot of butter, a second pound of meat, or a second bottle of wine for the poor. Whenever you drink an extra glass of wine after your meal or whenever you eat a sweet cake, then you must set aside a gold piece for charity. And if you should forget to read the Sabbath scriptural lesson three times, then you must fine yourself one gold piece, to be put into the poorbox. These rules and strictures I now set upon your shoulders under the sight of the good Lord God of Israel, blessed be He, amen."

In this way, Reb Tanechum "salted his wealth with charity," as my grandmother used to say, may the good Lord bless her and keep her. And my grandmother reminded me that Rabbi Amram's decrees were in the tradition of the charitableness of all good Jewish wives. You remember, Rabbi, how in the Book of Proverbs it says:

> Who can appraise a capable wife?
> Her worth is beyond all else in life –
> Like a ship that is laden with merchandise,
> She brings from afar good food and sweet spice.
> And for the needy she opens her door:
> She is generous to all the poor.

Yes, Rabbi, my grandmother always told us: "A Jewish wife is the most blessed gift to the Jewish community." Have you ever heard of little Doeg ben Joseph, Rabbi. No? Well, they say that his mother weighed her child every day and then she distributed his increased weight in gold to the poor. This mother was killed in Regensburg during the Thirty Years' War, and the epitaph on her grave is:

She gave Bibles to scholars, and she gave prayer books to paupers. She helped out at weddings and at funerals. She asked the poor to dinner in her own home. She gave clothes to beggars, she sewed shirts for the needy, and she loved all children like her own.

h, good evening, Rabbi. You are having difficulty sleeping again? Just put your feet up on the side bench here, and I will open the stove door. Let me push this coal back; there is nothing like that white glow to wash away the cares of a hard day. I heard your final prayers tonight, and there is no use denying it, Rabbi—you are overworked. Even a nearsighted shammas like me can tell. I kept one eye on you when I was cleaning the dishes; I saw that you were watching the door, hoping that Reb Elbaum would leave early. But then Reb Anton stayed late to argue about the Midrash passage.

That Midrash passage reminded me of old Rabbi Jehuda ben Saul. (Rabbi Jehuda? He was two rabbis before you.) One day he gave a Midrash sermon to his yeshiva students. "How do we know that God puts on *tefillin*?" he asked and he looked sternly at the young men on the benches. There was silence, so the Rabbi answered his own question:

First, it is said in Isaiah: "The Lord has sworn a fearsome oath with a raised right hand and with His strong and mighty arm." Now, said Rabbi Jehuda, the "strong and mighty arm" means the *tefillin*—*tefillin* are the strength of prayers bound to the arm. Then, it is said in the 29th Psalm: "The Lord gives strength to all His own people." This strength is, of course, the strength of the *tefillin* prayer parchments. And, my young scholars, how does one know that *tefillin* are a strength to the Jews and to Israel? Because, said the Rabbi, it is written in Deuteronomy:

> Then all people on earth shall see that the Lord has named Israel as His own special nation, and they shall go in fear of you.

The yeshiva students were puzzled, and a young man named Moshe ben Samuel asked: "Good Rabbi, if the Lord God, blessed be He, has prayer parchments bound to His arm, then what could possibly be written on these holy *tefillin* that are bound to the Lord God himself?"

Rabbi Jehuda looked fiercely at the student and he answered: "Do you not know the Books of Chronicles?"

"Yes I do," said Moshe, "but where in those two books is the answer to my question?"

"In the First Book of the Chronicles," said the Rabbi, "it is written":

> And Your people Israel, to whom can they be compared? Is there any other single nation on earth that God has gone out to redeem from slavery in order to make them His people? O Lord, You have won a name for Yourself by great and terrible deeds, driving out nations before Your people. You have made the one people—the nation of Israel—Your own people for ever, and You, O Lord, have become their one God.

"In other words," declared Rabbi Jehuda, "as the nation of Israel professes just one God, so their Heavenly Father correspondingly embraces just one people."

The students looked at one another unsurely, but Rabbi Jehuda continued; he pointed out that this also explains the words of the Lord God to Moses near Mount Sinai, late in Exodus:

> "Here is a place beside me," said the great Lord God, blessed be He. "Stand on this rock, and when I and My glory pass by, I will put you in a crevice of the rock and cover you with My hand until I have passed. Then I will take away My hand, and you shall see My back, but My face you will not see."

Rabbi Jehuda told his students that this means that God showed to Moses only the knot by which the *tefillin* are tied around the back of the head.

Yes, Rabbi, clearly *tefillin* are magical amulets. Do not look at me like that—I mean no blasphemy: I have heard that "phylactery" is actually a Greek word meaning "guard," in the sense of guarding against misfortune. Phylacteries—*tefillin*—are talismen. And, of course, there was the miracle of the *tefillin* of Amram. Exactly, Rabbi, that was the very same German Amram whom I have told you about before. Rabbi Amram was a fine and pious man; he was the chief rabbi of Cologne. Alone, he held together the tiny Jewish community that lived in Cologne on the River Rhine, in those medieval years. He had originally moved to Cologne from Mainz where he was raised, where his parents were buried, and where he first studied in the yeshiva. Amram came to Cologne as a young man, and it was in those young years that the miracle of the doves occurred. . . .

What? Of course there is more, Rabbi: I only closed my eyes for a moment. Can an old man not take a little rest? Now you have interrupted my thoughts. Let me see, where was I? Yes, yes, as my grandmother said: "Prayers to the Lord are like the wings of a dove."

What, Rabbi—*tefillin*? Well, Rabbi Yanai has said: "To put on the *tefillin*, a Jew must be clean and pure; he must be as clean as the white wings of a dove." Ah, Rabbi, you wonder: Why must a pious Jew be so clean? The answer is simple: a Jew must be free from physical impurities while wearing the *tefillin*.

And Rabbi Yanai also said: "One may wear his *tefillin* all day, but a man cannot sleep wearing *tefillin*." (And Rabbi Yannai did not get this interdiction from the Pharisees, who were the first Jews to wear *tefillin*: no, Rabbi Yanai was quoting the great Rashi.)

I suppose that you wonder, Rabbi, how all of this relates to Reb Amram and why he was called the "man of the dove's wings"? The answer is Hermann. Yes—Hermann. You see, once upon a time the Archbishop of Cologne—Archbishop Hermann III—had forbidden the Jews to wear *tefillin*. Archbishop Hermann set forth the following decree: if a Jew is seen with a phylactery on his head, then he will be beaten and thrown in jail. Now, not only were *tefillin* worn daily at the morning prayers (on arm and on head); in those days many Jews also wore their *tefillin* all day, in accord with Rabbi Yanai's proclamation. These Jews were very pious, and Amram wished to be pious like them. But what should the Jews of Cologne do now? After the first few Jews were beaten and jailed, all the Jews feared to wear their *tefillin* in public. Ah, but Amram was young, and he paid no attention to the order; he continued to wear his *tefillin* daily and wherever he went.

Of course, Rabbi, *tefillin* are not worn on the Sabbath or on any of the Festivals, because special days are already "signs" between God and Israel and no further signs are needed. For this reason, the miracle of the doves must have occurred on an ordinary day – on one ordinary day when two officers appointed by the Archbishop to enforce his decree discovered Amram wearing his *tefillin*.

As you remind each young yeshiva student, Rabbi: a Jew must wear his *tefillin* each morning when he prays. Four passages in the Pentateuch command us: "You shall bind them for a sign on your hand, and they shall be as frontlets between your eyes." Thus as soon as he awoke, Amram put on his hand *tefilla*; he wound the black leather strap seven times around his arm below the elbow, and he recited thanks to "He Who has commanded us to lay *tefillin*." Then, Amram put on his head *tefilla*. The special knot sat behind his head, and the black leather straps hung down his neck. Amram recited: "Thanks be to He Who has commanded us about the duty of *tefillin*." Finally, Amram wrapped the strap of the hand *tefilla* around his hand and fingers, reciting from Hosea:

> I pledge my troth a thousand-fold
> To be a righteous, truthful ward.
> I speak in modesty: this is told
> Full humbly and with God's accord.
> I betroth myself, to have and hold –
> And then I'll truly know the Lord.

The weather was fine, the sky was blue. Amram stood at his window praying, and two of the city's officers passed by. Amram heard them talking, he saw their uniforms, and he jumped from the window and ran down the street. The two officials ran after him. In Cologne, the Jews lived in the parish of St. Laurence near one of the four gates through the city walls. Amram ran down the street and through the nearby gate, the Wuefeltor Gate, which was also known as the Porta Judaeorum. Unfortunately, just outside the gate stood another of the city's guards. The guard took hold of Amram—but just as Amram was being stopped, he took off his *tefillin*, and he hid them in his hands.

The two officers who had been chasing Amram reached the Gate. "What do you have in your hands?" they asked. Amram looked down and then he looked up; a bird was flying far and high. Amram replied: "In my hands? It is the wings of a dove—I have the wings of a dove in my hands."

"Show me," said an officer.

Amram looked down, and then he looked up; the bird was nowhere to be seen. The officer grabbed Amram's two hands and pulled them apart. Amram took a breath. A white fluttering was in his hands, and then out of his hands flew a pale dove. It beat its wings, and it rose high into the heavens and it disappeared into the distance. The officers stood still. Amram stood still. The four men looked at the sky, and then quickly Amram walked back to his home. He did not stop, of course, but went to the synagogue, and he prayed all day.

Ah, Rabbi, you wonder why he said that he had a *dove* in his hand? It must have been because the Israelites always have been compared to the dove. And why did Amram say specifically the *wings* of a dove? It must have been because the dove uses her wings to protect her: she uses her wings as a defense in a fight, not her mouth or her beak or her feet. The *tefillin*, with its sacred commandments written in Hebrew on the white parchment scroll, are like the white wings of a dove—they protect the Israelites from all trouble; they defend us against all evil. Keep these commandments, says the Holy Scriptures, and no harm shall befall you. Clearly, this was the case with Amram. Although Archbishop Hermann had forbidden the wearing of *tefillin* on pain of death, nevertheless Amram knew that the good Lord God, blessed be He, had given a sacred commandment and that He would protect His children.

Oh? I am glad that you like that moral, Rabbi, but there is also another interpretation. You see, the wings of a dove protect her more than the wings of any other bird. When other birds tire in flight, they rest on a rock or a tree or a wall. On the other hand, when the dove tires, she rests by soaring, first with one wing and then with the other. The dove's wings are an escape and a refuge–as it is written in Psalm 55:

> O that I had the wings of a dove
> To fly away and escape distress
> In clouds that tower far above
> The clean and ancient wilderness.
>
> My wings would carry me like a wren
> Above the storms of hail and rains
> To havens free from wicked men
> And far from any vile campaigns.

Just as the wings of a dove protect her from harm, so the commandments of the *tefillin* protect the children of Israel from their enemies.

Yes, yes, Rabbi, this too is a fine moral, and yet I have heard another possible meaning of this miracle. Did you know that at one time a Jewish bridegroom wore his forehead *tefilla* under the marriage hood? Oh–well, then, you must also know that in a sense the *tefillin* countered the ashes that the rabbi rubbed onto the groom's forehead in memory of the destruction of the Great Temple at Zion. (May it be rebuilt speedily in our days, amen.) Just as a dove is both a symbol of prayer and of marriage, so the *tefillin* represent the sacred prayer-covenant between a man and his wife and the Lord.

However, Rabbi, I myself prefer my grandmother's interpretation. The dove is a messenger, and it is a holy messenger. When you see a pale bird flying high in the clouds, she is taking our prayers to the good Lord God, blessed be He. It has been so since the very beginning. You see, Rabbi, my grandmother (may her soul rest forever in the bosom of the great Lord God) reminded me that this is the meaning of the famous passage in Genesis:

> Noah waited for seven days, and then he released a dove from the ark to see whether the water covering the earth had subsided. The dove flew far and wide, but she found no place where she could settle; therefore, she returned to the ark because there was water over the whole surface

of the fresh-scrubbed earth. And Noah stretched out his hand, he caught the dove, and he took her into the ark.

Noah waited another seven days, and again he released the dove from the ark. Late in the evening, the dove returned with a newly plucked olive leaf in her beak. Then Noah knew that the waters were subsiding throughout the earth. And Noah waited yet another seven days; this time when he let the dove fly free, she never came back. So it came about that, on the first day of the first month of Noah's six hundred and first year, the flood waters had dried up on the earth; therefore, Noah removed the hatch from his boat and he looked out of the ark. The surface of the ground was dry again.

**Each week, Rabbi, Noah sent out his prayers, and when finally the dove did not return, then Noah knew that the good Lord God had taken her into His heart, and He had heard the prayers at last.**

hat is that, Rabbi? No, I was just resting my eyes—please join me here by the stove. (I think that you will be too warm on that bench: try the one nearer to the wall.) An old man like me can doze forever by a warm stove; I suppose that my mother did not use enough oil when I was a baby. What do I mean? Why, Rabbi, certainly you know the proper treatment of a baby: bathe it daily in hot water, and then rub it with olive oil. My grandmother told me that this routine accounted for her amazing agility, even in old age. When she was older than me (I am eighty, you know), she could stand on one foot while taking off her shoe and putting it on again. Grandmother could balance two plates of fish on one arm while serving wine, and she could sew tiny, even stitches along the entire edge of a shirt. And why was this? Grandmother always said: "It was my good mother (may she rest forever in peace, blessed be the Lord) who kept me fit and trim. My mother bathed me every day in hot water when I was a child, and then she rubbed me from top to bottom with olive oil." What more could you ask, Rabbi? . . .

What? No, no—do not get up on my account, Rabbi: I was just resting my eyes a moment. I was resting and musing. . . . Well, to tell you the truth, Rabbi, I was remembering little Erinna-anne; she was my tiny daughter who died many many years ago. It was before you came here – I still remember the story that my grandmother told me then:

Once upon a time, said my grandmother, in the congregation of Rabbi Amram of Cologne, there was a devout man named Reb Meir ben Jacob ben Gabirol. Reb Meir had two sons, who were two and four years of age. Every day Reb Meir's wife, Hannah, bathed them in hot water and then rubbed them down from tip to toe with olive oil, and after prayers each evening Reb Meir hurried home to tell them a bedtime story before they had fallen asleep.

It was the autumn, and Reb Meir was studying late in the old Cologne yeshiva. Rabbi Amram was bent over a book; he had just read a discussion of the passage from Job:

Hearing this, poor Job stood up, and he rent his cloak; then, he shaved his head and fell prostrate on the ground, saying:

"Naked was I when I came from the womb,
And naked I shall reach my reward.
The Lord gives life, and He sends to the tomb –
Blessed be the name of the Lord."

Suddenly, the Rabbi heard a noise, and he looked up. He looked up, and it seemed to him that Reb Meir became dark and misty for a moment. Rabbi Amram rubbed his eyes, and the vision passed. After the evening prayers, Reb Meir seemed shaky, and Rabbi Amram decided to walk him home.

The two men walked silently down Engegasse Street. They reached the door of Reb Meir's house, and both men walked in.

"Excuse me, Rabbi," said Reb Meir, "I will just go and say a few words to the children."

Hannah was pale. She stood directly in front of Meir. "Let me ask you a question, Meir."

"Can it wait?"

"No, it cannot," said the wife.

"Very well – what is it, Hannah?"

"I am not certain how to say this, Meir. You see, a few years ago, someone came here and entrusted two valuable articles to my care – two very precious things. And now – well, now he wants to have them back. What could I say, Meir? What could I do? I had to return them," said Hannah.

"Of course, you did the right thing, Hannah," said Meir.

Rabbi Amram looked sadly at the two of them.

"I gave them back without your consent, Meir. But I had no choice."

"And that was proper," said Meir.

"They were our children," said Hannah quietly.

Meir ran to the back room. He saw two small figures laid out on the bed. Meir threw back the sheet that covered them, and he fell down upon the floor and he cried. . . .

What, Rabbi? Yes, that is the whole story; there is no more.

abbi, I am glad to see you here alone. I want to apologize for my outburst during the service this evening. It was just that Reb Anton yawned. Yes, I know that it was warm in here, Rabbi – but it was inconceivable that he should yawn and then not cover his mouth during prayers. Why in the olden days, in the strict and pious days of our fathers, Reb Anton would have been ordered to leave and never to return. Undoubtedly, Reb Anton did not have bread for breakfast. What? Why of course it was a lack of bread. Does it not say in the Talmud: "There are thirteen benefits from eating bread in the morning"?

How can you not remember, Rabbi? I will list them for you:

Bread protects a man from heat and from cold, it wards off injurious spirits and demons, and it makes the simple man into a wise scholar. Bread helps the plaintiff to win his lawsuits. Bread allows the student to learn and then to teach the Torah – it makes his speech worth listening to. With bread, one's learning is remembered. After a meal of bread, one's mouth is fresh, one retains one's wife, and one does not have evil thoughts. Moreover, bread destroys tapeworms, it drives forth envy, and it causes love to enter unto your soul.

Also, remember Psalm 102, Rabbi:

> My days are consumed like smoke,
> My bones are brittle as the dead,
> My heart is like a withered oak;
> For I have neglected my daily bread.

So, Rabbi, I say that if Reb Anton did not take the time to have bread for breakfast, then he deserved his dressing down – he has no one to blame but himself. However, in the olden days, said my grandmother, it was not always a Jew's fault if he were grumpy all day: a Jew could not always get bread. Oh? You find that hard to believe? Well, listen to me, Rabbi, I am not inventing this: it is well known that in Regensburg the Jews bought all their bread from Gentile bakers – there were no Jewish bakers. Yes, that is a fact, Rabbi. There were not enough Jewish workers to provide for all our daily needs, and Jews were forced to contract with Gentile bakers and Gentile slaughterers and Gentile potters. (Yes, yes – I said Gentile slaughterers, Rabbi.) And so, in times of crises, we Jews were held hostage by boycotts – for instance, I think that it was about the year 1500 when all the bakers of Regensburg refused to sell bread to Jews. Those Jews suffered from more than grumpiness, I would wager.

I know what you are thinking, Rabbi. Oh? Well no one's mind is ever really blank, Rabbi, and I am certain that you were thinking *"matzohs."* . . . Then perhaps you were not aware of it. Jews may not always bake their own bread, but Jews always bake their own *matzohs* – they always have and they always will. And my grandmother – may the good Lord God cradle her immortal soul – began thinking of *matzohs* on the new year day each year.

What is that, Rabbi? No – of course not months early, during *Rosh Hashanah*: my grandmother thought of *matzohs* during the *real* new year. I do not have to remind you, Rabbi – you, a scholar and a man of learning – that the Holy Scriptures count *Nisan*, the Passover month, as the first month of the year. The day that we now call *Rosh Hashanah* is known in Leviticus and in Nehemiah as the first day of the *seventh* month.

Now, on the true new year (the old and holy new year, the first day of *Nisan*), my grandmother said *matzoh* as the first word that she

uttered when she awoke. This annoyed my grandfather, because my
grandmother felt that she must say the word loudly. Grandmother
maintained that she was merely following the dictates of Rabban
Gamaliel, who said:

> The good Jew has a duty on Passover to pronounce three words loud
> and clear—these words are *Pesach, matzoh,* and *maror.* The Jew says *Pesach*
> (Passover) because the vengeful Lord God passed over the houses of our
> fathers; he says *matzoh* (unleavened bread) because our fathers were
> delivered from Egypt hurriedly, with no time for proper baking; and he
> says *maror* (bitter herbs) because the Egyptians embittered the lives of our
> fathers in the land of the Pharaohs. In every generation, a man should
> look on himself as if it was he personally who had gone forth from
> Egypt—as it is written in Exodus: "You shall tell the full story to your
> son on that Passover day, saying: For the sake of freedom the Lord did all
> this for me, when I myself went out from the land of Egypt, amen."

Today, the Jewish wife is reponsible to her family for baking the
*matzohs,* just as in the days of the Egyptian exodus. Therefore, my
grandmother felt that it was her bound duty clearly to declare *matzoh*
whenever she could.

So, Rabbi, that is why *matzohs* were important to my grandmother, and it was my grandmother who told me the famous *matzoh*
story of Eliezer and Rabbi Juddah he-Hasid. No, Rabbi, that was not
the famous Rabbi Eliezer ben Hyrcanos of Lydda. Eliazer the mystic of
Worms? No, it was not him either—it was the Rabbi Eliezer ben Joel
ha-Levi whose father, Joel ben Isaac, had been the chief rabbi in
Cologne. Joel ben Isaac had succeeded *his* father, and eventually Eliezer
followed too, exceeding Rabbi Joel's reputation—but that was later,
well after Eliezer had met Rabbi Juddah.

You see, Rabbi, at first the young Eliezer was taught quietly by
his father in Cologne; then, he studied in the famous talmudic academies of Mainz, Metz, Regensburg, and Speyer. But the boy was a
wanderer. He was absentminded, and somehow he was not devoted to
the regimented, religious ways. His father was worried. Rabbi Joel ben
Isaac thought to himself: "My son is bright and deep, but he has a
strange distance from daily Judaism. What shall I do?" Rabbi Joel was

at a loss – but, as my grandmother used to say, Rabbi: "Who can tell the future in a thing like this?"

So there in the town of Cologne, between his rabbinical chores, Rabbi Joel ben Isaac thought and he worried. Finally, he decided that only time would shepherd his son into the correct life-style. O Lord, just let Eliezer grow and live without falling prey to extremes, hoped Rabbi Joel. Then, thought the Rabbi, I had best help God by keeping my son sheltered from certain disturbing ideas. Thus, when Rabbi Joel was about to die, he left a will forbidding his son to cross the River Danube. He wanted his son to remain in Cologne and to become the chief rabbi following his own death. Most especially, though, Rabbi Joel ben Isaac wanted his son to stay away from the mystical and disconcerting ideas of Juddah he-Hasid.

As a boy in the many yeshivas, Eliezer had heard whispered rumors of the great Rabbi Juddah he-Hasid. Of course, the young man was eager to go to see Rabbi Juddah in Regensburg and to study with this mystic Jew. Therefore, it came to pass that, contrary to his father's explicit wishes and against his father's written will, Eliezer crossed the Danube and came to Regensburg in order to visit the pious man, Rabbi Juddah he-Hasid, the mystic of Regensburg. Outside of Regensburg, Eliezer walked to the holy man's house. When Rabbi Juddah saw Eliezer, he greeted him, and Eliezer returned the greeting. Then, Rabbi Juddah said to him: "Perhaps I should not have said 'Hello,' young man, for I know that you have disobeyed your father's wishes and will. However, I greet you cordially out of respect for your father's memory; he was a fine rabbi, and he was my distant cousin." Eliezer was greatly frightened on hearing the words of the pious man. Then, Rabbi Juddah turned around, and Eliezer, having come so far, followed.

Eliezer remained with Rabbi Juddah he-Hasid, living in the Rabbi's house for the first three months. The young man followed Rabbi Juddah about daily: Eliezer hoped to learn mystical knowledge, he wished to understand the secrets of the hidden universe, and he was eager to see strange things at dusk and to hear odd sounds at dawn. But life seemed very ordinary with Rabbi Juddah in Regensburg on the Danube. The pious man arose, and he prayed. He ate a simple breakfast; he walked to the yeshiva. He taught the Talmud and he interpreted the Torah. Rabbi Juddah recalled famous sayings of the wise rabbis of earlier times. Where was the secret lore? How could one cause sticks to move on their own? What did the bending of leaves mean in the fall? Were certain rocks necessary for curing warts? Eliezer watched intently, but he gained no hints.

After three months, Eliezer began living in the yeshiva and he slept on the floor. He ate with the other students; he attended their lessons. He had been away from his home for one term and then for two. Although he had gone on a long journey and had disobeyed the sacred commandments of his father, he had learned nothing new. Finally, it was the day before his second Passover away from home, and Eliezer felt very sad, for he thought: "At this season I ought to be home. My father is gone, and it is my responsibility to give the *seder* in my own house. I have broken my father's sacred commandments and I have let my family down. Here I am, sitting at another man's table; once again, I have not taken the honorable course of action. I have learned nothing. If only I could live my life over again."

Rabbi Juddah he-Hasid saw young Eliezer sitting distractedly on the prayer bench. The Rabbi said: "You should be studying, young man."

"Of course you are correct, Rabbi," said Eliezer, "but I should also be at home. My first responsibility is to my family; I have failed on all accounts."

"You wish to be home for Passover," said Rabbi Juddah.

"Exactly, master–but now it is impossible; it is the morning of Passover eve."

Now, Rabbi, the pious man looked intently at Eliezer. Something sparkled in the corner of Rabbi Juddah's eye. Was it the morning sun glinting off the edge of an eyelash? Was it the hint of the moon to come? Rabbi Juddah smiled and said quietly to the young Eliezer: "What will you give me if I bring you home before the holy day begins?" Eliezer became sadder still, and he said to the holy Rabbi: "Master, please do not torment me. Cologne is three hundred and fifty kilometers away."

The pious one said: "I am quite serious, Eliezer."

"Ah, good Rabbi, I would give anything to be home with my family."

Suddenly, the Rabbi changed the subject: "It is getting late, young man; we must go and bake our *matzohs*." Eliezer was puzzled, but he followed the Rabbi into his house.

Rabbi Juddah he-Hasid went to bake the *matzohs* himself, and Eliezer stood at his side. Before this, Eliezer had seen only round *matzohs*, but Rabbi Juddah made many strange shapes with the dough, and on their surfaces he imprinted many strange signs. Then, just before the baking was finished, the pious one threw a handful of flour into the oven, and a puff of smoke rose to Heaven as thanks to the good Lord God, blessed be He. The two men took the finished *matzohs* out of the oven. The thin cakes were golden brown, and young Eliezer saw that they were square and that each one had a letter of the alphabet neatly indented in the center. Rabbi Juddah took a linen cloth and wrapped it around the third matzoh (the *gimel matzoh*); then, he gave it to Eliezer. "Take this special cake for your family; put it in your shirt now, in order to keep it warm."

Carefully, Eliezer tucked the wrapped *matzoh* in his shirt, and the two men walked out into the open countryside. Eliezer was happy, and yet he was also sad: he was going home, but had he learned anything?

Rabbi Juddah he-Hasid said: "I know what is bothering you, young man. You came here eager to learn from me the *mysteries*."

"True, Rabbi, that is what I had thought at first."

"Why?"

"Why, Rabbi?"

"Yes—why did you want mystical knowledge?"

"I suppose that I had dreamed of gaining some of your magical powers, Rabbi," said Eliezer.

"Dreamed? Yes—that is a good word: magic is a dream."

"I see. Then do you mean that I can never attain it?"

"Certainly not, Eliezer: I mean exactly the opposite. You can attain it every night in your wondrous and magical dreams."

Rabbi Juddah looked off toward the horizon; he looked off, and then he looked back. Rabbi Juddah took the walking staff that he held in his hand, and with its tip he wrote strange words in the sand. "My dear young Eliezer," said the Rabbi, "touch your tongue three times to these words." And as he did so (and with Rabbi Juddah he-Hasid's blessing humming quietly in his ear), Eliezer found himself in Cologne sitting before his home again, on the beginning of the feast of Passover, and a warm *gimel matzoh* was wrapped within his shirt.

He looked around him. What should he do first? Eliezer walked to the synagogue. He removed his shoes; friends and neighbors greeted him. Where had he been? they asked. How was it that no one had reported him home before? Ah, said Eliezer, at noon I was in Regensburg helping the famed Rabbi Juddah he-Hasid to bake *matzohs*. Why, look here, said Eliezer, I have in my shirt a special square *matzoh* inscribed with a *gimel* and still warm from the oven of that pious, mystical man.

The Jews looked at one another. They smiled and patted Eliezer gently on the shoulder; then they turned away. Happily, Eliezer said his prayers and he hurried home. His family hugged him and kissed him, and they thanked the good Lord God (blessed be He) for Eliezer's safe return. Eliezer dressed for the holiday; then he reclined at the head of the *seder* table. He presided over the Passover service, he drank the wine, and he broke Rabbi Juddah's *gimel matzoh* into many pieces, which each member of the family ate. Later, he told his story, but did they believe him? . . . .

What? No, I was merely thinking – and resting my eyes a bit. When you reach eighty years, Rabbi, you enjoy the quiet heat of the stove as much as anything else in life. Yes, Rabbi, my grandmother told a fine story – and the ending is as you would expect. You see, Reb Eliezer settled down. He became a scholar of repute. He traveled often to Bonn, to Worms, and to Wurzburg, consulting on esoteric matters. His father had left him much land in these cities. Eliezer was now quite well off economically, so he devoted himself to study; he could live without taking on the burdens of an official position. He even became a renowned chess player. For hours a day, Eliezer played with men in the study houses, and he carried his own silver chess set. (It is said, Rabbi, that Eliezer is the author of the little chess poem:

> With craft and guile their battle is fought –
> With cunning and art their contest wrought.
> And when one prevails, breaking his opponent's wall
> And wreaking havoc as the brave men fall,
> Then yet from death the pawns will rise again
> To test the mettle of the opposing men.

Of course good Eliezer followed Maimonides' stipulations: he never played chess for money, and he did not play on the Sabbath.) For a time, Reb Eliezer worked to raise money for the poorest of the Jews in the Judengasse of Frankfort on the Main; there, he also became an advisor to the local ecclesiastical council, and he befriended a young Frankfort Jew named Anselm Moses Bauer, great-great-grandfather of the patriarch of the famous Rothschild family.

Ah, Rabbi, but the world does not stand still – as my grandmother said: "The good Lord God, blessed be He, whirls our little earth in His holy palm." A fierce fire in the city of Bonn destroyed most of Eliezer's property there. The remainder of his wealth and holdings was stolen during the wars between the brave Duke Philip of Swabia and the anti-king, Duke Otto of Brunswick. At one point, Reb Eliezer barely escaped Frankfort with his life. With no home and no money, he finally yielded to the wishes of his father: at the age of sixty-one, Eliezer took over Joel ben Isaac's rabbinical post in Cologne.

Unfortunately, Eliezer was not satisfied as a simple rabbi. He was intolerant of petty problems, and he did not like routine. His congregation seemed to think so slowly – and would his local Jews never learn from their mistakes? The same problems arose again and again and again. Eliezer found it so painful to earn his livelihood through the normal rabbinic chores, that at one point he tried to escape by taking on the office of cantor, also. (However, in a strange turn of events, Eliezer soon resigned as cantor when the Archbishop officially confirmed this appointment. You see, Rabbi, it was contrary to Jewish policy for a Jew to accept a religious post from a Christian ruler: to do so would leave the way open for the non-Jewish authorities to dictate the religious policies of the Jewish community.)

Rabbi Eliezer could never be still; his mind raced even at night. He wrote books and books and more books, books on legal subjects, on Jewish customs, and on religious rules; he wrote on matters of prayer and of Sabbath observance, and he set down explanations of the Torah and its commentaries. In this way, his influence upon later generations was even greater than his effect upon his contemporaries.

Yes, exactly, Rabbi: this was the Eliezer ben Joel who authored the *Sefer Rabiah*, the *Sefer Abiasaf*, and the *Tosafot*. Then one day, his wife died suddenly; next, his oldest son lost a leg in an accident, and a grandson was drowned. Had the Rabbi broken some commandment? Was he too lazy? Was he not appropriately pious? Had the sins of his youth caught up with him in old age? Should he have been less headstrong – should he have accepted earlier the rabbinical post of Cologne? Only the good Lord God (blessed be He) knew for certain. These sad misfortunes led Eliezer to write a volume of penitential poems, six of which my grandmother remembered.

Eliezer sought no fame; nonetheless, Rabbi Eliezer ben Joel became recognized as the most erudite Jew of Germany, and in those days his Rabbinical Court of Law (the *Bet Din* of Cologne) was the final resort for all German Jews. When he was seventy-eight years old, Rabbi Eliezer gave up his post in Cologne, and he transferred his activities to Wurzburg, where he died. Why did he move? I do not know, Rabbi. I only know that he was buried in the Wurzburg *House of Life – The Garden of the Jews.* . . . Ah, yes, Rabbi, Gentiles always raise their eyebrows at these names, but the last refuge from day-to-day storms in any Jewish community is the most sacred spot of all for the living: all Jewish cemeteries are Gardens of Life. My grandmother used to sit happily by her mother's grave in one of these Gardens, embroidering for hours and hours in the good weather. That cemetery was at the end of a back street in the ghetto – far from the houses and alongside a park – in order to fulfill the old custom of burying the dead at least fifty paces from the nearest house. Grandmother would say to me: "Walk fifty steps, my golden young man, and you will always find a lasting happiness, amen."

abbi, I am glad to see you here tonight: I need your advice, although it is really a small matter. This afternoon one of our young students found two pennies out on the street; they were lying just beyond the front door of the yeshiva. He is an honest boy, and he brought the coins to me. Now, should I return the coins to him—after all, he is the finder. Or should I put the pennies in the poorbox? Of course, Rabbi, after all these years of sitting in the study rooms during lessons, I have learned a bit of Talmud. And I recall what the great rabbis decided about found articles: some objects immediately become the property of the discoverer—others must be advertised. And the Talmud's list of free treasures includes scattered fruit, sheaves of corn in the public road, cakes of pressed figs, baker's loaves, fishes strung together, pieces of meat, fleeces of wool (in their natural condition), stalks of flax, and strips of wool dyed purple.

I know that you remember these sections of the Talmud, so you will remember how it continues:

> Any found object that has something distinctive about it must be advertised. For example, one might find a cake of figs in which there is embedded some pottery, or one might find a loaf of bread in which are

hidden some coins – these must be advertised. Also the following articles must always be advertised: a piece of pottery, fruit in a container, a purse (and any money it contains), distinctive heaps of fruit, three coins one on top of the other, small sheaves of vegetables lying in private property, loaves of bread that are homemade, fleeces of wool that had been removed from the workshop, and pitchers of wine or oil.

I remembered these rules, and when I was remembering them I became confused. We have here *two* pennies: the Talmud speaks only of three coins (or of money in a purse). What is the proper thing to do? . . . Give the coins to the boy? All right.

At first I was thinking of advertising. I know that two pennies are only a small amount of money, but if the shammas does not maintain some standards in a congregation, then who will? My grandmother would always say: "Maintain some standards, young man." She repeated that phrase almost daily – did you ever hear her say it? You never met my grandmother, Rabbi? Ah, that is a pity, for she was a fine woman. She told me that in Jerusalem it was not the job of the shammas to advertise lost articles in the synagogue each week. Instead, there was a central meeting place in the market; it was a stone bench, and it was called the "Claiming Stone." If you lost something, then you went there and waited; whereas, if you found something, you went there and made an announcement. The finder was obligated to stand by the bench and to report that he had found an object, and the person who lost the object could reclaim it by describing any distinguishing marks. This was in the Golden Era. Things changed after the Temple was destroyed (may it be rebuilt speedily in our days, amen): then, announcements and claims began to be made by the shammases in the synagogues and in the study houses. . . .

What is that, Rabbi? Certainly there is more to tell: I was just resting my eyes a moment. Now let me see, what was I saying? Yes, found articles were very important to my grandmother: a pin lying in the street meant good luck all day – a dark button meant that a misfortune was coming. It was my grandmother who told me all about found articles. I remember her story about Rabbi Eliezer, who found gray hairs. What is that, Rabbi? No, Rabbi Eliezer did not find them in the mirror, and he did not find them in the street; he found them in the head of Rabbi Jochanan ben Azariah, the eighteen-year-old scholar from Sieburg.

Rabbi Eliezer? Yes, it was the same Rabbi Eliezer ben Joel ha-Levi whose father, Joel ben Isaac, had been the chief rabbi in Cologne. The father, Joel ben Isaac, had succeeded his own father, and eventually his son, Eliezer, followed too, exceeding even Rabbi Joel's fine reputation. Rabbi Eliezer was known for justice and for fairness. For instance, one winter morning, he was stepping into the yeshiva when a man offered the Rabbi his hand as a balance on the ice. The Rabbi thanked the man.

"You are quite welcome," said the stranger. "Have a good morning, Rabbi, I will be seeing you this afternoon in the rabbinical court."

"Why is that?" asked Rabbi Eliezer.

"Oh," replied the man, "I have a case pending today."

"Then you will not see me. For after accepting a favor from you, I must remove myself from judging your case," answered the Rabbi.

Rabbi Eliezer did not enjoy his normal rabbinical chores, but he did take great pride in the perceptive justice that he dispensed. Do you remember, Rabbi, how the talmudic rabbis discussed articles found in shops? If a person found something lying on the floor in a shop, then the object belonged to the finder and not to the shopkeeper. I know – that sounds unfair to me, also. I presume that the rabbinical thinking is this: the object was lost by some previous customer, the object was lost in a public place, and therefore there is no hope of the owner being identified. Of course, the finder must still advertise: the Talmud requires that one's neighbors learn about the found object and that they have an opportunity to claim it. And, as a shammas, I know that these advertisements should only report that something has been found – the claimant is responsible for correctly identifying the article. If the claimant cannot describe the distinguishing marks, then the finder does not give the article to him. Furthermore, if the claimant is a crook, then he cannot be trusted, and the article should not be turned over to him under any conditions. Of course, such judgments can only be made by rabbis, like Rabbi Eliezer. For example, my grandmother told me that once a man came to Rabbi Eliezer with a beautiful hand *tefilla*; the prayer box was made of polished brown wood, and it had fine black leather straps:

"I found this on the floor of my shop," reported the store owner. "Reb Johusan claims that the hand *tefilla* is his. I would gladly return it, if it actually belonged to him; unfortunately, he cannot identify the initials carved on the bottom of the box."

Then Reb Johusan replied: "There are no initials carved on the bottom of the box."

The Rabbi took the hand *tefilla* and he turned it over – sure enough, the letters *nun* and *mem* were scratched onto the bottom of the wooden box.

The Rabbi looked at the found object, and then he asked the shopkeeeper: "What will you do if I rule in your favor and decide to give you this phylactery?"

"Ah, good Rabbi, it is a beautiful prayer piece. I will set it gently on the shelf in my store; I will take care to guard and to protect it."

Then Rabbi Eliezer turned to Reb Johusan: "And how about you? What will you do if I rule in your favor and decide to give you this phylactery?"

"First," said Reb Johusan, "I will take some oil and rub out those scratches. Then, I will put on the prayer-piece and say my evening benedictions."

"Take the hand *tefilla*, Reb Johusan," said Rabbi Eliezer, and he turned to other matters.


Did you know, Rabbi, that Eliezer did not take over his father Joel ben Isaac's rabbinical post in Cologne until Eliezer was sixty-one years old? Oh, you knew this – then undoubtedly you also knew that Eliezer ben Joel quickly became famous throughout Germany. He was a rather aloof man; often, he looked bored. He dressed very neatly, and he kept the edges of his beard trimmed evenly. His judicial rulings were also neat, well trimmed, and even-handed, and his Rabbinical Court of Law (the *Bet Din* of Cologne) was widely respected; in those years, it became the court of last resort for all German Jews. Well, for *almost* all German Jews – you know that the Archbishop did not allow the Jewish Court of Cologne to prosecute murders. You did not know this, Rabbi? Then let me tell you. You see, Cologne Jews paid a special additional tax to the Archbishop, and in exchange they received the Archbishop's protection. Also, the Archbishop agreed to limit his own judicial authority over the Jews of Cologne to counterfeiting, murder, and adultery between Jews and Gentiles. Rabbi Eliezer's Court was empowered to decide all other cases, and the Archbishop agreed to lend his officers when they were needed to expel condemned Jews from the community.

Anyway, all manner of cases and informal decisions came to be decided by Rabbi Eliezer. For example, there was the case of the lentils and the divorce of Reb Joseph. One night, two Cologne scholars, Reb Joseph and Reb Samuel, found themselves arguing quite late in the yeshiva, so Reb Joseph said to Reb Samuel: "Come home with me this evening and have some dinner." Reb Samuel accepted the invitation.

Reb Joseph's wife was fiddling with her jewelry when she heard the men coming home from their studies. "What is this?" she thought. "Has Joseph again brought home some old man to bother me?" Quickly, she removed from the fire the meat that she had been cooking, and she put a small pot of lentils there instead.

Reb Joseph came in the door. "I have brought home my friend Reb Samuel," he said. "Have you anything for us to eat?"

"My dear husband," answered his wife. "I have been busy shopping, sewing, and cleaning all day—and you know how difficult these things are with my weak left arm. I am afraid that I have nothing much for you to eat; there is only this bit of lentils warming on the stove."

Reb Joseph took the pot of lentils, and he divided the small amount of porridge into two servings. "Is there any salt?" he asked his wife.

"Of course," she answered, "you can get it from the shelves over there."

When Reb Joseph went to the shelves to get the salt, he found the pot of meat hidden behind a flour container. "My goodness, Reb Samuel, you are truly a blessed guest," said Reb Joseph, "for you, the good Lord God has worked a miracle. Here, I have discovered a large pot of meat." And the two men had a fine dinner of meat with their lentils. . . .

What is that, Rabbi? Of course there is more. Can an old man not take a rest once in a while? I am eighty years old, you know. Now, where was I? Oh, yes—after dinner, Reb Joseph walked with Reb

Samuel toward his house. "I apologize for my wife's behavior," said Reb Joseph sadly. "I am afraid that she sometimes acts rather selfishly."

"Has this been going on for long?" asked Reb Samuel.

"Yes—it is typical of our everyday lives."

"Then I suggest," said Reb Samuel, "that you divorce your wife and that you find someone more friendly."

"I have thought of that," said Reb Joseph, "but I cannot divorce her. You see, when we were married, she brought a very rich dowry. Since then she has spent the money on clothes and jewels, and now I would not be able to repay her father if she and I were to be divorced."

Reb Samuel thought about this, but he did not answer. And the next day, he took Reb Joseph to Rabbi Eliezer for advice. Rabbi Eliezer listened to the two men discussing Reb Joseph's home life, and then Rabbi Eliezer said: "It is not only the dowry that must be repaid, gentlemen: the proper settlement for a divorce also includes a penalty of fifty percent more than the dowry itself (when there are no major transgressions by the wife). As judge in this case, I would certainly pronounce that additional stipulation. I would also remind you, Reb Joseph, that were you to accept a Bill of Divorcement, then you would continue to assume a financial responsibility for your wife—should she ever fall into dire need, you will have to stretch out your hand in order to aid her."

Poor Reb Joseph looked at the floor. "Fifty percent more than my dowry?" he repeated. "Then there is no hope: I am destined to remain with my wife forever." And Reb Joseph sat down on the bench along the wall of the studyhall.

Rabbi Eliezer looked at Reb Joseph and asked: "Are you that unhappy?"

"I do not know, Rabbi—I suppose that I should thank the good Lord God (blessed be He) for my health," said Reb Joseph.

"Perhaps," said Rabbi Eliezer to Reb Samuel, "we can help this man. How about taking up a collection among the men of the community? If you will organize this project, then I will lend my support."

With the backing of Rabbi Eliezer, the Jews of Cologne contributed the full dowry, and the Rabbi himself added the required fifty percent more. A Bill of Divorcement was drawn up, the Rabbi held a formal court session, and the dowry money (plus the fifty percent penalty) was returned to the father of Reb Joseph's wife. Reb Joseph signed the divorce decree. Reb Joseph's wife signed the decree. The father of Reb Joseph's wife signed, and Rabbi Eliezer signed. Later Reb Joseph married another woman–she was the daughter of a poor shopkeeper, she had no dowry, and the couple lived together happily for the rest of their days, amen.

I agree, Rabbi–that is a good example of how simplicity and modesty are the best of virtues. And old Rabbi Eliezer ben Joel (ben Isaac) believed that even one simple or modest trait was a sufficient basis for all final rewards. For instance, once there was an old man who never came to the synagogue. Yes, Rabbi, he was a Jew–but he was also a hermit: he never talked to anyone. When he died, his neighbors were not certain whether he deserved a Jewish funeral, and they asked Rabbi Eliezer. "Can you think of any good thing to say about this man?" asked the Rabbi.

"No," they replied, "we are afraid that we cannot."

"Tell me," said Rabbi Eliezer, "how did you discover that this man had died?"

"Well," said one neighbor, "every night, I see an oil lamp burning inside the window of this old curmudgeon's house. But last night, there was no light. I knocked on the door. I loudly called his name. No one answered, so I went in and I found him lying dead, slumped over in his chair."

"The lamp was unlit?"

"Yes," replied the neighbor, "it was filled with olive oil, but it was still unlit."

"Did you say 'olive oil'?" asked Rabbi Eliezer.

"I did," said the neighbor.

"Ah," said Rabbi Eliezer ben Joel, "the Talmud tells us that to burn olive oil in a lamp is a holy and pious act: therefore, this man deserves a proper Jewish funeral."

And, Rabbi, that was exactly like the case that Eliezer heard involving the perfect corpse. What is that, Rabbi? By "perfect," I mean the corpse that was unravaged in the grave–have you never heard of this famous incident? My grandmother told me that it happened in Gladbach. Were you ever in the little city of Gladbach, northeast of Cologne? No? It is a dark mining town with four old Catholic churches, and it has always had a tiny Jewish community.

Once upon a time, said my grandmother, an old Jewish man died in the outskirts of Gladbach. There is no Jewish cemetery in Gladbach, so the man was buried at the edge of a field. Not long after his death, his grave was dug up mistakenly by some workmen, and the dead man was found to be in perfect condition – worms, animals, and time had done no harm to his body. (I am not inventing this, Rabbi: my grandmother told me every detail.) The local Jewish scholar, Rabbi Nachman ben Moyses, was consulted, but he had no explanation, so a delegation of Jews traveled to Cologne to consult with the famous Eliezer ben Joel.

Rabbi Eliezer was sitting with his colleagues from the rabbinate of Cologne – these scholars were the famous rabbis Shealtiel ben Menahem and Menahem ben David. Rabbi Nachman told the story of the corpse, and he added: "Is this a miracle? If so, we cannot understand it in Gladbach. Here was the most ordinary of men. What could he possibly have done in his lifetime to deserve such favored treatment after death?" And Rabbi Eliezer asked: "What was the name of this man who is now dead?"

"He was Jacob ben Saul."

"Tell me," asked Rabbi Eliezer, "what was outstanding about Jacob ben Saul?"

"Nothing," replied the people from Gladbach.

"Nothing?"

"Absolutely nothing," they answered. "If you had met him in the street, then you would not give him a second glance."

"Do you mean," asked the Rabbi, "that Jacob ben Saul was not showy?"

"Exactly," they replied. "He dressed in plain and simple clothes. Moreover, another reason that you would hardly notice him is that he spoke so softly."

"Do you mean," asked the Rabbi, "that Jacob ben Saul never said a harsh word?"

"Exactly," they replied. "He was exceedingly mild, even to those who were mean to him. Apparently, in all his life he never did any harm, and he did not seem to envy anyone."

"Do you mean," asked the Rabbi, "that Jacob ben Saul was gentle to all his fellow men?"

"Exactly," they replied. "You are describing our timid and unobtrusive Jacob ben Saul precisely. He was not notable in any way."

"He may not have been notable to you," said Rabbi Eliezer, "but clearly he was notable to the good Lord God, blessed be He."

Now that was when Eliezer ben Joel was already quite old himself, Rabbi. Did you know that Eliezer did not take up his father's post until he was sixty-one years of age? Oh, you had heard that? Then undoubtedly you have heard of another of his famous cases, the one involving an astrologer. No? Well then let me tell you:

One time a Gentile astrologer told the mother of little Aaron ben Nathan that her boy would grow up to be a thief. The mother was very upset. Daily, she made her son report every single thing that he touched. Also, she never allowed him to be bare-headed; she repeated: "Keep your head covered, little man, so that the fear of Heaven shall be upon you–and pray for mercy." Aaron did not know why she told him this. Most other boys played without hats. (You see, Rabbi, at that time many Jews in Cologne went about their daily lives and even prayed bare-headed–or so my grandmother claimed. Why is that? I do not know. You would have to ask my grandmother; unfortunately, she has now gone to join her parents beyond the grave, so we will have to be content with those few words that she has left us.)

Grandmother said that one day, Aaron was sitting and studying beneath a tree–a carob tree–and his little woven hat fell off. It fell because he had lifted his head to look up at the carob fruit on the tree. Aaron was now bare-headed, and suddenly he felt that he had to have a piece of carob fruit. Perhaps he had forgotten to eat breakfast, or perhaps an evil spirit was whispering in his ear. Anyway, he climbed the tree, he took down a carob pod, and he ate it. Poor Aaron–this was the tree of a mean Gentile who spent the entire day guarding his fruit trees. Aaron was immediately caught by two of the Gentile's servants, and he was dragged off to the Jewish Court. That afternoon, young Aaron ben Nathan appeared before Rabbi Eliezer ben Joel ben Isaac, the head rabbi of Cologne.

Silently, the Rabbi listened to the Gentile's presentation. "There is no question that Aaron is guilty of theft," said the Rabbi.

"I knew it," cried his mother, "as much as I warned him, as much as I pleaded with him–nonetheless, the astrologer was correct: my son has become a thief."

"Yes," said the Rabbi, "your son is a thief. But I see that he is also a good boy—and the Almighty Lord God, blessed be He, forgives him and loves him. Remember, my fine woman, in Psalm 116 it says":

> I am blessed: the good Lord hears
> My voice, my hopes, my prayers.
> The Lord is righteous; He reveres
> Even one who errs.
> With His kind, compassionate gaze
> God uplifts the fallen man:
> Once, I fell to evil ways
> Yet God saved my soul again.
>
> In my heart, I held to Him
> (Even when I said in spite:
> "Men despise the cherubim.")
> Now, I greet the Lord, contrite
> In His House, where truth is read;
> In His courts, I bow my head
> With others whom He's shepherded –
> I'll praise the Lord till my deathbed.

Of course, Rabbi, it was not always a matter of making decisions and of passing judgments or of pointing out the appropriate scriptural references: sometimes, Rabbi Eliezer just reminded the Jews to wait patiently for God's Divine will and for His holy plans. For instance, my grandmother told me about the Sieburg miracle, a miracle that only involved Rabbi Eliezer ben Joel ha-Levi peripherally. This event occurred at a time when the infighting and conflict of the Sieburg congregation had reached a boiling point. What is that, Rabbi? No— the Cologne yeshiva had no direct influence on Sieburg; Sieburg is some distance from Cologne, perhaps twenty-five kilometers southeast, on the River Sieg.

In the days of Rabbi Eliezer, there was a small Jewish community in Sieburg, and it had its own yeshiva. One day, a pupil in the yeshiva came to Rabbi Joshua and asked that famous and unresolved question: "My dear master, tell me about the evening prayer. Is one obliged to say it or is it optional?" Rabbi Joshua replied: "It is optional; it is not obligatory." Then the pupil left Rabbi Joshua and went to Rabbi Gamaliel, who was the head of the college in Sieburg. The student said to Rabbi Gamaliel: "Tell me, Rabbi. Is the evening prayer optional or is it obligatory?" Rabbi Gamaliel replied: "It is a necessary duty for the pious Jew. Now, because the good Lord God, blessed be He, requires the necessary, then of course it is obligatory, and one must say the evening prayer." The pupil listened; then he said to Rabbi Gamaliel: "But I have heard from Rabbi Joshua that one is not obliged to say it if one does not wish to." And Rabbi Gamaliel said: "Wait until all the scholars come to the college and sit upon the benches and are ready to speak their minds, for that is a good time to test my opinion—when, of course, I will then hear their opinions, also. Then we will see what Rabbi Joshua has to say."

When the various scholars had finally gathered in the main study hall, the pupil stood up and he asked again: "Rabbis, I wonder: Is the evening prayer obligatory or is it optional?" And Rabbi Gamaliel stood up and, looking sternly at Rabbi Joshua, he said: "The evening prayer is a requisite for the devout of our faith, the children of Israel—we are they, and therefore the evening prayer must be obligatory."

Rabbi Joshua looked out one of the twelve synagogue windows. So Rabbi Gamaliel said: "Perhaps there is someone who would have another opinion on his mind when thinking about these matters. If anyone here has thought these things through and has come by some peculiar means to another conclusion—if there is in fact someone who differs from my decision, then let him speak forth now. He should state his misguided opinion clearly for all the assembled and for their friends and for their brethren, amen."

Rabbi Joshua studied his prayer book. So Rabbi Gamaliel asked loudly: "Is there no one who differs from me on this point?"

A moment of silence followed, and Reb Leitner, an old member of the congregation, said: "Apparently, no one disagrees."

Then Rabbi Gamaliel said: "What is this? How can I hear this silence? How can you all sit there saying in essence that there is no one who differs from me? I have been informed on this very day and in this very study house, and by one of these very students here, that there is in fact someone who disagrees completely and who holds exactly the opposite opinion. I have been informed that someone—a certain rabbi of our own congregation – has decided that the evening prayer is not obligatory and that the recital of evening prayers can be left done or undone according to one's whim. Now, anyone championing this strange opinion had best stand up honorably and speak now and defend with full and appropriate citations and authority this backward idea, because I cannot understand it at all."

And Rabbi Joshua said: "Frankly, Rabbi Gamaliel, I suspect that there are many things that you cannot understand at all – and the length of your sentences adds no substance to the weakness of your opinions. Clearly, the evening prayer is optional."

"Ah," replied Rabbi Gamaliel, "so it is you who has put forth this blasphemous stance without thinking and with no care at all for our young. You are encouraging the casual ways that boys have fallen into, in these evil times of excess Gentile influence and comradery. Defend your statements, Rabbi Joshua – if that is even possible. Because I doubt whether you could muster the slightest or the weakest or the feeblest support for such an untenable and radical position . . . ." Rabbi Gamaliel went on and on – with commentary from a certain Reb Huzpit, who felt obligated to help explain the deep sentences of the good Rabbi Gamaliel.

Soon, as my grandmother (may her soul have found the souls of her parents) would say: "His audience had already forgotten the beginning, and the end was still not in sight." Yet Rabbi Gamaliel lectured on and on. One scholar turned to his neighbor, saying: "Will the man never stop?" Another said: "If he is not badgering Rabbi Joshua, then Rabbi Gamaliel is preaching to Reb Solomon, or he is castigating young Saul ben Moshe. This is more than tiresome: this is painful." And another said: "How long will we let him torment our congregation? We must depose Rabbi Gamaliel. Remove him from his leadership, and let us elect another head rabbi." "But whom shall we put in his place? Shall we set Rabbi Joshua in the place of old Rabbi Gamaliel? Rabbi Joshua is also a quarrelsome person: as head of the yeshiva, he will annoy Rabbi Gamaliel even more than Rabbi Gamaliel annoyed him. The two men will argue interminably. However, there are no other elder scholars, and how can we choose between these two old and cranky men?"

They argued back and forth and back and forth. Finally, old Reb Leitner spoke up: "Let us consider someone else entirely."

"Who else could we possibly call upon?" asked one man.

"How about Rabbi Jochanan?" said Reb Leitner.

"Jochanan ben Azariah? Why, he is a mere boy."

"True–but he has an incredible knowledge of Jewish law and lore. We should make him head of the college because he is a fine scholar. (Also, he is rich and he comes from a well-respected family.)"

"Rabbi Jochanan is rich?"

"Certainly–do you not know that his family owns the major pottery factories here in Sieburg?"

"Oh? I did not realize that this is the family of our young, devout, and learned Jochanan."

"Absolutely–young as he is, pious as he is, and learned as he is, he is also quite wealthy. With his money, he would be in a good position to obtain favors from the government, and with his notable ancestry he would give the Jews a good standing in the Gentile community."

So in the end, various representatives of the congregation approached Jochanan ben Azariah. "It would be a great pleasure and a great honor to us if you would become the head of our yeshiva here in Sieburg," they said. Rabbi Jochanan looked at them for a moment, and then he replied: "I will think about your kind request." Then, Jochanan went home.

Jochanan asked his wife whether he should accept the post of head of the college. And she replied: "Why accept these headaches? You will work hard and then you will suffer the same fate as old Rabbi Gamaliel–tomorrow, you will be deposed."

Rabbi Jochanan thought about this, and then he said to his wife: "You may be right. But let me tell you a proverb: 'If one drinks from a beautiful goblet today, then it does not matter if the cup is broken tomorrow.' In other words, if I can be a good leader for the yeshiva today, then what does it matter if I am no longer the head rabbi tomorrow?"

But his wife shook her head: "I am not certain that I agree with you, Jochanan. However, there is another, practical matter. You are too young: you will never command the necessary respect."

Rabbi Jochanan thought about this, and then he said to his wife: "My wise wife, you are correct. I do not have even one gray hair in my head. The leader of the yeshiva must be old and respected. I had best decline the offer."

Rabbi Jochanan told the Sieburg scholars that he was still too young to be accorded the appropriate respect from the older members of the congregation. "A leader must command respect," said Jochanan. "Thank you for your offer, good friends, but I must decline."

The rabbis and scholars of Sieburg returned to their discussions and conferences. After long arguments, they decided that no other candidate in all of Sieburg could match Rabbi Jochanan; therefore, the council of the yeshiva decided to seek the advice of the famed Rabbi Eliezer of Cologne. Could the Sieburg rabbis actually appoint such a young scholar to head their aging congregation? Perhaps Rabbi Eliezer ben Joel would know. The rabbis collected their papers together, and they traveled from Sieburg to Cologne.

In Cologne, the rabbis arrived on Judengasse Street. They walked down the alley that led back to the courtyard of the House of Study; they entered the front door of the synagogue, and they sat on the wooden benches that filled the main prayer hall. The shammas greeted them courteously, and Rabbi Eliezer came over to them. The rabbis from Sieburg explained their problem, and Rabbi Eliezer heard them out. Then, without a word, Rabbi Eliezer turned and walked out of the main prayer hall with its many wooden benches; he passed the twelve stained glass windows with their colored lions and snakes, he went by the Holy Ark made of stone, and he retired to the back room of his yeshiva. An hour later, the Rabbi emerged. "Listen, good scholars of Sieburg," said Rabbi Eliezer, "go home." "Go home?" they asked. "What kind of advice is that?" But Rabbi Eliezer said simply: "Go back home again – the good Lord God (blessed be He) shall provide."

The rabbis returned to Sieburg. They were puzzled and disappointed. Some of them searched the skies; others kept their eyes on the Holy Ark in the synagogue. Then one morning a miracle happened. Rabbi Jochanan, who was eighteen years old, found that eighteen strands of gray hair had grown on his head, and eighteen white hairs were in his beard. His wife said that it was the will of the good Lord God, blessed be He: now people could think of Jochanan as an elder of the community. When the scholars of the yeshiva saw Rabbi Jochanan, they too felt that it must be a Divine signal. Even Rabbi Gamaliel spoke only in short sentences for a while. So Jochanan ben Azariah was immediately appointed to be the head rabbi of the yeshiva of Sieburg. And this experience is why Jochanan could say: "I have found myself, and I am like a man of seventy – in some ways."

ello, Rabbi, I will be with you in a moment—I cannot leave until every tablecloth is folded, otherwise the day has not ended properly. Do you remember Elisha ben Avram? I am like him. Every night Reb Elisha spent at least an hour closing up his house. First, he locked the front door; then, he locked the back. He checked each of the candleholders, and he banked the coals in the stove. He straightened the cloth napkins, he centered the pots hanging over the stove, he brushed crumbs from the table and the countertops, and he pushed the chairs into their nighttime places. And then on and on, for at least an hour—every bit of his house was checked and rechecked and neatened. His wife gave up on him long ago; she knew that he could not sleep without carrying out this meticulous routine, so she would go to bed and ignore him. Anyway, Rabbi, now I am finished, and I can sit next to you by the stove.

I am not sleepy either. It is too bad that I never learned chess, otherwise you and I could play a game. Oh? How could you have avoided learning chess when you were young; I thought that all rabbis knew chess. Really? That is not what my grandmother told me. (And I learned never to doubt her word.) Grandmother often told me stories about the great Rabbi Eliezer of Cologne, who was a renowned chess player. Exactly, Rabbi—it was the Eliezer ben Joel ha-Levi whose father, Joel ben Isaac, had been the chief rabbi in Cologne. Joel ben Isaac had succeeded *his* father; eventually, Eliezer followed too, exceeding Rabbi Joel's reputation—but that was later; it was well after Eliezer had met the Silent Shammas Amitai.

What is that, Rabbi? You have never heard of the Silent Shammas, Amitai of Prague? No—he was not Amitai ben anything. . . . Well, obviously it is that he had no father, and if you will listen a moment, then I will tell you how that could be. . . . Just be patient a moment, Rabbi. I learned this long ago from my grandmother, who told me that young Eliezer once met the Silent Shammas, before Eliezer became a rabbi. You see, when he was a boy, Eliezer had been taught by his father, Rabbi Joel, in Cologne. Then, Eliezer went and studied in the famous talmudic academies of Mainz, Metz, Regensburg, and Speyer. Eliezer was precocious, and soon he became a scholar of repute. He traveled often to Bonn, to Worms, to Wurzburg, and to Frankfort consulting on esoteric matters. Rabbi Joel was an astute businessman, so his son Eliezer was independently wealthy. Therefore, Eliezer devoted himself to study—he could live without the burdens of an official position. Later, of course, Eliezer suffered financial reversals, and at the age of sixty-one, he finally took over Joel ben Isaac's rabbinical post in Cologne.

Perhaps this late ascension to the rabbinate was a good thing, Rabbi. There is much to be said for a mature man taking such serious and holy positions. My grandmother always pointed out to me that giving important positions to one's children can even be a sin, and to make her point she told the story of Reb David ben Moses, a very pious man:

Once upon a time, said my grandmother, there lived a very pious man named David ben Moses ben Judah. Reb David was a serious scholar. In his later years, he was invited regularly to read all the special prayers, such as those at *Rosh Hashanah* and *Yom Kippur*; the congregation selected him for this honor because of his devotion, his scholarship, and his dedication.

One year when Reb David was already very old, he suddenly refused to read the *Rosh Hashanah* and *Yom Kippur* benedictions. "What is this?" asked the shammas. "We have counted on your leading the congregation."

"I only wish that I could conduct these wonderful services, my good Shammas," said Reb David.

"Then what is stopping you?"

"I am very old," answered David ben Moses.

"So?"

"So, if I should read the prayers now and if I should die during the year, then my son could claim the right to read next year as my successor."

"True—and what is the problem with that?"

"I love my son," said David ben Moses, "but to be honest, good Shammas, my son is not worthy of this honor. He does not always come to the yeshiva, he does not think hard and long about the Lord, and he does not put his prayers above all else in life. Let me do my holy obligation and ensure a worthy successor while I am still able. This year I will invite someone else to read on the high holy days."

Saying this, Reb David appointed Meir ben Abraham to read the *Rosh Hashanah* service. Reb Meir was a quiet old scholar who always sat in the very back of the study room. Meir came to the yeshiva every day rain or shine, and he rehearsed the prayers and benedictions during all his free moments at home. I think, Rabbi, that Reb David was driven, in all this, by the scriptural story from the First Book of Samuel. You know what I mean: Eli's two sons, Hophni and Phineas, were scoundrels, and they were selfish. Nonetheless, they were his sons, so Eli allowed them to remain as high priests of Israel—and because of this, the Philistines defeated the Israelites at the battle of Eben-ezer, the Holy Ark of the Lord was captured, and Eli and his sons died. In fact, it is this biblical story that my grandmother cited to show why it is that only old, proven, and unrelated men should be awarded such important positions.

In any case, Rabbi, this was the situation with Eliezer ben Joel: he became a rabbi only when he was already a mature man. I think that he even stopped playing chess after he took over the leadership of the Cologne yeshiva. Yes, that was quite a change, because at one time he played chess daily in the study houses. He even carried his own silver chess set wherever he went. Grandmother told me that Eliezer was a chessmaster in the days when the game had just been introduced to Europe. . . . Rabbi, where have you been? Chess started in India; then it crossed over from India into Persia—it passed from the Hindus to the Persians and from the Persians to the Arabians.

How did chess get to Cologne from Persia and Arabia? Undoubtedly, the Spanish learned chess from their Moslem invaders, and the Italians learned chess from the Byzantines—then the game marched north with travelers and merchants and wanderers of all sorts. People at the big fairs in northern cities (cities like Worms and Cologne) soon marveled wide-eyed at young foreign men who sat intently for hours before finely carved figures lined up on inlaid wooden boards.

As for the Jews, Rabbi—in Europe, chess quickly became a Jewish obsession. At first, men did not play chess every day but only on holidays; in contrast, women had the freedom to play games whenever they liked. Grandmother said that Jewish chess began as a woman's game. (But, then, my grandmother claimed that the Scriptures were originally set down on paper by women scribes.) In any case, men soon began to play chess daily in the study houses, and there was no religious opposition. What is that, Rabbi? Yes, it is true: Maimonides is sometimes said to have been an opponent of chess. But that is wrong. Maimonides only included chess in the list of games that are forbidden when played for money. All the Sages were against gambling. Chess, on the other hand, is a game of insight: it is a game of mental wrestling. Some scholars felt that chess is so like wrestling with the holy word that these men taught their children chess in order to improve their minds (and also to wean the boys from cards and from other games of chance). Even well-known rabbis, such as the young Eliezer, played chess among themselves.

And Eliezer played chess with a passion. You know, Rabbi, Eliezer ben Joel wrote books and books and more books. He wrote books on legal subjects, on Jewish customs, and on religious rules; he wrote on matters of prayer and of Sabbath observance, and he set down explanations of the Torah and its commentaries. It is also said that he wrote (under the pseudonym Jacobus de Cessolis) the first book on chess: it was called *The Game and Playe of Chesse*. In those days—in his chess playing days, before he took on his father's rabbinate at the age of sixty-one—Reb Eliezer traveled widely, he spent much time in the Judengasse of Frankfort on the Main, and once when in Prague he had a very strange experience, said my grandmother. In Prague, Reb Eliezer met the Silent Shammas. You do not know about the Silent Shammas? Then let me tell you:

It was late in the day – Eliezer ben Joel arrived late in the day in the Jewish Quarter of the city of Prague. Eliezer walked down the main street; he stopped a local Jew, he asked for the study house, and eventually he found his way to the yeshiva. There, he was received quietly by a tall hooded shammas who motioned for him to enter: apparently, the shammas did not have the ability to speak. After prayers, the Rabbi himself came up to Eliezer, and the two of them talked of news from western Europe. Eliezer proposed a game of chess; however, the Rabbi declined politely, and the shammas led them both to a corner table where he set out dinner in silence. As the shammas was serving, his hat (which was more like a cowl) slipped back. On his forehead was engraved a word, a single Hebrew word: the word *emet* (truth) was written above his brow.

Eliezer was taken aback, but he did not say anything. After the shammas had left the room, the Rabbi turned to Eliezer and he said: "You have seen Reb Amitai's forehead. I suppose that it was a bit of a shock."

"You must admit, Rabbi," said Eliezer, "it is an unexpected sight."

"Would you like to know his history?"

"I would."

"Well," said the Rabbi, "it begins in Regensburg. In the days of Rabbi Juddah he-Hasid, the mystic of Regensburg, a child suddenly appeared with the word *emet* engraved upon its forehead. At that time, Juddah the Pious was already very old. Rabbi Juddah could not see well, and the Regensburg yeshiva was dark and small and crowded. One evening after prayers, Rabbi Juddah he-Hasid heard a squeak and a creak. Was there a weak little cry? He stepped to the back benches, he bent down, and he peered among the scattered prayer books. There, in a low uncovered box and wrapped in a white cotton blanket was a tiny clay-colored child.

"Rabbi Juddah looked up and he looked down and he saw a strange and holy thing – on the blank little forehead of the clay-colored child was written the word *emet*. 'Emet,' whispered Rabbi Juddah, and he lifted up the infant. He took the child, and he carried it into the back room of the yeshiva. No one ever came to claim the little boy; no one inquired of a missing child. So Rabbi Juddah himself raised the child. Wherever Juddah he-Hasid went, he took the child with him, and as the little lad grew stronger and as the mystic Rabbi grew weaker, the boy began to care for Juddah he-Hasid, the mystic of Regensburg.

"There were secret understandings that passed between the Rabbi and the boy. Juddah he-Hasid taught the young child personally; the Rabbi taught him Hebrew and old knowledge and even archery. The boy learned quickly, and he became a great scholar in the Torah, and Rabbi Juddah named him 'Amitai.' Amitai was an artful and a prodigious writer; however, he never spoke a word – he was unable to make a sound.

"Eventually, Juddah he-Hasid died a quiet and mystical death. The boy was heartbroken. He remained in the Regensburg yeshiva as an assistant, but the men did not speak to Amitai, and he put no effort into communicating with them. Silently, he walked about the yeshiva, cleaning and organizing, straightening and tidying. He wore a hat with a cowl, and he always looked at his feet. Then one day Amitai simply disappeared; he walked out, and he never returned. Did he have adventures? Did he travel to the Holy Land? Did he go off by himself and meditate? No one knows – he has certainly never told me – in any case, it was not until many, many years later that he finally arrived here in Prague.

"It was many, many years later when finally he arrived here – he came late in the fall. Our old shammas had just died during a miserable cold and rainy spell, and we had not had the heart to look for a replacement. One night, Amitai appeared in my study. I looked up and there he was, a silent, pale, clay-colored man wearing a hood that covered his forehead. I spoke to him, but he did not respond. Was he not listening? Was he deaf? Perhaps he could not speak. After a moment, he tilted his head, he stepped to my desk, he took up a pen, and he wrote: 'Rabbi, I am Amitai. Once I was a shammas in Regensburg. I have heard that your poor shammas has passed on to the Great Hereafter, by the desire of the good Lord God (blessed be He). May I take on his position, the post of shammas here in the Prague yeshiva?' 'Can you speak?' I asked him. He shook his head 'no,' and as he did, the cowl slipped backward from his head.

"At first in the dim light of the back study room, I did not notice anything. Then it suddenly struck me: something was written on the man's forehead. I looked again. The word *emet* was engraved clear and deep above his eyes. I must have gasped, for he stepped back a moment. Then, he bent his head, he pulled down his hood, and he turned to leave. 'Wait a moment,' I said, 'listen here: we will try you as our shammas.' That was ten or twelve years ago; we gave him a room in the yeshiva attic, and he has lived here silently ever since. As you see, Reb Eliezer, Amitai remains with us now, strong and quiet still; perhaps he will remain with us in Prague forever—may the Lord (blessed be He) convert all evil hearts to good, amen," said the Rabbi of Prague.

No, I am not inventing this, Rabbi: my grandmother swore that this is exactly what she had heard.

ood evening, Rabbi. Of course—feel free to sit here by the stove: the night fire helps me to become sleepy, also. You and I are not blessed like old Reb Elbaum. Once again, I saw him nodding off during the last prayers this evening; he has learned to sway piously even while asleep—he must have gained some magic from the mystic Achselrad. I suppose that you and I could use a dose of Achselrad ourselves. My grandmother said that Achselrad could put men into a sleep-trance by waving a gold coin before their eyes. You have never heard of Achselrad? He was a German rabbi—Rabbi Abraham ben Alexander, also called Achselrad of Cologne. Achselrad was a pupil of Eliazer ben Judah, the mystic of Worms.

Rabbi Abraham Achselrad was always conjuring visions in the synagogue. I doubt whether he would be tolerated nowadays, but my grandmother said that Rabbi Abraham was also a scholar, and he always claimed that his visions came from devout and pious study. Many an astonishing event took place in his yeshiva—or so my grandmother (blessed be her memory) was told. One day, old Reb Honi even showed up. What, Rabbi? Yes, I will gladly tell you about Honi the Circle-Drawer, although he had nothing to do with Spain.

Did you not ask about Spain? Well, undoubtedly you would

have asked had you known that Rabbi Abraham once visited the Christian King Ferdinand II of Castile. (Although on that occasion, Abraham Achselrad found it necessary to call himself "Nathan" for some unknown reason.) Actually, Ferdinand II was only king of the Spanish province of Leon. His reign of thirty years was unremarkable; there was constant petty fighting, and he was forced to behead a number of unruly local nobles. When he died, Ferdinand II was remembered as a good knight and a hard fighter but as a rather simple man with no political abilities. What is that you say—Rabbi Abraham Achselrad? Well, my grandmother reported that Abraham (alias "Nathan") had spent one Sabbath in the court of Leon. There, in the company of many rabbis, Abraham Achselrad made a young page boy disappear during dinner. No, I am not inventing this, Rabbi—my grandmother swore that this is exactly what she had heard.

And this same Rabbi Abraham Achselrad was a writer, too; he authored kabbalistic tomes of mystical knowledge, including the *Keter Shem Tov* (which, I am told, was never published and only exists as a secret manuscript hidden in a loft above the old Cologne yeshiva). Grandmother said that it was one night while writing this very book that Rabbi Abraham looked up, and in the light of the candle he saw Honi the Circle-Drawer standing in the doorway. . . . No, "Circle-Drawer" is not a profession: Honi was a roof tiler.

Well, I will tell you—Honi was known as "the Circle-Drawer" because he was a very pious man. Of course, a devout life-style does not necessarily require drawing circles, but one day Honi's village began to suffer a terrible dry spell. The drought lasted for a week and then for a month. The rabbis prayed, but no rains came. Honi was a devout scholar, and he prayed also—still, the skies remained clear and dry.

Now, Honi always loved the Psalms, and in regard to weather, he remembered the words of Psalm 147:

> Praise the Lord, He's bountiful;
>   glorify His name, O Israel.
> He dropped thick snow like fleecy wool;
>   He scattered frost and hail.
> In winter, His ice was cast around –
>   who could stand before His cold?
> In spring, He melted frozen ground:
>   the warm winds blew, and waters rolled.

Honi thought of this verse and he prayed to the good Lord God, but no rains came. Finally, Honi stood in the yard outside his front door and he drew a circle about himself in the dust; he drew it neatly and cleanly, and he declared: "O Lord God, King of the Universe, please grant me this small mercy: let it rain. I will wait patiently, my God of all this earth, and I will not move from this circle until the rains come."

Why did he draw a circle, Rabbi? Clearly it was because of the famous section in the Book of Proverbs:

> In the beginning, the Lord created me,
> The first work of His new household.
> I was made from the primal scree,
> From the dust of the earth of old.
>
> Before the mountains, hills, and more,
> I sat below the first Garden tree
> When God formed the edges of the shore
> And set a circle upon the sea.
>
> (And when the fountains of the sea
> Spewed their thunderous tides,
> He gave forth His first decree:
> Stay within your rock-rimmed sides!)
>
> Then I was but a nursling child
> Full of joy and warm delight
> Playing at His feet, beguiled
> By His newborn earthly light.

Honi sat within his circle, and he waited all day. In the evening, the rains began to fall, but they were a gentle mist. So Honi said: "O Lord God, King of the Universe, I must have spoken too quietly, because your rains are falling rather quietly. I need loud rain: I need rain that will fill cisterns, ditches, and caves."

Honi remained inside the circle, and he waited all night. In the morning, the rains began to fall more heavily. Then Honi said: "O Lord God, blessed One, it is true that I spoke loudly before, but actually I should have shouted. I need rain of flood proportions."

In his circle, Honi waited through the morning. The rains increased and increased. They fell in sheets and in torrents; they flooded the town, but also they filled all the wells and the reservoirs. The people were happy, and Honi stepped from the spot where once there was a circle and where now there was only rain-splattered mud.

That was why Honi the roof-tiler became known as pious Honi the Circle-Drawer ever after. Moreover, it was because of this very same Honi that we have the proverb: "Either companionship or death." What is that? Well, if you will listen patiently, Rabbi, then I will tell you.

Now as I was saying about Achselrad: my grandmother claimed that it was one night while writing the *Keter Shem Tov* (which was never published and which remains only as a secret manuscript hidden in the loft of the old Cologne yeshiva) that Rabbi Abraham looked up, and in the light of the candle he saw Honi the Circle-Drawer standing in the doorway. "Good Rabbi," said Honi, "may I stay the night on your yeshiva floor?"

"Certainly," said Achselrad; and then he added: "Would you like some food?"

"No," answered Honi, "I am on my way to die: I do not need to eat."

Well, Rabbi, you can imagine that even the mystic Abraham ben Alexander was taken aback by that reply.

"If I may be so bold as to ask, my good man: Why are you going to die?" said the Rabbi.

"I am living seventy years past my time," said Honi. "My friends are gone, my family is gone, and really I am gone, too. Now it is only for the good Lord God, blessed be He, to take me home in His warm and loving arms again."

Rabbi Abraham looked a moment at Honi: "I am afraid that I do not understand, my friend. . . ."

What, Rabbi? Yes, yes—of course there is more, I was just resting my eyes a bit. The warm glow of the coals seems to slow me down in my old age: I am eighty, you know. Now, where was I? Oh yes—as my grandmother told me: the pious Honi ha-Me'aggel the Circle-Drawer was a scholar with an orderly but rather literal mind. Far and wide, he was known for his careful and methodical exposition of the

Talmud, especially the fine legal points of the *Halakhah*. Honi the Circle-Drawer loved precision, exactitude, and detail. Among his other chores, he was the Gabbai for the congregation: Honi kept the records of all the synagogue's financial transactions, and he was never happier than when he was entering figures in the proper columns of the congregation's leather-bound volumes. Honi the Circle-Drawer loved to write neat numbers. Honi was not much of a romantic, and he accepted only that which accorded cleanly and neatly with the well-worn, well-understood features of his orderly world.

Honi studied the old Jewish books sentence by sentence. Sometimes, he was satisfied with the standard teachings—sometimes, he was not. But all his life, the pious Honi ha-Me'aggel the Circle-Drawer remained worried over one particular section in the Scriptures; it was the first verse in Psalm 126:

> When the Lord returned the Israelites to Zion
> We were like men who awaken to find new health.

Apparently, thought Honi, the good Lord God (blessed be He) regards the seventy years of the Babylonian exile as an extended dream; it is as though we had been asleep for seventy years. But said Honi: "Is this really possible? Is there any man who can sleep seventy years in one stretch? I simply cannot believe this."

(What is that, Rabbi? The Babylonian exile lasted only fifty years? Ah, but it was seventy years from the time that the Temple of Solomon was destroyed until it was finally rebuilt—I am certain that is what Honi had in mind.)

One day, as Honi was riding on a mare through the fields not far from his home, he saw a man planting a carob tree. Honi stopped, and he said to the man: "My good friend, you are obviously a patient fellow. Tell me: How long will it take before this tree grows up?"

The man replied: "It will be seventy years before this seedling can produce fruit."

Honi said to him: "My dear sir, are you sure that you are going to live seventy years more? Will you ever be able to eat the fruit of this tree? Will you ever see even immature pods to feed to your pigs?"

And the man answered: "Ah, Rabbi, let me explain. I found a carob tree when I came into this world—it was a tree that had been planted by my father. I have enjoyed the fruit pods from that tree for all my life; therefore, I will also plant a carob tree for my son to enjoy after me."

Honi the Circle-Drawer dismounted from his horse. He sat down on the ground and ate some bread, he drank some wine, and he had a bit of goat cheese. The hills seemed far away. The clouds were light and gentle. A breeze came and went. Honi became drowsy, and he fell asleep. Then, a rock grew up around him, and no one knew what had become of him. And so Honi the Circle-Drawer slept the sleep of a rock for seventy years and a day – for seventy years and for one day more.

After seventy years, the rock suddenly broke in half. Honi awoke, and he found himself in the same field. There, he saw a man shaking the fruit pods from the carob tree and then picking them up to eat. The man looked younger than Honi had remembered, and Honi asked: "Are you the man who planted this tree?"

The young man looked strangely at Honi and replied: "No, of course I did not plant this tree – it was my grandfather who planted this tree, seventy years ago."

Then Honi said to himself: "It seems that I have had a long sleep this afternoon. In fact, could it be that I have slept for seventy years and a day?"

Pious Honi ha-Me'aggel the Circle-Drawer stood up, and he looked for his horse, but he saw around him a whole herd of young horses – they had multiplied three or four times during the seventy years that he had slept in the rock. Then Honi said to himself: "I am afraid that no one will believe this when I tell it to them." And he set off for home.

Honi the Circle-Drawer walked to his own house. He found strange people standing in his yard, and he said: "Is the son of Honi the Circle-Drawer still living?" The people replied: "No. Honi's son is dead, but his grandson is still living." Then Honi said: "You will not believe this: *I* am Honi the Circle-Drawer." Unfortunately, Honi was correct – his own descendants did not believe him, for they thought that he had died long ago.

Then Honi went to the yeshiva. The men were busy discussing a point of law, and Honi listened for one hour and then for two. Eventually, Honi could remain quiet no longer: he interrupted, and he offered his own interpretation. The scholars were silent. Finally, one man turned to his neighbor and said: "Who is this greybeard? He is spouting ancient *Halakhah*: these rules are coated with spiderwebs – they are from generations ago. Why, it sounds as if they had been taught in the days of the old scholar Honi the Circle-Drawer."

Yes, Rabbi, in his day Honi the Circle-Drawer had been known as a great halakhic scholar. He had been proud of his interpretations of the legal sections of the Talmud. Whenever he had come to the yeshiva, he answered all the difficult questions about Judaic formal codes. Now, Honi heard the various scholars talking among themselves and he said: "My good students, it is I, Honi. I am Honi the Circle-Drawer." But the rabbis did not believe him. They thought that Honi had died many years before, and they knew nothing of his long sleep. The men of the yeshiva ridiculed him; they considered Honi to be a confused old man, and they showed him no respect because they found his story incredible.

Poor Honi grew despondent: the yeshiva scholars would not take his words seriously, and his family would not welcome him. Honi wandered about the streets. People nodded at him, but they did not really see him. Men patted him on the shoulder but they did not really touch him. Children ran past, women talked to someone else. Honi went for weeks and weeks and there was no one to hold his hand – so, the pious Honi ha-Me'aggel the Circle-Drawer prayed; he prayed to the good Lord God (blessed be He) to erase those seventy years of sleep, those seventy years and one day. And shortly afterwards, said my grandmother, the Lord God appeared to Honi in a dream and commanded him to take a pilgrimage north. So Honi set out. He walked from Regensburg to Cologne, where he stayed one night in the yeshiva with Rabbi Abraham Achselrad. The next morning, Honi continued walking north, and soon thereafter, Honi the Circle-Drawer fell down by the roadside and he died.

ello, Rabbi. I know—it is always hard to sleep on a night with a bright moon. Just put your feet up on the side bench here and I will open the stove door. Let me push the coal back: there is nothing like that white glow; it washes away the tensions of a hard day. I heard your final prayers tonight, Rabbi: there is no use denying it—you are overworked. Oh yes, even a shammas like me can tell. I kept one eye on you when I cleaned the dishes, and I saw that you were watching the door, hoping that Reb Elbaum would leave early. And then, Reb Anton stayed to argue that passage about miracles in the *Avot* of the *Mishnah*. Of course you must still be worn out.

What chapter of the *Avot* was it? Chapter 5? Then why am I thinking of Chapter 10? . . . . Oh yes, Rabbi, of course you are right— Chapter 5 is about "tens": the ten generations from Adam to Noah and the ten generations from Noah to Abraham, the ten plagues of Egypt, the ten at the Red Sea, the ten times that the Israelites tempted God in the wilderness, and the ten wonderful things bordering on the miraculous that were noticed in the great Temple. What is that, Rabbi? Ah, the most noteworthy "ten" of all:

Ten things were created on the eve of Sabbath during the first twilight— namely, the mouth of the earth, the mouth of the well from which the

Israelites drank in the wilderness, the mouth of Balaam's ass, the rainbow, the Manna, the rod of Moses, the Shamir (the worm that cut the stones for Solomon's great Temple), the alphabet, the ten command-ments written on the tablets, and the stone tablets of the covenant themselves.

These are certainly miracles, but they are orderly miracles. The good Lord God, blessed be He, has created a miraculous world, but at the same time he has a Divine plan. Is that not what you would say also, Rabbi?

It is exactly what you would say, word for word? Ah, then I knew that I had heard it somewhere before. So why is an old man like me talking at all? I should learn to be a bit quieter. What is that, Rabbi — a story from me? Rabbi, all I know are the old-fashioned children's tales, the grandmother fables. You need something new and fresh to keep your mind keen. Otherwise you will become an old man like me, a shammas who is constantly musing and dozing and nodding off in front of the stove.

What do you mean you are already an old man, Rabbi? Do you think that sixty years is old? Why, you are still a child: when you reach eighty, *then* you will be old. You doubt that you will live to see eighty years? If so, Rabbi, then you will never grow old. . . . All right, all right, Rabbi — as I have said, I know no special stories. But listening to you and Reb Anton put me in mind of miracles, and of course, when I think of miracles then I think of Rabbi Abraham. Yes, Rabbi, it is the same mystic Abraham ben Alexander, Achselrad of Cologne, of whom I have spoken in the past.

I remember my grandmother telling me that one evening Rabbi Abraham Achselrad was praying after the Sabbath. He had just said:

> You have favored us to know Your law, and You have taught us to do the ordinances of Your will. Moreover, You have divided, O Lord our God, between holy and unholy, between light and darkness, between Israel and the nations, and between the Sabbath and the six days of work. Our Father, our King, let the coming days begin in peace: let them be free from all sin, clean from all wrong, and firm in the fear of You.

And then Rabbi Abraham stopped, horrified by what he had just said.

Yes, yes — horrified. I know, Rabbi, that there is nothing wrong with that passage: it is the same one that any pious Jew would repeat

after the Sabbath. But Rabbi Abraham was an exceedingly cautious
and devout man, and he began to worry about the last line. He had
said: "Let the coming days begin in peace"—but which days were
those? Were they all possible days? If so, then he should not have to
say this part of the prayer ever again—having asked for peace once, it
should suffice forever. And did not the other rabbis overrule the great
Rabbi Akiva when he attempted to insert needless repetitions into the
benedictions?

(What? That is not exactly the same thing? Of course it is
different, Rabbi—if it were the same, then the problem already would
have been corrected by the great Rabbi Akiva, and Rabbi Abraham
would not have gotten into this dilemma in the first place.)

Now what should Rabbi Abraham do? Clearly, he must change
the line a bit; he should be more specific, saying: "Let the coming *six*
days begin in peace." He repeated the prayer with this new addition,
and he felt better.

However, his unease returned. How many times had he mis-
spoken the prayer after the Sabbath? The answer was startling: he had
prayed improperly all his life. Rabbi Abraham Achselrad sat down
hard upon his bench. His entire life! There were fifty-two Sabbaths
each year, and the good Rabbi had been praying seriously on the
Sabbath since he was thirteen years old—that made more than eighteen
hundred Sabbath prayers. More than eighteen hundred prayers had
been said wrongly. He was overwhelmed. There was nothing to do
but to correct them all. So the Rabbi went into the back room. He took
a drink of water, he sat beside his desk, and he found a pen and a piece
of paper. Then, he began to repeat the correct version of the last part of
the prayer:

> You have favored us to know Your law, and You have taught us to do
> the ordinances of Your will. Moreover, You have divided, O Lord our
> God, between holy and unholy, between light and darkness, between
> Israel and the nations, and between the Sabbath and the six days of
> work. Our Father, our King, let the coming *six* days begin in peace: let
> them be free from all sin, clean from all wrong, and firm in the fear of
> You.

Each time that he said the prayer correctly, Rabbi Abraham made
a mark upon his paper. One hour passed and then two. The night

deepened, and the dawn approached. Rabbi Abraham Achselrad began to feel hoarse, but he continued praying and marking, praying and marking. And then, just in time for the morning prayers – seven hours after he had begun correcting his past mistakes – Rabbi Abraham marked the eighteen hundred and thirty-third repetition. Before his voice gave out completely, the Rabbi launched into the morning prayers, and afterward, he collapsed exhausted in his chair.

Poor Rabbi Abraham slept all morning. Now, the Rabbi's wife had been sick the day before, and so the Rabbi had promised that he himself would bring the morning milk and eggs home from the milk wagon that passed by the yeshiva. Unfortunately, Rabbi Abraham Achselrad slept all that afternoon, too. Late in the day, he was awakened by his students, and they immediately began the afternoon devotions. By the evening, the milk and the eggs were gone. When the good Rabbi returned home, his wife was feeling better, but she was still weak. "Have you any milk and eggs for me?" she asked her husband.

Rabbi Abraham looked blankly for a moment, and then he remembered about the milk and the eggs. He hurried back to the yeshiva. There was nothing on the yeshiva steps. Sadly, he turned to go home, when a young Jewish woman stopped him. "Rabbi," she said, "I feel a bit foolish. I have bought an extra pitcher of milk, and I cannot use it before it spoils. Do you know anyone who might be able to use it this evening?" Rabbi Abraham could not believe his ears, for it seemed to him that it was a miracle. . . .

What is that, Rabbi? I only closed my eyes for a moment – can an old man not take a little rest? Now let me see, where was I? Oh yes: you think that this free milk was a miracle. Well, perhaps it was; then again, perhaps it was just a coincidence. In any case, that is not the miracle of the milk – not the miracle that my grandmother told to me. As my grandmother said: "There are many ways for the good Lord God, blessed be He, to provide milk." Did you ever hear her say that, Rabbi? You never knew her? That is too bad; you missed a fine woman. Ah, well – anyway, Rabbi, I first heard about Rabbi Abraham Achselrad of Cologne and the miracle of the milk from my grandmother (may her soul visit happily with her parents forever).

Once upon a time, said my grandmother, there lived in Cologne on the River Rhine a mystic scholar named Rabbi Abraham ben

Alexander–"Achselrad" they called him. Rabbi Abraham had a ye-shiva in which the scholars of Cologne argued abstruse matters nightly. What is that? Please do not interrupt, Rabbi–I am just reminding you that many miracles and visions occurred in the old Cologne yeshiva in the days of Rabbi Abraham Achselrad; for in-stance, there was the miracle of the milk.

Now, I am not inventing this, Rabbi, my grandmother heard the tale from both of *her* grandmothers. You see, it began when a poor and pious man–Reb Samuel ben Moses–lost his wife, and she left behind a tiny baby boy. Of course, this was a tragedy many times over. The care and the education of all Jewish boys was the province of their mothers until the children were five years old. (Although, I must admit, Rabbi, young women are rarely well versed in Hebrew.) How-ever, education was a future problem for the son of Samuel ben Moses. Would this child live even until next year? The tiny infant was still a suckling baby, and the widower, Reb Samuel, was so poor that he could not afford to hire a Jewish nurse for the child. (And Gentile nurses were absolutely forbidden in the Jewish homes of Cologne.) Reb Samuel was so poor that the table on which he ate was the same table on which his wife Jutta was washed before she was buried.

During the week of mourning, Reb Samuel was dazed. His little baby cried constantly. A neighbor woman recommended mixing cow's milk and cereal for the newborn child. The baby swallowed some of the cold gruel, but then the child coughed and it spit and it cried all night. Somehow, the week of mourning passed. At first, Reb Samuel felt numb and dead, but he reminded himself that he must nonetheless be alive because (as the Talmud says): "A childless person is accounted as dead." And did he, Reb Samuel, not have a child–therefore, he must still be alive. But would that child itself live for long? Reb Samuel was afraid: the baby cried all the time, and it seemed weaker and paler and more wrinkled than ever.

Reb Samuel felt sick; he spent all his free time at home praying to the good Lord God, blessed be He. Then one evening, Reb Samuel felt very strange. He was dizzy and his head ached; his chest felt heavy. When he removed his shirt for the night, he was horrified: his breasts had begun to enlarge like a woman's. Reb Samuel was afraid to look down at himself. He lay in bed sweating; he did not fall asleep. By the next morning, he realized that his breasts had grown so large that now he was able to feed his little infant like a nurse. Dare he try? He did, and sure enough the tiny child suckled happily; for the first time in weeks, his little son seemed content.

Reb Samuel remained greatly frightened. He knew that the Talmud said that three classes of persons are susceptible to attack by evil spirits. Three classes of persons need special protection from demons: invalids, brides and grooms, and new mourners. So Reb Samuel recited incantations:

> Be split, be accursed, be broken and be banned—
> You son of mud, you demon from an evil land.

He followed the old rules for ridding oneself of malevolent spirits: he put a root through his ring, he recited the *Shema* in bed while holding a knife, and he buried a lock of his hair beside a dead tree. The charms did not work—but Reb Samuel was secretly relieved, because he felt that without human milk his little son might die.

Reb Samuel continued to suckle the infant day after day. The child became strong and happy, but poor Reb Samuel became weak and sad: he was too upset to eat or to sleep. Finally, he went one evening to the yeshiva. In the back room, a number of scholars were conversing with Rabbi Abraham ben Alexander, Achselrad of Cologne. Reb Samuel stood in the doorway, but the old men did not stop their serious argument. Reb Samuel stood for one hour and then for two. Eventually, Rabbi Abraham said: "Good friend, we will be talking for many hours more. Is there something important that you wish to say?"

Reb Samuel looked down at the floor, and he said weakly: "No, Rabbi."

Rabbi Abraham Achselrad looked silently at Reb Samuel for a full minute. "I think," said the Rabbi, "that you had best come in and tell us what is the problem."

Reb Samuel stepped into the room, and he sat on the bench that was nearest to the door and that was farthest from the other men. After a moment, he told his whole story. He looked only at his feet, and after he finished there was silence in the little study room in the back of the old Cologne yeshiva.

The scholars looked at Reb Samuel and they looked at each other.

Reb Shimshon ha-Zaken spoke first: "We should see in this strange situation the lesson that Reb Samuel has been a good man, because the great Lord God, blessed be He, performed a wondrous miracle for him."

But Lewe ben Anselm shook his head and said: "No, we should see in this that Reb Samuel has been a bad man, because he forced the great Lord God, blessed be He, to change the sacred order of creation."

Then another sage, Menahem ben Joel, said: "My friends, we should see in this that Reb Samuel was neither a good man nor a bad man, because the great Lord God, blessed be He, only made the change temporarily. Undoubtedly after the child grows, Reb Samuel will again become normal."

Rabbi Abraham Achselrad looked silently at Reb Samuel. "I think," said Rabbi Abraham after a moment, "that we should see in this simply one thing: the good Lord God, blessed be He, performs miracles. Daily, the Lord performs innumerable difficult tasks in order that we be fed and clothed and nurtured. But do we recognize these miracles? No, we rarely do. The Lord provides our air, that we might breath. He gives us rain and He gives us sun. He gives us wool and cotton and wood and clay. The good Lord has offered laws and rules and an orderly way of living. And daily the good Lord God, blessed be He, provides our food. But we forget how miraculous this is. Why has God changed the order of creation for the sake of one tiny infant? It is to remind us how miraculous is every tiny bit of our daily world."

That was Abraham Achselrad's view. And my grandmother would smile at me, Rabbi–she would smile at me and say: "Rabbi Abraham reminded us that the good Lord God, blessed be He, performs many miracles for us. We do not always recognize them: some seem insignificant. But all of these miracles protect us and keep us, for we are His little children." In any case, Rabbi, this poor widower, Reb Samuel, was transformed by a miracle; the good Lord God (blessed be He) transformed him in order that his little baby son, Joshua ben Samuel, might live and might care for his father in turn. Joshua ben Samuel grew into a fine and scholarly man who loved his father. Joshua and Samuel both lived into a ripe old age, and then one day, much later, they were both buried side by side, together in the old Jewish cemetery in Cologne along the River Rhine. Now they walk forever hand-in-hand, father and son–and, no doubt, the mother, too.

ood evening, Rabbi. No sleep for the weary? That is what my grandmother said—and she said it almost nightly. If you are cold then sit down here on the bench and I will stoke up the oven. You know, Rabbi, this reminds me of the passage from the Holy Scriptures that you and Reb Anton were discussing earlier, the passage where the good Lord God, blessed be He, said:

> Now go and speak to Eliazar, the son of Aaron the priest. Tell him to take the fire-pans out of the burning flames and then to scatter the fire yonder, for now they have all become holy. Even the fire-pans of these men who have sinned at the cost of their lives and who have let them be made into beaten plates for a covering of the altar—even these fire-pans are now holy, and they may now be a sign unto the children of Israel.

So, Rabbi, let me just "take up the fire-pans" and "scatter this fire yonder" a bit in the stove. There—I love that white glow, so warm and sleepy. As it is said in the Holy Scriptures: "And now ye shall sleep."

I agree, Rabbi: I quote the Scriptures because a knowledge of the holy books is a great comfort. Did you ever know Joseph ben Joshua (son of Reb Joshua ha-Levi)? No, he was not a member of this congregation. Actually, I never met him myself, but my grandmother knew him well. I was thinking about him because of the time that he became very ill.

Once upon a time, said my grandmother, Joseph ben Joshua became very ill. He had a burning fever. He thrashed about in his bed, his head was sweating, and finally he fell into a coma. His mother wrapped him in sheets, the sick room became damp and hot, and everyone spoke in whispers. Joseph's sister was sitting alone with him, when suddenly Joseph ben Joshua sat up stiff in his bed.

Joseph opened his eyes, but he did not seem to be able to see. His sister was frightened, and she brought her father, Reb Joshua, into the room. "Joseph?" asked his father, "are you all right?" At first, Joseph did not answer.

"Joseph?"

"Yes, Father?"

"Are you all right?"

"I think so."

"Can you see me?"

"No, I am afraid that I cannot."

"Then what is it that you see?" asked Reb Joshua.

"The world is upside down, Father."

"Upside down?"

"Yes," said Joseph, "the furniture is on the ceiling, and in fact everything is the opposite of our normal life. Trees grow with their roots in the sky; cattle lie upon their backs. And as for the people— why, kings are the servants, and servants are the kings."

"Ah, my son, you have seen a corrected world: it is the world of the Great Hereafter," said Reb Joshua. "But tell me, my son: What is the position of us students of the Torah there?"

And Joseph answered: "We scholars are the same there in the Great Hereafter as we are here now. I saw many learned men contentedly studying in the glorious golden prayer halls of Heaven, and I heard one scholar say: Forever happy is he who comes here possessed of holy learning."

Yes, Rabbi, we are told that learned men will continue to be comforted in the Great Hereafter. I wonder what form we will take.

Do you believe that we will be resurrected as men after we die, Rabbi? Of course the second benediction begins:

> You are mighty forever, O Lord. You revive the dead.

And the same prayer ends:

> W ho is like You, master of mighty deeds? Who compares with You, O King Who kills and Who brings to life again, and Who causes salvation to grow; You are entrusted to revive the dead. Blessed be You, O Lord our God, Who revives the dead.

But is this literal, Rabbi? Will we really be reconstructed after the grave?

Ah yes, Rabbi, the good Lord God (blessed be He) *is* the Master Craftsman, the Holy Architect. But nonetheless I remember the debate between Reb Meir and Rabbi Channina in the Talmud:

> First, Reb Meir asked: "How do you know that we will be reassembled and resurrected in the Great Hereafter? Is this really possible?"
>
> And Rabbi Channina answered: "If a glass vessel is broken, can a glass blower not remelt the pieces and then reform the vessel?"
>
> But Reb Meir responded: "Of course, Rabbi—but man is not glass: he was created from clay; as it is written in Genesis:

> Then the good Lord God formed a man, Adam, from the dust of the ground, and God breathed into Adam's nostrils the subtle breath of life.

And then consider pottery, Rabbi Channina. Once a piece of clay pottery has been shattered, it cannot be repaired by the potter; as it is written in the 2nd Psalm":

> You shall break them with an iron rod today
> And shatter them forever like a pot of clay.

Rabbi Channina listened carefully, and he asked Reb Meir: "Did you say that the good Lord God, blessed be He, breathed the breath of life into a lump of clay?"

Reb Meir said: "Yes."

And Rabbi Channina asked: "How could He do this?"

Reb Meir answered: "Frankly, it is a mystery to me. The good Lord is Holy—He is the most Holy of Holies. How should I, a mere mortal, know the answer to your question, Rabbi? There are many holy things that I shall never understand."

So Rabbi Channina said: "Then you have answered your own question, Reb Meir. The great God of all heavens, the most Holy of Holies, can resurrect man in ways that we mere mortals can never understand."

Reb Meir considered this; then, he said: "I see. But now I wonder, Rabbi—if it is true that we shall all be resurrected beyond the grave, then what will we look like?"

And Rabbi Channina responded: "I do not know."

"You do not know?"

"Well," said Rabbi Channina, "some scholars say: 'As a generation goes, so will it come back.' Specifically, he who goes lame to the grave also comes back lame, and he who goes blind to the grave also comes back blind. 'This,' say these scholars, 'is so that people shall not say that the good Lord God (blessed be He) put to death persons who are any different from those that He restored to life.'"

Reb Meir said: "So, we will all look the same?"

Rabbi Channina replied: "Perhaps we will—but then again, Reb Meir, perhaps we will not."

And Reb Meir asked: "Oh? How can you say both 'yes' and 'no' at the same time, Rabbi?"

"Because," said Rabbi Channina, "in Isaiah it says":

> Behold—our God will remake thee,
> With awesome powers to save all men.
> The blind man's eyes shall be opened,
> The deaf man's ears will be cleared,
> The lame will leap like a young deer,
> The dumb man's tongue will laugh aloud.

At last, the masses shall be free:
His children finally come home again
Happy, entering Zion. Good friend,
With holy joy you will be cheered.
Yes, gladness and comfort shall persevere –
No sufferings or cares will be allowed.

And Reb Meir asked: "Well, Rabbi, if you cannot tell me exactly how we will look, then can you at least tell me how we will be dressed? Will the resurrected bodies be naked or will they have clothes?"

Rabbi Channina answered: "On that point, the Sages agree – the resurrected will have clothes. Remember: even the naked come out of the earth with some garb. For instance, a seed is buried naked in the soil, but the newlygrown plant rises up clothed in leaves. And, Reb Meir, we humans do not bury our dead naked; we clothe them in shrouds. Therefore, the resurrected person must come back with even more coverings."

What is that, Rabbi? You do not remember that part of the Talmud? Undoubtedly it is from an old version. As my grandmother would say: "Who can ever know for certain about these things?" She said this often – and, of course, how could you question that?

What did she mean? Clearly she was referring to miracles, Rabbi – let me illustrate with a story of hers. (It is always best to use my grandmother's own words.) In relation to miracles, I remember that she told of a certain Rabbi Abraham Achselrad. Exactly, Rabbi – this was the very same Rabbi Abraham ben Alexander, Achselrad of Cologne, who wrote the famous kabbalistic treatises and who performed miracles and who had visions in the old Cologne yeshiva. You may not know this, Rabbi, but Abraham Achselrad once journeyed to Spain where he made a page boy disappear in the court of King Ferdinand II of Leon. Oh, you knew that? Did you also know that he met Honi the Circle-Drawer just before Honi's death? . . .

What is that, Rabbi? Of course there is more – I was just resting my eyes. Let me see now, where was I? Oh yes, I was telling you about the mystic Rabbi Achselrad. Once upon upon a time, said my grandmother, Rabbi Abraham Achselrad was sitting quietly on the back bench of the main study room, listening to his students argue. After reading and rereading a portion of the Talmud (a section about Gehinnom, the fate of the wicked), a young and serious scholar named Isaac ben Safir turned to the Rabbi.

"Excuse me, sir," said Isaac. "Is it true that the body crumbles to dust in the grave?"

"Why do you ask, young man?" said Rabbi Abraham.

"I am thinking of the Great Hereafter, Rabbi. If a body crumbles to dust in the grave, then what is left for the Hereafter? What distinguishable relic is there in the grave from which the resurrected person can be reconstructed?"

And another young scholar added: "Yes, Rabbi–what will the Holy One, blessed be He, use in order to rebuild a human being in Heaven?"

Then Rabbi Abraham said: "The good Lord uses a bone."

"But, Rabbi," said young Reb Isaac, "there are many, many different bones. I remember how the Talmud enumerates them":

There are two hundred and forty-eight parts in the human body. Thirty bones are in the sole of each foot – specifically, there are six bones in each toe. Ten bones are in the ankle, two are in the foreleg, five are in the kneejoint, and one is in the thigh. Three bones are in each hipjoint. There are eleven ribs. There are thirty bones in each hand – specifically, there are six bones in each finger. There are two bones in the forearm, two in the elbow, one in the arm, and four in each shoulder. In other words, there are one hundred and one bones on each side. In addition, there are the middle bones of the body: eighteen vertebrae in the spinal column, nine bones in the head, eight bones in the neck, six bones in the thorax, and five in the genitals.

The Rabbi answered: "Quite true, my young friend, and it is from one bone in the spinal column – a particular bone called the 'Luz' – that all of a person can be reconstructed."

(Yes, Rabbi – "Luz" . . . Well, the reason that the name is familiar is because of Jacob. Exactly, Rabbi, our Jacob of the Scriptures. You remember Jacob's dream of the ladder: he dreamed that he saw a ladder that rested on the ground with its top reaching to Heaven, and the angels of God were going up and down upon it. Yes, yes, Rabbi, of course you know this. And of course you know the name of that holy spot: "Beth-El," the House of God.

Jacob dreamed of this ladder, and when Jacob awoke from his sleep, he said: "Truly the Lord is in this place, and I did not know it. How awesome is this spot! This must be none other than the House of God; this is the gate of Heaven." That is why Jacob named the place Beth-El. Then Jacob took the stone on which he had laid his head, and he set it up as a sacred pillar and he poured oil on top of it. Oh, of course you know all this–but, Rabbi, do you remember what that place was called before it was renamed by Jacob? Yes–it was called Luz: the original name of that area was Luz. Likewise, that is why this particular spinal bone–the vertebra of resurrection–is called *Luz*: it is the Beth-El of the body. The Luz bone is the House of God within ourselves.)

Anyway, young Isaac ben Safir asked: "What is this Luz bone, Rabbi, and how do you know that it is immortal?"

But Rabbi Abraham said: "That is enough discussion for today."

The scholars were puzzled, but they respected the Rabbi's wishes. Then Rabbi Abraham Achselrad left the main study hall, passing the Holy Ark made of stone and the twelve stained glass windows with their colored lions and snakes, and he went into the back room of the yeshiva. He took out his pen, and he wrote a long letter to Rabbi Petahiah ben Jacob of Regensburg. After writing, he slowly reread the letter, he sealed it with wax, and then he set it aside. He could not entrust the letter to a Gentile merchant: he would wait for a Jew who was traveling to Regensburg, the old city on the Danube.

The next afternoon, young Isaac asked the Rabbi if he would be so good as to tell them more about the resurrection bone. Rabbi Abraham replied: "Perhaps in a few weeks, if we are fortunate."

During the following week, Rabbi Abraham heard that a local tradesman, Benjamin ben Samuel, was going to Salzburg on business and that Reb Benjamin was planning to stop in Regensburg along the way. Yes, said Benjamin, he would deliver a message to Rabbi Petahiah in Regensburg, and yes, he would be happy to retrieve a reply letter on his return journey.

One month later, Reb Benjamin brought a small brown envelope to the shammas, who gave it to Rabbi Abraham Achselrad. The Rabbi took the envelope into the dim back room of the Cologne yeshiva, he read the letter, and then he burned both the letter and the envelope in the yeshiva stove. At the study session that afternoon, Rabbi Abraham said to Isaac: "Young man, I am ready to answer your question now."

"What question was that, Rabbi?"

"Did you not ask me: What is the Luz bone, and how do you know it is immortal?"

"Yes, I did," answered Isaac ben Safir, "many weeks ago."

"Do you still wish to know?"

"I do."

"Very well," said Rabbi Abraham, "then go to the *shochet*. Have him clean the backbone of a calf, and bring the entire backbone to me."

The students did as the Rabbi asked.

That evening, Rabbi Abraham Achselrad set the backbone of a calf on a wooden table in the yard behind the yeshiva—for it was not clear to him that the subsequent events should be permitted alongside the holy books within the study house. The young scholars gathered around, and Isaac asked: "Does a cow have an immortal bone just as does a person?"

"The cow does indeed," replied Rabbi Abraham, "for in the golden Hereafter we shall all feast on milk and honey. And whence comes the milk in Heaven? It comes from immortal cows. Remember: in Isaiah it is said that in the resurrected world":

> The calf and the lion cub shall walk together
>   And a human child will be their guide;
> The cow and the bear shall be gentle friends
>   And their young will lie down side by side.

"I see, Rabbi," said Isaac. "Then show me: Where is the Luz bone of the cow?"

"The Luz is a backbone in the lower spine, here."

"But, Rabbi, all these backbones look the same to me."

And Rabbi Abraham said: "Take this hammer and smash the backbones."

Isaac ben Safir looked at his fellow students; then, he lifted the hammer and brought it down on the column of bones, and when he did, all the backbones were broken into bits. All the backbones were smashed into shards–all except one bone. One ordinary backbone with a flat middle and with wings on either side, a bone near the bottom of the spine, a bone that looked identical to all the others around it–this one bone still remained intact, while all the other backbones were shattered. The young men hesitated to touch the intact bone, but the Rabbi immediately picked it up. With the hammer, Rabbi Achselrad struck the bone another mighty blow, but the bone did not shatter.

Then the Rabbi said: "Now *this* is the Luz bone."

In the yard, there was a tool shed. The Rabbi brought out a heavy iron file from the shed, and he rubbed and rasped the Luz, but the bone remained unmarred. The Rabbi set the bone on an anvil, he hit it with a large iron hammer, and he beat it with the iron tongs–still the bone was unharmed. The Rabbi picked up the Luz bone, and he walked back into the yeshiva; the students followed. Inside, the Rabbi opened the door of the little stove, he stoked up the coals, and he tossed the Luz bone into the hot white fire. After a few minutes, Rabbi Abraham Achselrad scraped the bottom of the coals with a stoker until the bone fell through the grate; then he picked up the bone with a cloth, and he dropped it into a bucket of water.

The Rabbi picked up the bone as soon as it was cool. He held it for the students to see. Rabbi Abraham passed the Luz to Isaac, and all the young men crowded around. They bent their heads over the bone, and they studied it carefully. They each held it intently. It looked like an ordinary backbone; it looked like one normal backbone from somewhere down on the spine of a calf. Was it really immortal? Was this the bone from which the good Lord God, blessed be He, would resurrect a new calf in the Great Hereafter? The young men looked up. The fire had died down in the little yeshiva oven, and the Rabbi was gone.

What is that, Rabbi? The letter that Rabbi Abraham ben Alexander, Achselrad of Cologne, wrote to Rabbi Petahiah ben Jacob of Regensburg? I am afraid that I cannot answer you. No one knows what the two rabbis discussed in that correspondence. Rabbi Petahiah was the brother of the famous Rabbi Isaac ben Jacob of Prague. (Yes, that was Isaac "the Wise" of Prague.) In the days of Abraham Achselrad, Rabbi Petahiah was already very, very old; his skin was brown and thin, his hands were weak and shaky, and he walked with two canes. He was retired from his rabbinical chores, and he could not bring himself to the yeshiva every day. I can only say that the older he grew, the closer he was to God. Perhaps that meant that he began to understand resurrection more clearly than us young men. Who knows? Soon after, he died in Regensburg–Rabbi Petahiah died far from the Holy Land in the cold lands of Europe, but it does not seem to have mattered.

Oh yes, Rabbi, I know–my grandmother used to say it too: "Resurrection will only take place in the Holy Land. Those who die outside the holy land of Palestine will not live again." When I first heard that from my grandmother, I began to cry and I said: "Grandmother, Palestine is so far away. What if I die here instead?" Then she took me on her lap and she said: "My dear little boy, it is true that now you live in the cold lands of Europe, and someday (far, far in the future) you may die in the cold lands of Europe. But, my golden one, don't you know that God loves you? The Holy One, the good Lord God (blessed be He) will burrow, and He will make a tunnel through the earth. And when you die, your body will roll through that smooth round space like a happy bottle; and when you arrive at the holy land of Palestine then you will be resurrected–and you and I shall see each other once again. That is as certain as the rising of the sun."

ood evening, Rabbi. You are having difficulty sleeping again? Put your feet up on the side bench here and I will open the stove door. Let me push this coal back; that white glow will wash away the cares of the day. I heard your final prayers tonight, and there is no use denying it, Rabbi—you are overworked, even an old shammas like me can tell. I kept one eye on you when I was cleaning the dishes; I saw you were hoping that Reb Elbaum would leave early. But then Reb Anton stayed late to argue about the Midrash passage.

That Midrash passage reminded me of our Rabbi Jehuda ben Saul. (Rabbi Jehuda was two rabbis before you.) One day he gave a Midrash sermon to his yeshiva students.

"How were angels created?" asked Rabbi Jehuda. He asked this, and then he stood looking down sternly at the young men on the benches. There was silence, so the Rabbi answered his own question: "The angels were created by the utterance of the Lord, for it is written in the 33rd Psalm":

> By the word of the Lord
> Were the Heavens made,

All the heavenly horde
Formed from words that He said.

The Rabbi looked around. Then he asked: "And, my young scholars, when were the angels created?" Again there was silence, so Rabbi Jehuda answered his own question: "Clearly, the angels were created on the second day, for it is written in the 104th Psalm":

First, the Lord spread His heavenly tent,
Then on the waters set supporting posts;
In clouds He put beams of the firmament,
Where winds can be wings for all His hosts.

"Note, my aspiring young men," continued Jehuda, "the Psalm says 'wings for all His hosts': this must mean wings for all God's angels. And the separation of the waters (of which the psalmist speaks so eloquently) occurred on the second day of creation—as you will recall":

Then God said: "Let there be a vault between the waters, to separate water from water." So God made the vault, and He separated the water under the vault from the water above the vault—and God called the vault "Heaven." And evening came and morning came, a second day.

"Therefore, young men, clearly angels must have been created on the second day."

Rabbi Jehuda ben Saul looked down sternly at his yeshiva students. "Now, I know that this sounds quite logical," he said, "but do you young men think that there may be other opinions?"

There was silence; so, once again the Rabbi answered his own question: "Certainly there may be other opinions. In fact, the famed Rabbi Channina actually proposed that angels were created on the fifth day."

Rabbi Jehuda looked up to the ceiling. "The fifth day," he repeated. "And why was this? It was because it is written in Genesis that winged things, flying above the earth, were created on the fifth day."

"But I ask you, young men," continued Rabbi Jehuda, "is this *really* what it says in Genesis?"

The students did not know what to say; there was silence, so the Rabbi replied: "No, it is not really what it says in Genesis—not in *my* Genesis. In my Genesis, it speaks only of birds. In my Genesis, the passage reads":

Then God said: "Now let the waters teem with countless living creatures, and let birds fly above the earth across the great vault of Heaven." God then created the great sea-monsters and all the living creatures that move and that swarm in the waters, and He created every kind of bird— and God saw that it was good. So He blessed them all, and He said: "Be fruitful and increase. Fill the waters of the seas, and let the birds increase on land." And evening came and morning came, a fifth day."

So I suppose, Rabbi, that Jehuda ben Saul was correct and that angels must have been created on the second day—but regardless of when they were created, I am thankful for them nonetheless. When I think of angels, I cannot help remembering the angel that followed Reb Samuel ben Shimshon into the presence of Rabbi Abraham Achselrad. Yes, Rabbi, that was the very same Abraham ben Alexander, Achselrad of Cologne, about whom I have spoken before. He was a pupil of Eliazer the mystic of Worms. Did you know that Rabbi Abraham once visited the Christian King Ferdinand II of Castile. (Although on that occasion Abraham Achselrad found it necessary to call himself "Nathan Alexander" for some unknown reason.) You knew that, Rabbi? Then you also must have known about his angel. You did not? Then let me tell you. Now I am not inventing this—my grandmother swore that this is exactly what she had heard:

Rabbi Abraham Achselrad was a writer of kabbalistic tomes of mystical knowledge, including the *Keter Shem Tov* (which, I am told, was never published and which only exists as a secret manuscript hidden in the old Cologne yeshiva). The good Rabbi was always conjuring visions in the synagogue. I doubt whether this would be tolerated nowadays, but my grandmother said that Rabbi Abraham Achselrad was a renowned scholar, and he always claimed that his visions came from devout and pious study. Many an astonishing event took place in his yeshiva—or so my grandmother (blessed be her memory) has heard. One night, said my grandmother, Samuel ben

Shimshon came into the back room of the yeshiva where Rabbi Abraham was studying by candlelight; the Rabbi was writing the late chapters of his *Keter Shem Tov*. Reb Samuel was pale and wide-eyed, and behind him came an angel.

Yes, yes, Rabbi, an angel—a faint misty holy angel of the Lord. Samuel sat, the angel hovered, and Rabbi Abraham put down his pen. No one spoke, not a sound was uttered for a full five minutes. Finally, Reb Samuel said in a weak voice: "Rabbi, I need your help. . . ."

The candle flickered, although there was no breeze, and after a moment Samuel ben Shimshon continued: "I must go to the cemetery again this evening, and I must find and retrieve a sack of money that my father has hidden. This angel is to follow me, but I am weak and faint—I need your support."

Rabbi Abraham looked at the angel, and then he looked at Samuel. The Rabbi remained silent, so Reb Samuel told this story:

As you know, good Rabbi, I am Samuel son of Shimshon. Apparently, my father Shimshon ben Isaac ben Samuel had been entrusted with some money belonging to the orphans who are being raised by Sarah, the wife of Joshua ha-Kohen. I do not know how this money originally was designated for these children, and I do not know why my father became the caretaker of the funds. However, it seems that for many years Shimshon ben Isaac guarded a significant fund for these young orphaned children. The money was a secret, and I knew nothing about it.

Last month, my father traveled to Regensburg, and unexpectedly he died. My mother (may she rest in peace) had passed on long ago, and my father and I had been living alone, so I traveled sadly to Regensburg and I brought back my poor father's body. My mother and my father's parents are buried in the old Cologne cemetery—the *Am Toten Juden*—just outside the southern gate of the city, and there I laid my father to his final rest also.

After the week of mourning, I went out and I resumed my daily affairs. I admit that the world seemed thinner, but the skies were still blue on sunny mornings, and I said my prayers and I went about my routines. One day, as I was walking down the Obernmarspforten Street along the edge of the Jewish Quarter, I heard some women talking. "There goes the son of the thief who stole the orphans' money," they said.

What is this? I thought. I turned back in order to talk to these women, but abruptly they walked away. The next day, Sarah the wife of Joshua ha-Kohen appeared on my doorstep. "Where is the money that your father kept for my children?" she asked. I was mystified, and after hearing her out, I tried to explain that I knew nothing of this money. But Sarah was angry. She claimed that we had stolen the funds of her orphans. She hurled curses upon my head. The neighbors appeared; they comforted her, and they reviled me. Soon, I was being shunned by all my old friends.

Was there a sack of money belonging to the orphans? If so, then it was well hidden—I had never seen it anywhere around the house. Nonetheless, I made a diligent search inside and out. But I could not find a single trace of anything unusual, let alone any extra money. We have been a poor family, Rabbi, and there was not much to search.

I became an outcast, and my life was increasingly miserable. I prayed and I ate, and I worked and I prayed; I slept fitfully at night. Then one night this very angel, who now sits beside me, appeared to me in a dream. She said: "Samuel, go to the cemetery, and bring an earthenware cup filled with blood-red wine. Question your father, find out where the money is hidden, and return it to the orphans."

To be honest, Rabbi, I did not believe that this was a holy dream: I thought that it was a nightmare, and I ignored it. However, the same dream was repeated every night for a week. Finally, tonight I followed the angel's directions. I walked to the cemetery with a wine cup. I was quite frightened, and I felt cold and stiff. I stood uncertainly in the middle of the graveyard. Suddenly, I saw the shape of an old friend of mine, Levi ben Mordecai. The shape floated toward me, and it bent down and took a sip from the earthenware cup that was filled with blood red wine. A chill damp wind slipped out from among the far tombstones.

"Samuel," said the spirit, "it is me—Levi ben Mordecai." "Are you dead?" I asked. "Yes," said Levi, "I am dead but I am not in Heaven." "Why is that?" I asked. "Do you remember, Samuel, how I would skip the afternoon sessions in the yeshiva?" "Yes." "Now I am condemned to hover here in the cemetery for as many weeks and months and years as I missed my studies with the scholars." "Afterward, will you then be admitted to Heaven?" I asked. "I am hopeful, my friend," answered the shade of Levi, "but I do not know."

The spirit of Levi floated away, and another ghostly mist approached. The vague shape floated toward me, and then it bent down and took a sip from the earthenware cup that was filled with blood red wine. A chill damp wind slipped out from among the far tombstones. "Samuel," said the spirit, "it is me—Solomon ben Asher." I recognized the bearded grandfather of one of my friends, Jacob ben Meir. "Tell me, Samuel: How is my grandson Jacob?" "Reb Solomon, I have not seen Jacob in many years, but the last I heard was that he was doing very well. Jacob traveled to Bonn, where he has become a respected scholar in their yeshiva." "Ah, that is good. And has he married?" "Yes," I replied, "I understand that he is now married and that he has two sons—but tell me, O spirit, what is the other world like and how does God appear and. . . ." But Solomon ben Asher had floated off, happy with the news of his grandson Jacob.

The night was absolutely silent, and now another ghostly mist approached. The vague shape floated toward me, and it bent down and took a sip from the earthenware cup that was filled with blood-red wine. A chill damp wind slipped out from among the far tombstones. "Samuel," said the spirit, "it is me, your father."

I bit my lip and reached out, trying to embrace my father. Three times I tried to put my arms around him, but each time the spirit of my father passed through my hands, impalpable as the shadows are, wavering like a dream. "I am dead, my son," said Shimshon ben Isaac ben Samuel.

This was too much for me, Rabbi. I turned and I ran. When I could run no more, I walked—and I came straight here. And the angel from my dream has been following me ever since.

Rabbi Abraham Achselrad did not say a word; he arose and put on his coat, and he walked from the back room into the main prayer hall filled with wooden benches. He passed the twelve stained glass windows with their colored lions and snakes, he passed the Holy Ark made of stone, and he walked through the front door and and out into the dark night. Reb Samuel arose and followed, and the misty angel hovered behind. Out into the night they went. There was no moon, there were no stars, the winds were quiet. The old synagogue in

Cologne was in the block bordered by the two streets Engegasse and Judengasse. The night walkers passed silently down Judengasse, south toward the Jewish cemetery just outside the St. Severin gate on the road from Cologne to Bonn. The three night walkers traveled through the streets and out to the cemetery.

On the ground in the middle of the cemetery was the earthenware cup, and inside the cup were only a few drops of the blood-red wine. The three of them waited—the Rabbi, Samuel, and the angel. One hour passed and then two. The night was absolutely silent. And then a ghostly mist approached. The vague shape floated toward them. It bent down, and it drank the last sips of blood-red wine from the earthenware cup. A chill damp wind slipped out from among the far tombstones. "Samuel," said the spirit, "it is me, your father." And then it said: "I am now dead, my son, my son."

Samuel had tears in his eyes: "Where is the orphans' money, father?"

The voice of Shimshon was like a dry wind: "I did not steal it, my son—I did not take it for myself, and I did not spend it. I only hid the money where no one might find it."

There was a silence, and Samuel said quietly: "Now I must return it, Father. Tell me: Where is the orphans' money hidden?"

"Go back to our house, my son, and look at the space where the bolt of the back door fits into the wall. There you will find a recess: put your hand deep down in the space, and you will come across two bags of money. The top bag is the dowry that came to us when I married your mother, fifty years ago. I have saved it all, and now that money belongs to you. Below this bag is the sack that belongs to the orphans—return it to them. I put their bag on the bottom so that if thieves should come, perhaps (in their haste) they would only steal our money and the funds for the orphans would still remain safe and secure."

Then, Reb Samuel went home. He found the hidden money and he returned it to the orphans, and the angel of the Lord was satisfied and she departed. The angel was satisfied because the little children were now protected. Ah, Rabbi, how fortunate are we Jews that angels have always watched over our little children—and it has been so since the very beginning. When I would become afraid at night, my grandmother (may her soul rest forever in the bosom of the great Lord God, blessed be He) always reminded me that angels guarded all little children. And sometimes, my grandmother would repeat the story in Genesis:

Hagar, the young outcast mother, was given some food and some water in a skin container. She set her tiny child on her shoulder, she tied the waterskin about her waist, and she set off early in the morning. Hagar wandered in the wilderness of Beersheba, far from any other person. Soon her food was gone, and then her waterskin was empty.

When the water in the skin was completely finished, Hagar gave up all hope: she put the child under a bush, and she went and sat down some way off. Hagar thought: "We will both soon be finished, but how can I watch my own child die?" Hagar sat far away from the child, and she wept.

God heard the child crying under the bush, and an angel of the Lord called from Heaven to Hagar: "What is the matter, my dear Hagar? Do not be afraid: I have heard your little boy crying. Go and get him, lift him up, and hold him in your motherly arms – he will yet grow into the father of a great nation."

So Hagar opened her eyes, and she saw a pool of water. Hagar went to the pool, she filled her waterskin, and she gave the little child a drink. And the little boy was quieted. In time, the tiny infant grew up and lived in the wilderness of Paran; eventually, he became a renowned archer, and he married a woman from Egypt and together they had a fine large family and they lived long and full lives, amen.

hat is that, Rabbi? No, I was just resting my eyes. Of course–please join me here by the stove. (I think that you will be too warm on that bench: try the one nearer to the wall.) An old man like me can doze forever by a warm stove; I must have eaten my vegetables before untying the bunch. What do I mean? Why, Rabbi, certainly you know the misfortunes that befall a man who forgets to untie his onions or garlic or radishes before eating them–he becomes a lazy, sleepy old coot. Oh yes, I learned many such important rules from my grandmother, who had heard them from her grandmother. I think that, originally, these descended from the mystic Rabbi Abraham ben Alexander, Achselrad of Cologne.

My grandmother told me that she always carefully untied vegetables, and then she folded the string into neat and even lengths. This accounted for her ability to walk with a neat stride, even when she became older than me–and now I am eighty, you know. Grandmother could walk up and down hills without varying her pace, and men marveled at her strength, Rabbi. My grandmother always said: "Deal evenly, neatly, calmly, and strongly with your vegetables, my boy, and you shall grow even, neat, calm, and strong in your old age." What more could you ask, Rabbi?

What? No, no—do not get up on my account, Rabbi. I was just resting my eyes a moment. I was resting and musing. Well, to tell you the truth, Rabbi, I was remembering all the rules that my grandmother knew. There were rules about food, like: Always untie your vegetables before eating them, and never store food beneath a bed or it will become filled with evil spirits. There were rules about strangers: Expect a neighbor if a flame leaps up in the fireplace, and a traveler will fall into the water if you pour water onto the fire, and if you meet someone who has eaten soup without bread, then a wound will begin to bleed. There were also other omens about the future, for instance: Itching of the foot foretells an imminent journey, itching of the ears foretells strange news, itching of the eyes foretells new sights, and itching of the hand foretells new money.

Why do these things work? It is spirits, Rabbi. Spirits hide in caves, witches and ghouls eat lost children, and wizards can put the bone of a certain animal (my grandmother would never tell me which one) on their tongues and then the bone will speak all by itself. And why do birds grow from thin air deep in the forest, and how is it that some men have no shadows? It is spirits, spirits, and more spirits.

As you know, Rabbi, if you find drops of blood on a tree, then you cannot chop down that tree or the spirits within will be let loose. Evil spirits are also found in wells and in ponds, not only in fields and forests. I remember the story that my grandmother told me about Rabbi Abraham Achselrad and the water spirit. Perhaps you know it. No? Then let me tell you:

Once upon a time, said my grandmother, in the congregation of Rabbi Abraham ben Alexander, Achselrad of Cologne, there was a man named Solomon ben Sheshet ben Israel. Actually, Solomon lived outside of Cologne in the village of Stommeln, just to the north. One sunny morning, Solomon was sitting and studying out-of-doors; he was leaning against the edge of a well, when the spirit that lived in the well arose like a mist and said: "Solomon!"

Poor Solomon jumped, and he dropped his book.

"Solomon," continued the apparition, "I have lived deep in this well for many, many years."

"You have?" asked Solomon ben Sheset.

"Yes I have, and yet you and your wife and your children come out here day and night. You come here even in the new moon. But I have done you no harm."

"That is true," said Solomon.

"Then I want you to believe me when I say that I wish you no ill," said the spirit.

"All right – I believe you," said Solomon.

"I am an old spirit," said the misty figure.

"Fine," said Solomon.

"Unfortunately, a new and ill-tempered demon has arrived. He intends all manner of evil, so you must drive him away."

"Why has he come?"

"Who knows why anything bad happens, Solomon," responded the spirit. "The good Lord looks away for a moment and the darkness flows in immediately. As you know, evil spirits begin as dogs – so, perhaps thirty-five years ago a dog was maltreated here. As the Talmud tells us":

> After seven hard years a dog becomes a rat
> Seven years later the rat becomes a bat
> Seven years more and the bat becomes a crake
> After seven years of flying the crake becomes a snake
> Then into the earth and after seven years at most
> A demon returns when the snake becomes a ghost.

"And I am afraid," continued the spirit, "that a malevolent ghost has returned here to haunt this well."

So Solomon ben Sheshet asked: "What should I do?"

"First," said the spirit, "put a second amulet on your door – this will protect any newborn babies against evil. Second, bury a ring of woven roots behind your house – this will protect older children against evil. Do that now, and then return."

Solomon hurried home. "What are you doing to the door?" asked his wife.

"Please do not bother me, wife," said Solomon. "I am in a hurry."

"Now what are you digging behind the house?" asked his wife. Solomon did not answer; instead, he followed the spirit's orders, and then he returned to the well.

"Next," said the spirit, "tomorrow morning you and your wife and your oldest son must come to the well. Each of you should have a hoe or a shovel or a spade with a handle long enough to reach the surface of the water. You will not be able to see the demon, but you should –"

"Excuse me, O spirit."

"Yes?"

"Why can I not see this demon?"

"Solomon, had the human eye been given the power of seeing demons, then no person could bear living because of the overwhelming tide of evil spirits. Ghosts outnumber people: they surround you like ridges around a plowed field. Everyone has a thousand dybbuks on his left hand and ten thousand cruel sprites on his right. Let me ask you, Solomon: Have you ever felt hemmed in when you were inside the synagogue, even though the hall was not full?"

"Yes."

"Of course, you have – the crush that you feel is actually the pressure of a myriad evil spirits; they wish you to feel uncomfortable so that you will stay away from holy places. Under the crush of throngs of demons, your knees become weak and your eyes tire and your feet get sore. And it is due to the evil spirits that the clothes of rabbis wear out so quickly: rabbis are constantly rubbing up against these rough and hirsute devils."

"I see."

"No, Solomon, that is just the point: you do not see. The evil spirits cannot be seen. Of course, you can detect their presence on land by sprinkling ashes and then finding the chicken-scratch footprints that appear. In the water, one must notice the ripples where there is no wind. And this, Reb Solomon, is precisely what you must do tomorrow. When you or your wife or your oldest son notices a ripple on the water, then beat it fiercely with your iron tool and say:

> Be split, be accursed, be broken and be banned –
> You son of mud, you demon from an evil land.

You must repeat this – beating and chanting – until you notice drops of blood floating on the water; then you must say: 'The victory is ours.' Finally, return home and bury your tools for seven days."

Solomon carefully noted all these instructions, and then he went back home to prepare for his afternoon study in the yeshiva.

Later, Solomon went to the yeshiva, and all during the prayers he reviewed the spirit's directives. Rabbi Abraham Achselrad saw how distracted Solomon was, and the Rabbi went up to him after the services. "Is something bothering you, Solomon?" asked Rabbi Abraham.

Solomon was not certain whether he was planning a profane act. He looked at the Rabbi, but he did not know what to say.

The Rabbi looked at him strangely. "Come into the back study room with me," said Rabbi Achselrad.

The Rabbi sat down at his desk and looked at Solomon. Solomon looked at the benches along the wall. Finally, Solomon told the entire story to the Rabbi. Rabbi Abraham Achselrad remained quiet a moment, then he said: "You have not asked my advice, but I will give it anyway: Do not do this thing."

"But, Rabbi, my well is haunted, and the spirit said that –"

Rabbi Abraham looked down at the papers on his desk. He picked up his pen and he began to write, and after a while Solomon left the room. Solomon walked into the main prayer hall filled with wooden benches, he passed the twelve stained glass windows with their colored lions and snakes, he looked up at the Holy Ark made of stone, and he walked out the front door of the old synagogue of Cologne.

Solomon was worried, and he walked home slowly. When he came in the door, his wife began to talk, but Solomon said: "Please do not bother me, wife – I must think." Solomon did not feel like eating dinner; he undressed and lay in bed, and he tossed and turned all night. Just before dawn, the spirit appeared at the edge of his bed. "Awake and arise, Solomon," said the wraith. "Wake your wife and your son too, and bring your tools to the well."

Solomon got up. He dressed, he woke his wife and his oldest son, and they collected their hoe and their shovel and their spade – each with a handle long enough to reach the surface of the water in the well. Then together they went down to the old well. The sun was not yet up; a damp mist hung over everything and there was no wind. Suddenly, they saw a ripple on the surface of the well water. They beat the surface fiercely with their tools, and they chanted the incantation. A dark wave began to roll back and forth in the well. The wave grew larger and larger and like an ocean tide it leaped up over the edge, it caught the three people, it washed them into the depths of the well, and Solomon ben Sheshet ben Israel of Stommeln and his wife and his oldest son were never heard from again.

What, Rabbi? Yes, that is the whole story; there is no more.

abbi, I am glad to see you here alone. I want to apologize for my outburst during the service this evening. It was just that Reb Anton was swaying so violently that I feared he would fall over on old Reb Elbaum. Of course I know that a Jew prays with his whole body, as Psalm 35 says:

> Now I shall rejoice in the Lord
> And delight in His love and mercy.
> My very bones shout to the Adored:
> "O Lord, who is like unto Thee?"

But surely, Rabbi, the psalmist was speaking of whole and healthy bones, he did not mean broken bones. In any case, the most famous swayer that I know of, Hanan the Hidden Gardener, only prayed outdoors. What is that, Rabbi? How could you not have heard of Hanan? Oh—then let met tell you: you see, Rabbi, in the days of Abraham ben Alexander, the mystic Achselrad of Cologne, there lived an old recluse named Hanan.

Hanan lived in the village of Rondorf just south of Cologne. As far as anyone knew, Hanan had no family and no living relatives, although it was rumored that he was a grandson of Honi ha-Me'aggel the Circle-Drawer (who, you will remember, had been known as a rainmaker). What is that, Rabbi? Yes, it is true that Rabbi Abraham Achselrad also met Honi himself–but in those days Honi was living seventy years after his time. Hanan, however, lived in his own era. He was a gardener, a wondrous gardener; he lived alone and he raised his own food, and he hardly spoke to his neighbors.

Hanan was a hermit, but the people of Rondorf did not fear him: he was as gentle a soul as ever you could meet. Hanan was very poor, but he said his prayers regularly, and when he did he swayed so wildly that he took to standing outdoors in order not to hurt himself and not to break any of his few pieces of furniture. Sometimes, people would stand along the road and watch old Hanan rocking back and forth, moving his lips silently. Children whispered and giggled, but Hanan did not mind. In fact, to Hanan children seemed to be little wispy-haired plantlings, and Hanan loved children and he loved to watch them grow.

In those days, most Jews of Rondorf attended the synagogue in Cologne. The Rondorf Jews told all manner of tales about Hanan to their Cologne friends: they recounted how Hanan swayed so wildly when he prayed that he often fell over, they told how he worked in his garden at night (regardless of whether the moon was shining), and they wondered that he could manage to remain healthy for he never ate any meat–he ate only vegetables. Some of the Rondorf Jews speculated aloud that Hanan might be bewitched. Rabbi Abraham ben Alexander, Achselrad of Cologne and head of the Cologne yeshiva, was well versed in mystical lore; Rabbi Achselrad said that Hanan did not sound dangerous, but some Rondorf Jews remained worried. So Rabbi Abraham Achselrad agreed to come to Rondorf and see for himself.

One sunny afternoon, Rabbi Achselrad walked to Rondorf. A group of Jews accompanied him, and then they stood back at a distance as the Rabbi stepped up to Hanan's door. The Rabbi knocked, but there was no answer. Then, the Rabbi walked around to the back, behind the old shack and into the neat, thick garden. Was there a rustling somewhere by the vines of peas and beans? Was there a movement by the grove of sweet chestnut trees? The Rabbi looked up and he looked down. He closed his eyes and remained silent for a full five minutes; then he opened his eyes again. Finally, the Rabbi walked back among the tangle of vines and bushes and trees. A few quiet minutes passed, and the Rabbi returned. He looked back at the neat, thick garden with the chestnut trees beyond, he looked up at the fine summer sky, he looked at the collection of Rondorf Jews, and he said: "I am satisfied that Hanan must be a pious and gentle man." Then, Rabbi Abraham Achselrad turned and walked back to the old Cologne yeshiva on that fine summer afternoon.

Now perhaps, Rabbi, it was because Hanan was descended from Honi ha-Me'aggel (on his mother's side), or perhaps it was because he understood the feel of the soil, or perhaps it was because he was a devout and pious man of the out-of-doors – as my grandmother would say: "Who can tell, for this sort of thing?" Grandmother said this often. Did you ever hear her say this, Rabbi? You never met my grandmother? Ah, that is a pity, for she was a fine woman. What is that, Rabbi? Why, obviously I am speaking of *rainmaking* – did I not tell you that Hanan could bring forth the rains?

Hanan was a natural rainmaker, and all of Rondorf knew this. However, it was not easy to get Hanan to make rain: Hanan the Hidden Gardener was called "the Hidden" because he was extraordinarily shy. Whenever an adult tried to call on him, Hanan seemed to be somewhere else, somewhere far in the back of his garden or somewhere off beyond the trees. When Hanan was much younger, he had planted some sweet chestnuts that he had gotten in trade from a Spanish merchant who came to the Cologne fair. From these seeds, chestnut trees had grown, and they now had begun to bear fruit. (Grandmother claimed that this was the only grove of sweet chestnuts in all of northern Europe, in those days long ago in the Middle Ages; but frankly, Rabbi, I do not know how she could be certain of this.) Anyway, it seemed that Hanan could blend in among the chestnut trees whenever he needed to be alone.

But it was different with children. Children did not frighten Hanan, and little children always seemed to be popping up in various corners of the garden. Hanan would give them bunches of onions or radishes. He would break off stalks of rye or barley, he would pull up turnips for them to munch on, he gave them small cucumbers and yellow gourds, and he would put garlic bulbs into their baskets. So, when the Jews of Rondorf were in need of rain, they would send their young children to the house of Hanan the Hidden Gardener in order to ask him to pray for rain. When the children came to him, they took hold of the hem of his long gardening shirt and they chanted: "Gardener, gardener—give us rain. Give us flowers, give us grain."

And old Hanan would smile at them and he would begin to pray. He swayed back and forth wildly and he said: "Lord of the universe (blessed be He), Who has brought forth the sun and the wind, now please bring the rains. Let the clouds amass, let the downpours come."

> Roll the dark clouds
> Now for hours,
> Water the winds
> And misty towers
> With drenching sheets
> Of rainfall showers.
>
> Now, good Lord
> With weather powers,
> Rain the rains,
> Wash the bowers.
> Children ask me
> For thundershowers –
>
> But You're the Gardener
> Of trees and flowers.

And inevitably, the skies would darken and the rains would come.

Hanan was a rainmaker all his life, hidden and happy and finely weathered, and when he was an old, old weathered man, Hanan died; one day he was found in his yard lying beneath a chestnut tree. A Jew should be buried beside his parents so that he will be able to hold their hands for ever and ever in the Great Hereafter, but no one knew where Hanan's parents lay buried. The neighbors in Rondorf came to Rabbi Abraham. Abraham Achselrad closed his eyes and after a he moment declared: Hanan shall be buried beneath the chestnut tree where he has fallen. The Rabbi returned with the delegation from Rondorf, and Abraham Achselrad himself helped to dig the grave; then Abraham Achselrad himself washed the body—he wrapped it in a white shroud, and he covered it with spices. Then, Abraham Achselrad bent Hanan the Hidden Gardener into a fetal position in order that he might one day roll to the Holy Land. And so old Hanan was buried. It was a fine summer afternoon when they buried Hanan the Hidden Gardener, and Abraham Achselrad cried a bit as he walked back to the yeshiva in Cologne.

abbi, I am glad to see you here tonight: I need your advice. It is really a small matter. This afternoon one of the older students was complaining that the study hall is too noisy in the afternoons. Some of the youngsters read out loud; they get carried away—but should I say something to them? Speaking aloud and speaking one's mind are certainly honorable traits, and I hate to discourage them. It is difficult to know what is best. Should you speak your mind, or should you hold your peace? I remember the Talmud's story of Rabbi Safra, the teacher who boldly spoke his mind aloud.

One sunny spring day, Rabbi Safra went for a walk with his students. After a few minutes, he met a pious man—a stranger—coming along the road. The man looked up, and he saw the Rabbi who was a well-known figure in the community. The man said to himself: "Well, how kind of the Rabbi to come out and meet me; he must have recognized what a devout scholar I am."

So the man stopped the Rabbi and said: "Rabbi Safra, it really was not necessary to humble yourself and to come out specially in order to greet me."

Rabbi Safra was puzzled, and he answered: "Good sir, you are mistaken. I merely came out in order to take advantage of the fine weather. My students and I have met you by chance."

The poor stranger was terribly embarrassed, he mumbled something, he glanced quickly at the people passing by, and he hurried off down the street.

Then one of the students turned to the Rabbi and said: "Why did you shame that man? Is this not a sin?"

"Why should I have lied?" asked the Rabbi.

The student answered: "Rabbi, you need not have lied—you could have just kept silent."

But Rabbi Safra said: "If I had kept silent, then the man would have thought that he had spoken the truth. In this case, I would not have lived up to the requirements of the Holy Scriptures, for it is written in the 15th Psalm":

> Lord, who shall enjoy Your heavenly tents?
> Who shall bask in Your holy light?
> He who speaks honest sentiments
> And tells the truth from his heart aright.

"The psalmist means that you should speak with your mouth that truth which is in your heart.

"And, my good students, do you really think that I would have done this man a favor if I had pretended?" continued the Rabbi. "Had I kept silent, then I should have 'outwitted him and stolen his heart' (as it is written in Genesis). Why would I have stolen his heart? It is because through silence I would have outwitted him—I would have made him foolish. This poor man would have thought that I had actually come out for a walk in his honor, and when he discovered this deception then his heart would have been broken.

"Remember, young men, the name of the good Lord God (blessed be He) is 'Truth,' and He desires that we *always* speak the truth. Never lie, friends: if all men shall observe this requirement, then the Lord will send rain in its due season, whenever it is needed, and the sun will shine afterward. As the Holy Scriptures say in Psalm 85:

> Love and Fidelity have come together;
> Justice and Peace have joined their hands.

Hope and Trust grow from God's verdant earth;
From Heaven, Goodness falls on all the lands.

The good Lord God will ensure prosperity:
We'll reap rich harvests without cease.
God rains down Truth upon His children,
And the path of His feet shall be at peace.

Therefore, speak truthfully – and speak that truth loudly."

Of course there are always two sides to any story. After all these years of sitting in the study rooms during lessons, I have learned some of the ins and outs of the Talmud. And I recall that the great Sages followed the story of Rabbi Safra with a warning: the tongue is unruly. Therefore, pointed out the Rabbis, the good Lord God (blessed be He) provided the tongue with exceptional controls:

The Holy One, blessed be He, said to the tongue: "All the limbs of man are erect, but I have kept you horizontal. All the limbs of man are outside the body, but I have kept you inside. Moreover, I have found it necessary to surround you with two walls, one of bone and the other of flesh."

I know that you remember these sections of the Talmud, Rabbi, and I know that you also remember how the discussion continues: "Too much talk is a bad habit" and "A word is worth a coin, but silence is worth two" and "Silence heals all ailments" and "Although silence is good for the wise, it is even better for the foolish" and "I have grown up among thoughtful men – where I have found that silence serves me best."

For these reasons, my grandmother would always say: "Maintain your silence, young man." She said that daily – did you ever hear her? You never met my grandmother, Rabbi? Ah, more is the pity, for she was a fine woman. Grandmother was especially fond of the 39th Psalm, the verses:

Closely I will watch my word
And not fall to evil slanderings,

My agile tongue will not be heard
Speaking any hurtful things.

In the face of wicked men
I will be quiet and calmly pray,
I will keep my silence then
And cast my eyes the other way. . . .

What is that, Rabbi? Certainly there is more to tell: I was just
resting my eyes a moment. Now let me see, what was I saying? Yes,
silence was very important to my grandmother: she would arise early
every day, in order to have some quiet time to herself. Often, during a
noisy day she would go and sit by her mother's grave where it was
quiet, and she would work on her embroidery. It was my grandmother
who gave me an appreciation of silence. I remember her story about
Rabbi Abraham and the silent child. Do you know about the mystical
Achselrad and the silent infant? No? Then let me tell you. You see,
Rabbi, once, in the time of Rabbi Abraham Achselrad, a silent child
was born.

It was in the time of Rabbi Abraham ben Alexander, Achselrad of
Cologne, when a child was born unable to utter a sound, and the little
boy remained this way as he grew older. His mother bathed him daily
in hot water, and she rubbed him from tip to toe with olive oil. She
tried all manner of charms and incantations. She talked to him for
hours without stopping. She sang to him. She crept up on him when he
was playing, in order to scare him into speech. Nothing worked. The
mother had heard a great deal about the mystical Rabbi Abraham
Achselrad, so eventually she went to see the famous Rabbi. She told
him of her trouble – namely, that she had a child that was still unable to
speak – and she asked the good Rabbi what she should do.

The Rabbi was in the back study room in the old yeshiva of
Cologne. He listened to the young woman's story; then he put his head
in his hands, and he closed his eyes. Abraham Achselrad sat so long and
so quietly that the woman finally asked: "Rabbi, are you all right?"

The Rabbi replied: "My good woman, I have had a vision."

"A vision?"

"Yes – a vision. Now, listen carefully to these instructions: put on your walking clothes and travel south toward Bonn. First you will pass the old Jewish cemetery, next you will reach the village of Rondorf, finally you will get to the town of Bruhl.

"Bruhl sits at the edge of the Eifel mountains. Just before you enter the town and at the base of a hill, you will find an old man sitting on a bench. Stop and say to him: 'I have a speechless child. What am I to do in order to make him talk?' Then, do whatever he tells you."

The woman shrugged her shoulders—it sounded strange, but this was the great Achselrad of Cologne, so she did as she was told by the pious man. When she came to the village of Bruhl, she met an old Gentile man sitting on a bench. She said to him: "Good sir, I have one child, a lad of three years old, named Asher. He has not said a single word since birth. What am I to do?"

The Gentile man narrowed his eyes, and he spit at her feet and said: "You are a Jew—throw the boy into the fire."

The woman could not believe her ears. She stepped back. Then she said: "Why, may you go to the devil for your evil speech!" And she turned around, and angrily she walked back home.

In Cologne, the woman went back to Rabbi Abraham Achselrad and she reported her ill-fated adventure. The Rabbi sat back in his old chair and said: "Young woman, you were wrong in not doing what this man told you to do. You did not have to burn the child. All that you had to do was to put the little boy on a warm board on the hearth. You could have covered the little child with a cloth and let him lie there a while. Then, you would have uncovered the infant and picked him up. The child would have been able to speak. Now, madam, go back to Bruhl again. Find the same man, make the same speech, and then—as I told you before—find some way to do whatever he tells you."

The woman was surprised, but this was the great Achselrad of Cologne, so she did as she was told by the pious man. When she came again to the village of Bruhl, the same old Gentile man was sitting on the same old bench. The young woman said to him: "Good sir, I have one child, a lad of three years old, named Asher. He has not said a single word since birth. What am I to do?"

The old Gentile man narrowed his eyes and spit at her feet, and he said: "You are a Jew—beat the boy with a stick."

The woman was furious: How could this vile old man say such things? The little boy was her only child. "You blasphemous old man – may you go blind and may your feet rot," she called, and she walked angrily back to Cologne.

In Cologne, she went home. She picked up little Asher, she hugged him, and she played with him. He seemed to be a happy child, but he did not make a sound. She set the little boy on the floor, and she said: "Something must be done." So she went back to Rabbi Abraham Achselrad and reported her ill-fated adventure.

The Rabbi sat back in his old chair; he closed his eyes and he opened them again, and he said to her: "Young woman, why did you not follow my instructions? You did not have to harm the child. All that you had to do was put the little boy on the ground, cover him with a cloth, and tap him three times with a stick. Then, you would have uncovered the infant and picked him up. The child would have been able to speak. Now, go back to Bruhl again. Find the same man, make the same speech, and then – as I have told you twice before – find some way to do whatever he tells you."

What could the woman say? This was the great Achselrad of Cologne, so she did as she was told by the pious man: the poor woman walked out the southern gate of Cologne toward Bonn. First, she passed the old Jewish cemetery; then, she traveled through the village of Rondorf. Finally, at the foot of the beautiful Eifel mountains, she saw the village of Bruhl, and there, just before the village, was the same mean Gentile man sitting on the same worn bench. The woman felt silly repeating her speech, but she built up her courage and she said to him: "Good sir – as you may recall – I have one child, a lad of three years old. He has not said a single word since birth. What am I to do?"

Again, the Gentile man narrowed his eyes and spit at her feet, and this time he said: "You are a Jew – throw the boy into the water; throw him deep into the wide River Rhine."

At first, the woman could not believe her ears – however, she stopped herself from making any remarks. She stepped back, but she said nothing. Then, the woman turned, and without looking at the old man, she returned home. She went to her bedroom; she was afraid to tell anyone what she planned to do. Late at night, she took her little child and she tied a rope around his waist. She walked down to the edge of the deep black River Rhine, she gave her little boy a last hug, she covered him with a cloth, and she threw him into the river.

The young mother threw her only son, Asher, into the River

Rhine, one cold, cold night. She heard a splash; a minute passed and then two. Had she drowned her only son? Would God ever forgive her? Then she heard a whimper and a whisper, and a small voice said: "Mother, mother—I am so cold." Quickly, she pulled in the line. She wrapped her wet and crying little boy in her apron, and she carried him home. From that day on, the child spoke as normally as any other little boy, and later when he attended the yeshiva he was an outstanding pupil, one of the favorites of Rabbi Abraham Achselrad. When he grew up, this little boy became a famous rabbi, Rabbi Asher ben Yehiel (also known as "Rosh"). And when he was old, Rabbi Asher would always say: "I never spoke when I was young, and for this reason I learned to listen well with my littlest and tiniest and softest ears."

ello, Rabbi, I will be with you in a moment. I cannot leave until every tablecloth is folded – otherwise the day is not properly ended. There, that is the last one. What is that, Rabbi? You are not sleepy? Well, set your eye on the glowing flames in the stove. That will lull you to sleep: it washes away all thoughts and cares and angers. My grandmother used to say that you can even wash out the Evil Eye by staring at a white flame. Yes, that is what my grandmother told me – and I learned never to doubt her word.

My grandmother told me many wonderful things. Often, she related tales of her favorite rabbi, Abraham ben Alexander, Achselrad of Cologne. Abraham Achselrad (a pupil of Eliazer the mystic of Worms) was always conjuring visions in the synagogue. I doubt whether he would be tolerated nowadays, but my grandmother said that Rabbi Abraham was also a scholar, and he always claimed that his visions came from devout and pious study. Many an astonishing event took place in his yeshiva, or so my grandmother (blessed be her memory) was told. And Achselrad was not cowed by strange events and disquieting manifestations – no, he knew how to deal with these visions. Why, one day he even stared down the Angry Simeon of Cologne.

You have never heard of the Angry Simeon of Cologne? Grand-mother said that this Simeon was a perenially angry man. You might say that he was the proverbially angry man – you know the sayings from the Book of Proverbs:

> Just as the north wind brings forth rain,
> So a biting tongue brings an angry face.

> He who angers quickly acts foolishly,
> And a wicked man is widely hated.

> An angry man stirs up strife,
> And a wrathful man encourages sins.

What is that, Rabbi? Yes, I also know the proverb:

> A spiteful man stirs up discord,
> But if slow to anger, he avoids strife.

> A good man gets angry very slowly
> And overlooks most others' sins.

> He who angers slowly is better than royalty;
> He who tempers his spirit is better than a conqueror of cities.

Undoubtedly, Rabbi Achselrad also knew these proverbs by heart. Now, proverbs are all well and good, Rabbi, but Abraham Achselrad had to deal in a practical way with the strange anger of Simeon. No, no, Rabbi, he is not the angry Simeon ben Moses. . . . Well, if you will listen a moment then I will tell you about Achselrad's angry Simeon – just be patient. My grandmother said that it all began when Simeon appeared one day with his son in the old Cologne yeshiva. In the middle of prayers, the men in the back stopped their swaying and they stared, for Simeon ben Joshua had stepped into the synagogue. Reb Simeon had a strange fierce look on his face; the men looked at one another – there was no doubt that the Evil Eye had entered the Cologne yeshiva.

Yes, the angry Evil Eye, Rabbi. Of course, that is not entirely unheard of, even for a holy place of study. The Talmud reports that wherever certain Sages directed their gaze either death or some other dire calamity occurred. And my grandmother said that such was the curse of Reb Simeon ben Joshua, who lived outside of Cologne, far back in those old days of Abraham ben Alexander, Achselrad of Cologne. When this fearsome Jew became angry, a strange expression took over his face – Simeon's forehead became wrinkled and creased, his eyebrows almost covered his eyes, and wherever he looked disaster struck. For some reason, the fearsome Reb Simeon suddenly took to attending services in the Cologne yeshiva one winter, and for those dark months all the men were ill at ease.

Then one day at the end of winter, Reb Simeon was walking by the Cologne cathedral. (That is the Dom, the cathedral in which the three kings of Cologne are buried. Those kings – Kaspar, Melchior, and Balthazar – were the three wise men who came from the East to see the infant Jesus.) It was after the morning service on a Sunday, and a Gentile – the church beadle – hurried down the steps without looking, and he bumped into Reb Simeon. Simeon ben Joshua stumbled and fell. Then Simeon turned, and he looked up at the beadle. A strange expression took over Reb Simeon's face, his forehead became wrinkled and creased, and his eyebrows almost covered his eyes. Reb Simeon glared fiercely at the man. The Gentile shrunk back, and soon afterward, the beadle died of a strange and painful disease.

Parishioners from the morning service had witnessed the bump, the stumble, and the stare, and when the beadle died, the entire story was reported to the Archbishop, Archbishop Philip von Heinsberg. Clearly, a Jew had killed an official of the Church with the Evil Eye. The Archbishop issued a warrant for Simeon's arrest – promising a sentence of death by hanging.

Word passed quickly through the Jewish Quarter, and Reb Simeon ben Joshua and his son hid in a cellar in order to save their lives. The two men lived underground in one of the houses deep within the main block of the Jewish Quarter in Cologne. Yes, Simeon and his son concealed themselves in a cellar, and they never dared appear outside in the light of day. Simeon was a fearsome man – but was he not a brother Jew? For this reason, uneasy neighbors cared for them and brought them food.

Simeon and his son walked about in their small cell, they prayed regularly by themselves, and somehow they lived an orderly daily existence. As it is written in Psalm 141:

> In the Lord I take my refuge where
> He will conceal my soul secretly
> And keep me hidden from the snare
> That evil men have laid for me.

So Simeon and his son stayed concealed in the basement, and they remained there for twelve long years.

After a full dozen years, the old Archbishop of Cologne, Philip von Heinsberg, died suddenly. The new prelate was Archbishop Adolph; he was a scholar, and he was sympathetic to the Jews. As head of the Jewish community in Cologne, Rabbi Abraham Achselrad petitioned Archbishop Adolph to redress the wrongs instituted under Archbishop Philip, and among the requests was a pardon for Simeon and his son. The new Archbishop declared a general amnesty, and Simeon and his son finally came out of their cellar hiding place.

For the first time in twelve long years, Simeon ben Joshua emerged into the light of day in the Jewish Quarter of Cologne. He looked about, and he saw life as he had remembered it. Or was it worse? Women were hurrying about the streets with large baskets and with small children who trailed behind, holding onto their mothers' skirts so as not to get lost. Bearded men argued and laughed loudly. Girls shouted and teased each other; boys jumped and pushed. Horses jostled each other aside. A large pile of rags and old cloaks leaned against the side of a house. A smokey smell rolled through the streets.

Simeon turned to his son and said: "These neighbors of ours, are they really Jews?"

"What do you mean, Father?" asked his son.

"Look at them here in these dirty streets: these people forsake the life of eternity. Instead, everyone is caught up in petty, mortal trivialities," said Simeon. Then he almost shouted: "Today is transitory— tomorrow is forever!" A strange expression took over Reb Simeon's face, his forehead became wrinkled and creased, and his eyebrows almost covered his eyes. Reb Simeon glared fiercely at the things around him. A nearby woman limped off, a cart fell broken, a fire broke out in a trash heap.

You think that this is unheard of? Why, the mystic Eliazer of Worms was known to get angry like this often. One time, he stared his deep stare at a Gentile who had stoned a Jew: the Gentile shriveled and turned into a heap of bones, right then and there. Or, Rabbi, consider the hermit Sheshet the Pious – he was blind, yet his sightless stare could turn a man into a rock. And as for Reb Simeon, small disasters followed and preceded him everywhere as he angrily strode about the Jewish Quarter. Men ran to the yeshiva in fear, and Rabbi Abraham came out into the streets. Abraham Achselrad went up to Simeon: "What is going on here, Simeon? Have you left your cellar hide-away simply to destroy our little Jewish world? Perhaps you should go back to living underground."

Simeon stared at the Rabbi, but the Rabbi stared back. The two men looked at each other for a full minute, then Rabbi Abraham Achselrad turned and left. Simeon stared at the departing Rabbi; he stared at the buildings and the people and the carts and the street. And then Simeon ben Joshua walked off down Judengasse and out the south gate of Cologne, and he was never seen again.

Of course Rabbi Abraham Achselrad himself became very angry at times. One afternoon, he was walking down Judengasse Street. He heard some yelling, and he found that two young Jews were arguing and were throwing pieces of bread at one another.

"What is this?" asked the Rabbi.

"Oh, Samuel here is just being unpleasant," said one of the men.

"You seem to be returning his behavior in kind," noted the Rabbi.

"Should I just let him act like a child?" responded the man.

"It is true – I suppose that a child might waste food when others need it," said Rabbi Achselrad angrily. The Rabbi stared fiercely at the two men, who looked aside and stopped their arguing. Then abruptly the Rabbi walked on. Later in the day, it began to rain. It rained and it rained and the bread on the street was washed away, and when the two men returned home, they found that their kitchens had flooded and all their food had been ruined by the waters.

No, I am not inventing this, Rabbi: my grandmother swore that this is exactly what she had heard. The Evil Eye is a mystical but holy fact, Rabbi. You know, of course, that the good Lord God (blessed be

He) has set an example with His fearsome, righteous stare. Remember how it says in Psalm 92: "Mine eye has fiercely gazed on them that lie in wait for Me." And does it not also say (in Psalm 33): "Behold, the eye of the Lord stares down fiercely on them that fear Him"? . . . What is that, Rabbi? Of course I remember Psalm 117—it is the shortest psalm of all. It goes":

> Praise our God, all you nations;
> Join with Him, all His children.
> For He loves His congregations,
> He is gentle, kind, and open;
> He forgives the wicked person;
> All God's Truths will rise again
> And smile down on us like the warm sun –
> Hallelujah, joy and amen.

ello, Rabbi. Of course – feel free to sit here by the stove: the night fire helps me to become sleepy, also. You and I are not blessed like old Reb Elbaum; once again I saw him nodding off during the last prayers this evening. He can sway piously even while asleep – he must have learned some magic from the mystic Achselrad. And, Rabbi, I suppose that you and I could use a dose of Achselrad ourselves tonight. My grandmother said that Achselrad could put men into a sleep-trance by waving a gold coin before their eyes. Exactly, Rabbi, I am speaking of Abraham ben Alexander, also called Achselrad of Cologne. As you know, he was a pupil of Eliazer the mystic of Worms.

Rabbi Abraham Achselrad was always conjuring visions in the synagogue. I doubt whether he would be tolerated nowadays, but my grandmother said that Rabbi Abraham was also a scholar, and he claimed that his visions came from devout and pious study. Many an astonishing event took place in his yeshiva – or so my grandmother (blessed be her memory) was told. One day his vision from a Psalm saved poor Daniel ben Jacob ben Judah. Yes, I will gladly tell you about Daniel, although he had nothing to do with Spain.

Did you not ask about Spain? Then I suppose that I was drifting off – for a moment I was thinking of the time when Rabbi Abraham visited the Spanish King Ferdinand II in his court in Leon and when he made a young page boy disappear during dinner. Oh? You knew this already—then perhaps you have heard about Achselrad's vision from Psalm 121. You have not heard about this vision? Well, then, let me tell you what I learned from my grandmother:

As you know, Rabbi Achselrad was the author of the mystical treatise, the *Keter Shem Tov,* which was never published and which only exists as a secret manuscript hidden in the loft of the old Cologne yeshiva. Grandmother said that it was early one cold winter morning, while writing this very book, that Rabbi Abraham looked up and in the light of the candle he saw a young man, pale and shaken. "Rabbi," said the boy, "I am Benjamin, son of Daniel ben Jacob of your congregation. They have arrested my father for murder this morning—please come quickly, we need your help."

In Cologne, St. Laurence parish is the Christian area directly south of the Jewish Quarter, and just beyond is St. Albans parish, which borders on the St. Laurence parish. Early in the morning, a group of Gentiles came into the Jewish district from the St. Albans parish. These Gentile young men had with them two officers of the Archbishop. They marched up to the house of Daniel ben Jacob, and they declared that Reb Daniel had killed a young Gentile named Otto. Daniel protested, but when the group looked in the backyard of Daniel's house, there lay the dead body of a man. Daniel was dragged off to the guard house, and Daniel's son Benjamin ran immediately to Rabbi Abraham.

Rabbi Abraham put on his hat and his coat; he left the small back study room of the yeshiva, and he walked through the main prayer hall filled with wooden benches. He passed the twelve stained glass windows with their colored lions and snakes, he went by the Holy Ark made of stone, he stepped out of the main door, and he strode off to the courthouse, with Benjamin hurrying behind. The Archbishop himself was there in court; this was the Archbishop Adolph of Cologne, a noble and honorable prelate. Archbishop Adolph knew the Rabbi. "Rabbi," said the Archbishop sadly, "I am afraid that one of your Jews has committed murder. We have accusers, and we have the body—so, Mr. Daniel Jacob must be hanged."

"I see," said Rabbi Abraham. Abraham Achselrad looked at the

*Rabbi Abraham Achselrad* 119

accusers, he looked at Daniel, and he looked at the Archbishop. Rabbi Abraham closed his eyes a moment; then he asked: "Have you a Bible here, good Archbishop?"

"Of course," replied the Archbishop, and he instructed one of the officers to pass a leather volume to Rabbi Achselrad.

"Now, let us read from the Psalms," said the Rabbi.

"I respect your religious views, Rabbi," said Archbishop Adolph, "but is this really relevant now?"

Rabbi Abraham Achselrad was holding the Bible. Suddenly, his eyes opened wide, and then they closed tightly; he became weak, and he sat on a nearby chair. Then, the Rabbi gently set down the Bible.

"Are you all right, Rabbi," asked the Archbishop.

"I have just had a vision: I have seen the Heavens at night. I have seen the good Lord God (blessed be He), Who never sleeps – and now I have seen also that Psalm 121 is quite important," said Abraham Achselrad. "If you will be so good as to hand me that holy book, I will read a bit of those verses":

> The Guard of Israel never slumbers, He never sleeps.
> The Lord is your saviour, He defends your soul
> So that foes will not strike from the nighttime deeps;
> God lets no evil crawl from the midnight hole.

"Of course," said the Archbishop, "that is a noble and holy sentiment."

"You are a noted cleric, Archbishop Adolph. What would you say that this verse means?" asked the Rabbi.

"Clearly it means that He Who guards us from all evil neither sleeps nor slumbers."

"I would say that it means more," said the Rabbi.

"You would? Then pray tell, Rabbi Achselrad: What more do you read into this Psalm?"

"First I would say, good Archbishop, that the Lord God (blessed be He), Who is the Guardian of all Israel, does not sleep. In addition, the good Lord God does not let *others* sleep, in order to protect His people Israel against false accusations," said the Rabbi.

"Exactly what are you saying, Mr. Alexander?" asked the Archbishop.

"I am saying this, Archbishop: I have had a vision. I have seen that somewhere in this city is a man who could not sleep. He is an old man, with a drooping mustache. He will tell the truth, and he will vindicate poor Daniel ben Jacob ben Judah of our congregation – for Daniel has been accused falsely."

Then one of the officers laughed and said, "The Psalm has told you all this, old man?"

"Yes, it has," said the Rabbi.

The Archbishop conferred with his councilors, and after an argument, Archbishop Adolph of Cologne agreed to send out word into the town. His officers were instructed to ask around the community for a man who could not sleep last night – specifically, they looked for an old man with a drooping mustache who had seen some strange events in the vicinity of the Jewish Quarter. Other court business filled the morning; but later that day, an officer returned with an old Gentile man. And the man told his story to the court.

"I am an old man," he began, "and I fall asleep early in the evenings. However, I often awaken in the dead of the night, and then I have trouble falling back to sleep. Last night I could not sleep. I looked out the window, I got back into bed, I tossed, and I turned. Finally, I went into the kitchen and had a bit of bread. It was of no use – I was not sleepy, so I put on my shoes and my coat and I decided to take a walk.

"I walked down Obernmarspforten Street and along the Jewish Quarter – you know, down the Judengasse Street. I stopped at the corner of Engegasse because I heard voices. There, I saw two men carrying what looked like a dead body. The men were whispering and arguing. Suddenly, they flung the body over a fence into the yard of one of the Jews and they ran off. All was silent, and for a moment I was not certain that I had seen the event at all."

"Perhaps you dreamed it," suggested the Archbishop.

"I was not sure until now, your holiness," replied the man.

"Something now convinces you that your vision was real?"

"Yes."

"What is that?" asked the Archbishop.

"Now, I see both those men once again."

"Do you mean that you are having a vision?"

"No, this is no mirage – the two men are right here in the courtroom. I recognize them clearly," said the man, and he pointed to two of the Gentiles from the St. Alban's Parish, the two men who had brought the charges against Reb Daniel.

With the testimony of this witness, Archbishop Adolph of Cologne turned to his officers; he had the two Gentiles arrested for murder, and he freed Daniel ben Jacob ben Judah. The Lord protects the Jews, said my grandmother, even in the dead of night.

ood evening again, Rabbi; I know how hard it is to sleep when the moon is bright. Just put your feet up on the side bench here and I will open the stove door. Let me push this coal back: there is nothing like that white glow – it washes away all cares. I heard your final benediction tonight, and there is no use denying it; you are overworked. Oh yes, even a shammas like me can tell. I kept one eye on you when I cleaned the dishes, and I saw that you were watching the door, hoping that Reb Elbaum would leave early. And then, Reb Anton stayed to discuss that passage from Exodus, the place where the good Lord God (blessed be He) speaks to Moses from the burning bush:

> And Moses hid his face, for he was afraid to look upon God. . . . And shielding his eyes, Moses said unto the Lord: "Who am I, that I should be allowed to bring forth the children of Israel out of Egypt?"

Yes, after the analysis of these holy passages, of course you are worn out. What is that? A story from me? Rabbi, all I know are the old-fashioned children's tales, the grandmother fables. You need something new and fresh in order to keep your mind keen. Otherwise you will become an old man like me, and you will find yourself constantly musing and dozing and nodding off in front of the stove.

What do you mean you are already an old man? Do you really think that sixty years is old? You are still a child. When you reach eighty, *then* you will be old. You doubt that you will live to see eighty years? Well if you are correct, Rabbi, then you will never grow old. . . . All right, all right—I really know no special stories—however, listening to you and Reb Anton reviewing the modesty of Moses put me in mind of a story about the modesty of Rabbi Shealtiel ben Menahem.

You have not heard of Rabbi Shealtiel? Then let me tell you: Rabbi Shealtiel was a student of Rabbi Amram of Cologne. Like his teacher, Shealtiel ben Menahem was a scholar and a poet. He was also a legal expert: along with Rabbi Eliezer ben Joel and Rabbi Menahem ben David, Rabbi Shealtiel ben Menahem was on the Rabbinical Court of Cologne in the years when it was the court of last resort for all German Jews. Rabbi Shealtiel was modest and shy, and he would rather look at the wall or at a chair than look at another person. Grandmother described Shealtiel as a thin man with big ears and reddish brown hair; he squinted, and when he walked he bent slightly to the left.

My grandmother told me that once upon a time there lived in Cologne a man who was called Makir ben Isaac. Makir was too old and too sick to come to the synagogue. Each week, Rabbi Shealtiel would take eight students with him to Makir's house, in order to pray with the old man. Makir's house was like Makir himself: it was old and tumble-down. (Also, in the attic, Makir had a large quantity of wine, which he used in order to protect himself against the ravages of old age and cold weather.) Makir loved to review the Holy Scriptures and other Jewish learning, so sometimes Shealtiel ben Menahem would deliver lectures in Makir's kitchen or he would discuss items of *Halakhah*.

As you know, Rabbi Shealtiel was a shy and modest man, and he rarely looked at anyone else. Usually, he looked at the ceiling or at the corner of the room or at a board in the floor. One day Rabbi Shealtiel, a group of yeshiva students, and Reb Makir were sitting in Makir's kitchen and were arguing about the puzzling sentence from Isaiah:

Then the Lord spoke again unto Ahaz, saying: "Ask for a sign of the Lord your God, either from the depths of Sheol below or from the heights of Heaven above."

Suddenly, the Rabbi looked up to the heights above and there in the ceiling he saw a large, newly formed crack in the center beam.

"What is this?" he asked.

Makir looked at the ceiling, and he replied: "Well, Rabbi, I have never noticed this crack before, but old houses are always getting wrinkles, just like old men."

"Perhaps, Reb Makir," said the Rabbi, "but this looks dangerous to me." And he sent one of the students up to the attic to see what was happening above. The student climbed up and then he ran down; many wine casks sat right above the center beam, he reported, and it looked as if the ceiling were about to collapse.

"Fear not: the good Lord God (blessed be He) will protect us Jews," said Makir calmly. "We have a holy man here below the crack."

Rabbi Shealtiel was not certain that the Lord was watching them at that particular moment, but how could he deny that the good Lord God (blessed be He) protects the Jews? So the Rabbi kept his eyes on the ceiling, and he finished his lecture. Rabbi Shealtiel talked more quickly than usual, and as soon as he finished, he and all the students hurried out of the house; Reb Makir hobbled out the front door after them in order to bid them good-bye. Just at that moment, the ceiling of the kitchen collapsed, wine casks fell and broke, and purple wine spilled onto the floor and ran throughout the ruined house.

The men all stood in amazement. When Rabbi Shealtiel realized that a miracle had happened and that it had happened for his sake, he was very troubled. The Rabbi looked around rather wildly and he said: "My goodness, a person should not remain presumptuously in such a dangerous place." Then the Rabbi said: "We cannot count on the good Lord God (blessed be He) to be watching everywhere at once. We cannot think that a miracle might happen to us – because it is quite possible that the miracle will *not* happen."

"And," continued Rabbi Shealtiel, "what if a miracle does happen to happen? We are not necessarily better off. Do not forget, young men: every miracle is deducted from the final reward that is due to each of us for his good deeds." Then the Rabbi paced back and forth, and he felt ill at ease and very angry with himself. . . .

What is that, Rabbi? Of course there is more: I only closed my eyes for a moment. (Can an old man not take a little rest?) You have interrupted my thoughts; now, let me see, where was I? Yes, yes— Shealtiel was a quiet, modest man. As my grandmother (may her soul visit happily with her parents forever) said: "Rabbi Shealtiel reminds me of Psalm 131." Do you remember Psalm 131, Rabbi? No? Then let me repeat it for you:

> I do not wear haughty masks,
> My eyes are not on lofty tasks:
> I only do what my God asks.
>
> I stay within the modest shores
> Avoiding all impossible chores:
> I do not open profane doors.
>
> I hold in check my inner pride,
> Tempering arrogance deep inside:
> I quiet my soul and am satisfied.
>
> I am a contented little child:
> The Lord's my Parent, strong and mild.
> Hallelujah—God has smiled.

That Psalm was a favorite of my grandmother. Just like Shealtiel ben Menahem, the psalmist was a humble and modest man: yes, as my grandmother said many times, Rabbi Shealtiel was devout, wise, humble, and modest. When leading a service or when delivering a lecture, the Rabbi modestly looked everywhere but at his audience; Shealtiel always seemed distracted, and so he could surprise you with his intense piousness.

Rabbi Shealtiel had a special ability to intercede with the good Lord. As I mentioned, Shealtiel ben Menahem headed the famous yeshiva in Cologne. Cologne is twenty-five kilometers from the town of Kerpen, and in Kerpen lived a superstitious man named Meir ben

Saul. One day, said my grandmother, the little son of Meir ben Saul fell ill; he had a fever that got very high each afternoon and that cooled down each morning. The child became weak, he had pains in his back, and sometimes he had strange and frightening dreams even when awake.

Meir's wife prayed to the good Lord God (blessed be He): Hallelujah, she said. Amen, returned her husband – we will follow the dictums of the Talmud. So, Reb Meir took a clean new cup and he filled it precisely to the top with salt. Then his wife sewed the cup into a white cloth, she affixed a white braided cord to the salt pouch, and she tied the whole packet onto her little son's shirt. The parents waited through the night, but the boy still had a high fever the next day.

Meir's wife prayed again: Hallelujah, she declared. Amen, returned her husband, let us continue to follow the sacred Talmud. So, Meir walked to the crossroads near his house, and he watched for ants. Eventually, he saw a large black ant carrying a leaf. Meir picked up the ant, he dropped it into a copper tube, he closed off the end of the tube with lead, and he sealed it with sixty seals. Then Reb Meir shook the copper tube, and walking back and forth and back and forth, he said: "Let your load be set upon my back, and let my son's evil load be set upon you." The parents waited through the night. Unfortunately, the little boy still had his fever the next day.

Reb Meir's wife said: "Perhaps another person has already used this ant, and now the ant is carrying *his* fever. You had best repeat your incantation with a different request." So again Meir walked to the crossroads near his house, and he watched for ants. Eventually, Meir saw another large black ant carrying a leaf. Meir picked up the ant, he dropped it into a copper tube, he closed off the end of the tube with lead, and he sealed it with sixty seals. Then Reb Meir shook the copper tube, and walking back and forth and back and forth, he said: "Let your load remain with you, and let my son's sorry load be set upon you, too." Unfortunately, the little boy still had his fever on the next day.

Reb Meir's wife prayed: Hallelujah, she said. Amen, responded her husband – let us try another recipe from the Talmud. This time, Reb Meir took a clean pitcher, and he walked down to the river, the Erft River in Kerpen. He filled the pitcher with water, and he said: "River, river, lend me water for my long, long journey." Meir waved the pitcher seven times around his head, he threw the water behind him, and he said: "River, river, take back the water that once you gave me. Now, the long, long journey is finally done: I have gone, and I have returned on this the selfsame day."

Nonetheless, Meir's son remained ill. Meir and his wife felt desperate. For a time they even considered an old and profane remedy. Perhaps they should steal a nail from the cross on which a person had been hanged and then gently string the nail around their son's neck on the Sabbath. Of course this was explicitly forbidden by all the Sages, and Meir and his wife did not dare to try such black magic.

However, the parents did try all manner of other chants and incantations and amulets – but nothing worked. Their poor little son's fever persisted, rising and falling regularly each day. Each day, the little boy sweated and yet felt chilly, and his teeth chattered violently when the fever was the highest. Reb Meir and his wife became more and more worried, and they decided to call upon the well-known Rabbi Shealtiel of the Cologne yeshiva. Hallelujah, said the wife. Amen, said Meir. So Meir and his wife asked two of their neighbors, Reb Etan and Reb Lavan, to travel to Cologne and to ask Rabbi Shealtiel ben Menahem to pray that their poor young son might recover from his illness.

Rabbi Shealtiel was in the back room of the Cologne yeshiva. The two men from Kerpen walked through the main prayer hall filled with wooden benches, they passed the twelve stained glass windows with their colored lions and snakes, they looked up at the Holy Ark made of stone, and then they walked into the dim back room. There, the Rabbi was bent over a book.

"Excuse me, Rabbi," said Reb Etan.

"Yes?"

"Rabbi, you know Meir ben Saul. Well, his son –"

"Is this Meir ben Saul ben Jacob?" asked Rabbi Shealtiel.

"No – this is our Meir ben Saul ben Judah ben Moses, from Kerpen."

"I see."

"Anyway," continued Reb Etan, "poor Reb Meir – his son is very ill with a fever. Would you be so kind as to say some prayers and to intervene with the Holy Lord God in order to stop this sickness? Can you perhaps break the fever and return the little boy's good health?"

Rabbi Shealtiel squinted at the wall, and he stared at a corner of the study room. "Tell me," he asked, "does the fever appear every day?"

"Yes."

"Does the boy shake and does he chatter his teeth?"

"He does."

"I see," said Rabbi Shealtiel, "well, I will do my best."

Rabbi Shealtiel went back to reading his book. Reb Etan and Reb Lavan stood there a moment. They looked at each other; then they looked at the Rabbi. After a few minutes, Reb Etan said: "Excuse me, Rabbi – I do not want to be impolite, but Reb Meir is rather worried. What shall I tell him?"

"Is this Meir ben Saul ben Jacob?" asked Rabbi Shealtiel.

"No – this is our Meir ben Saul ben Judah ben Moses, from Kerpen: he has a young boy who is very ill with fever."

"Ah."

"Will you pray for him?"

"Of course I will," said Rabbi Shealtiel, looking at a dark corner of the study room.

The two men remained standing in the doorway. Should they leave? Should they sit down on the benches and wait? The Rabbi looked down at his book, and then he looked at the ceiling. Finally, he turned his back on the two men, and, facing Jerusalem, he began to pray silently. Soon the two men could hear Rabbi Shealtiel mumbling, and after a moment, they could also distinguish words. Finally, they heard the Rabbi repeat out loud the end of this ancient and little-known prayer:

> Were our mouths full of song like birds of the air
> Were our tongues as gleeful as waves of the seas,
> Were our eyes as shining as the stars out there,
> Could our voice fly like the eagles of the trees,
> Were our feet as swift as the woodland hare,
> Were our hearts as deep as the fathomless seas,
> Still, we could not praise God enough in prayer.
> When we were in bondage He answered our pleas;
> The Lord protects us from evil everywhere –
> So too will He deliver us from this disease.

As soon as he had finished his chanting, Rabbi Shealtiel turned around and he said: "Very well, my friends, you can return home to Reb Meir's house in Kerpen. Now the little boy's fever has left him, and he is healed."

The two men from Kerpen were surprised, and they asked: "Kerpen is twenty-five kilometers away: Who told you that the boy is suddenly well, Rabbi? Are you a seer? Are you a prophet?"

Rabbi Shealtiel was staring at the edge of the door and he replied: "I am no seer, and I am no prophet – I am not even the son of a prophet. But my father's father knew the old and sacred prayers, and I heard them chanted frequently when I was young.

"Morever, my good friends, I know that if one of these special prayers runs smoothly, then it is a sign that it has been heard by the good Lord God (blessed be He). Just now, my prayer flowed as smooth as a gentle spring rain. Therefore, there can be no doubt: our entreaty has been heard, and the young boy should be getting better this very minute."

Reb Etan and Reb Lavan looked at each other; they looked at the Rabbi and they waited a moment. Nothing more happened, so the two scholars from Kerpen noted the time when Rabbi Shealtiel had finished his prayer. They thanked Rabbi Shealtiel, who was now reading a book, and they left the back room of the old Cologne yeshiva. The two scholars walked into the main prayer hall filled with wooden benches, they passed the Holy Ark made of stone, they walked under the twelve stained glass windows with their colored lions and snakes, then they stepped out the front door and they returned to Kerpen.

In Kerpen, Reb Etan and Reb Lavan went directly to Reb Meir ben Saul. Meir and his wife were sitting with their little boy in the front room of their house. The boy was smiling, and although he was still damp with perspiration, his fever was gone, and he was eating some hot cereal. Reb Etan and Reb Lavan asked Meir: When was it that the boy's fever left him. Reb Meir and his wife were not certain, but they did know when it was that the boy had sat up suddenly and had asked for a drink of water. Comparing times, the scholars found that this had occurred exactly when Rabbi Shealtiel had finished his special prayer.

Yes, Rabbi, as my grandmother said: "The great Lord God (blessed be He) protects the Jews. And I pray," continued my grand mother, "that the example of Rabbi Shealtiel ben Menahem will make us appreciate all modest rabbis, and I hope that it will also cheer the weary pilgrim on his way to that great celestial city above." And then my grandmother added, quoting Meir and his wife: "Hallelujah, amen."

ood evening, Rabbi. "No sleep for the weary." That is what my grandmother said, and she said it almost nightly. If you are cold, then sit down here on the bench and I will stoke up the oven. This stoker? It is one of the iron shoe scrapers from the front hall—you probably do not recognize it because it is covered with soot and also because I bent it in order to make it fit through the oven door. Of course there are still two scrapers in the anteroom for dirty shoes—but I myself think that all men should remove their shoes before coming in to pray. Do you know that when the Messiah arrives, he will be barefoot? How could you not know this, Rabbi?

Yes, when *mashiach*, the anointed one, arrives, he will usher in the new, wonderful, Golden Age of the Messiah. As you know, the Talmud tells us that seven things were created before the good Lord God (blessed be He) actually set to work building our world: God made the Torah, repentance, the Heavenly Garden of Eden, Gehinnom, the Throne of Glory, the Temple, and the name of the Messiah. In difficult times, my grandmother always reminded me of this—the Messiah has been planned for us from the very beginning.

What is that, Rabbi—barefoot? Clearly, Rabbi, shoes were not thought of until well after our mortal world was formed, so undoubtedly the Messiah will arrive barefoot. Yes, yes–barefoot. Why, he might be any one of those barefoot and pious pilgrims that come through here weekly from the Holy Land. Barefoot means holy. But, Rabbi, beware of men in ancient sandals. My grandmother told me of the strange, sandaled man who appeared one black night in the back study room of the old Cologne yeshiva; he appeared in sandals, and he cast a pall on the studies of the modest Rabbi Shealtiel. What is that, Rabbi? Certainly I will tell you about it:

In medieval Europe, wandering pilgrims were constantly returning from the Holy Land; they came barefoot, and they came filled with tales of ever new potential Messiahs. All Jews remained hopeful: the Messiah was never far from their thoughts. Did you ever hear the old hymn that was sung at home at the Sabbath dinner table in those days?

> Here comes Hope–
> The Messiah arrives–
> A barefoot stranger
> Bringing eternal lives.
> Rebuilding the Temple;
> Repopulating Zion,
> Your everlasting city.
> And like a proud lion
> With glory as a mane
> And dressed in white
> We will go there, too,
> Following in Your light
> Singing new songs
> Praising You forever,
> Singing joyous songs
> To praise the Lord forever.

All Jews hurried to have more children and to marry their children and then to see crowds of grandchildren. And why was this? Without a doubt it would speed along that Great Day. Once upon a time, long, long ago, God had created every single soul from the primeval chaos; but the Messianic era could not dawn until all those souls – the souls originally created by the good Lord God – had been fitted into the earthly bodies that were destined for their reception here below. Then the one last soul would be the Messiah. And each mother dreamed that in the child of her own offspring God would deign to plant the soul of the longed-for redeemer.

In the days of Rabbi Shealtiel, a thin, wild-eyed, barefoot young man appeared in Spain. "I have been to the Holy Land," he reported. "I lived in a cave at the edge of the Dead Sea, and there late at night I heard a voice from the blank wilderness: 'The Messiah is finally arriving,' it cried.

"And when is that joyous arrival to be, my brethren? 'When?' you ask. It will be on the last day of the fourth month. I tell you, friends: it is the twenty-ninth day of the month of Tammuz. Then cometh the Messiah – praise the Lord, amen."

Ah, the Messiah had come at last. In those medieval days, the Jews of Germany lived in a wretched state: they were constantly tormented. When they heard of the coming of the Messiah to Spain, many Jews in northern Europe resolved to leave the cold European soil behind. Together with their wives and their children and with their sons and their sons' wives and children, Jews emigrated to Spain from Mainz, Worms, Rothenburg, Speyer, Oppenheim, Regensburg, and Cologne. And leading these emigrants was one of the most famous rabbis of Germany, Rabbi Benjamin Shalom of Oppenheim; Rabbi Benjamin was revered as a saint. He, too, took his entire family. And in Spain, Rabbi Benjamin and all the ecstatic Jews prepared for the great Coming. They fasted and they prayed. Many gave their clothes, their furniture, and their dishes to charity, they donated their money to the poor, and they tithed to their congregations. This philanthropy was to prove their piousness; it was to ensure that they would be worthy in the eyes of the soon-to-arrive Messiah.

I doubt whether anyone slept on the nights preceding the end of Tammuz. On the wondrous morning, throngs of Jews collected outside the synagogues, looking down the roads. Children stared up at the pale sky. Everyone was dressed as if for the Day of Atonement, and everyone was barefoot. Would shofars sound? Would the skies lighten, or would they darken? Would the earth crack? Would angels descend? Would the good Lord God (blessed be He) lead a mighty army Himself?

The morning dragged on; the people milled about. Where was the Messiah? A whispered rumor began: the people had collected too early, because the Messiah would arrive at nightfall. Some Jews returned to their homes; children were hungry and had to be fed. The afternoon passed, the nightfall came, but no Messiah appeared. Should the Jews remain through the night? Then some people noticed strange designs on their shirts: faint crosses could be seen by the candlelight. Was it just the shadows? Panic passed like a wave through the crowds. Jews hurried home; they lit Sabbath candles, they said prayers, and they sat uncomfortably all night long. The next morning there were no crosses on any of their clothes, and the Messiah had not come. The people felt dulled, and they did not know what to say. The day was hot. Businesses reopened, men and women milled about the markets, and children played in the streets. Somehow, life continued as before.

You are a hopeful man, Rabbi – do you think that you and I shall see the Messiah before we pass on to the Great Hereafter? Grandmother was optimistic. Sometimes she would remind me of God's promise to the Jews in Leviticus:

> If you conform to My statutes, if you observe My commandments, and if you follow My rules, then I will give you rain at the proper time. The rich lands will produce abundantly for you; the trees of the countryside will be filled with fruit. Each harvest will last until you must clear your storehouses to make room for the new harvest. And I will give you peace throughout the land. Then I will establish My Tabernacle among you, and I will walk beside you forever.

Obviously, the good Lord God (blessed be He) was speaking of the day of the Messiah – and, Rabbi, how could you question that? Grandmother smiled at the thought. It did not matter that many a strange claimant had already appeared: my grandmother would know the true Messiah when he arrived. *Mashiach* will come shining and barefoot and dressed in white, calm and wise and happy, ready to lead us back to the Holy Land. There is no confusing the true Messiah with the pale, sandaled, ill-clad specters haunting the old Jewish Quarters in northern Europe – these were wraiths from the darkest eras, wraiths like the one who appeared to Rabbi Shealtiel late one dark night in Cologne.

Exactly, Rabbi–this was the very same Rabbi Shealtiel ben Menahem who wrote the eighteen liturgical poems about the Sabbath that have since been lost. As you know, Rabbi Shealtiel was a shy and modest man. He preferred working alone, so he could often be found in the back room of the old Cologne yeshiva late at night. . . .

What? Of course there is more–I was just resting my eyes. Let me see, where was I? Oh yes, once upon upon a time a sandaled man came to Rabbi Shealtiel from England; he came by way of Belgium and France, and then from France he traveled to Cologne on the River Rhine, begging alms. Bearded ageless men like this wandered into the Jewish Quarter daily, begging and preaching, trading strange wares and relating news and tales and folklore.

It was a dark night: yes, my grandmother was positive that it was a dark night. The moon was tucked deep into a black pocket in the sky, and only a rim peeked out. Rabbi Shealtiel ben Menahem was reading late, in the back study room of the old Cologne yeshiva. Was the wind blowing against the shutters? Was an animal making a strange noise far away? The Rabbi looked up, a stranger stood in the doorway. The light was dim, and the Rabbi squinted. The man had long hair. He was dressed in an old and faded coat, and he had sandals on his feet. Was he a wandering peddler? He carried no belongings. Was he a pilgrim from the Holy Land?

The Rabbi looked up and past the man. After a moment, the stranger said in an old dry voice: "Rabbi, may I sleep on the floor in the study hall tonight?"

There was something very odd about this voice. Rabbi Shealtiel tilted his head, and he stared at his thumb. "Rabbi?" said the stranger quietly.

"Oh," said the Rabbi, "yes certainly, sir. You are welcome to spend the night here." Then the Rabbi stood up, and he took a blanket from behind his desk, and he led the pilgrim to a warm corner near the stove. "Feel free to spread out on the benches or on the floor and to make yourself as comfortable as possible. I am afraid that we have nothing fancy here. I have some bread left over from dinner. Would you like to eat a bit?"

"I would–that is very kind of you, Rabbi."

The Rabbi brought over a thick slice of bread. The man sat on the floor, and the Rabbi sat on a bench. "Tell me," asked the Rabbi, "are you a Jew?"

"Yes, Rabbi–I am an old Jew. My name is Isaac, Isaac ben Laquedem."

"Where are you from, Isaac?"

"Rabbi, I can honestly say that I am from everywhere."

"I see."

The stranger finished his bread. "Rabbi, might I have a bit of water?"

"How about some wine?"

"I would like that."

Rabbi Shealtiel brought over a cup of wine. "Usually, I can recognize a man's accent, but I cannot place yours," said the Rabbi.

The stranger looked down at his sandals: "As I said, Rabbi, I have been in a great many places. I have wandered so far and so long that my accent is probably an inextricable tangle of every accent in the world. Just last year, I was in England; I stayed with the monks of St. Albans. I must confess that I did not tell them that I was a Jew: there, I used the name Joseph of Arimathaea."

"Joseph of Arimathaea? That name is familiar."

"I have used that name before. . . . I have also been known as Cartaphilus."

There was a silence. Rabbi Shealtiel ben Menahem looked at the bench. Cartaphilus was a name that he recognized. . . .

What? Yes, yes, Rabbi, I am about to continue. I was just thinking quietly here in the glow of the stove. Now, where was I? Oh yes, there was silence. Perhaps it was five minutes. Or was it ten minutes? Finally, Isaac ben Lacquedem said: "You know the name."

"Yes, I do."

More quiet minutes passed.

"He was a thin man, Rabbi," said Isaac quietly.

The Rabbi continued looking at the bench.

"He was thin, and he looked very tired," said Isaac. "He carried two rough wooden beams lashed together as a cross. Jesus was his name."

Again there was silence.

Isaac continued: "I am a cobbler. I stood in my doorway, a

half-finished sandal in my hand. I will tell you the truth, Rabbi: I was irritated. I was expecting a wealthy customer momentarily. Suddenly, this man Jesus just collapsed on my steps, and he sat there for minutes and minutes. Finally, I said to him: 'Get up, young man – get up.' But he did not move. So I said: 'Please, get off my doorstep.' He did not even look up, and I said: 'Hurry up, move on. Get off the steps.' Then, he did look up at me. Slowly he arose and slowly he walked off, carrying the cross. He stood, he walked, he carried – then for just a moment he turned back, and as he shuffled ahead, I heard him say to me: 'Yes, Isaac the cobbler, I go – but you? You shall wait. You shall wait and wait and wait. Do not be in a hurry, Isaac, for you shall wait until I return once more.' "

Isaac had set down his empty wine cup, and he said no more. After a little while, Rabbi Shealtiel arose and walked into the back study room. He put on his coat and his hat, and he went home. In the morning, when the shammas arrived to open the yeshiva, Isaac was gone and his blanket was neatly folded and returned to its place behind Rabbi Shealtiel's desk, and there was no sign that anyone had ever slept on the floor beside the oven in the main study hall of the old yeshiva of Cologne on the dark River Rhine.

You probably do not know the Christian part of the Bible, Rabbi. Oh? You have read it? Then you will remember in their book called Matthew, there is a section that foreshadows an everlasting human witness to the crucifixion:

> Then Jesus said to his disciples: "Anyone who wishes to be my follower must leave his wordly self behind: he must take up his cross and come with me. Bring to me your true, inner self. Remember: Even if you win the whole mortal world, what can you have really gained if you have lost your true, inner self? . . . And then, good friends, what can you ever give that will buy back your true self once it is lost?"

Later in that same passage, Jesus says:

> I tell you this: some of those standing here before me today will not taste death until they have seen the Messiah coming again into his kingdom.

As my grandmother (may the good Lord God bless her and keep her in the Great Hereafter) pointed out: the wondrous kingdom has not yet come, and we still await the Messiah. The Messiah has not yet arrived – so, Rabbi, what if Jesus were correct? Could there be persons living today who had once been present at the crucifixion? Now, I have not invented the story, Rabbi – my grandmother swore that she had heard the tale of Isaac ben Laquedem from her grandmother. Was Isaac ben Laquedem an ancient wandering Jew? Did he still remember personally the details of those harsh Roman times? It is hard to believe, but perhaps Shealtiel ben Menahem met an everlasting Jew, an eternal Jew, a Jew who wanders the face of the earth until the end of the world, when the true Messiah shall come at last, amen. I wonder if we will see that golden day, Rabbi.

h, good evening, Rabbi. You are having difficulty sleeping again? Well, just put your feet up on the side bench here, and I will open the stove door. Let me push this coal back; there is nothing like that white glow to wash away a hard day. I heard your final prayers tonight, and there is no use denying it—you are overworked. Even a nearsighted shammas like me can tell. I kept one eye on you when I was cleaning the dishes; I saw that you were watching the door, hoping that Reb Elbaum would leave early. But then Reb Anton stayed in order to argue about the Midrash passage.

That Midrash passage reminded me of old Jehuda ben Saul—he was two rabbis before you. One day, Rabbi Jehuda gave a Midrash sermon to his yeshiva students. "What are the four reasons that we drink four cups of wine at the Passover service?" he asked. Then he looked sternly at the young men on the benches. One of the students, Moshe ben Samuel, answered: "Rabbi, we drink four cups because the good Lord God (blessed be He) made four promises to Israel through Moses."

"And what were those promises?" asked Rabbi Jehuda to Moshe ben Samuel.

"One—I will bring you forth. Two—I will deliver you. Three—I will redeem you. And four–I will take you as My people," answered Moshe quickly.

"Is this all?"

"That is four reasons, Rabbi."

"That one thing–a set of promises–is four reasons?" asked the Rabbi. "You have given me four *promises*. I want to know the four *reasons*. What are the four reasons?" Again Rabbi Jehuda looked sternly at his students, and there was silence. There was silence, so the good Rabbi answered his own question.

"First, of course, are the four promises. Second, there are the Pharaoh's cups (which are mentioned four times in the cupbearer's dream). Third, there are the four times in the Scriptures that the enemies of Israel are threatened with an evil cup. Fourth, there are the four times in the Holy Scriptures when a cup of joy or salvation is mentioned."

"And," asked the Rabbi, "how high are the booths?"

The booths? The yeshiva students were puzzled, and one asked: "Wine booths, Rabbi?"

"Wine booths? Certainly not–I mean *Sukkot* booths":

And you shall celebrate the pilgrim feast of ingathering at the end of the growing season, when you bring in the fruits of all your farming work upon the land–

"Exodus!" proclaimed Rabbi Jehuda, looking sternly at his students. Then he continued:

On the fifteenth day of this seventh month, the Lord's pilgrim feast of booths and arbors begins, and it lasts for seven days. Then you shall live in booths and arbors for seven days, all who are native Israelites; in this way, your descendants will be reminded how God made the Israelites live in booths and arbors when He brought them out of Egypt–

"Leviticus!" proclaimed Rabbi Jehuda. "And these booths," he asked, "how large can they be?"

The students looked at one another, unsure of how to reply; so the Rabbi answered his own question: "The booths (said Ezra the scribe) should be made of branches of olive, myrtle, and palm, and of other leafy boughs–and as you know from the Talmud, my young scholars, the Sages prescribed the height of the booths to be less than twenty cubits."

"Twenty cubits," repeated Jehuda. "Ah, but were they right, these Sages?"

No one spoke, so Rabbi Jehuda continued: "No, they were not right: the wise Rabbi Judah the Patriarch allowed booths with an interior height larger than twenty cubits high."

Then Rabbi Jehuda proclaimed: "He allowed booths more than twenty cubits high! And why was this?"

Again there was silence. Rabbi Jehuda looked down sternly at his charges: "Would the good Lord God (blessed be He), Who cares for us as if we were all His very own children, make us suffer more than Noah? No, he would not. And was not the length of the ark three hundred cubits and the breadth of the ark fifty cubits and the height of the ark thirty cubits? Yes, it was–so, Rabbi Judah the Patriarch knew directly from the holy word of the good Lord God (blessed be He) that the booths could be at least thirty cubits high, amen."

And how could you argue with that, Rabbi? Then, too, there was the time that Rabbi Jehuda proved that iron is mightier than charity. "Is not charity a mighty force?" he began.

"Yes," said one student.

"Is it mightier than iron?" asked the Rabbi. He looked around, but there was only silence, so Rabbi Jehuda answered his own question: "Yes, it is mightier. And why, my young men–why is charity stronger than iron? . . . You do not know? Then I will tell you.

"Iron is strong, but Iron can be melted by Fire. And Fire is powerful, but Fire can be subdued by Water–can it not?"

The study hall was quiet. The Rabbi continued: "Of course it can. And as for Water–why, Water can be carried by clouds; thus, Cloud is stronger than Water, because clouds hold the mighty rains. But are clouds the mightiest of forces? Well, are they? Certainly not, gentlemen–winds can shepherd clouds wherever they wish.

"Now, young scholars, does this mean that Wind is the strongest of all? Well? If you think so, then you are mistaken, for men can tame the winds: men can stand in the strongest gale, men can build houses to resist the hurricane, and men can harness the wild breezes with sails. Man is stronger than Wind.

"So, is Man then the mightiest of the natural elements?"

Silence greeted Rabbi Jehuda; thus, he continued and answered his own question: "Of course not—Trouble is mightier than Man, for Trouble can overwhelm the greatest king. But do not jump hastily to the simple notion that Trouble is the strongest of all forces. I warn you, young men, Wine can overcome Trouble: a drunken man forgets his problems. Wine temporarily wipes out Trouble. Nonetheless, mightier than Wine is Sleep, and stronger even than Sleep is Death.

"Death—dark Death—is a fearsome and a mighty force, young men. But now, consider Charity: why, Charity is mightier than Death itself, because Charity can save the starving man from Death.

"Therefore," concluded Rabbi Jehuda sternly, "Charity is mightier than Iron, praise the Lord and amen."

What is that, Rabbi? Yes, I agree: these conclusions might be presented a bit differently in different hands. But clearly such inferences are difficult to come by; they take serious thinking, they need knowledge of the scholarly books, and they require intricate reasoning from the holy words.

This was one of Rabbi Shealtiel's strengths: I am told that Rabbi Shealtiel was a master at the minute scrutiny of texts and that he was an accomplished dialectician. However, his skill was not apparent from looking at him. He spoke rather absently. His reddish brown hair was always askew. His ears were too large, his eyebrows were uneven, and he was always looking away. Yes, exactly, Rabbi, that was the very same German Shealtiel whom I have told you about before. Rabbi Shealtiel was a fine and wonderful man; he was the chief rabbi of Cologne, but he was exceedingly modest and shy. He actually appeared rather unintelligent. As you know, Shealtiel ben Menahem rarely looked at anyone else: when he talked his eyes were always on the ceiling or the floor or the corner of the room or the edge of the table.

My grandmother said that when Rabbi Shealtiel's wife, Leah, was in her sixties, she died suddenly. (No, Rabbi, I am not changing the subject—just listen a moment.) After Leah's death, the neighbor women came and washed her body; then they wrapped it in a clean white shroud. After a while, one of the women came over to the Rabbi, where he was sitting on a mourning stool, and she said: "I had never noticed before, but your dear wife Leah was missing the end of her small finger on the left hand." The Rabbi was astonished. "What is this? Is that true?" he asked. The neighbor assured him that this was the absolute truth: "Did you not know this, Rabbi?" He was embarrassed, but he did *not* know; Rabbi Shealtiel had been so shy that he had never looked closely at Leah's hands during the entire forty-two years that they had lived together. . . .

What? Of course there is more, Rabbi: I only closed my eyes for a moment. Can an old man not take a little rest? Now you have interrupted my thoughts. Let me see, where was I? Yes, yes – as my grandmother said: "Rabbi Shealtiel was modest, but he was an able speaker." Some have said that Rabbi Shealtiel ben Menahem was such an able speaker that he was never defeated in an argument. Have you heard that? Well, if you *had* heard, then I would have to tell you something, Rabbi: there were at least three times when Shealtiel ben Menahem, the head rabbi of the old Cologne yeshiva, was left without reply by others who were not scholars. It happened in Duren – once by a woman, once by a young girl, and once it was by a small boy:

Once upon a time, said my grandmother, Rabbi Shealtiel was called to Duren, and there he stayed in the house of an old woman who was a distant relative. The woman cooked a large pot of lentils for his meal. This woman had grown to an age where her tongue had worn down and she was not able to taste things very well, so she salted and seasoned food by eye. On his first day in Duren, Rabbi Shealtiel ate the whole plateful of lentils and left nothing. "A fine meal," said the Rabbi. "I particularly liked the seasoning."

Ah, thought the woman, a well-known Rabbi like this deserves my best seasonings. So the next day she doubled the seasonings and she doubled the salt. The Rabbi found the lentils much too strong and much too salty, but he hesitated to say anything to his venerable relative, and again he finished the whole plateful of lentils.

He loves my cooking, thought the old woman. My Shealtiel is a great and respected Rabbi (although I still can picture him as a small, absent-minded, red-haired boy) – if a little seasoning suffices for a little man, then great seasonings are needed for a great man. So, when on the third day she again made boiled lentils, the old woman added dollops of seasonings and she added salt, salt, and more salt. The Rabbi tasted the lentils. They were terrible—the salt was intolerable, and he stopped eating as soon as the old woman had turned her back. The woman busied herself with some pots and pans; then she returned to the table: "My good and holy Rabbi, my weak and overworked pious man, why do you not eat the lentils? Do not be shy. Go ahead, eat and enjoy yourself."

Rabbi Shealtiel replied: "I had a meal earlier in the day."

"That is silly, Rabbi—you came home directly from the synagogue. Where would you have gotten a meal?"

The Rabbi looked at his shoe and he looked at his spoon, and he answered: "Well, good woman, I guess that I am just not hungry today."

Then the old woman said: "Not hungry? Then why did you wash your hands and say the blessing and why did you go so far as to pick up your spoon if you really had no desire to eat?"

The Rabbi looked at his thumb, and he looked at the corner of the table; then he replied: "Well, it was just a habit."

Then the woman said to her relative: "Oh? And was this just a habit yesterday, and was it just a habit the day before? Tell me, dear Rabbi: Why did you eat all the food on your plate for the last two days?"

"Well—" began the Rabbi, but the woman continued: "Now, now—do not make a big story out of this. You know as well as I do that it is just your shyness and your modesty. Clearly you are hungry and you need to eat, but for some reason you have gotten it into your head that *I* will not eat if you eat. Put your fears to rest, Rabbi: I have already eaten my fill."

"Well—" began the Rabbi, but the woman continued: "Do you not know what the Sages say, my good Rabbi? They say: 'Leave nothing in the pot.' They say that once, and they say that twice. Are there not starving people in the world? And even if there were no one else who was hungry, do you think that a scholar such as yourself can study on air alone? Well, Rabbi, for a thoughtful man, you certainly have not thought much about food. Food and consistency, I always say. Now, Rabbi, you ate yesterday, so be consistent and eat today – praise the Lord, amen."

That was the woman – and as for the young girl: Later, on the same trip, Rabbi Shealtiel was walking along the road toward Duren. He wanted to hurry and to reach town before sunset; to his left there was a beaten path across the field, so he took that route. A young girl was sitting at the edge of the field playing with some straw. As the Rabbi passed her, she said to him: "Tell me, old man: Do you think that this is a public highway across the planted field?"

"What is that? What are you saying, young woman?" asked the surprised Rabbi.

"I said, sir: Is there not a law that one should avoid walking across a planted field?"

Then Rabbi Shealtiel said: "My dear daughter, there is a well-trodden path through this field."

"Oh yes, this is definitely a well-worn path," said the girl. "It is well worn because selfish people and lazy men like you have made it so. This path was beaten down by thoughtless men who hurry wherever they are going and who have no regard for others."

And what could he say to that? So the poor Rabbi walked back to the road. Soon, he came to a crossroads where a very small boy was sitting tossing stones. The Rabbi said: "Hello, young man, what is your name?"

"I am Ephraim," said the little boy.

"Ephraim, can you tell me which road leads to the town of Duren?"

"Both roads go to Duren, Rabbi," said Ephraim.

"Both roads? Then what is the difference?" asked Rabbi Shealtiel.

The little boy thought for a moment. "Let me put it like this, Rabbi: the road on the left is short, but it is also very long; on the other hand, the road on the right is longer, but in a way it is also short."

"Short-but-long and long-but-short?" asked the Rabbi.

"Yes – that is what I would say, good Rabbi."

"I see. Well I think that I will try the road on the left because it is short-but-long." Sure enough, the left-hand road quickly led to Duren. However, the road ended abruptly in a vineyard, where it was completely blocked by a fence. The Rabbi retraced his steps to the cross-roads. "Ephraim," said Rabbi Shealtiel, "did you not say that this road was short?"

The boy replied: "My dear Rabbi, I told you that it was short and yet long. What I meant was that it was a short road to the town but that you could not actually enter the town by the left-hand road; therefore, in the end it is the longer route.

"The right-hand road, although it seems much longer at the beginning, eventually leads into Duren without an obstacle. You did not ask – but I would recommend the right-hand long-but-short road, rather than the left-hand short-but-long road."

When Rabbi Shealtiel heard this discourse, he sat down and he laughed. "You are a typical Jew," said the Rabbi. "Someday, Ephraim, you will make a fine but irritating scholar in your yeshiva."


What is that, Rabbi? Yes, yes – my grandmother was exactly like you: she too was impatient with the endless raveling and unraveling of the scholarly words that is practiced in many yeshivas. But I am sure you know that this *pilpul* is God's will. I am referring to the famous story about Rabbi Akiva – surely you remember that story? No? Then let me tell you what I heard from my grandmother:


Once after a particularly convoluted and abstruse analysis of a passage from the Talmud, one of the yeshiva students asked Rabbi Shealtiel: "Rabbi, tell me the truth: Is this playing with words really appropriate? Are we learning anything at all? Or are we just twisting tiny nuances to no end whatsoever?"

The Rabbi bent his thumb; he looked at the corner of his desk, and then he answered: "Young man, you know about the great Rabbi Akiva – he was the finest rabbi among all the teachers of the *Mishnah* epoch. In fact, he was the founder of the school of study that derives all the laws – the full *Halakhah* – from minute interpretations of each word of the Torah, from painstaking analysis of even the tiniest ornamentations of the script."

"Yes, certainly I know that, Rabbi," said the yeshiva student.

"One time," said Rabbi Shealtiel ben Menahem, "Rabbi Akiva was asked whether he was perhaps overstepping the holy meanings.

Was the good Rabbi going beyond God's will in this detailed word analysis? Here is what the great Rabbi Akiva answered:

"When Moses saw God putting dots and other detailed marks upon the letters of the Torah he asked: 'Almighty Lord, what is this? Are you unsatisfied with your Divine decrees? Are you now decorating your holy words?'

"And the good Lord God (blessed be He) answered: 'Moses, my child, I must look to the far, far future. There will come a time when the plain, unadorned words of the Law will not suffice. Who can capture all possible situations in one brief, summary statement, Reb Moses? You men live in an intricate world, and you live tangled lives. No simple word can be sufficiently complete to match all the complexities of men's lives. The world, my child, is ornamented with thick and rich complexities. Therefore, the holy words, too, must be ornamented thickly and richly. So, my young Moses, I decorate the Law in order that future scholars—scholars like Rabbi Akiva—may interpret and reinterpret My word. And now they may do so unendingly, for ever and ever and ever.'"

hat is that, Rabbi? I was just resting my eyes; so please, join me here by the stove. (I think that you will be too warm on that bench: try the one nearer to the wall.) An old man like me can doze forever by a warm stove; I suppose this is because I was born on the Sabbath. What do I mean? Why, Rabbi, certainly you remember what the Talmud tells us:

> If born on a Sunday, you'll be purely wrong or right –
> On that day, the good Lord made pure dark and light.
>
> If born on a Monday, you're ill-tempered and hard to please –
> On that day, the good Lord, He split and cleaved the seas.
>
> If born on a Tuesday, you'll gain luxuriance –
> On that day, the good Lord, He created trees and plants.
>
> If born on a Wednesday, you'll be both wise and bright –
> On that day, He lit the sun and set the moon alight.
>
> If born on a Thursday, you'll be benevolent and fair –
> On that day, God created the creatures of the air.

If born on a Friday, you'll be an artisan –
On that day, God made the beasts, and also He made man.

If born on the Sabbath, you'll be lazy and content –
On that day, God rested, deep in His firmament.

I do not know for certain, Rabbi, but I would guess that my grand-mother (may she rest forever deep in the Lord's firmament) was born on a Wednesday: she was both wise and bright. On the other hand, she was always busy sewing or cooking or shopping or instructing her grandchildren – perhaps she was born on a Friday. I suppose that I will never know.

What? No, no – do not get up on my account, Rabbi: I was just resting my eyes a moment. I was resting and musing. . . . Well, to tell you the truth, Rabbi, I was remembering a sad tale that my grand-mother told me. Grandmother was always telling me the old tales. I wonder what day of the week story-tellers are born on? Anyway, this story was about Rachel. No, not the beautiful Rachel with whom Jacob fell in love. No – this was another Rachel, a little Rachel, a beautiful Rachel, but a German Rachel whom no one ever married. You see, Rabbi, in the time of Rabbi Shealtiel, there were many difficult years for the Jews of Germany. One of the worst problems was the rumor that kept surfacing: the Jews were said to kill a Gentile child each Passover.

Yes, I too find it hard even to say this, but that was the terrible accusation. Nonetheless, there were brave and noble Christians in that era. One was the Pope – Pope Innocent the Fourth. Pope Innocent the Fourth had been born Sinibaldo Fiesco; he came from a Genoese family of aristocrats, counts of Lavagna, and he was educated in both law and religion. Do you know that the cardinals of the Roman Catholic Church wear red hats? That tradition was begun by Pope Innocent the Fourth: he gave red hats to his cardinals as a symbol of their readiness to shed their blood in the cause of the Church. This Pope took strong stands in defense of the best teachings of the Holy Scriptures; back then, in the thirteenth century, he issued an imperial edict from Lyons saying –

What is that, Rabbi? Well, the Pope was in Lyons in France because his life had been threatened by the German emperor Frederick

II; one night, the Pope fled Rome secretly on horseback, and the next day he was pursued by three hundred of the emperor's troops. Anyway, from Lyons, Pope Innocent the Fourth issued his famous ruling:

> Despite the fact that their Divine Scriptures pronounces the law *Thou shalt not kill*, the Jews of Germany are falsely accused of sharing the heart of a murdered child on their Passover. In fact, no matter where a dead body is found, their persecutors wickedly blame it upon the Jews. Because of this and other imaginary crimes of which the Jews do not stand accused, of which they do not confess, and of which they are not convicted, their enemies rage in their midst. In subversion of God and justice, Jews are robbed, oppressed, imprisoned, tortured, and killed. We command you to show yourselves mild and kindly toward the Jews— restore to them their just status and do not permit them to suffer in these ways in the future. Persecutors of the Jews shall be put under ecclesiastical excommunication.

Rabbi Shealtiel ben Menahem had this edict copied into Hebrew. He also had copies in Latin deposited in the Cologne Seminary for Priests. Through his efforts, this edict was renewed by Pope Gregory the Tenth, and later it was even ratified by King Rudolph of Hapsburg; it was also endorsed by the Bishop Albertus Magnus, the great Christian philosopher of Cologne. Perhaps all these efforts protected the Jews of Cologne somewhat during those harsh years; however, it certainly did not protect the Jews of Mainz and of Munich. For a while, Cologne was a haven, and many Jews appeared in Cologne, stunned by their sad fates in the other cities of Germany. Rabbi Shealtiel could hardly believe their stories—but he knew, of course, that they were true.

Once at Easter time, a dead Christian child was discovered in a back alley of Mainz. The poor little boy had been hit with a stick or a rock and then left to die. The child was found at the edge of the Jewish Quarter, and people immediately said: "It was the Jews. The Jews have killed this boy in order to eat his heart at Passover."

The Archbishop, Werner of Mainz, Lord Chancellor of the kingdom, sent out an order: Do not take any action—wait until the murderer is discovered and is brought properly to trial. However, the officers who carried this proclamation thought that the Jews had killed the little boy; although they posted the official notices, the guards personally told the Christians that the evil Jews must be brought to justice. The child's parents carried his battered body through the streets in an open coffin. People screamed and wept and shouted and ran down the streets, and on that day, on the second last day of Passover, a mob of Christians broke into the synagogue in Mainz and beat to death ten Jews who were praying.

Terrified Jews left their houses at night, they collected what belongings they could fit into wagons, and they fled to other cities, especially to Cologne. The Christians of Mainz then seized the abandoned houses and all the furniture and clothes and utensils and books. The emperor, Emperor Rudolph, ruled that because the Jews had fled in secret, they must have been guilty. Therefore, all the citizens of Mainz were acquitted from any blame, and all the possessions that had been confiscated were now legitimate retribution—however, said Emperor Rudolph, the seized items must be given to Christian charities.

Rabbi Shealtiel did his best to help his community absorb the newcomers. Soon, the Jews from Mainz became sad but regular members of the old Cologne synagogue. However, they had barely begun to open businesses, to have children again, and to forget their problems by living the regular daily rituals of Cologne, when another wave of broken Jews arrived—this time they came from Munich. It was only two years after the Mainz tragedy when a terrible rumor spread in Munich: the Jews purchased a Christian child from a weak-minded old woman, and then the Jews killed the child and were saving its heart for Passover.

Suddenly one night, young men from the surrounding parishes broke into the Jewish Quarter in Munich and killed two young Jews who were walking home from the yeshiva. Somehow the news of this killing angered the Christians still further. Another crowd of Gentiles came with torches, and they set fire to the Jewish bakery, which was on the very edge of the Jewish Quarter. Jews fled to the synagogue.

The Jews fled to the synagogue for refuge. Would not the good Lord God, blessed be He, protect the Jews in their most holy of homes? Did He not deliver them from their bondage in Egypt? A little girl named Rachel was pulled from her bed by her mother: "My shoes, my shoes," she said. But there was no time; barefoot, she ran beside her mother into the main prayer room. Inside the synagogue, women sat with men, men sat with children, and grandparents sat side by side. Someone began to recite the *Shema*. Rachel's grandmother set the little girl on her lap and covered her with a shawl and hugged her tightly. Outside the building, the Gentiles hesitated a moment: "Dirty, murdering Jews!" called someone. Two men threw their torches against the side of the old wooden house of prayer; then everyone threw their torches. One hundred and eighty persons, old and young, were burnt to death inside the Munich synagogue on the eleventh of October in the year 1285. Rachel's grandmother said to her: "There is still an amazing Grace, my little girl; sweet will be the sound of Heaven." But Rachel cried in her grandmother's lap.

What, Rabbi? Yes, that is the whole story; there is no more.

abbi, I am glad to see you here alone; I want to apologize for my outburst during the service this morning. Reb Anton was fiddling with a pencil, and writing is strictly forbidden on the Sabbath. Yes, I know that he was just holding the pencil—but in the olden days, in the strict and pious days of our fathers, Reb Anton would have been ordered to leave and never to return. Of course, I suppose that was an especially German style: my grandmother always pointed out that the German Jews are more scrupulous than those of any other country. Why, the German Jews fasted for two consecutive days at *Yom Kippur* instead of fasting for one day.

Grandmother often used Rabbi Meir as an example of the strictness of the German Jews. At the time of Rabbi Meir, the French rabbis allowed the study rooms in the yeshiva to be warmed on the Sabbath by Gentile custodians. But as for Rabbi Meir—he insisted that no fires could be lit by anyone on the Sabbath, not by Jews or by Gentiles. In the cold weather, Rabbi Meir ordered that the doors and windows of the houses and the synagogue be tightly fastened in order to save the heat before the Sabbath began. One time, he found that a Gentile servant had made a fire in the yeshiva stove on the Sabbath, so the Rabbi took to bolting shut the oven doors every Friday.

153

Exactly, Rabbi – this was the famous Rabbi Meir of Rothenburg. Rabbi Meir was born in Worms and he was buried in Worms, ninety-two years later. In his day, he was the most famous Rabbi in all of Germany; he was the Rabbi who wrote the well-known talmudic *Tosafot* and the equally renowned *Responsa* and the beautiful elegiac poems called the *Songs of Exile*. Apparently, he wrote most of these works when he was in prison – he spent the last seven or eight years of his life in prison, and he died there at the age of seventy-eight.

What is that, Rabbi? Yes, I said that he died at the age of seventy-eight and that he was buried ninety-two years after he was born. You do not know the story of how he remained unburied for fourteen years? Then let me tell you. It is a curious tale – it concerns the chief rabbi of Cologne, Hayyim ben Yehiel; Rabbi Hayyim headed the delegation that unsuccessfully negotiated with Emperor Rudolph for the release of Meir of Rothenburg. Many years ago my grandmother told the story to me, and now I will tell it to you:

At the time of Rabbi Hayyim, there was an uneasy peace between the Gentiles and the Jews of Cologne; but elsewhere in Germany, Jewish life was very hard. Was their German homeland worth the daily fear? Venturing out of the Jewish Quarter, a Jew might have stones and garbage thrown on him by rude Gentile teenagers. Buying food in Gentile stores, a Jew would have to wait last in line, and often he would be given old or spoiled produce. Jewish land might be confiscated without explanation, extra taxes were regularly levied on Jews, and many parts of the city were considered off-limits to the average Jew. These regular persecutions, the total insecurity of their existence, and their generally wretched state drove the Jews of several German congregations to consider a drastic step: perhaps they should cast aside all their familiar everyday surroundings. Families from the cities of Mainz, Worms, Speyer, Rothenburg, and Oppenheim left their friends, their homes, and much of their possessions in order to go across the sea. Yes, Rabbi, these Jews hoped against hope that the Messiah would appear in the southern Mediterranean lands – there, he would shelter them in a new and joyous life, and he would protect them against all the evils of the world with his calm and pious prayers, hallelujah, amen.

It was late one winter, when word began to filter back to Europe that the true Messiah had appeared in Syria. Walking in from the desert, he came thin and barefoot – a young Jew in a white robe. He had sparkling eyes, and he sang the psalms sweetly, in a golden voice. If only they could reach him, all the children of Israel would be redeemed from their cruel daily toils in the dark cities of Europe. So, the Jews of Germany began to emigrate, and at the head of this wave of travelers was the most famous rabbi of Germany, Meir of Rothenburg. Rabbi Meir was a scholar, a devout man, and a poet; he was revered as a saint by his congregation. Together with his family, Rabbi Meir hoped to reach Syria in the spring, when the Messiah would then usher in a new spring for all the Israelites.

With a certain amount of organization and planning, Jews of the districts of the Rhine and the Main started on their journey to Syria. The Jews wanted to travel quietly, for they feared that local authorities might stop them or that local bandits might rob them; therefore, the Jews did not go all in one group. Instead, families left one at a time and with no fanfare. As the first stage in his trip, Rabbi Meir of Rothenburg quietly reached Basel, together with his whole family. As soon as he got into town, Rabbi Meir was received as a guest of honor at the local synagogue, and the head rabbi of Basel himself insisted on washing Rabbi Meir's feet. In the synagogue Rabbi Meir led the prayers every morning, in the yeshiva he taught the lessons from the Talmud, and on the Sabbath he read the entire scriptural passage. But Rabbi Meir was only biding his time: he was only waiting for the members of his congregation to arrive in order to take ship together from Italy. Then, the Rothenburg Jews would all steer a course toward the East and into the haven of safety promised by the barefoot Messiah.

One afternoon, Rabbi Meir walked from the Jewish Quarter of Basel to the Rhine River docks, looking for word of Jews arriving from Rothenburg. In the shadow of the great Cathedral of Basel (which was built of deep red sandstone on a terrace high above the Rhine) stood a former Jew from Worms who had since been baptized; this newly converted Christian was talking with a companion. The convert recognized the famous Rabbi, and wishing to show himself a loyal Christian, the former Jew reported Rabbi Meir to the Bishop of Basel. Why was this Rabbi from Rothenburg hiding in Basel? Was there some devilment afoot? The Bishop had his Captain of the Guard arrest the Rabbi and bring him to the courthouse.

Rabbi Meir answered the Bishop honestly: the Rabbi was planning to emigrate to Syria with members of his Rothenburg congregation. The Bishop reported this to the Archbishop, and the Archbishop reported to the Emperor of Germany.

"What is happening?" asked Emperor Rudolph. "Why are the Jews flooding out from Europe? This could be a disaster: our revenues will disappear."

The Emperor had been elected by a wrangling confederacy of princes, and he was under constant financial pressure from this loose coalition of local sovereigns. The high taxes paid by Jews throughout Germany represented a major income each year. Where would the money come from when all the Jews left Germany to go to the Holy Land?

"Clearly, they have lost all perspective: these Jews do not realize when they are well off. You had best hold the Rabbi," said the Emperor to the Archbishop. "Do not let him leave Germany, or all his followers will leave, too."

The Archbishop took the Emperor's orders to the Bishop of Basel, and that summer, on the fourth day of Tammuz and under the direct decree of Rudolph of Hapsburg the Emperor of Germany, the Bishop of Basel imprisoned Rabbi Meir of Rothenburg; the Rabbi was confined to the local fort in the tower of the small town of Ensisheim in the district of Alsace, about thirty kilometers north of Basel. The Emperor ordered the Rabbi to be arrested, but he was to be kept safe and he was to be treated respectfully. This was an economic decision and not a judicial punishment. For this reason, the Rabbi was permitted to receive visits, to instruct his pupils, and to perform all the usual functions of a rabbi. However, Rabbi Meir was not under any circumstances to leave the grounds of the old fort in Ensisheim.

But consider that, Rabbi—imprisoning the saintly Rabbi Meir of Rothenburg? When the Jews of northern Europe heard this, they were appalled. The Jews of Cologne were especially upset: not only was Rabbi Meir the spiritual head of all German Jewry; he also had many relatives in Cologne. In the old Cologne synagogue, the shammas was forced to repeat the announcement three times during the Sabbath service. Two prominent Cologne cousins of Rabbi Meir began to weep. Reb Baruch ben Urshraga ha-Kohen (a well-to-do property owner and a member of the Jewish Council of Cologne) tore his shirt.

Reb Jakar ben Samuel ha-Levi (also a member of the Jewish Council of Cologne and the author of eight religious poems) threw himself on the floor.

The German Jews could not rest – their most highly respected scholar was in custody. Therefore, a delegation of Jews was chosen to plead with Emperor Rudolph. Twelve rabbis from the Rhine communities set out to meet with the Emperor, and the head of the group was Rabbi Hayyim ben Yehiel of Cologne. As usual, the Emperor Rudolph of Hapsburg was in desperate need of money, and he proposed a ransom of forty thousand marks of silver for Rabbi Meir. The rabbis doubted whether they could raise that much money; instead, they countered with an offer of twenty thousand marks. The Emperor accepted their proposal.

The rabbis returned home, they organized collections in all the Jewish communities up and down the Rhine valley, and eventually they amassed twenty thousand marks in silver. Rabbi Hayyim returned to the Emperor with the money, and he received a formal agreement to present to the Bishop of Basel; this edict instructed the Bishop to free Rabbi Meir from his captivity.

Rabbi Hayyim decided to take the royal decree himself to Ensisheim, a small town on the River Ill. Rabbi Hayyim traveled up the Rhine to Basel, and then he followed the River Ill north. The River Ill is a dark and sleepy stream that begins in the meadowlands just beyond the city of Basel; from there it flows through the Alsace, and it waters the cities of Mulhausen, Ensisheim, Colmar, Schlettstadt, and Strassburg. After two days along the Ill, Rabbi Hayyim reached Ensisheim, where he walked to the old fort and was admitted to see Rabbi Meir. The Rabbi listened quietly while Hayyim ben Yehiel of Cologne explained that the Rabbi of Rothenburg was at last free to return home.

Rabbi Meir closed his eyes for a moment, and then he opened them. "Thank you, Rabbi Hayyim," he said. "However, I think that I must remain here in the Ensisheim prison."

"But, Rabbi – why? Why stay here? Please, think of your family. Think of your congregation; think of yourself. We need you."

"I do think of you – I think of you all, and my heart is breaking," said the Rabbi. "But also I must think of Jews everywhere, both now and in the future. Tell me, good Rabbi Hayyim: What would happen if I leave this prison? I have been ransomed, and this ransom money is an insidious evil. If emperors are permitted to gain financial wealth by capturing holy men, then what will stop common bandits? Soon any brigand with a weapon can capture a Jewish leader and refuse to liberate him until the Jewish community pays a ransom. All Jews will be held hostage by terrorists; no Jew will be free from extortion. Then, my friend, where will it ever end? If this evil is let loose in the world, then I cannot see how it can ever be stopped. Therefore, for the sake of all Jews of today and for all Jews of all times in the future, I must stay here in Ensisheim."

Now, Rabbi, as my grandmother used to say: "Who can tell the future in a thing like this?" But Hayyim ben Yehiel only looked down at the floor. Then, he bid good-bye to Rabbi Meir of Rothenburg, and sadly Hayyim made his way back to Cologne. In each Jewish community along the way, he patiently repeated Rabbi Meir's words; he explained that in order to ensure that the arrest of Jews would not become a profitable business, Rabbi Meir could never leave his prison for money. Rabbi Meir must remain in his prison in the old fort in the small town of Ensisheim on the quiet River Ill. So Rabbi Hayyim ben Yehiel returned to Cologne, and Rabbi Meir of Rothenburg remained imprisoned.

In prison, Rabbi Meir replied patiently to all the many letters he received, and he wrote a number of books, including his famous elegiac poems. And slowly Rabbi Meir aged–his hair got thin, his skin became spotted, and his eyes wrinkled and crinkled. He took to dozing and to nodding off every day in the late morning. One day at the age of seventy-eight, Rabbi Meir died there in prison; the guards found him lying peacefully in his old wooden chair by a window. By then, Emperor Rudolph had been deposed. When the successor to the Emperor learned of Rabbi Meir's death he said: "Fine–now the Jews must pay fifty thousand marks to bury the old Rabbi." And so the successors to Rudolph kept the Rabbi's corpse unburied for fourteen years, in order to extort money from the Jewish congregations of Germany. . . .

What is that, Rabbi? Of course there is more: I was only resting my eyes for a moment. Now let me see, where was I? Oh yes–one day, many, many years later, a wealthy Jew arrived in Cologne from Frankfort; his name was Suesskind ben Alexander. He was traveling on business, he stopped in the old Cologne yeshiva, and he sat through the afternoon prayers. Knowing no one in the city, he stayed at the synagogue for dinner, and after the evening benedictions he stopped to talk with Rabbi Hayyim in the back study room. Reb Suesskind was old and white-haired; his voice and his hands shook, and he seemed a little sad.

The two men chatted a while: "Yes, Rabbi," continued Reb Suesskind, "I am afraid that I remain childless – it is my only regret in life. Worse yet, I grew up as an orphan in Worms, and I do not know where my parents are buried. And now I will have no children to be buried beside me. With whom will I walk hand-in-hand in the Great Hereafter? I am doomed to remain lonely for ever and ever – praise the Lord, amen."

Rabbi Hayyim thought a moment. Then, he said: "My good sir, the great Sages tell us that your companion in Sheol will be whomever you are buried next to. Have you no friend to set your quiet grave beside?"

"No, Rabbi," answered the old man from Frankfort, "I am alone; I fear that there is no one at all."

Again Rabbi Hayyim remained silent. He looked down at the papers on his desk and at the holy books in a shelf at his side. Then, he said to Reb Suesskind: "I have heard that you are quite wealthy. Is this true?"

"Yes, Rabbi, I own ships and land and businesses; I have even loaned money to Emperor Albert himself."

Rabbi Hayyim looked at the old man for a moment. "Reb Suesskind, something has been preying on my mind for years and years," said the Rabbi.

"What is that?"

"There is a very holy man whose body remains unburied. He is in the small town of Ensisheim in Alsace. By now, his family has given up hope of ever laying him to rest in a Jewish cemetery."

"How can this be, Rabbi?"

"Originally, this saintly Rabbi was imprisoned by Emperor Rudolph. We tried to ransom him, but the Rabbi refused to be bought for money. Eventually he died in his prison, and the Emperor's successors (first King Adolph, and now King Albert) refuse to give us the Rabbi's body unless we pay an exorbitant sum of money."

"How much money do they demand?"

"They are asking for fifty thousand marks."

"Fifty thousand marks! That is incredible," said Reb Suesskind.

"Yes, it is," responded the Rabbi – then the Rabbi sighed, and the two men talked on into the night, as Rabbi Hayyim related the entire story of old Rabbi Meir of Rothenburg.

The next day, Suesskind ben Alexander returned to Frankfort. He borrowed as much money as he could from his friends, he called in all the debts owed him, and then – under the cover of a number of fictitious enterprises (in order to avoid panic and suspicion) – he liquidated all his businesses, he sold all his boats, his lands, his homes, and his belongings. All told, Suesskind ben Alexander raised more than fifty thousand marks in silver.

Reb Suesskind bought a small wagon, he bought a white shroud and a plain wooden coffin, and he traveled to Emperor Albert, who was a patron of the Jews; Reb Suesskind had known the Emperor indirectly because the Jew had once loaned the Emperor some money. "Your honor," said Suesskind ben Alexander to Albert, King of Germany, "I should like to ransom the body of an old Jewish scholar that lies in the prison tower in Ensisheim."

The King did not remember Rabbi Meir, and he did not recall the hostaging of the Rabbi's body; however, one of the King's councilors knew the situation. The councilor reminded the King that a fee of fifty thousand marks had been set as the condition for release of the Jew's body. "I am afraid," said the King, "that I cannot return the man's body. This decree has been in effect for more than a generation – even for a friend, I could not set the precedent of allowing a Jew to reverse an imperial ruling."

Suesskind ben Alexander said: "I expect no favors, your excellency." Then Reb Suesskind took out the fifty thousand marks that he had collected. The court was astonished: this was more than the entire taxes that were collected from all the Rhine districts for a full year. The King ordered his captains to guard the doors, and he assured himself that the money was in fact a full fifty thousand marks. Then the King issued a royal release, which he signed and sealed and presented to the Jew, Suesskind ben Alexander of Frankfort.

Suesskind immediately left for Basel and thence on to Ensisheim. Word had preceded him to the little town on the River Ill. Old

Suesskind ben Alexander presented the official papers, and the Rabbi's dry, partly mummified body was turned over to him. Gently and carefully, Reb Suesskind wrapped the Rabbi in the white shroud, which he had filled with spices. He placed Rabbi Meir in the simple wooden box; and then by wagon, the two old Jews—Meir and Suesskind—slowly made their way to Worms, their first home town.

The two old Jews journeyed along the wagon road beside the Rhine, past Strassburg, Karlsruhe, Speyer, and Mannheim. When they reached the city of Worms, they passed the famous cathedral of the Christian saints Peter and Paul with its four round towers and its two large domes, they rolled and bumped by the endless wine merchants in the market district, and eventually they reached the Jewish Quarter of town. They stopped in front of the synagogue, which was much like the one in Cologne. Reb Suesskind left his wagon outside; slowly he walked through the prayer hall filled with wooden benches, he passed the twelve stained glass windows with their colored lions and snakes, he looked up at the Holy Ark made of stone, and he walked, in his shaky old man's shuffle, to the door of the back study room. There, the Rabbi was bent over a book.

The Rabbi of Worms was the scholar Anschel ha Levi. He looked up at the old stranger. "May I help you?" he asked.

"Good Rabbi," began Suesskind ben Alexander, "my name is Suesskind ben Alexander; recently my home has been Frankfort, but originally I grew up in Worms. . . ." Then he told his entire story from beginning to end. "I would like very much," he concluded, "to bury Rabbi Meir here in Worms, in the old Jewish cemetery—the Garden of Life—beside his parents. I ask only that you reserve a grave for me also at his side, so that one day when the good Lord God (blessed be He) calls for me to return to His warm embrace, then I may rest beside Rabbi Meir."

Rabbi Anschel was quiet a moment, and then he said: "It shall be as you wish."

Rabbi Meir was buried the next day beside his parents and alongside his parents' parents. Few people heard of the funeral, for Reb Suesskind respected Rabbi Meir's desire: Rabbi Meir had hoped that it would not become common knowledge that Jews could be ransomed for money. After the service, Suesskind ben Alexander walked away from the cemetery and into the streets of the Jewish Quarter of

Worms. He gave his wagon to a local merchant. Reb Suesskind had no other belongings, and he had no money. At night he slept on the floor in the yeshiva, each day he sat quietly in the back of the synagogue during the prayers, and the next winter he died. Rabbi Anschel buried old Suesskind ben Alexander beside Rabbi Meir of Rothenburg. When Hayyim ben Yehiel of Cologne heard from his friend Rabbi Anschel that Suesskind had died, Rabbi Hayyim came to Worms. One afternoon, the two Rabbis walked to the cemetery in Worms and they stood beside the grave of Suesskind ben Alexander and they said nothing but only bowed their heads.

abbi, I am glad to see you here tonight: I need your advice. Really, it is a small matter—this afternoon one of the students said to me that he saw an omen in the clouds. Young Moshe was certain that he had seen the shapes of those most holy letters *gimel* and *bet*. What did that mean? I could not say. Of course, Rabbi, after all these years of sitting in the study rooms during lessons, I have learned a bit of Talmud. And I recall what the great Sages said about the clouds: "The whole Universe drinks from the ocean; as it is said in Genesis":

> Then from the earth there arose and went up a great and misty cloud, and it watered the whole face of the ground.

"These clouds swell above the seas, and they ascend to the firmament. Then, once they are high in the air, the clouds open their mouths like a bottle, and they receive the full rain waters. As it is said in Job":

> The good Lord God (blessed be He) draws up drops of water from the sea, and He distills rain from the mist that He has made. Then, the vast thundrous rainclouds pour down in torrents, descending showers on all mankind.

Yes, Rabbi, I also find it unclear exactly what this allows us to read into the designs of clouds. However, in relation to clouds, my grandmother would always remind me of the other passage from Job:

Can any man comprehend the sailing clouds,
Spread like a rug on the good Lord's knees?
God rolls mists o'er His fishy crowds –
Fog-bottomed cloudlets cover the seas.

Why do the clouds flow far overhead,
Thick and white and mountainous,
Unconcerned with the earthly tread
Of mankind tied to the dirt and the dust?

The glorious ceiling of skies at dawn
Is beaten hard as a metal mirror.
First, sunlight shines; then it's gone
And all is clouds and rainy weather.

Then God breathes – a wind rolls through;
It clears the flowing clouds away,
And sun-gold radiates from the blue
To coat us in a glorious day.

Yes, it is a beautiful verse. Why did my grandmother tell me this? I am not certain – perhaps she was referring to the cloud into which the famous Rabbi Hayyim jumped. You do not know about this? Well, it is a curious tale. As you know, Hayyim ben Yehiel was the chief Rabbi of Cologne many, many years ago. Late in his life, he headed the delegation that unsuccessfully negotiated with Emperor Rudolph for the release of the hostage, Rabbi Meir of Rothenburg. Much earlier, however, when he was still a young yeshiva student, Hayyim jumped into a cloud – my grandmother told the story to me, and now I will tell it to you:

Hayyim ben Yehiel, said my grandmother, was born in the little town of Seeheim, and he was sent to study in Oppenheim on the Rhine, where a famous scholar, Rabbi Benjamin Shalom, was the head rabbi. Rabbi Benjamin Shalom had a beautiful and intelligent daughter named Dinah. The Rabbi was in a hurry for her to marry so that she would not have to continue as a businesswoman and so that she would have a fine large family and in this way she would speed the day of the arrival of the Messiah, amen.

So Rabbi Benjamin said to his daughter: "Dinah, I am going to find a husband for you."

Dinah replied: "But, Father, who will attend to all of our businesses, the lending of money and the pawnbroking and so on, when I am occupied raising children?"

"Ah, my fine daughter," said the Rabbi, "this is exactly why I wish to find a husband for you—it is this young man who will take care of our family businesses."

"Very well," said the daughter, "if you insist on getting me a husband, then at least be sure that he is a learned man, for it is written that to give one's daughter in marriage to an ignorant man is like tying her to an ape."

Dinah was a wise young woman, and she hoped for a man of equal wisdom; she wanted to have a husband whom she could respect. Dinah remembered the talmudic injunction: "If your wife is tall, then stand on a chair and talk to her." (What is that, Rabbi? Yes, yes, the Talmud also says: "If your wife is short, then bend down and whisper in her ear.") In any case, Rabbi Benjamin was not concerned. "I will look among my students for a suitable husband," he said.

So Rabbi Benjamin Shalom went back to his yeshiva, and he cast a thoughtful glance among his students as he lectured. When the Rabbi finished his talk, the young men began to leave the study hall. Rabbi Benjamin said to himself: "Old man, have you among your students anyone who is an outstanding scholar? Is there someone whom you would be happy to have as a son-in-law?" He looked at the boys, and then he answered: "Yes, I see two young men, who are both very good students. One is Johanan and the other is Hayyim. And I think that I prefer Hayyim." Then Rabbi Benjamin Shalom returned home, and he told his daughter that there were two fine young men in his yeshiva, both good scholars, one called Johanan and the other called Hayyim, and that Hayyim was a young man of special and unique merit.

But Dinah said: "Tell me, Father, will this Hayyim grow to be a good man or will he be bad?"

"Will he be good or will he be bad?" asked the Rabbi. "Who can tell, my daughter? Only the good Lord God knows now—no mortal ever learns the answer to that question before his death, amen."

So Dinah said: "Then I will take Hayyim."

The next day Rabbi Benjamin Shalom went to the yeshiva, he waited until the pupils were leaving, and then he asked Hayyim to remain a moment. After everyone else had left, the Rabbi said to Hayyim: "Young man, do you want to get married?"

"Married, Rabbi?" asked Hayyim. "No, I do not think that I am ready—certainly I have not studied enough yet."

But the Rabbi said to him: "It is time for you to take a wife, Hayyim: you are nineteen years old. Remember what the Talmud says: 'Up to the age of twenty years the Holy One (blessed be He) waits patiently for a man to marry, but the Lord curses him if he fails to marry by then.' And so, Hayyim, I would like you to remain in the Lord's good graces and to marry my daughter Dinah."

"Well, Rabbi, that is very kind of you," said Hayyim, "but I really think that I am barely worthy of your daughter."

"Nonsense," said the Rabbi, "you may still be a bit skinny, but you are a fine young scholar, and after a few years of good food you will fill out and you will become a respected member of this community. Perhaps someday you will even become a rabbi."

"Ah, Rabbi, that would indeed be a fine day," said Hayyim. "However, to become a respected rabbi like yourself I must study more. So let me go off and devote myself to serious learning; then I will return (God willing), and I will marry your daughter."

Rabbi Benjamin Shalom went home, and he repeated this conversation to his daughter. Dinah thought that Hayyim sounded like a good choice for a husband, and so father and daughter decided on a wedding date. And in the end, Hayyim agreed to return to Oppenheim by a certain Sunday morning exactly ten months in the future; then a large wedding would take place, and Dinah and Hayyim would be married and Hayyim would become the son-in-law of Rabbi Benjamin Shalom.

Hayyim felt that he had much to accomplish in ten months, so he departed immediately. Hayyim traveled south to Regensburg on the Danube, and the good Lord God, blessed be He, helped Hayyim to become a student of Rabbi Juddah he-Hasid (the son of Samuel he-

Hasid of Speyer); Rabbi Juddah was, of course, the famed mystic who knew the whole Torah by heart and who knew much other strange and wondrous knowledge beside. In Regensburg, Hayyim was more than one hundred and twenty-five kilometers away from Oppenheim, so Rabbi Benjamin and his daughter Dinah and the other members of the Oppenheim community heard nothing directly from Hayyim for ten long months.

A few months passed, and Rabbi Benjamin Shalom awoke one night after a sad dream. The Rabbi had dreamt that Hayyim would not be able to come back at the appointed time and that the wedding would not take place. The next morning, Rabbi Benjamin told the dream to his daughter. "I am worried, Dinah," said the Rabbi.

"I am not afraid," said Dinah. "Remember, Father, the talmudic Sages tell us that no dream—neither a good dream nor a bad dream—is fulfilled in every detail. Besides, a bad dream is preferable to a good dream: when a dream is bad, then the pain that it causes drives us to prevent its fulfillment."

"I am still uneasy," said the Rabbi.

"Listen, Father," continued Dinah, "the other night I myself dreamt of traveling in a small boat. Now, if I remember correctly, the Talmud says that this dream means that a good name will proceed from me. Undoubtedly, my marriage will come to pass, and Hayyim and I shall have a large and a happy family, and you will have many fine and scholarly grandchildren, amen."

"Well, Daughter, I hope that you are right," said the Rabbi.

Meanwhile, Hayyim remained ten months with his mystical teacher Juddah he-Hasid, and the young scholar became well versed in holy lore and in archery. (Did you know that Rabbi Juddah was an accomplished archer? I am not inventing this, Rabbi: my grandmother swore that it was true.) One day, Rabbi Juddah was instructing young Hayyim in the advanced mental art of archery. Hold the bow taut, said the Rabbi. Close your eyes, and concentrate on that most holy set of letters *gimel* and *bet*. Hayyim stretched the bow. He stood firm and he stood calm, and he thought of *gimel* and then of *bet*. Suddenly, the letter *bet* reminded him of the name "Benjamin," and "Benjamin" brought to mind his old rabbi, Rabbi Benjamin Shalom. Oh my goodness, thought Hayyim, this very weekend is when I was to be in Oppenheim in order to marry Dinah, Rabbi Benjamin's daughter. Sunday is the wedding day; however, today was already Friday, and in Regensburg, Hayyim was far more than two days' journey away from Oppenheim.

Hayyim went to his teacher, who was somewhat of a prophet, and Hayyim told him the story. Rabbi Juddah closed his eyes and then he said: "Hayyim, if you do not arrive at the appointed time, then your bride will wed another man."

"My dear teacher," said Hayyim, "what can I do?"

"Well, Hayyim, we must always begin by trusting in the Lord," said Rabbi Juddah. "Then, let me tell you what to do next: you must start out immediately for Oppenheim, and I will send along with you five of my best pupils."

"But, Rabbi, we will have to travel more than one hundred and twenty-five kilometers," said Hayyim.

"True," said the Rabbi, "but you must trust in the Lord."

That Friday afternoon, Hayyim and five fine young men left Regensburg with the blessings of Rabbi Juddah sounding softly in their ears. The six men followed the River Altmuhl, which runs between the Danube and the Rhine. (Do you know that river, Rabbi? Grandmother reported that it winds interminably and that it is filled with many weird and romantic gorges.) The day began to darken, and soon the young men reached a small dark town along the bank of the winding River Altmuhl. Hayyim rested on a bench outside the town while his companions went on ahead. When they entered the town, the young men looked around, and it seemed as if they were inside a maze and they could not find their way out. Bewildered, the young men began to walk blindly up one street and down the next.

After an hour had passed, Hayyim stood up, and going to the edge of the town, he called to his companions, but they were not there. Hayyim sat down, and he felt like crying. He said a brief prayer; this made him feel stronger, and he stood up again and he began to walk, hoping that somehow the Almighty Lord would help him to reach Oppenheim on time. However, it was now almost the Sabbath eve. "I had best stop and find some place to pray rather than violate the Sabbath," thought Hayyim. So Hayyim returned to the dark little town along the bank of the River Altmuhl.

Hayyim thought: "In this dark town there surely are many Gentiles who would harm or even kill me, but it is better to lose my life than to break the Sabbath." So he entered the town. It was four o'clock in the afternoon, and as it was the autumn, it was very near the beginning of the Sabbath. "I should hurry and find some Jewish home," thought Hayyim.

Hayyim wandered about the streets until he saw a small wooden building with a *mezuzah* on the door. "Ah, a Jewish house," he thought. Boldly, he opened the door and he went in; Hayyim found himself inside the prayer hall of a little synagogue. Slowly, he walked through the main prayer hall filled with wooden benches, he passed the twelve stained glass windows with their colored lions and snakes, he looked up at the Holy Ark made of stone, and he walked to the door of the back study room. There, in the innermost chamber, was an old man sitting on a carved chair and reading a book. The old man had thin white hair, and he had a long beard that almost touched the floor.

Hayyim stood silently in the doorway, and the old man went on reading. After a little while, the shammas came in. "Hello," said the shammas, "have you come for the Sabbath?"

"Yes, I have," said Hayyim.

"Good," said the shammas, "you are quite welcome to join us." Then the shammas lit the Sabbath lights, he brought some water, and both Hayyim and the old man washed their hands and rinsed their faces. The water smelled of wonderful spices. Next, seven men came in for prayers, and together with the shammas, with Hayyim, and with the old man, they all made a group of ten. The old man stood and he led the benedictions, and everyone else followed with quiet responses; something fine and gentle was in the old man's voice, and Hayyim felt very calm and very happy. The old man finished by saying: "O Lord, may Your loving kindness warm me so that I can again be a child of whom You shall be proud for ever and ever, amen."

When they had finished the prayers, the old man sat down, and the shammas served a Sabbath meal. The wine was golden, the bread was warm, and the cakes were lightly sweetened. No one spoke, but everyone was happy. After the meal, Hayyim thought of his obligation to Dinah and to Rabbi Benjamin, but he knew that he must not violate the Sabbath, so he remained quiet and he waited. Eventually, the shammas brought Hayyim a blanket. Hayyim went into the main prayer hall, he lay down on the blanket in front of the stove in a corner of the room, and he fell fast, fast asleep.

In the morning, Hayyim awoke to the sound of the old man reading in his beautiful old man's voice in the back study room. Hayyim himself said his morning prayers, and soon the shammas appeared. "My good Shammas," said Hayyim, "you have been more than kind and generous to me, but I must be on my way now. I have an impossible journey to take. Unless I get to Oppenheim by tomorrow morning, I will fail to marry the fine woman to whom I have been betrothed for ten months."

The shammas smiled at Hayyim. "Listen, young man," said the shammas, "and I will tell you what to do: first, go out into the street in front of the synagogue here. Turn to your left, and then turn to your right. Count seven streets and pass by the old cemetery on your left. Suddenly you will come to an empty wooden store. There, you will find the five companions whom you have lost. Do not say a word to them; just stand silently. A cloud will descend at your feet. Then jump, my young friend—jump and the good Lord God (blessed be He) will smile upon you so that in your old age, you will be able to remember the jump and then you will smile again, too."

Hayyim was puzzled. "I should go out into the street, good Shammas?"

"Yes."

"And then I should turn left, and then turn right? And I should count seven streets and pass by a cemetery on my right? And I will see my five companions?" asked Hayyim.

"Exactly," said the shammas.

"Then I should say nothing at all, but a cloud will descend—and then I should jump?" asked Hayyim.

"Yes," said the shammas.

"And then what?" asked Hayyim.

"And then, Hayyim, trust in the Lord," said the shammas.

So Hayyim followed these directions. When he came to the old wooden store, he found his young friends, who began to talk to him excitedly, but Hayyim remained silent. Suddenly a mist appeared and then a fog arose, and Hayyim realized that a cloud had descended from Heaven. And as the shammas had instructed, Hayyim jumped—Hayyim jumped, and in a moment he seemed to be stepping onto an old wall in some far-off town.

On the appointed Sunday morning, Rabbi Benjamin Shalom

awoke early. The sky was still gray. Something strange was in the air; the Rabbi was worried, and he glanced out his window constantly. After a while, he went to the synagogue and he sat, just watching the Holy Ark. Then a miracle happened. A fluffy white towering cloud floated in from out of the south, and it approached the town. Have you ever been to Oppenheim, Rabbi? The city is set on the slopes of vine-clad hills along the dark River Rhine. Above the town is a fortress (nowadays the fort is just ruins); this was the fort of Landskron, and there on the thick old walls of Landskron the cloud touched down. Out of the cloud walked Hayyim and his five companions, and they climbed down the old walls, and they walked into the town toward the Jewish Quarter where Rabbi Benjamin and his friends waited.

As Hayyim came out of the cloud with the five young men, Rabbi Benjamin Shalom recognized his future son-in-law, and when Hayyim reached the town, the Rabbi kissed Hayyim and he hugged him and he patted him on the back. Then Rabbi Benjamin asked young Hayyim what he had learned during the last ten months, and Hayyim replied: "I have learned much Torah, Rabbi, and I have also learned to trust in the good Lord God (blessed be He)."

Then Dinah went up to Hayyim and she held his hand, and Rabbi Benjamin Shalom took them both to the synagogue, where he himself performed the marriage ceremony. They had the wedding feast right there in the synagogue, and the full festivities went on for seven days and seven nights. Eventually, Hayyim ben Yehiel and his wife Dinah had many, many healthy children, the family moved to Cologne, and of course Hayyim became the head rabbi of the old yeshiva there, and all manner of young scholars came and studied with him. And this marriage adventure is why, in his later years, Rabbi Hayyim would smile and say: "Once I jumped and I touched a cloud— I smile when I think of it to this very day." And, Rabbi, may the good Lord God (blessed be He) grant that you, too, can remember the day when once you jumped and touched a cloud, hallelujah and amen.

ello, Rabbi, I will be with you in a moment—I cannot leave until every tablecloth is folded; otherwise the day has not ended properly. There, now I am finished at last, and I can sit next to you by the stove. What is that? No, at the moment I am not sleepy either; although I would swear that just before you came, I was about to fall asleep. Yes, yes, I know that one should never swear to anything casually. "Let no oath rise to your lips," said the Sages. "Hold yourself far from frivolous vows, light-minded oaths, and hasty solemn promises—and swear not at all, amen."

My grandmother always reminded me that a false oath, even if made with honorable intent, is a great sin, and it can be punished with the full wrath of the Omnipotent Lord God. Now *you*, Rabbi—you are much too easy on your congregation. I have heard you releasing men from all manner of hastily made vows. However, in the olden days, in the strict and pious days of our fathers, rabbis would not forgive a solemn vow. The strict rabbis denied absolution for thoughtless oaths.

My grandmother would say:

> If you only swear to what is true,
> Healthy children will the Lord give to you.

174

But false oaths are a different matter. The great Lord God Almighty punishes wrong vows with a vengeance. Therefore, the stern German rabbis resisted with all their will having any oaths sworn in the synagogue or in the *Bet Din*. Of course, I suppose that was the German style: my grandmother always pointed out that German Jews are much more scrupulous than Jews of any other country. Why, the German Jews fasted for two consecutive days at *Yom Kippur* instead of fasting for one day. Grandmother often used Rabbi Meir of Rothenburg as an example of the strictness of the German Jews. At the time of Rabbi Meir, French rabbis allowed the study rooms in the yeshiva to be warmed on the Sabbath by Gentile custodians. But as for Rabbi Meir— he insisted that no fires could be lit by anyone on the Sabbath, not by Gentiles and certainly not by Jews. In the cold weather, Rabbi Meir ordered that the doors and windows of the houses and the synagogue be tightly fastened in order to save the heat before the Sabbath began.

You knew this already? Did you also know that one time Rabbi Meir found that a Gentile servant had made a fire in the yeshiva stove on the Sabbath, so the Rabbi took to bolting shut the oven doors every Friday afternoon. Oh, you knew this too? Well then undoubtedly you must know of Rabbi Hayyim and the fatal oath? No? It is a curious tale—it concerns the chief rabbi of Cologne, Hayyim ben Yehiel. Many years ago my grandmother told me the story of the fatal oath, and now I will tell it to you:

Once upon a time, said my grandmother, in the town of Cologne on the River Rhine there lived a pious rabbi named Hayyim ben Yehiel. Rabbi Hayyim was a renowned legal scholar, and at one time he headed the delegation that negotiated with Emperor Rudolph for the release of Rabbi Meir when Meir was held hostage. In the days of Rabbi Hayyim, there was an uneasy peace between the Gentiles and the Jews of Cologne; but elsewhere in Germany, Jewish life was very hard. One of the institutions of German life was the Jewish Oath— Jews had to take a special oath in order to establish proof in all lawsuits. Now, the German authorities reasoned that the best way to ensure that Jews would consider their oaths legally binding was to have the ceremony agree with the precepts of Jewish religious laws. Therefore, the Jewish Oath had a strong dose of Jewish law, although it was mixed with medieval German custom.

In any case, Rabbi, one year there was a widespread famine throughout northern Europe. At this time, a wealthy man – one Baruch ben Urshraga ha-Kohen, the Parnas of the Cologne congregation, a well-to-do property owner, and a member of the Jewish Council of Cologne – gave two gold pieces to a poor, starving widow who was a neighbor of his. The woman cried with thankfulness. Then Reb Baruch said to her: "My good woman, you are certainly welcome. And now I need a favor from you. Please store these two additional gold pieces for me: otherwise, I am afraid that I will spend them, although I know that I should really save them for next year." The woman promised to hide the second set of coins and to give them back to Baruch during the next Passover.

At the same time, Reb Baruch also gave the widow a large stone jar of oat flour. Old Baruch was a strange man: he was always hiding coins to keep himself from spending them, and when he gave the flour to the widow, he forgot that he had hidden two more gold coins at the bottom of the jar. Again, the poor woman was tearfully grateful. She took the flour, she made an oven full of cakes for her small child, and she baked them to a golden brown. Little did she know that inside one of the golden cakes were two gold coins.

Not long afterward, Baruch ben Urshraga ha-Kohen remembered the gold coins in the flour jar, and he went back to the woman. "I think that I mistakenly gave you two gold coins," he said.

"Was that a mistake?" she asked. "I thought that you told me to hide them. However, if you want them back now, then here they are." Saying this, the widow went to her bedroom, and she got the two coins that Reb Baruch had given her to hide. Then, she gave the money back to the Parnas.

"No," said Baruch, "besides those two coins, I am missing two more. I think that you have them."

The woman replied: "Well, I certainly appreciate the kind charity that you have shown me, Reb Baruch. But if you are implying that I am a thief, then you are sadly mistaken. In fact, if I have wrongly made use of any of your gold coins, then may the good Lord strike down my child, amen."

"Do not say this," said Reb Baruch.

But the woman said: "I am no thief, Baruch. May my child die if I have your missing gold coins."

Poor Baruch ben Urshraga ha-Kohen covered his ears.

"Listen to me," shouted the woman to a neighbor passing by, "I am being accused unjustly: I will swear to my innocence in court!"

Baruch hurried away, but the woman ran after him. "I may not be wealthy, but at least I am honest," she cried, and she followed Reb Baruch down Judengasse Street. Baruch walked quickly into the alleyway that led to the synagogue, and the widow followed, yelling at the poor man all the while.

Rabbi Hayyim ben Yehiel was in the back room of the old Cologne yeshiva. When the Rabbi heard the commotion, he sent one of the scholars, who had been sitting with him, out into the courtyard to see what was going on. The young man returned and said: "Rabbi, I think that this is the situation. A woman has sworn an oath. She claims that she has not misused some gold coins of Reb Baruch ben Urshraga ha-Kohen, our Parnas. Unfortunately, Baruch is convinced that the woman used the coins mistakenly, and now he is afraid that her false oaths will bring some terrible misfortune down upon her."

When he heard all of this, Rabbi Hayyim ben Yehiel ordered that the front door of the synagogue should be locked; he feared that the widow would profane the synagogue with a false but sacred oath. However, the woman had seen legal transactions before, and she knew that in lawsuits involving minor amounts of money a sacred oath could be sworn in front of the synagogue. In such cases, the swearing Jew must grasp the chain or the ring or the handle of the synagogue door. So the woman held tight to the front door handle, and she said loudly: "I solemnly swear that I have not misused this man's gold coins – so help Thee God, amen."

Reb Baruch was beside himself with fear. Certainly, the great Lord God (blessed be He) must be angered by this profligate oath-taking and this wild vow-swearing. Would thunder roll and would lightning strike them, right then and there? Or would the earth crack and swallow them all, as if the ground were a hungry fish?

At that time, however, the good Lord held his wrathful action, so the woman began to pound on the front door. She pounded and she yelled and she stamped her foot, and the rabbis stood inside looking at one another. What should they do? Finally, Rabbi Hayyim ordered the doors to be unlocked, and in stormed the woman.

"Rabbi, Rabbi," she exclaimed, "I am being accused unjustly. I am not a thief, and I demand to take the full Jewish Oath once and for all times, amen."

Rabbi Hayyim looked at Reb Baruch, who was very, very unhappy. "Now," said the Rabbi, "an oath is a sacred matter. We must do this properly." The assembled yeshiva scholars nodded. "As you all know," said Rabbi Hayyim, "according to Jewish law, the person taking a sacred oath is obliged to stand and to touch the Torah. I am afraid that a Torah is not immediately available; so, my good woman, let us postpone the oath until another time."

"What are you talking about?" asked the woman. "I see a copy of the Holy Scriptures right there on your desk."

"Ah, that is true," said the Rabbi, "but it is best to touch the actual Holy Scrolls themselves, not a manuscript copy." Again the various scholars nodded.

"Then we will go to the Holy stone Ark," said the woman, and she marched out of the back room and into the main prayer hall.

The Rabbi looked at the other men; slowly, they all followed the woman into the hall. "My good woman," said the Rabbi, "the Jewish Oath requires that the swearer face the rising sun, in order that he might turn east toward Jerusalem. Unfortunately, it is now the afternoon and the sun is in the west."

"What does that matter?" said the woman. "I will face east anyway."

Rabbi Hayyim looked helplessly at the other men standing around him.

Then the Rabbi said: "Let us take a moment, my good woman, to reflect on this matter. Specifically, I would remind you of the proverb from Scriptures: 'A man may think that he is always right, but the good Lord God (blessed be He) does not always agree, for it is *He* who fixes a standard for the heart.'"

"Oh? Well that may be true for a *man*," replied the widow, "but a *woman* does not fool herself so easily. Women know secrets that men shall never know, Rabbi."

And what could the Rabbi – a man – answer to that?

So in the end, the woman put her right hand out and she touched the Holy Ark; then she recited the medieval Jewish Oath, while all the scholars stood by, very uncomfortable indeed. The widow faced east and she said: "This is my oath, as I shall swear it, full and true and right":

> About all matters hereto broached I will keep no secrets in my soul nor will I hide any facts above or beneath the ground nor will I keep any secrets locked within walls.

> So help Thee God Almighty, Who created Heaven and earth, Who set out the valleys and the mountains, Who planted the woods, the foliage, and the grasses, and Who first created all the creatures of the land, the sea, and the air–I will tell the truth.

> So help Thee God Almighty, Who with His own hand gave to Moses the Law on Mount Sinai, the five books of the Torah–I will tell the truth.

> Otherwise, may I eat a horrible food and become defiled all over, as did the king of Babylon. Otherwise, may sulfur and pitch rain upon my neck, as it rained on Sodom and Gomorrah and as it poured upon two hundred men at Babylon. Othewise, may I become leprous, like Naaman. Otherwise, may the ten scourges come upon me as they did upon the Egyptians at our captivity. Otherwise, may the earth swallow me, as it did Datan and Aviram (when the great Lord God split the earth and when He sent a great fire to burn their two hundred and fifty followers). Otherwise, may my clay never mingle with other clay and may my dust never mix with other dust in the bosom of Abraham for ever and ever, amen.

> Thus, I now swear a solemn oath that what I claim is true and right and honest, so help Thee God Almighty, our Lord, King of the Universe, Who appeared to Moses in the burning bush. On this I stake my immortal soul and the souls of my children, which on doomsday You must bring to righteous judgment, amen.

Then the woman removed her hand from the Holy Ark, she turned, and she strode from the main prayer hall, which was filled with worn wooden benches. She did not look up as she passed the twelve stained glass windows with their colored lions and snakes. Without a glance back at the Holy Ark made of stone, the widow stepped out the front door of the synagogue. She walked through the courtyard and down the alleyway, and then she went down Judengasse Street and finally reached her home.

My grandmother said that it was not long after this – it may even have been the next day – that the poor widow fed her child the cake with the two gold coins in it. The child choked on the coins, and he died instantly. Rabbi Hayyim ben Yehiel sadly performed the funeral service, and the child was buried at the side of his father in the old Jewish cemetery beyond the southern gates of the city of Cologne. Now father and son walk hand-in-hand together in the Great Hereafter. But does their mother walk with them, too? That I do not know, Rabbi.

ood evening, Rabbi. Of course – please sit here by the stove; the night fire helps me to become sleepy, also. You and I are not blessed like old Reb Elbaum. Once again I saw him nodding off during the last prayers this evening. He has learned to sway piously even while asleep: he must have acquired some magic from the mystic Achselrad. And I suppose that you and I could use a dose of Achselrad ourselves. My grandmother said that Achselrad could put men into a sleep-trance by waving a gold coin before their eyes. Exactly, Rabbi, that is the same German rabbi whom I have told you about before – Rabbi Abraham ben Alexander, also called Achselrad of Cologne. He was a pupil of Eliazer the mystic of Worms.

Rabbi Abraham Achselrad was always conjuring visions in the synagogue. I doubt whether this would be tolerated nowadays, but my grandmother said that Rabbi Abraham was also a scholar, and he claimed that his visions came from devout and pious study. Many an astonishing event took place in his yeshiva – or so my grandmother (blessed be her memory) was told. For instance, one day Rabbi Abraham looked up while writing a chapter in his famous kabbalistic tome of mystical knowledge, the *Keter Shem Tov* (a book that was never published and that only exists as a secret manuscript hidden in the loft of the old Cologne yeshiva), and he saw a vat of wine hovering in the doorway.

No, I am not inventing this, Rabbi – my grandmother swore that this is exactly what she had heard. After the Rabbi rubbed his eyes, he realized that it was not actually a vat of wine; instead, it was one of the members of the congregation, a rather portly man named Solomon ben Isaac. Behind Solomon stood a group of the regular yeshiva scholars, and when they had caught the Rabbi's eye, they all trooped into the little back room where Abraham Achselrad was trying to study. Solomon said hello, and the other scholars also greeted the Rabbi politely. They stood for a moment, and then some of the men sat on the benches.

"What can I do for you, gentlemen?" asked Rabbi Abraham.

"Ah, Rabbi," said Solomon ben Isaac, "as you know, I am a wine merchant, a wholesaler."

"Yes, I know," said the Rabbi.

"I have been negotiating a large deal, and at the moment I own four hundred vats of wine. Yesterday (praise the good Lord – may He have mercy on me), I discovered that every single vat of wine has turned to vinegar. I am ruined, Rabbi," said Solomon.

"This does not sound very good," said the Rabbi.

" 'Not good' is an understatement," said Solomon ben Isaac.

"Yes," said one of the other men, "it is very, very bad."

"Well," said another man, looking up at the ceiling, "I would recall to you, good Reb Solomon, the saying in the Talmud":

Justice is a key attribute of the Almighty Lord God (blessed be He); therefore it follows that He deals justly with all His creatures.

"This does not seem like justice to me," said Solomon sadly.

Then another of the scholars, Shimshon ha-Zaken, said to Reb Solomon ben Isaac: "Examine your deeds, my friend: review your life. Have you committed some wrong? Undoubtedly, the good Lord God (blessed be He) is punishing you in this world. Of course, He is only punishing you now in order that you will not lose any of your reward in the Great Hereafter."

And Reb Solomon ben Isaac replied: "My dear friends, do you suspect me of having done something wrong?"

Shimshon said: "It is not important what *we* suspect, Solomon. The good Lord God (blessed be He) does not levy pain and He does not inflict evil and He does not rain down woes on His pious ones without cause."

"That is true," added another man, Baruch ben Jacob. "In the Holy Scriptures there is a very apt proverb":

> A righteous man shall eat his fill,
> But the wicked will go hungry.

Now, Solomon, does this not mean that the righteous man drinks mellow wine, but that the wicked man must drink vinegar?"

Then Reb Solomon ben Isaac became worried and he replied: "If any of you knows anything against me, then please tell me my sins. What have I done wrong?"

Reb Shimshon asked: "Did you perhaps stand in the field of your neighbor when his wheat was in full ear?"

"I am not sure," said Reb Solomon. "Is that a sin?"

"It is expressly forbidden in the Talmud," said Shimshon.

And Reb Baruch said: "In the Scriptures there is another apt proverb":

> A wicked man earns a false profit fraudulently,
> But a good man reaps a sure and honest reward.

"Now, Solomon, in this regard, I have heard rumors that you have not paid your gardeners their full wages."

But Solomon ben Isaac said: "That would be stealing, and I am not guilty. I am ready to take an oath that I have paid them all that I owe—it was just that I had to delay the payment for a few days."

Another man said: "Have you perhaps brushed crumbs from your table with a broom? That will cause poverty, you know."

"Or," said yet another scholar, "could your wife have sewn a button on your shirt while you were still wearing it? Clearly, this will invite disaster."

"Perhaps you have sat upon a chair with no legs?" asked Reb Shimshon.

"With no legs?" asked Solomon.

"Yes, you may have been enticed to sit upon a bewitched stool, my friend," said Shimshon.

There was silence in the back study room. Then, Baruch ben Jacob said: "In the Talmud it is written":

> He who prays must turn his eyes downward
> and he must turn his heart upward.

"Undoubtedly, good Solomon, at some time you have prayed upside down, with your heart looking down and with your eyes looking up."

Reb Solomon became more upset because he had never thought of this iniquity.

Then another man said: "You enjoy good meals, Reb Solomon. Have you eaten meat and vegetables together on the night of a full moon? That is forbidden in the Talmud."

"That is against the Talmud?" asked Solomon ben Isaac. "I had not heard that."

"Certainly," said Reb Baruch, "as it is written":

> Whoever eats the flesh of a fat ox with turnips on the night of the fourteenth or fifteenth of the month and whoever sleeps in the light of the moon, even at the summer solstice, his blood is on his own head. (In addition, he will be seized with ague.)

And Reb Shimshon nodded and he said: "Now, Solomon, let us be honest with each other. Have you recently eaten food that a mouse nibbled? This is a sin, say the talmudic Sages."

"That is against the Talmud? I had not known about this either," said Solomon.

"Yes, it is definitely forbidden – as it is written: 'Whoever eats what had once been nibbled by a mouse or by a cat makes his learning to be forgotten,'" quoted Reb Baruch.

Then one of the other scholars spoke up: "Now that we are being helpful, Reb Solomon, I might remind you that crumbs left in the house cause poverty, because on Wednesday and Saturday nights harmful spirits alight on these bits of food and nibble and gnaw them. Also, my friend, hanging up a basket of food causes poverty."

"Exactly," added Baruch, "in the Holy Scriptures there is a very apt proverb":

> He who suspends a food basket in the air
> Suspends his sustenance

"(although I think that this applies only to bread)."

At this, Solomon ben Isaac dejectedly sat down again on a bench by the wall. Then Reb Samuel said: "We must consider carefully all the possibilities, gentlemen. Now it is quite likely that poor Reb Solomon has gotten into the habit of twisting his hands behind his back—as we all remember, the Talmud tells us that this is quite bad. It is unpious, and it slows one's work immeasurably. I would also mention that we know how Solomon can become absent-minded when walking and talking; at some point, he must have stepped between a passing couple when he was in a crowd of three people. This is bad, bad luck."

"You know, Reb Samuel," said Baruch thoughtfully, "I wonder whether Reb Solomon forgot to eat either pumpkin, leeks, beets, or dates on *Rosh Hashanah*?"

"Or," someone else inquired in a low voice, "did he perhaps read aloud the inscriptions on a tombstone?"

Until now, old Reb Moyses ben Nathan had been silent, but here he spoke up: "My good scholars, it is nothing that poor Solomon has done. It is the planets. Remember how the Talmud says: 'Longevity, offspring, and sustenance depend not upon merit—they are decreed by the influence of the planets.'

" 'Once upon a time,' say the talmudic Sages, 'there were two learned, righteous, and eminent rabbis, Rabbi Chisda and Rabbi Jochanan. Each was a fine man, a pious scholar, and a modest teacher. However, their fates were exactly opposite from each other.

" 'Rabbi Chisda prayed for rain and it came immediately; whereas, all the weather-prayers and the holy entreaties of Rabbi Jochanan were totally useless. Rabbi Chisda lived to the age of ninety-two and he was not sick for a day in his life, whereas Rabbi Jochanan died at the age of forty after many years of crippling pains. In the house of Rabbi Chisda, sixty marriages were celebrated, whereas in the house of Rabbi Jochanan, sixty funerals were mourned. In the house of Rabbi Chisda, bread of the finest flour was eaten even by the dogs and no one was concerned, whereas in the house of Rabbi Jochanan, there was not enough barley bread for the humans. And why did the two men differ? Was it piety? No, it was not—the two men were born under exactly opposite planetary configurations.'

"Clearly, gentlemen, poor Solomon was born under the wrong planets," said Reb Moyses.

At that moment, said my grandmother, Rabbi Abraham Achselrad awoke with a start. He had been writing his book all night, and now he had fallen asleep during the discussion. Well, asked the many scholars, what do you think, Rabbi. Rabbi Achselrad asked for a brief review of the situation. Then he said: "Ah, good rabbis, this reminds me of a story that I once heard. However, I seem to be a little tired at the moment, so I will not bother you with all the details. Let me just say this: Reb Solomon ben Isaac must take a pilgrimage east."

"A pilgrimage?" asked Solomon.

"Yes," said Rabbi Achselrad.

"East of Cologne?"

"Exactly," said Rabbi Achselrad.

"Very well," sighed Solomon ben Isaac.

So, on the next morning, Reb Solomon set out on his holy walk. From Cologne he crossed the River Rhine to Kalk, the brewery town. From Kalk he went on to Overath (on the Agger River), to Waldbrol, and finally to Morsbach. Morsbach was too small to have a synagogue, and Reb Solomon stayed one night at the house of the local Jewish scholar, Nathan ben Moyses Joselin. Then bright and early on the next morning, Reb Solomon began his return journey. When he reached Cologne again, he found that his wine was still vinegar.

However, one day a few weeks afterward, Reb Solomon succeeded in selling all of his many vats, and he even made a small profit. . . . How was that possible? Either the vinegar had suddenly turned back to wine, or the cost of vinegar had risen so high that it could then be sold at the same price as wine. My grandmother told me what had happened, Rabbi, but at the moment I forget which it was.

h, good evening again, Rabbi. I know how difficult it is to sleep on the night of a bright moon. Just put your feet up on the side bench here, and I will open the stove door. Let me push this coal back. There is nothing like that white glow: it washes away the cares of a hard day. I heard your final benediction tonight, Rabbi; clearly you are working too hard. Oh yes, even a shammas like me can tell. I kept one eye on you when I cleaned the dishes, and I saw that you were watching the door, hoping that Reb Elbaum would leave early. And then, Reb Anton stayed to argue about the scriptural passage from Leviticus – in particular, I remember the difficult part where the good Lord God (blessed be He) said to Moses:

> A priest (a *kohen*) shall not participate directly in any funeral rites, except for the death of his nearest blood-relations – father, mother, son, daughter, brother, or full sister (when unmarried).

After wrestling with these holy words, of course you are worn out. What is that? A story from me? Rabbi, all I know are old-fashioned children's tales, the grandmother fables. You need something new and fresh to keep your mind keen. Otherwise you will become an old man like me, and you will find yourself constantly musing and dozing and nodding off in front of the stove.

What do you mean, you are already an old man, Rabbi? Do you really think that sixty years is old? You are still a child. When you reach eighty, *then* you will be old. You doubt that you will live to see eighty years? If so, Rabbi, then you will never grow old. . . . All right, all right, – I know no special stories, but listening to you and Reb Anton discussing *kohens* and funerals put me in mind of the smile of the grandfather of Rabbi Asher and of his friend, Solomon, who was a *kohen*.

Exactly, Rabbi – this was the same Rabbi Asher ben Yehiel who, when he was old, would always say: "I never spoke when I was young, and for this reason I learned to listen well with my littlest and tiniest and softest ears." You see, this tale has to do with Asher's ears, because Rabbi Asher heard the story of his grandfather's smile from the son of Reb Solomon ha-Kohen, who actually saw it happen himself. What is that, Rabbi? Of course Asher's grandfather smiled many times during his living days – I am speaking of the time that he smiled after he had died. . . . Well, if you will just be patient a moment, then I will tell you:

Once upon a time in the town of Cologne, there lived a pious Rabbi named Asher ben Yehiel, and Rabbi Asher's grandfather had also been named Asher. As you know, Rabbi, the Sages in the Talmud tell us that the highest of all benevolences and the greatest of all good deeds and the kindest of all fine acts are those that are done for the dead. And why is that? Of course it is because such deeds give no practical reward. "If you do me an act of kindness after my death, then it is *truly* an act of kindness – for I will not be able to repay you," said Benjamin Shalom, the Pious. And that, Rabbi, is why Asher's grandfather smiled.

As my grandmother reminded me, Asher ben Yehiel (the younger Asher) sprang from ancestors who centered their whole world on the Talmud: these rabbis revered the holy words for their own sake. Asher himself studied in a number of talmudic academies, and he even spent time with the mystic Juddah he-Hasid of Regensburg. Later, Asher became a disciple of Meir of Rothenburg. Asher was a fine writer; so, when finally he was a rabbi himself, Asher became a *Tosafist* – writing the extensions and additions to the Talmud that were the great contribution of those medieval rabbis. After the death of his master, Meir of Rothenburg (whose corpse the German emperors refused to give up for burial without remuneration), Asher ben Yehiel became the most influential rabbinical authority of Germany. . . .

What? Of course there is more, Rabbi: I only closed my eyes for a moment—can an old man not take a little rest? Now you have interrupted my thoughts. Let me see, where was I? Yes, yes—as my grandmother (may her soul visit happily with her parents for ever and ever, amen) said: "A smile is a reflection of the good Lord God's radiance—it even transcends death, my child." She said this about Rabbi Asher's grandfather (who was also named Asher). You see, once upon a time, said my grandmother, there lived in Cologne on the River Rhine a pious scholar named Asher. Rabbi Asher headed the Cologne yeshiva for a number of years before he emigrated to Spain. Asher's father, Yehiel ben Asher, had also been a Rabbi, in the small town of Gladbach, just northeast of Cologne. What? Please do not interrupt, Rabbi—I was just getting to the grandfather's smile.

The grandfather the elder Asher was Rabbi Yehiel ben Asher's father. This Asher, the elder Asher, was born and educated in Gladbach, a mining town of ironstone, of lime, and of peat. When this Asher was ten years old, he became firm friends with a boy of the same age, Solomon ha-Kohen. It seemed to happen overnight. The boys had known each other since they were barely able to walk, but suddenly they became inseparable. They went to the yeshiva together, they played together, and they even devised their own secret language. One day they found a bird, a jackdaw, with a broken wing in the yard behind Solomon's house. They tried to feed it worms and oat-mash, but the bird weakened and in a few days it died. Together the two boys secretly gave the jackdaw a Jewish burial. Asher washed the little body, and he wrapped it in a white linen napkin that he had stolen from his mother's cabinet. Solomon said the benediction:

> Happy is the man who does not forget You, O Lord. Those who seek You will not stumble and they will be saved, for the memorial of every single creature comes before You. O Lord, You watched over Noah and his animals: You rained down upon him a merciful salvation, and You remembered Noah and his sons and his wives and his sons' wives and all

the beasts and all the cattle that were with them in the ark. And finally, O Lord God, King of the Universe, we remember how You said in the Scriptures: "Cease your loud weeping, shed no more tears, for you shall leave many descendants behind you." So, praise the good Lord God (blessed be He), amen.

Asher and Solomon made a pact that each should share all of the other's treasures, and they held to this agreement all their born days. If one boy learned a passage from the Talmud, then he taught it to the other; and if one man made a profit in business, then he gave some of the money to his friend. And together they shaped each other's fine spirits—as the Holy Scriptures say in the Proverbs:

> As iron sharpens iron,
>   So one man sharpens the wits
> Of his boon companion,
>   Especially when they are young.

The two men grew up together and they aged together, and one day on the eve of the Day of Atonement, early in the night, the candle of the elder Asher went out in the synagogue. (In those days in medieval Germany, it was the custom for every man who was a member of the congregation to light a wax candle on the eve of the Fast of Atonement. These candles were large enough to burn the whole night and the whole of the next day.) Seven days later (on the seventeenth of *Tishri*) during the middle of the Feast of the Tabernacles, old Asher died. At his death, great honor and respect were paid to his family; people from neighboring places such as Cologne and Bonn and even Duren and Dusseldorf attended his funeral.

As you know, Rabbi, dying on the Sabbath or on any other holy day indicates that the deceased person has lived a most righteous life. Asher died during the Feast of the Tabernacles, and when Solomon ha-Kohen heard the news that afternoon, he said: "Blessed are You, O Lord our God, King of the Universe, Who is the only true Judge, amen." Then Solomon tore the hem of his shirt.

The day of the funeral was drizzly and dismal. As the mourners walked silently to the cemetery, water dripped from Solomon ha-Kohen's long nose. Everyone's socks became wet through their shoes.

The fog was thick, and although you could hear voices, you could see only the person walking next to you. Trees were wet, bushes were water-logged, and all was an ocean of dreary, muddy puddles.

In those days, it was the practice to set the coffin on a special stone (which was set aside for just this purpose) near the cemetery; then the pallbearers opened the casket, in order to see whether the body had been dislocated or disarranged by the jolting of the coffin during that last solemn walk. The men set Asher's coffin upon the rock, and they opened the top. When they did this, Reb Solomon ha-Kohen stepped toward the coffin, and he stopped at a distance of four cubits, which was as near as a respectful person was allowed. But from there, old Reb Solomon could see that the face of his friend Asher was wet. Water was puddling in the old creases. Rain was dripping on the old brows. So, as the gathered people watched in stunned silence, Reb Solomon walked closer and closer to the coffin. Solomon walked up and he stood right next to the coffin, he took out his handkerchief, and he carefully dried the dead face of Asher. Then, Reb Solomon turned and he walked away. And he stood back again the required four cubits from the body of his childhood friend.

Was it the wind that made a bit of fog swirl over the open coffin? For a moment, the face of old Reb Asher became obscured by mist. Then the mist cleared, and there was a gentle smile on his face. Asher smiled, and the pallbearers closed the coffin and buried the old man. And my grandmother told me, Rabbi, that old Solomon ha-Kohen smiled, too.

ood evening, Rabbi: I see that there is no sleep for the weary. (That is what my grandmother said, and she said it almost nightly.) If you are cold, then sit down here on the bench and I will stoke up the oven. This stoker? It is one of the iron shoe scrapers from the front hall – probably you do not recognize it because it is covered with soot. (Then, too, I bent it into this strange shape in order to make it fit through the oven door.) Of course there is still another scraper in the anteroom for dirty shoes. But I myself am of the old school: I think that all pious men should pray barefoot. Did you know that the famous Rabbi Asher prayed barefoot?

Oh yes, my grandmother told me that he always prayed barefoot, and of course he wrote barefoot – this was to ensure that all his writings were humble and devout. Rabbi Asher even wrote barefoot when he acted as the scribe for his flock, as when he wrote ethical wills. Now there is a fine tradition, Rabbi: my grandmother often reminded me of the charge that the good Lord God (blessed be He) put upon Abraham:

> For I have known him and I have taken care of him, and I have charged
> him to instruct and to command his children and his children's children

and all his household after him. Let his descendants conform to My commandments, let them keep the way of the Lord, and let them do what is right and what is just and what is true and what is holy. Then, I shall give to him and to his children and to his children's children all the joy and the happiness that I have promised.

Yes, my grandmother often quoted this passage—and, of course, how can you question the Holy Scriptures? Every father is bound by the good Lord God (blessed be He) to leave moral rules for his children's guidance. Let me illustrate with one of my grandmother's stories. I remember that she told me about the ethical will that a certain Eleazer ben Samuel ha-Levi of Mainz asked Rabbi Asher ben Yehiel to write.

As you know, Rabbi Asher was a famous writer. He wrote the great *Compendium* of talmudic commentaries, and he wrote many minor manuscripts and poems and essays on religious thought—throughout Germany, all Jews knew that Asher ben Yehiel was the foremost Jewish writer of the day. Therefore, when Eleazar ben Samuel ha-Levi decided to have a will written, he went immediately to Rabbi Asher.

You see, Rabbi, Eleazar ben Samuel ha-Levi was a plain and simple man from Mainz. When he reached the age of fifty-six, his brother Nathan said to him: "Eleazar, if you should die (may the good Lord God, blessed be He, let you live another twenty years, amen), where can I find your will?"

"My will?"

"Yes, yes," said Nathan, "your will."

"I do not have a will," said Eleazar.

"What!? You have not written a will?"

"Nathan, you know as well as I," said Eleazar, "that I have almost no money and that I have no property; my store and my house are rented. What could I possibly will to my children?"

"Eleazar," said Nathan, "where have you been all these years? Have you lived in a cave? You must will your whole life's philosophy to your children. Remember, Eleazar, it is written in Genesis":

For I have known him and I have taken care of him, and I have charged him to instruct and to command his children and his children's children and all his household after him. Let his descendants conform to My commandments, let them keep the way of the Lord, and let them do what is right and what is just and what is true and what is holy. Then, I shall give to him and to his children and to his children's children all the joy and the happiness that I have promised.

Now, good brother of mine, sit down immediately and write out a will," said Nathan.

"Nathan, I am not certain that I know my whole life's philosophy – also, I am not too good at writing. I must confess," said Eleazar, "that setting many serious words on paper seems a rather formidable task."

"Then go to a good writer, my brother," said Nathan, "but please do not put this off any longer. Write out a will immediately."

So, after a little thought, Eleazar told his wife to take care of the store for a few days, he kissed his children, and he set off north for Cologne in order to ask the great Rabbi Asher to help him write his last will and testament.

Eleazar traveled north along the River Rhine, through Bingen, Coblenz, and Bonn, and on the second day he reached Cologne. There he found the Jewish Quarter, and he went to the old synagogue. Eleazar walked through the main prayer hall filled with wooden benches, he passed the twelve stained glass windows with their colored lions and snakes, he looked up in wonder at the Holy Ark made of stone, and he walked to the door of the back study room. In the little back room, Rabbi Asher ben Yehiel was bent over a book, studying barefoot.

The Rabbi looked up. "May I help you?" he asked.

Eleazar said: "Are you Rabbi Asher ben Yehiel, the writer?"

"I am."

"Rabbi, my name is Eleazar ben Samuel ha-Levi. I live in Mainz. My brother has reminded me that it is my duty to leave a will for my children, but I am not a man who is comfortable with long sentences. Will you help me to write a good will?"

The Rabbi looked at the papers on his desk, and then he said: "Give me a few minutes to finish what I am doing, Reb Eleazar."

After about ten minutes, the Rabbi said: "Now I am ready to write for you. Let me take out a new sheet of paper."

The Rabbi got ready to write, and Eleazar took a worn parchment from his pocket and he handed it to the Rabbi.

"What is this?" asked Rabbi Asher

"It is an old cantrap, Rabbi. It has been in my family for many generations, and my brother says that we must begin the will and testament with this, as did my father and as did his father before him."

The Rabbi read the old charm aloud:

> Lord, protect my beloved children
> From disease and sores of skin,
> From fiends and demons and from sin,
> And from painful deaths, amen.
>
> Lord have mercy on my heirs.
> Keep them whole—guard their affairs.
> Defend them from all evil snares
> Which might entrap them unawares.
>
> And may Your sacred holy angel
> Guide my children toward where You dwell.
> Bless them, Lord—I love them well
> As You love all of Israel.
>
> Mighty is our God of awe—
> Lord, raise these young of mine to draw
> Upon Your great and holy Torah,
> To study humbly from Your Law.
>
> Give them each a fine household
> And give them children many fold,
> Let them do good deeds untold,
> So gently they'll grow wise and old.

"Shall I write this first?" asked Rabbi Asher.

"Yes, please," said Eleazer.

After a moment, the Rabbi said: "All right, Eleazer—continue."

"This, then," began Eleazar, "is my Will and my Testament to my children. These are the things that my sons and my daughters shall do at my request. My children, you shall go to the house of prayer every morning and every evening, and you shall be certain to pray with your *tefillah* and to say the *Shema*. Then, when the service is over, read and study the Torah, the Psalms, or the Proverbs. (Or, you can also do good deeds of charity, amen.)

"As to your business lives—always be scrupulously honest in your dealings, both with Jews and with Gentiles. Do not forget to be gentle in your manners, and try your best to fulfill every honorable request. Remember the scriptural proverb":

> Continue to live honorably, loyally, and honestly,
> And your days will always be happy.

"Hold on a moment, Reb Eleazer," said the Rabbi. "Speak a little more slowly please."

"I am sorry, Rabbi. . . . Now, my good and obedient children, do not talk more than is necessary: this will save you from slander, falsehood, and frivolity. Again recall the scriptural proverb:

> The good Lord God (blessed be He) detests a liar,
> But He delights in the honest man.

"And my fine and charitable children: never turn away a poor man empty-handed. Give him whatever you can, be it much or be it little. (If he begs a lodging overnight and if you do not know him, then at least give him enough money to pay an innkeeper.) As the Holy Scriptures tell us in the Proverbs":

> Refuse no man any favor or help
>   When it lies in your power to give it.
> And then, do not procrastinate.
>   Never say to a beggar: "Come back again;
> You shall have it tomorrow"
>   When, in fact, you can actually help
> The poor man today.

"When you go off and set up your own households, my sons and my daughters, live in Jewish communities so that my grandchildren may learn all the many ways of Judaism. This is very important. Moreover, even if you must ask for charity, find the money to pay for teachers for your children: do not let my grandchildren grow up uninstructed in the Torah. As the Scriptures tell us in the Proverbs":

> There are always gold, rubies, and corals –
> These will decorate the outside of your body.
> But the words of knowledge are the most precious of all jewels,
> For they adorn your mind.

"And marry your children, O my sons and –"

"Slowly, please, Eleazar," reminded the Rabbi.

"Of course, Rabbi – Marry your children, O my sons and daughters (as soon as they are of marriageable age) to members of respectable families. But do not hunt up the best dowry; instead, search out the finest and the most learned person. (Remember, good children, as the Scriptures have told us in the Proverbs: 'It is better to be poor and above reproach than to be rich and crooked and dishonest.') Marriage produces children, and children and grandchildren are great gifts – the talmudic Sages have said: 'A father's first love is for his children, and the children's first love is for *their* children' – amen, my first loves.

"In this regard, my good descendants," continued Eleazer, "let me remind you of a few practical matters about your own children (may you have many); these are practical matters that I and your mother (blessed be her name for ever and ever) found of great use in raising all of you. First, of course you should not name your children after any living person; instead, choose a revered relative who lived a long and fruitful life. Never, never allow your pregnant wife to look at anything frightening or to step over nails. Then, when the infant is young, do not step over it yourself, otherwise it will not grow properly. Remember, of course, to pull the baby's right ear (rather than its left) when it sneezes. Do not let it see its reflection in a mirror, or no teeth will ever grow in its little mouth. And if the child does not begin to walk early enough, then you can hurry him along by drawing a line in front of him as he crawls."

"Slowly, slowly, Eleazer," said Rabbi Asher.

"I am sorry, Rabbi," said Eleazer. "May I continue now?"

"Just a moment . . . . all right."

"Good—now, my children, every Friday morning, prepare yourselves for honoring the Sabbath. Be sure to light the lamps while the day is still bright, and in winter light the furnace before dark in order to avoid desecrating the Sabbath by kindling fires during the holy time.

"Now that I think of it, I would like to remind you: be very fastidious, and keep your houses clean and tidy. I was always scrupulous on this point, for all diseases and sicknesses and poverties arise in dirty houses. Also, remember that when you visit the houses of others you should bring a gift—a sweetcake or some bread are nice. Then repay all the gifts that you yourselves receive—and in this regard, pray carefully. Why do I bring up the subject of prayer here, my children? Prayer is your grateful acknowledgment of God's Divine gifts, amen."

And Rabbi Asher said: "What about prayers for others?"

"What do you mean, Rabbi?" asked Eleazer.

"Remember, Eleazer, it is written in the Talmud":

One must not only think of oneself when praying: you should also be mindful of the needs of your fellows. Whoever can pray on behalf of his neighbor and fails to do so is thereby a sinner. On the other hand, whoever prays unselfishly for his fellow man, he will receive the good graces of the Lord first.

And as the Scriptures say in the Second Book of Samuel:

Moreover, as for me, God forbid that I should sin against the Lord by not praying for you also. In fact, I will show you by my example what is good and what is right: it is to revere the Lord and to worship Him faithfully, with all your heart.

"Oh, yes, Rabbi—well then, please write this: On Holidays and on Festivals and on Sabbaths try to make happy the poor, the unfortunate, the widows, and the orphans. These people should always be guests at your table; their care and their entertainment are religous duties."

And Rabbi Asher asked: "Now, Eleazer, will you include any advice on education?"

"I suppose that I must," said Eleazer.

"You suppose? Eleazer, you had best recall the story from the Talmud":

Balaam, the son of Beor and Oenomaos of Gadara, was one of the greatest of all philosophers. One day, the many peoples of his race came to him for advice. "Tell us, wise Balaam," they asked, "how can we overcome the Israelites?" Balaam looked at the crowd of his people, and he answered: "First, my friends, go to the schools and the study houses of the Israelites. Do you hear the clamor of little children? They are rehearsing their lessons; they are studying the laws and the wisdom of their people. You will hear this noise, and you will know that you cannot prevail. Temporarily, you may subdue them  but in the long run they will endure. Scholarship and wisdom are eternal and invincible."

"So," continued Rabbi Asher, "you must offer some counsel on the education of your descendants."

"Very well, Rabbi—how about this: Every good quality that you must acquire will become a habit when you study the Torah, my children. Holy study forms a noble character; in fact, God's words are translated into our very bodies. Therefore, read and read and reread the Torah. I suggest that you set aside regular times for this each day—and then stick to your schedule. As for group prayer, be certain to arrive at the synagogue early. Pray steadily with the congregation, and give each word and every sound its full time and its complete value: the holy words are like the parts of the body—there are in the *Shema* two hundred and forty-eight words corresponding to the two hundred and forty-eight limbs in the human body, amen.

"Now, as the Scriptures remind us in the Proverbs":

> Listen, all Israel, learn My refrains
> And you shall live—

"Just a moment," interrupted Rabbi Asher, "please go a bit more slowly, Eleazer."

"Certainly, Rabbi. . . . as I was saying, remember the scriptural passage from Proverbs":

Listen, all Israel, learn My refrains
And you shall live long golden days
And I will show you sunny lanes
And lead you along My glorious ways.

As you walk you will not slip,
As you run you will not fall,
If you keep to scholarship:
For study is the safest life of all.

"So, good children," said Eleazer, "my sons and my daughters of Israel – attend to your prayers. When you come to the prayer for redemption, follow it immediately by the eighteen benedictions. Do not talk during the prayer services. Listen to the Precentor, and respond with 'Amen' at the proper times. After the morning prayer, read the chapter in Exodus about the *mannah*, read all the accompanying passages, and read the eleven holy verses, with due attention to clear enunciation. Then recite a Psalm. And when day is done and when your prayers are ended, think about the words of the good Lord God (blessed be He) as you fall asleep."

There was silence. "Is that all, Reb Eleazar?" asked Rabbi Asher.

"Yes – I think that is all," said Eleazer.

"How about instructions for your funeral?"

"Should that be included?" asked Eleazer.

"Well," said the Rabbi, "I think that a word about your burial would be appropriate here."

"Very well, Rabbi: Now, my children, as to my funeral. I ask you all – my sons, my daughters, my wife, and my friends – that no funeral oration be spoken in my honor. Just say the benedictions quietly. Do not use a fancy coffin: I would like a plain wooden box. When I die, wash me clean, comb my hair, and trim my nails, as I would have done in my lifetime; I would like to go fresh and neat and bright to my eternal rest in the same way that I went fresh and neat and bright to the synagogue on every Sabbath day. (And if the ordinary community officials should dislike this duty, then find some poor man who will not mind preparing my body, and please pay him well for this last service to me.)

"Now, children, at a distance of thirty cubits from the grave, set down my coffin. Put it on the ground and drag me the final distance to the grave by a rope attached to the front of the coffin box. Every four cubits, stand and rest a moment, and do this seven times – in this way I will find a final atonement for all my many sins, amen.

"Finally, put me in the ground at the right hand of my father. And, good children, if the space be a little narrow, then I am sure that my father loves me well enough to slide over and to make room for me by his side.

> *"Signed, your loving father,*
> *Eleazer, son of Samuel the Levite"*

Then Rabbi Asher ben Yehiel read the entire will back to Reb Eleazar. Eleazar listened happily with his eyes closed. Afterwards, Eleazar signed the will, he thanked the Rabbi, he put three gold coins into the poorbox, and he returned to Mainz. Eleazar ben Samuel ha-Levi remained a plain and simple man. My grandmother said that he lived another twenty years; then he died peacefully on the first day of *Rosh Hashanah*, and he was buried the next day beside his father's grave, on the righthand side, amen.

ood evening, Rabbi. You are having difficulty sleeping again? Just put your feet up on the side bench here and I will open the stove door. Let me push this coal back; there is nothing like that white glow to wash away the cares of a hard day. I heard your final prayers tonight, and there is no use denying it, Rabbi—you are overworked; even an old shammas like me can tell. When I was cleaning the dishes I saw that you were watching the door, hoping that Reb Elbaum would leave early. But then Reb Anton stayed late to argue about the Midrash passage.

That Midrash passage reminded me of our Rabbi Jehuda ben Saul. (Rabbi Jehuda? He was two rabbis before you.) Jehuda was a stern man. One day he gave a Midrash sermon to his yeshiva students; looking down at his pupils, he asked: "Tell me, young men: Was Light created as the first of all things?"

For a moment there was silence. Then a bright student, Moshe ben Samuel, said: "Good Rabbi, Genesis tells us: 'In the beginning of creation, God said: "Let there be Light," and there was Light.' So the answer to your question is 'yes'—Light must have been created as the first of all things."

"I see," said Rabbi Jehuda. "And why was this? Why did the good Lord God (blessed be He) create Light first?"

The Rabbi looked pointedly at each student, but there was silence; so the Rabbi said: "Well, there is a useful story here, my young men. Once there was a king who wished to build a new palace. But his favorite locality was in the shade of a great mountain, and it was forever enshrouded in darkness. So what did the king do first? . . . Well, students, what have you to say for yourselves?"

Apparently, the students had nothing to say, so the Rabbi himself said: "It is obvious, young men – the king lit torches and lamps and lanterns, in order to know where he had to set the foundations for his palace. Does this not suggest why the good Lord God created Light first of all?"

Some of the students nodded, and Rabbi Jehuda continued: "However, my story is not yet finished. Now, my good and serious students, there was a neighboring king who also wished to erect a magnificent palace, and this king too favored a spot that was in the shade of a vast and towering mountain. In fact, he too picked an entirely black region for his mansion. So what did this king do first of all?"

Moshe said: "Rabbi, the second king lit torches and lamps and lanterns first, in order to see where to locate the foundations for his palace."

"Ah, that is an interesting idea, my young and attentive pupil," said Rabbi Jehuda. "Unfortunately, you are incorrect."

"I am?" asked Moshe ben Samuel.

"Yes, you are," said the Rabbi. "You see, Moshe, the second king decided to build the palace first; in this way, he had some place on which to affix the torches and the lamps and the lanterns. Now, what does *this* teach us about the good Lord God (blessed be He)?"

The pupils looked silently at one another. Rabbi Jehuda said: "Here is a hint – consider the Holy Scriptures, my young scholars. There it is written":

God said: "Now, let there be lights in the vault of Heaven in order to separate day from night. And let these lights serve as signs both for Festivals and for seasons and years. Let them also shine in the vault of

Heaven in order to give light on earth." So it was: God made the two great lights, the greater – the sun – to govern the day, and the lesser – the moon – to govern the night, and with these He also made the stars.

God set all these lights in the vault of Heaven to give light on earth, to govern day and night, and to separate light from darkness. And God saw that it was good. And evening came and morning came, a fourth day.

This, young men, is what the Scriptures say. But now I ask you, students: The sun and the moon and the stars were not created until the fourth day, so where did any earlier light come from?"

Again there was silence in the study hall. Rabbi Jehuda stared down at his students. No one spoke, so the Rabbi himself answered the question: "I will tell you whence came the earlier light: the Holy One, blessed be He, enwrapped Himself in Light like a garment. In this way the brilliance of His splendor shone forth from one end of the Universe to the other. At least that is what one set of Sages tells us – but, my boys, are there any other possibilities?"

No one answered, so the Rabbi said: "Perhaps, my quiet students, the earlier Light first emanated from the site of the Temple, which, as we all know, was the center of the whole earth's creation. Is this not possible?"

The Rabbi looked at the young men on the benches. The young men looked up at the Rabbi. Then Rabbi Jehuda said: "Yes, anything is *possible*. But, young men, is this possibility true?"

Jehuda looked up at the ceiling. "Is this possibility a fact?" he asked. "Or is it fiction?"

The Rabbi continued without pausing: "Now, does not Exodus tell us that the glory of the Lord filled the Tabernacle built by Moses and that this glory was a cloud of fire visible at night at every stage of the journey of the Israelites? And does not Ezekiel tell us that the glory of the Lord rose high above all the angels and filled His holy temple with a splendrous radiance? . . . Certainly this is what the Holy Scriptures tell us. So, my fine young men, did the good Lord God Almighty need anything other than His glorious radiance in order to light the universe from the very beginning? No, He most definitely did not, amen."

With that, the yeshiva students thought that the lesson was over, and they began to gather their books. "Just a moment, young men," said Rabbi Jehuda, "does this mean that the first Light did *not* emanate from the site of the Temple, which, as we all know, was the center of the whole earth's creation?"

The students were puzzled, and they looked at one another. "Well?" asked the Rabbi. There was silence, and so the Rabbi said: "Of course this does not mean any such thing. There can never be too much light – so the first Light radiated both from the good Lord God (blessed be He) *and* from the site of the Temple. Moreover, does it not say in Psalm 41":

> Happy is he who tends the helpless;
> The Lord will spare him from all sickness.
> The Lord gives him health, protects from harm:
> He guards him with His sheltering arm.
> Then God never unleashes his enemies,
> And He keeps him safe from cruel disease.

"And does it not say in Chapter 19 of the Book of Proverbs":

> He who is generous to the poor
>   Lends to the Lord Himself,
> And God will repay the charitable man
>   From the fullness of His shelf.

"Certainly it says these fine things. And, my lads, just as there can never be too much light, so there can never be too much charity. Remember that – amen." And the Rabbi gathered up his papers, and he left the study room. . . .

What is that, Rabbi? Yes, yes, there is more – I was just resting my eyes a moment. Now, let me see, where was I? Ah yes, once upon a time, said my grandmother, there was a fine and pious scholar in Cologne named Asher ben Yehiel. (Please do not interrupt, Rabbi.) Now Asher was as charitable a man as could be imagined. My grandmother told me that before he was the chief rabbi in Cologne, he had been in charge of the distribution of the communal charity. At that time, there was a year of dismal famine in the surrounding countryside, and a poor woman came to him from the neighboring city of Duren and said: "Dear Rabbi, my family has nothing at all; please, sir, would your congregation give me some food or some money."

Asher knew that the Cologne congregation was penniless; nonetheless he looked hopefully in the poorbox. It was empty. Sadly, he swore by the good Lord God (blessed be He) that there was no money in the charity box, no money in the community fund, and no food at all in the yeshiva. But the woman said to him: "Dear Rabbi, if you refuse me food, then–by all that is holy–a poor woman and her seven children are sure to die of hunger." When Rabbi Asher heard this, he took the woman to his own house and he emptied his pantry stock into a basket, which he gave to the woman, who wept and thanked him and left.

Soon afterward Rabbi Asher fell very ill. He coughed ceaselessly, he had a high fever, and he became delirious. Everyone believed that Asher was destined to die. Dumah, the Angel of Death, hovered over Asher's bed with a drawn sword. The sick room was quiet and damp, and some of the neighbors began to prepare for mourning. Then, two young angels happened by, and they looked in the window.

"My holy Dumah," said one of the little spirits, "what is going on here?"

"Rabbi Asher is about to die," said Dumah.

"Just a moment," said the young angel, and she flew off to the glorious throne of the Almighty One. The little spirit could not stare directly at the radiance of the good Lord God (blessed be He), so she looked at His feet and said: "O Lord our God, King of the universe, You have said that he who feeds an Israelite should be likened unto him who feeds the whole world. Have You not?"

"Yes, I have," replied the Lord.

"Now, my dear Master, in the German town of Cologne there is a dying man–one Asher ben Yehiel. Earlier this year, he fed a woman and her seven children, and he kept them alive during a difficult time in Duren. Asher is still young, good Lord. Is it right that he should die now?"

When the great and powerful Lord God, blessed be He, heard the spirit speak this way, He looked again at young Rabbi Asher, and then He revoked the decree of death that had been pronounced against him. The holy Bill of Death was torn into sixty times sixty pieces and it was forgotten, and Asher's life was prolonged another forty-two years. Therefore, said my grandmother, every man should dispense charity — as the scriptural proverb points out:

> Wealth is weightless
>   On Judgment Day,
> But goodness and charity
>   Shall heavily weigh.
> Generosity, mercy,
>   Kind words with each breath —
> These will protect you
>   Against a sad death.

Later, Asher ben Yehiel — this fine and charitable man — became the chief rabbi of Cologne, but then he was forced to emigrate to Spain. In Spain, he was the spiritual head of all the Jews in the region of Toledo. (When he died, it is said that his body was finally returned to Germany and that he was buried in Regensburg, but that may be just a legend.) Anyway, in Spain, Asher wrote many well-known religious books; most of these works organized and commented on the halakhic parts of the Talmud. Asher ben Yehiel was a tireless writer, and he also authored an old text entitled "Rules for the Health of the Soul." Because of Asher's inherently generous nature, there are a great many stipulations about charity in this text, and the section on helping one's neighbors begins with the well-known quotation from the Talmud:

> Practice charity and you will fill the whole world with loving kindness. Charity is equal to all other good deeds put together — it is greater than any sacrifice, and it brings the Day of Redemption and the coming of the Messiah ever nearer. When a beggar stands at your door, then the Holy One (blessed be He) stands at the beggar's right hand.

And, as Rabbi Jehuda said, there can never be too much charity — although Eleazer ben Solomon once gave Rabbi Asher pause to wonder. This was before Asher had moved to Spain, and it was when he was still the chief rabbi of Cologne. Of course I am thinking of the time that Eleazer was blessed with the miracle of the oats; undoubtedly this miracle influenced Asher's later writings on charity. You do not know of the miracle of the oats, Rabbi? Then let me tell you:

Once upon a time, said my grandmother, there was a man living in Cologne, named Eleazer ben Solomon ben Moses ben Joseph. Eleazer was very charitable, in fact, he was so charitable that when the collectors who went around to gather money for charity saw him at a distance, they avoided him. The Gabbai of the congregation carefully neglected Reb Eleazer, for Eleazer would give the shoes off his feet and the food from his family and the hat from his head if he had the slightest opportunity.

One day, Eleazer went to the market to buy a few things that his daughter needed for her wedding. The wedding was to take place on the next Sunday, and Eleazer's wife felt it important that her daughter should have new shoes. As he was walking through the marketplace, Eleazar saw the collectors of charity making their rounds. However, as soon as they caught sight of Eleazer, the collectors crossed the street, they looked the other way, and they began to hurry off.

Eleazer ran after them. "Tell me, good friends – what is the cause for which you are collecting?"

"Oh, it is nothing at all," said one man.

"Nothing? And how can you spend your morning out for no purpose? Should you not be studying in the yeshiva?" asked Eleazer.

"Well actually, Eleazer, there is an orphan boy who needs to be married."

"Ah, well, in that case – here, have some money."

Eleazer pushed his money on the men, leaving just one penny for himself. Then Eleazer said: "The weather is getting cool, gentlemen. Perhaps this young orphan needs a hat? Here, take mine."

Eleazer gave them his hat, and he turned and walked back toward the main section of the market. Eleazer had the one penny in his pocket, and with this coin, he bought a small packet of oat seed that a seller was giving away because the seed had spoiled. Then Eleazer ben Solomon returned home. At home, he put the oats in the bottom of the grain jar, where it hardly made even a tiny little pile.

When his wife and daughter returned, he reported that a problem had arisen and that now he could not afford to buy the new shoes. "But never fear, my good wife – the Lord is charitable, and He will provide," said Eleazer. Besides, he continued, he had purchased some oats on sale, and now he would use those as a dowry for his daughter. The poor girl began to cry, and she ran from the room. However, Reb Eleazer shrugged his shoulders, and he went to the yeshiva to study.

That afternoon a tremendous rainstorm swept the town. When the sun finally appeared again, there was a rainbow. Eleazer's daughter felt better, and she went into the pantry to see her father's dowry of oats. As she opened the cupboard door, oats, oats, and more oats spilled out upon the floor. The entire cupboard was filled to overflowing with oats, and on top of the oat jar were seven gold coins. The daughter could not believe her eyes. She felt light and happy, and she ran out the front door of their house. As she passed the *mezuzah* on the doorpost, she touched it gently and, then she kissed her fingers and skipped away. Quickly she sped to her father in the yeshiva, and she said to him: "Father, come home immediately! Then you can see what your friend the good Lord God has done for us!"

What is that, Rabbi? Well, my grandmother said that when Eleazer returned home, he looked at the vast pile of oats and at the seven gold coins, and he praised the good Lord God, the most Holy of Holies; then, he gave all the oats and the gold coins to charity. Many years later, Eleazer died, a happy man—my grandmother said that charity makes you happy, especially when you are old. As the Talmud reminds us:

> Go into the world and occupy yourselves with charity;
> then you will be worthy of reaching old age,
> and when finally you do become old and gray,
> you will also be content.

o, Rabbi, I was just resting my eyes. Please, join me here by the stove. (I think that you will be too warm on that bench: try the one nearer to the wall.) An old man like me can doze forever by a warm stove; I suppose that is because I am thin.

What? Well, I am referring to the scriptural proverb: "Love sleep, and you will end in poverty – but keep your eyes opened, and you will eat your fill." Undoubtedly, the proverb means that if you do not eat enough, then you will become like me and you will love sleep. You do not think that is logical? Well, it may not be logical, but it is certainly holy because it is from the Scriptures. And my grandmother told me: "Be holy, say your prayers devoutly, my golden young man, and it will go well with you in the other world." She repeated that on many a morning, amen. Grandmother also said that one should be careful not to forget anything when dressing dead bodies. What did she mean? Obviously, Rabbi, she was referring to the famous torn sleeve incident in Cologne.

No, no – do not get up on my account, Rabbi: I was just resting my eyes a moment. I was resting and musing. . . . Well, to tell you the truth, Rabbi, I was remembering Rabbi Asher ben Yehiel's grandfather.

You see, six months after his death (on the seventeenth of *Tishri*, during the middle of the Feast of the Tabernacles), this old man appeared to his daughter Miriam at midnight one Sabbath eve; the grandfather hovered in her bedroom and he warned her of bad weather. (No, I am not inventing this, Rabbi—my grandmother swore that this is exactly what she had heard.)

The old man appeared as a vague mist, and he said: "My good daughter Miriam, hurry and get up. Take your family and leave. There will be a flood."

Now, the weather had been fine and warm, and Miriam was a bit sleepy, so she just turned over in bed. But the old man floated to the other side of the room. "Miriam, Miriam," he whispered, "get up. A terrible storm is coming, and the house is in danger."

Miriam opened her eyes, but the spirit was gone. She wrapped a robe around her, and she looked out the window. Clouds were beginning to swirl over the moon, and there was a strange cool feel to the air. So Miriam woke the children, she put on their clothes, and then she took them to her sister's house in the middle of the night. The sister said: "What is going on, Miriam? What are you doing here at this hour?"

"Father suddenly appeared to me tonight, Hannah. He warned me that my house would be flooded."

"That was just a nightmare," said the sister.

"It may have been a dream, but I am not certain," said Miriam, "and, Hannah, there is something strange in the air tonight."

"Well, it is too late to be wandering about—come in and stay the night."

Sure enough, Rabbi, the next morning brought a terrible rainstorm. Lightning and thunder slashed and flashed. Rain fell in sheets, and one wall of Miriam's house was washed away. All of her bedrooms were flooded, and the children may well have been killed had they not fled in the night. This is a good example of the strength of love, Rabbi: as my grandmother pointed out, a father's first love is his children and then come his grandchildren, amen.

One of these well-loved grandchildren was, of course, Rabbi Asher himself. Picking up and hurrying about became a way of life to Asher—hasty travel was a feature of his childhood, and his family developed a history of fleeing from place to place. As he moved around,

Asher studied in many different yeshivas. Eventually, he became a student of the great Rabbi Meir of Rothenburg, of blessed memory. When Rabbi Meir was later imprisoned, the general climate was extremely uncomfortable for Jews in Germany; at that time, Rabbi Asher left Cologne because of his fear of the authorities, and he settled in the city of Toledo in Spain.

A great many Jews were leaving then, but King Rudolph (the emperor of Germany) hoped to keep most of the Jews in Cologne so that they would continue to pay their yearly taxes. Therefore, in the first year of Asher's residence in Spain, Rudolph sent him a written communication: "To–Mr. Asher Yehiel," said the formal letter. "We invite you to return to Cologne. In this regard, I have instructed fifty officers to meet you at the German frontier; they will give you safe-conduct. We hope that you and your fellow Jews will remain in Germany, which is a fine country for an industrious people such as yourselves. From–Rudolph of Hapsburg, Emperor of Germany." And the letter was affixed with the official seal of the Emperor of Germany. Of course, Asher was tempted: one always hopes to live in one's childhood home. But in the face of the frequent ill-treatment of the Jews in Germany, Asher could not bring himself to go back.

So Rabbi Asher settled into Toledo. There, he continued in his strong opposition to secular culture. He did not like casual dress. He frowned on slang expressions. Most of all, he was upset by modern science; he thought that science was incompatible with a holy life. Today's young men, thought Rabbi Asher, give quick and simple answers to deep and complex questions. Does a description of the movement of the planets help one to understand *why* the good Lord God (blessed be He) actually created planets in the first place? Should a mortal be able to heal a man whom the Almighty Holy One decided, in His unknowable wisdom, to afflict with disease? And what of these new and more deadly weapons of war? Can any man think that these are better aides to life than are the sacred understandings of God's Holy words?

Asher looked carefully at the men in his yeshiva in Toledo. How could the pious Jews in southern France and in Spain occupy themselves with subjects outside of the Talmud? asked Asher ben Yehiel. Asher devoutly thanked his Creator, the good Lord God (blessed be He), that He had protected Asher from the baneful influence of science.

I am afraid, said Asher repeatedly, that there is some profane miasma in the warm climates. It is the German Jews and the Jews in northern France who have inherited the devout will and the pious humble wisdom that come down to us from the time of the destruction of the Temple (may it be rebuilt speedily, amen).

Rabbi Asher's antipathy to secular culture had always been with him, even in Cologne. Grandmother told me that one time, when Asher was still the head rabbi in Cologne, a rather worldly member of the congregation, a man named Jedaya ben Abraham, died quite unexpectedly. Jedaya was a voracious reader; he spent all his meager moneys on books and manuscripts, and he left behind a large and wonderful library of very beautiful books. His family was poor, his children were hungry and in need of shoes, and so his widow decided to sell the books to the Gentiles in the surrounding parishes.

When the Jews heard that these treasures were leaving the Jewish community, they were very upset. Jedaya had had Spanish manuscripts by Hivi of Balkh and by Hushiel and by Hushiel's son Hananeel of Babylonia. There were books by Nissim ben Jacob of Kairawan and by Samuel the Nagid of Spain. There was poetry by Solomon ibn Gabirol and Hafz al-Quti and Behai ibn Paquda of Saragossa. Jedaya also had rare copies of French literature including commentaries by Gershom ben Judah (the "Light of Exile") and his pupils Jacob ben Yaqar and Moses of Narbonne, all predecessors of Rashi. Of course, there were works by Rashi himself and by Maimonides. How could the children sell the wonderful scholarly books of their father to the heathen Gentiles? What else did the Jews have to treasure but their literate culture?

Neighbors complained, but Jedaya's wife and his children replied: "We are very poor. We needed the money. But we, too, were uncertain whether we should sell these unusual books. Therefore, we first consulted with Rabbi Asher. The Rabbi looked at all the books—he studied them carefully; he found books on astronomy, medicine, and pharmacy, and he declared most of them to be too secular and too distracting. 'Keep to the holy word. Study the Torah and the Talmud, first and last and always,' said the Rabbi. Therefore, he allowed us to sell them all. In fact, he encouraged us to disperse the entire library, because he felt that it posed a danger to the Jewish community."

What is that, Rabbi? The tale of the torn sleeve? Yes, yes—I was just coming to that. You see, it was just after the sale of these books that yet another poor scholar, Mannes ben Joshua, died in the Cologne community. At that time, said my grandmother, the shammas of the synagogue was a devout man named Baruch ben Isaac. Baruch was a simple man, and like his master Rabbi Asher, Baruch attended only to the Holy Scriptures, and he turned a deaf ear to the airy talk of bright young men – the young yeshiva scholars whose talk was filled with "Avempace," "aviaries," "Acherons," "aconites," "Averroes," and "avocets."

Baruch ben Isaac kept the yeshiva clean, he kept the rituals orderly, and he assisted in all the burials of the dead. One day, old Mannes ben Joshua died and, as usual, Reb Baruch accompanied the body to the grave. The next morning, when Reb Baruch went to the synagogue to open it up for the early morning prayers, he saw at the door a man dressed in a shroud with a wreath around his head.

No one else was about, and Reb Baruch was frightened. What manner of demon was this? Baruch ben Isaac turned to run away, but the man in the shroud called after him: "Do not be afraid, Baruch. Come here."

Baruch stopped and he looked at the spirit: "Are you not Mannes ben Joshua, the old man whom I accompanied to the grave yesterday?"

"Yes," said Mannes, "and I must thank you, good shammas. In the Talmud it is written: 'He that is gracious to the poor gives alms unto the good Lord God (blessed be He).' And, my fine friend, there is certainly none so poor as the dead, amen."

"Amen," said Baruch, and he came a bit closer. "Of course you are quite welcome, Reb Mannes." The two men were silent for a moment. Reb Baruch did not know whether to open the synagogue in the presence of the dead man, so he said: "Good Mannes, it is also written in the Talmud that to assist at a funeral is a duty of the most sacred importance. Even the study of the Torah may be interrupted in order to carry a coffin."

"That is true, my shammas," replied Mannes ben Joshua. "Moreover, if you see a poor dead soul being carried to its last resting place and if you do not join in the burial procession, then you are committing a sin. We know this from the scriptural proverb":

He who mocks the poor,
Blasphemes his Maker.

"And, I repeat, Baruch – there is none so poor as the dead."

"Yes, amen," said Baruch. Baruch stood uncomfortably by the locked building: "Tell me, Reb Mannes (if it is not too bold of me to ask): How are you getting along in the other world?"

"Oh, I am getting along fairly well – actually, they seem to respect me in the Great Hereafter."

"That is good to hear," said Baruch.

"Yes – you see, Reb Baruch, when I was a living man I arose early and I read my prayers and my blessings with great devotion, every single morning. Even when I was sick, I would manage to tie on my *tefilla* and to say the holy benedictions. When I was weak, when my head ached, when I was depressed and sad, I nonetheless repeated the holy words. At times, I had to force myself. But in the end, I was happy. Now I lightly say the blessings in Paradise; my soul is at peace, and I rest easily."

"Ah yes, amen," said Reb Baruch. The spirit wavered in the breeze, there was a quiet morning silence, and Baruch ben Isaac looked at his feet. Then he looked at the spirit and he asked: "O spirit, let me ask you a question: What does the wreath on your head mean?"

The dead man said. "This wreath? It is made of the good holy herbs of Paradise; it is woven of myrtle and wild olive twigs, and it keeps the evil demons from doing me harm as I visit here in this dangerous mortal world, a world thickly filled with all manner of dybbuks and ghouls."

Again there was silence. Baruch looked down the alleyway behind him, but no one was coming. Mannes ben Joshua continued to hover at the door of the old synagogue, so Baruch said: "My good Mannes, is there something more that I can do for you? I must say that it is not often that the dead return here to our humble house of study."

"Actually," answered Mannes ben Joshua. "I have come to ask a small favor."

Baruch felt worried. "Yes?" he asked. "What favor is that?"

"When you put the shroud on me yesterday, you tore one of my sleeves," said Mannes.

"True," said Baruch, "I am sorry. If I remember correctly, it is just a small rip."

"Do not feel badly, Baruch," said the dead man. "However, remember the part in the Talmud that says: 'It must always be the practice of the living to attend to the needs of the dead.'"

"I remember," said Baruch.

"Good," said Mannes. "Now, my fine shammas, I must confess that I am ashamed to be seen by the other spirits. They all have clean white robes with not a speck or a spot or a spiven of dirt, and everyone's shroud is even and neat and there are no holes or rips or tears. Will you mend this sleeve for me? I will feel happier, my friend—I will rest more easily for ever more, amen."

"Certainly," said Baruch, "I will do that now."

"Thank you," said the dead man, and then he disappeared.

Then Baruch ben Isaac opened the front door of the yeshiva, he got a needle and a thread, and he went to the cemetery. Baruch uncovered the grave and he opened the coffin. Carefully, he mended the torn sleeve on the white shroud of Mannes ben Joshua. Then, Baruch brushed a few bits of dirt from Mannes's white robes and he closed the coffin, he replaced the dirt over the grave, and he patted it down gently on top. Finally, the old shammas walked back to the yeshiva, to start another day of study.

What, Rabbi? Yes, that is the whole story; there is no more.

abbi, I am glad to see you here alone. I want to apologize for my outburst during the service this evening. It was just that Reb Anton was twisting a piece of string, and he had turned it into a mass of knots. Yes, yes, I know that it was absent-minded fiddling, but in the olden days, in the strict and pious days of our fathers, Reb Anton would have been ordered to leave and never to return. The Talmud explictly lists the thirty-nine forbidden acts for the Sabbath, and that list includes knotting and unknotting; we must be severely religious on the Sabbath.

What is that, Rabbi? The Book of Isaiah says that we must: "Call the Sabbath a day of joy and a delight"? Ah yes, well that must be a more recent interpretation. My grandmother pointed out that in the olden days every rule was strictly enforced. For instance, you know the prohibition against going out carrying a burden on the Sabbath? The German Rabbis said that this forbade even walking about with a gold tooth in one's mouth. Oh yes, I am not inventing this, Rabbi.

But this strictness just made life all the more sweet and poignant: a strict Sabbath hallows life. In fact, the Talmud tells us that an additional soul is given to each man on the eve of the Sabbath (and it is then taken from him the next night, on the termination of the

Sabbath). This means that strict observance of the most holy day of the week heightens the power of the soul. That is why the Sabbath was so important to my grandmother, and it was because of the Sabbath that grandmother told me of the famous river letter of Rabbi Petahiah of Regensburg.

Exactly, Rabbi–that was the Petahiah ben Jacob (the brother of Rabbi Isaac "the Wise" of Prague), who undertook a tour of the entire world. Eventually, Petahiah wrote about his adventures in a book *Sivuv ha-Olam* ("Around the World"). What is that? Well, if you will just be patient a moment, then I will tell you what rivers and Rabbi Petahiah have to do with the Sabbath. Now, all of this adventure took place before the time that Asher ben Yehiel was the chief rabbi in Cologne.

As you remember, Asher ben Yehiel feared the persecutions inflicted on the German Jews in those dark Middle Ages, so after a time Asher fled Germany and went to Spain, where he was then made the chief rabbi of Toledo. Rabbi Asher left Cologne hurriedly and with no possessions, and the Jewish community of Toledo decided to give him a regular salary. Up until then, most rabbis made their livings by having another, secular profession, like medicine. But Rabbi Asher said that he was a rabbi and only a rabbi. In fact, he hated secular callings. Asher's sole interest was the Talmud. He was a man of austere piety, he was profound, and he was narrow.

Asher was a determined opponent of the study of non-Jewish philosophy. How, he asked in wonderment, can Jews–pious, devout, religious Jews–bother with anything other than the Talmud? Daily, Rabbi Asher thanked his Creator that He had protected Asher from the baneful influence of science. When in Toledo, Asher claimed that the Jews of Spain and of southern France had a weak and superficial knowledge of the Torah and the Talmud. It is the northern Jews who maintained the devout piety passed down from the time of the destruction of the Temple, said Asher. . . . What is that, Rabbi? Yes, rivers and Sabbaths are about to come up–please be patient.

Before Asher left Cologne, he spent all his time writing and reading, studying the Torah and the Talmud in the little back room of the yeshiva. There, since time immemorial, the rabbis passed hours and hours working and thinking and arguing with themselves. Above the back study room was a loft for storage. One day, when he was rooting around among the manuscripts in the loft, Rabbi Asher found a letter from Rabbi Petahiah of Regensburg to one of Asher's predecessors, Rabbi Abraham ben Alexander, Achselrad of Cologne:

"*My dear Rabbi Abraham*—(began the letter)

"I have just met a fine young man, a Jew from Frankfort. He has agreed to carry this letter to my good friend, Rabbi Benjamin of Frankfort, who I am certain will then arrange to transport it to you. I write to wish you and your family well, to convey my fondest greetings to all the Jews of your blessed community in Cologne, and to praise the good Lord God (blessed be He) and His Almighty Name for ever and ever, amen.

"I will not trouble you with the details of my many wagon rides and my subsequent sea voyages. Suffice it to say that they safely brought me here to the Oriental regions that are so near to the great Holy Land, the Holy Land where someday the Messiah shall return and deliver us and resurrect all souls and rebuild the Temple on Zion, amen. Now, I write in order to record for you the most remarkable details of a waterway; this is a river that, you will recall, you and I heard of one time at the spring fair in Worms. Yes, good Abraham, it is that wondrous river story that you and I marveled at but never believed: I can now report that it is, in fact, true—praise the Lord and amen.

"Needless to say, my old friend, I have had many, many adventures in arriving here. I hope—with the good Lord willing—to relate these to you in person. Let me just say that after setting sail from Venice, we arrived at Jaffa here in Palestine. (Jaffa is called "Joppa" by the ship captains, and it is called "Yafa" by the local Arabs.) This is an old city. It is a city of pirates and sea monsters, and apparently the Christian Saint Peter lived here; supposedly, he had many visions, and it is said that here he once resurrected a benevolent widow (named Tabitha) after her mistaken death. The town of Jaffa can be seen from far asea because it sits on a rounded hillock. The harbor itself is quite small, and only moderate-sized craft can fit inside the natural breakwater of reefs. We were fortunate to arrive in calm weather, and small oriental boats from the town ferried us to the shore.

"From Jaffa, I traveled by camel and by cart southward and inland one day's journey, to the town of Jamnia. You would know this town as the holy Jabneth (the Arabs call it Yebna); it is, of course, the town where the Sanhedrin set up the great rabbinic system of study after the destruction of Jerusalem. Jamnia is on the border between Dan and Judah. As you come into town, you see garden after garden of olive trees. The village itself sits on a sandy hill; many fine farms of fig, citron, orange, and olive groves roll away to the north, the east has mainly vineyards, and there are only sand dunes to the west. This is a Jewish town with a fine old yeshiva, but there is also a rather well-known church that was built recently during the Crusades. I spent two glorious nights here arguing and studying from old versions of the Talmud. These manuscripts have been preserved in the Jamnia synagogue, and the glory of the good Lord God radiated down upon us like the warm desert sands and the fine and gentle holy sun, amen.

"The next morning was gleaming and bright. A group of scholars and rabbis was delegated to guide me to Jerusalem. The rabbis told me that we were going to take an abstruse and circuitous route, in order that they might show me one of the most holy of sights. We left in a caravan with a number of Persian friends and guides. I must say, Abraham, that I am quite taken with the Persians that I have met: they are a wonderful race. Persians are easygoing, and they try to make everything pleasant. Each one to whom I have been introduced was hospitable and obliging and welcomed foreigners. What a difference from the native Germans. The Persians whom I have seen show a tremendous deference for mothers and especially for grandmothers, and they are kind and indulgent to their children. The little ones dress just like adults, in miniature shirts and robes – but the strangest thing, Rabbi Abraham, is that the Persian mothers dress little girls as boys, and they dress little boys as girls. Until about the age of seven or eight years, the costumes remain reversed; I think that this custom is to keep away the Evil Eye or to fool Dumah, the Angel of Death, praise the good Lord God, amen.

"There is one Oriental trait that is very striking: the Persians are in no hurry whatsoever. It was only after the local rabbis became visibly impatient that finally we set off on our journey. I would say, from my small experience here, that procrastination is an innate Persian attribute. 'Tomorrow, my friend' is the universal answer to any proposition, and 'tomorrow' really means an indefinite delay. This shows up in their legal affairs, for they dislike any written contracts that bind the parties to some fixed date. On breaking a contract, a Persian always appeals for (and then he expects to receive) repeated delays without penalty and with endless days of grace.

"In spite of this leisurely view of time schedules, we managed to leave Jamnia within a few hours of our initially intended departure time. After a full half day's dusty travel, we had crossed two rivers; then we came across another river, a beautiful full river, running strong and clean and blue. There were reeds aplenty along its shore, it was filled with fish, and birds flew overhead and waded along the banks. I would estimate that at the place where we stopped that afternoon, the river was perhaps one hundred meters wide.

"Now, good Abraham, this was on a Friday afternoon. My companions immediately began to set up tents for the evening. 'Are we not going to press on to Jerusalem?' I asked. 'I would dearly love to celebrate the Sabbath in that holy city.'

" 'We must remain here until tomorrow,' they answered. However, they would not tell me why. I was puzzled, but I helped them to prepare for the Sabbath. There were no women with us, so we ourselves set up candles and oil lamps and recited: 'Blessed are You, O Lord our God, King of the Universe, Who has sanctified us by Your commandments and Who has commanded us to light the Sabbath lamps.' We prepared a table, we set out two loaves of bread (covering them with a fine linen cloth), and we stood an empty cup close to the wine jug. Ah, my old friend Abraham, how reverent it is to celebrate the Sabbath under the glorious stars of our good Lord God (blessed be He) in the Holy Land. May you, too, have this fine experience before Resurrection, amen.

"After all of our benedictions and before we retired to bed, we sat around a fire, and one of the old rabbis said":

> Do you know, my friends, that even the sufferers in Gehinnom enjoy a respite every Sabbath. The Talmud reminds us of this with a dialogue between the Roman governor, Tineius Rufus, and the great Rabbi Akiva.
>
> First, the Roman asked: "How is the Sabbath different from any other day?"
>
> And Rabbi Akiva answered: "Tell me, sir – how are you different from any other man?"

Then Rufus said: "Well, Rabbi, the Emperor decided to honor me."

So Rabbi Akiva said: "In just the same manner, the Holy One (blessed be He) decided to honor the Sabbath."

"How can you prove that to me?"

"Have you heard of the river Sabbation?" asked the Rabbi.

"No," said the Roman.

"Well, Governor Rufus, the Sabbation is so strong that boulders are rushed downstream for six days of the week. But on the Sabbath, the entire waterflow disappears, because the pious river rests on the Sabbath."

"That sounds like an old grandmother's fable," replied Rufus.

"Perhaps," said the Rabbi, "but you can prove the strength of the Sabbath and its great holiness yourself, Governor."

"Oh–and how is that?" asked the Roman.

"Any necromancer can demonstrate this fact to you. For a necromancer, the dead will ascend from Gehinnom all the days of the week, but no one can call forth the spirits on the Sabbath. You can test my statement by calling up the spirit of your dead father."

"We will see," said the Roman. The next day, the Roman governor went to a Chaldean necromancer, and he had this wizard call up the dead spirit of Rufus's father. Then, Rufus found that his father's spirit could be contacted every day that week. However, on the Sabbath the necromancer could not make the spirit appear–although on the following day, a Sunday, the spirit again arose.

"Tell me, Father," asked Rufus to his father's spirit on that Sunday, "have you become a Jew since your death? Why did you appear to me on every other day of the week but not on the Jewish Sabbath?"

Then the spirit of the father answered: "My son, on earth one may choose voluntarily to observe or not to observe the Sabbath. On the other hand, here one is compelled to keep the Sabbath holy for ever, amen."

"And is there, then, no work where you reside?"

"Oh, there is endless work and heavy toil, young man. However, all spirits rest on the Sabbath. It is the universal rule that the good Lord God set from the very beginning. First, the Heaven and the earth were created with all their mighty throng, and on the sixth day the good Lord

God completed all the creation that He had been doing. Then, on the seventh day He stopped: on the seventh day, the Lord ceased from all His work. God, the King of the Universe, blessed the seventh day and He made it holy, because on that day He finished all the work that He had set Himself to do."

"My father, you are beginning to sound like a Jew."

"My son, in the Great Hereafter we are all, in a sense, Jews."

"The next morning we arose early to pray. Something strange was in the air, Abraham – I was struck by the silence. Where once the air had been filled with the rush of waters and with the wingbeats of many birds, there was now nothing at all. Yes, Abraham, my childhood friend, it is exactly as we had heard at that magical fair when we were young and when the entire world was a wonderment. Here I was at the great River Sabbation, the river that completely stops running in pious devotion on each Sabbath. On that Sabbath morning, the stream bed was dry, the fish and the birds were gone, and the reeds were all fallen over. No turnstones or tanglepickers soared overhead, no knotroot grass flourished on the banks, and no waters could be seen either upstream or downstream at all.

"I was stunned – and my companions swore that this magical event happened every single Sabbath. Normally, the Sabbation is a strong and vital river, Abraham, but one day each week it is empty and it is filled only with sand and with stones. When it runs, its current is strong, it has plenty of water, and its streams rush and gush over the boulders – just as Titus Caeasar has reported: the springs of the mighty Sabbation run boldly for six days together. Then, suddenly on the seventh day, the whole river dries up and the springs disappear. But on the very next day, the river rushes and flows along, just as it did before; on Sunday the waters roar, the fish and birds teem, and the reeds grow green and strong. Men swear that the Sabbation has kept to this schedule ever since it was first seen. Therefore, it has been called the Sabbatic River, for it rests and it keeps sacred the Sabbath of the Jews, hallelujah, amen.

"So, Abraham son of Alexander, think of me now as you read this letter in your holy study in Cologne. Think of me, and remember the magic days of our childhood. I write to tell you, my friend, that magic is truly abroad in the world; magic is the holy spirit of the good

Lord God (blessed be He), Who gives wondrous gifts to us as children in our youth and Who redeems us again as children in our old age—hallelujah and amen, good Abraham.

*Your childhood friend,*
*Petahiah, the son of Jacob"*

abbi, I am glad to see you here tonight: I need your advice—although it is really a small matter. This afternoon one of the youngsters in the study hall put his shirt on backwards for a joke. Now, my grandmother always said that if you reverse your shirt then you will have prophetic dreams. (Also, she told me that sitting on a broom will induce stark visions of the future, in the dead of the night.) I warned the young man, but he and the other students only laughed. Dreams are sacred, Rabbi: they are not things with which one trifles. If you are sick, then a vivid dream means that you will get well; whereas, if you dream of a hoe or an axe (with a handle) or of an elephant or of unripe dates or of turnip heads or of things blue or of owls and bats, then you are destined for misfortune. After all these years of sitting in the study rooms during lessons, Rabbi, I have learned a bit of Talmud, and I recall what the great Sages decided about dreams. The Almighty One communicates with us, his children, through dreams: "I have hidden My face from Israel," says the Talmud about the good Lord God (blessed be He); "therefore, I will communicate with the Israelites through their dreams."

I know that you remember these sections of the Talmud, so you will recall how it continues. The Sages say: "An uninterpreted dream is like an unread letter – it has no effect. An unread dream is neither good nor evil. In order for it to operate, a dream must be unfurled. Moreover, no dream is fulfilled in every detail: do not completely fear your evil dreams, and do not completely rejoice in your good dreams.

"There are some general principles concerning dreams," continue the Sages. "First, dreams are interactions with the Lord, and someone who goes for seven days without a dream is not being appropriately pious. Second, good dreams are not squandered on good men; likewise, dreams of warning are not wasted on the bad. Generally, when one has had a dream, the next morning he does not know the meaning of what he has seen. Therefore, dreams must be interpreted.

"If you are a good man with a clear conscience and if you have had a strong and vivid dream and if you are feeling depressed about that dream, then follow this advice. Find three holy scholars, sit them down, and say to them: 'Gentlemen, I have had a vivid dream.'

"The scholars should respond: 'Was it a good dream?'

"Then say to them: 'Yes – it must have been a good dream, because I am a pious man, I have a clear conscience, and the dream was sent by the holy Lord God (blessed be He).'

"Then the scholars will say: 'Very well – good is the dream, and good may it ever be. May the Merciful Almighty God turn all your dreams toward good.'

"And finally, the scholars should end by saying: 'It shall be decreed seven times – good is the dream and may it ever be good, amen.'"

Yes, *seven* times, Rabbi – my grandmother always reminded me: "Do a good deed seven times, my golden one, and that will make it holy." She said that almost daily. Did you ever hear her? You never met my grandmother, Rabbi? Ah, more is the pity, for she was a fine woman. She told me that three types of dreams are always fulfilled: a morning dream, a dream that your friend has about you, and a dream that is interpreted in the midst of another dream. (Some people also say that a dream that is repeated on the next night will then come true, but my grandmother did not hold to that thinking. "To be certain, a dream must be repeated seven times," said Grandmother.)

What is that, Rabbi? Certainly there is more to tell: I was just resting my eyes a moment. Now let me see, what was I saying? Yes, dreams were very important to my grandmother. I remember her story about Salomo ben Jacob, whose friend dreamed a strange and vivid dream once in the synagogue, when they were both young men. Later, Salomo grew up to became a renowned scholar – eventually, he was the chief rabbi of the Cologne yeshiva – but this dream took place many years earlier, long, long ago:

Once upon a time, said my grandmother, when Salomo was just a little boy in the yeshiva, his best friend was Aaron ben Nathan ha-Levi. One lazy afternoon the two boys were alone in the main prayer hall of the old Cologne synagogue. They had said all that they had to say to each other, they had played all that they had to play together, and they were leaning against the benches in a far corner of the room, idly thinking each his own little thoughts. Aaron closed his eyes, and after a while, Aaron ben Nathan ha-Levi fell asleep. Salomo looked at his friend; Aaron was snoring there on the floor, fine and easy and calm. "What a strange thing is this sleep," thought Salomo. And then with no warning, suddenly out of Aaron's mouth flew a little white moth.

The moth fluttered out, and it landed on Aaron's shirt. Salomo bent over to look more closely. The moth had pure white powdery wings, and each wing had seven fine white stripes. The moth began to hop and to walk down Aaron's shirt, and then it crept along his pants. "This is even more strange than sleep itself," thought Salomo. Down over the sleeping boy hopped and walked the little white moth, and when it came to Aaron's toe, it jumped up into the air and it began to fly. Aaron's little white moth flew through the prayer hall filled with wooden benches, it fluttered past the twelve stained glass windows with their colored lions and snakes, it bumped the air currents beside the Holy Ark made of stone, and it flew out the open front door of the old synagogue in Cologne, one lazy afternoon long, long ago.

"Curiouser and curiouser," thought Salomo, and he got up and followed the moth. The little white moth flew through the courtyard, it wafted down the alleyway between the houses, and it fluttered out into Judengasse Street. Then the moth turned left down Judengasse, flitting and floating in the breezes. It passed the intersection of Engegasse Street, and it fluttered on and on until it came to an iron fence. There, the moth alighted and it began to climb the bars of the fence, from rung to rung, slowly and easily. When it came to the top of the fence, it continued right on, and it climbed down the other side. Salomo stood watching every turn that the moth was taking.

On the other side of the fence was a yard, and in the yard was the skull of an old cow, which had been sitting there looking blankly at the world for years and years and years. In through one of the eye holes went the moth, and then Salomo could see nothing more of the moth for many minutes. Salomo looked at the skull, and he looked at the sky. Light clouds passed far above; turnstones and tanglepickers soared on high. A few people hurried by on Judengasse Street. A baby cried in the distance.

"I wonder," thought Salomo, "whether Aaron is still asleep?"

Salomo was about to return to the yeshiva, when the moth appeared again; this time, it came out between the teeth of the skull where there was an open space. The moth crept out of the skull and it jumped into the air and it flew back to the iron fence. There it alighted and it climbed up the bars of the fence, from rung to rung, slowly and easily, up one side of the fence and then down the other. Again, Salomo followed as the moth flitted and floated down Judengasse Street toward the yeshiva. The little white moth passed Engegasse Street and, turning neither right nor left, it fluttered to the alleyway leading to the synagogue. Fascinated, Salomo watched every move of this little insect. Through the alleyway the moth wafted with the breezes, and then it went into the front door of the yeshiva. The moth fluttered past the Holy Ark made of stone, it floated by the twelve stained glass windows with their colored lions and snakes, and it flew down the main prayer hall filled with worn wooden benches.

Next, the little white moth dropped right into the mouth of Aaron ben Nathan ha-Levi, and it was never seen again. Salomo sat down next to his sleeping friend, and in a moment Aaron awoke. "My goodness, Salomo, have I had a strange and vivid dream," said Aaron.

"Oh," said Salomo, "and what is it that you dreamt?"

"You will never believe this, Salomo. You and I were out walking; we were playing in a vast and beautiful hall filled with golden-colored lights and holy stones and long, long benches. Then I lost sight of you, and I walked for miles and miles. But you know, Salomo, it was quite wonderful: it was not like ordinary walking, it was almost like floating on air. After a while, I came to a strange iron hill made of smooth bars like a huge ladder. Up I climbed on one side, and then down I climbed on the other.

"All along the way I called out to you: 'Salomo, Salomo – where are you?' But you did not answer, and I was alone. Still I walked on and on, until I came to a big bright white house and I went up to it. The house was round like a hill, and there seemed to be no door; however, there was an empty round doorway. I stopped, and I looked. May the good Lord God (blessed be He) save my soul, I thought, what sort of awesome place is this? There was no *mezuzah* on the doorpost. Do I dare go inside?

"This is what I really dreamed, Salomo. Shall I go on?"

"Yes, yes – please do," said Salomo.

"All right. Well, my friend, I was brave and I was bold, and I went in. But there was no one alive or dead to be seen in this strange round white house. I walked from room to room to room. All was empty; I began to be overcome by fear. A cool tingling was in my back, and my legs began to tighten. I thought that perhaps I would never find my way out. Where were you, Salomo? Would I spend the rest of my days wandering that fearsome white palace? I was groping my way along, through empty hall after hall after hall, until at last there was an opening in the walls: finally, I had reached the back doorway. Quickly, I hopped and I jumped out. I ran, ran, ran over to the neat iron mountain and, without looking back, I climbed up one side and down the other. And then like the wind, I ran back and back until I came again to the golden holy land, and suddenly I awoke and here I am reunited with you at last, Salomo, my friend. And glad I am to be awake, amen," said Aaron ben Nathan ha-Levi.

Yes, Rabbi, that is all – that is the entire dream that my grandmother told me about. In fact, said my grandmother, it was this very experience that led Rabbi Salomo to say in his old age: "I once knew a boy whose life was a holy dream, as white as a little moth sent from the mouth of the good Lord God, blessed be He for ever and ever, amen."

ello, Rabbi, I will be with you in a moment – I cannot leave until every tablecloth is folded, otherwise the day has not ended properly. There, now I am finished at last and I can sit next to you by the stove. Watch that coal, Rabbi – it flew out like an arrow. Have you ever dreamt of flying? My most wondrous dreams are of flying over housetops and streets and trees, gliding along. It is a very religious experience; as the psalmist says: "O my soul, flee to the mountains like a bird." Do you think that our old souls will ever fly about, Rabbi? If so, then undoubtedly we will fly to Zion when the Messiah arrives, amen.

Souls must be able to fly when they are young – I can picture all the little baby souls flying among the clouds. My grandmother said that in that great cloud Heaven of Aravot all the waiting souls and spirits are crowded, hovering and floating together. They watch the unborn babies below. Which little baby body will pop out next? To which body will the next soul be assigned? Some of those souls must be impatient by now, since the good Lord God created them all once upon a time, long, long ago; and of course the Messianic era will not dawn until all these unborn souls have had their term of existence here on this clayey earth.

Yes, Rabbi, a soul is certainly a light and wondrous gift from God.

Grandmother said that only when a man realizes how precious is this endowment can his life be suffused with holiness and guided by the Divine will. That is why the first morning prayer is:

> Dear God, Lord of the Universe, the soul that You have given to me is pure. You have set it within me, and You will take it from me —but I know that it will be restored to me in the Great Hereafter. So long as my holy soul is within me, I will give thanks unto You, O Lord my God and the God of my fathers and my grandfathers, Sovereign of all worlds, Lord of all souls. Blessed are You, O Lord of the Universe, Who restores souls unto dead bodies, amen.

Of course that jubilant day of restoration will finally dawn when the Messiah returns and when a great trumpet blast is heard throughout the earth and when all our souls will fly through the clouds once again.

Grandmother told me that the Messiah will come in the springtime. What is that, Rabbi? Well, it is written in the Scriptures (in Zechariah): "On that great day there shall be neither heat nor cold nor frost"—so Resurrection must be destined for the spring. My grandmother said that it was just such a mild springtime evening when a strange thin traveler arrived in the back room of the Cologne yeshiva where Rabbi Salomo was working.

As you know, Rabbi, all manner of barefoot and pious pilgrims came through Germany each week from the Holy Land in those olden days. Strange men appeared at all times of the day and night in the Cologne yeshiva; for, in medieval Europe, wandering pilgrims were constantly returning from the Holy Land. These travelers came wide-eyed and worn, and they came filled with tales of ever new potential Messiahs. All Jews remained hopeful: the Messiah was never far from their thoughts. Therefore, there was always a bit of wonder about the appearance of even the most pale, sandaled, and ill-clad of these peregrinating specters, like the one who appeared to Rabbi Salomo one springtime evening in Cologne.

You see, Rabbi, once upon a time (said my grandmother) there lived a very pious scholar named Salomo ben Jacob, who was the chief rabbi of Cologne. Exactly, Rabbi—this was the same Rabbi Salomo ben Jacob who wrote the eighteen liturgical poems about the Sabbath that have since been lost. As you know, Rabbi Salomo preferred working alone; so he could often be found in the back room of the old Cologne yeshiva late at night. One night, while writing a poem, Salomo looked up and he saw a thin, long-haired man standing in the doorway.

"Yes?" said the Rabbi.

"Good evening, Rabbi," said the stranger. "My name is Ezra. May I come in?"

"Certainly," said Rabbi Salomo, and he moved a pile of papers so that Ezra could sit on a bench by the wall.

The two men sat silently for a while. Then the Rabbi said: "It is late, but perhaps I can offer you some bread or some cold soup?"

"No thank you, Rabbi," replied Ezra.

Again there was silence. Ezra was staring intently at the Rabbi. Finally, he said: "Ah, good Rabbi, I see that you have a fresh soul."

"I do? What do you mean, young man?"

"I mean: it is clear to me that your soul is new, clean, and direct. Your soul comes straight from Aravot," said Ezra.

The Rabbi tilted his head a bit. "This is what you see?"

"Definitely."

"Have not all souls come from Aravot?" asked Rabbi Salomo.

"Oh, originally they have. But, Rabbi, as you well know, many souls of our fellow men are presently in the process of migrating from body to body, in order to try to recover their purity.

"In the beginning, Rabbi, all souls were created by the good Lord God (blessed be He)—praise the Lord, amen. Originally, all these many souls were bright and clean and pure, and they were destined to enter upon an earthly career. All souls will pass into bodies, and then they will remain connected to these bodies for a certain period of time. Is this not so?"

"Yes, that is what the Sages teach us," said Salomo.

"Exactly, Rabbi," said Ezra. "Now, during its earthly life a soul is subjected to the inevitable trials, tribulations, and tests. Lusty temptations abound. But can the soul remain pure? Can it avoid earthly errors, mortal mars, and temporary taints? Ah, if so, then the soul flies up into the heavens of the Great Hereafter; it ascends purified after death to the great domain of all clean spirits, and it becomes a part of the world of the ten *Sefirot* of the great Lord God (blessed be He)—praise the Lord and amen."

"Ah yes, the ten *Sefirot*," repeated the Rabbi somewhat doubt-fully.

Then Ezra said: "Of course, it is best not to speak too loudly about such secret knowledge, good Rabbi; it is secret knowledge that you and I share silently in our hearts. Anyway, those souls that fail the tests and that become tainted with earthliness – those flawed souls are compelled to return to the bodily life. Eventually, even these souls improve, and they become strong and they repent and after repeated trials they soar aloft to Heaven – hallelujah, amen."

"Amen," said Rabbi Salomo.

There was silence. Ezra closed his eyes, his breathing became strong and regular, and his head nodded. Then suddenly he opened his eyes: "Even the soul of the Messiah."

"Yes?" said Rabbi Salomo.

"Yes, Rabbi, even the soul of the Messiah," repeated Ezra.

"Even the soul of the Messiah?"

"In its aethereal preworldly existence, even the soul of the Messiah abides like the other glorious spirits in the Heavenly realm of the ten *Sefirot*. Of course," said Ezra, "the soul of the Messiah is the last in line, there high in the clouds of Aravot. . . . I see it now. Can you, Rabbi?"

Ezra was staring wide-eyed at the ceiling. The Rabbi looked up. "No," he said, "I am not certain that I can."

"I understand, Rabbi," said Ezra. "You must look way down the line, past all the other souls. Do you see that little golden soul fiddling with its fingers there? That is the second to last spirit in the line. Just beyond is the soul of the Messiah – praise the Lord, hallelujah, and amen."

The Rabbi looked at the dark ceiling, and then he looked at Ezra. "Amen," said Rabbi Salomo.

"With the length of that line of spirits, we clearly have a long wait, Rabbi," said Ezra. "We must wait patiently for the Messiah to come to earth. Then, of course, the great golden jubilee will arrive. All souls, purified and refined, will have returned from earth to Heaven. When the Messiah arrives, we will all be able to fly through the clouds; we will fly high and far away to Zion, under God's white clouds. That is, Rabbi, we will be able to soar when the *true* Messiah arrives. However, the long line of souls that we see bespeaks patience.

"Ah, Rabbi, *patience* I tell you. Now, now, do not interrupt, Rabbi. It is true that we hear tales and that we hear *tales*. But these are not really reports of the true Messiah. Why, remember Alroy. . . . Rabbi, you do not know about Alroy of Amadia? It is a tale from Persia about Menahem ben Solomon, Alroy of Amadia; let me tell it to you:

"David Alroy – also known as Menahem ben Solomon – suddenly appeared in Azerbaijan. He came from the town of Amadia in the mountainous corner of Persia north of Mosul, but his true childhood was shrouded in mystery. Was he really born in Turkestan? Was he the child of nomads? Did he study in a yeshiva? Was he given mystical knowledge? No one knew for certain. One day, however, there he was, standing handsome, clear-minded, and courageous. He spoke quietly with a low rolling voice; he had memorized the Scriptures, he knew the Talmud, and he was fluent in Arabic. Alroy could quote the Koran, and he claimed to have studied in Spain with the two great Moslem philosophers, Averroes and Abu-Bakr Muhammad ibn Yahya (that is, Avempace).

"David Alroy was a man of no small ambition. He declared that he was the true Messiah. The Messiah had returned – and as a base of operations, he needed a stronghold; so Alroy set about to capture the fort in Amadia. Secretly, he wrote to the Jews of the surrounding cities: he wrote to Erbil, Jeziret-ibn-Omar, Julamerk, Khorsabad, Mosul, Rowanduz, Tabriz, and Urmia. He even wrote to the large synagogues in Baghdad, Teheran, and Isfahan. Come in great numbers, he said, and bring swords and knives and other weapons concealed in your clothes.

"The Persian Jews believed Alroy to be the promised Messiah. Officially, they passed the word that David Alroy would deliver a prophetic religious sermon and that the Jews of the region would gather in order to celebrate. Vast throngs filled the town of Amadia: they came on the pretext that a great crowd was to worship with the renowned scholar Rabbi Menahem ben Solomon. Knives and cutlasses were tucked in their muslin cummerbunds and were hidden under shawl-cloth shirts and were folded within long white silk sleeves. At the appointed hour, Alroy appeared on the top of a building. 'Now!' he shouted. 'Storm the castle.' The Jews unveiled their sharp and hidden weapons, and they ran and yelled and stormed the fort, which was captured without incident. David Alroy had come, and he had conquered.

"Locally, Alroy instituted a religious council. The people of Amadia began to live a strict and pious life in which every single daily act had to follow directly from scriptural dictates. The Persian emperor, the Seljuk Sultan, was worried. The Empire of the Seljuk family was essentially military, but their authority over their own officers was so precarious that they only dared to entrust the major positions of command to Turkish slaves. Unfortunately, the Turkish officers were barely loyal to their Persian sovereigns, and they became quite independent locally. In the midst of these many local fiefdoms, David Alroy built a fanatic pocket of resistance in the Persian Empire; his region became independent and autonomous. Would this religious fundamentalism spread? The Seljuk Sultan felt that he had to act, and he devised a plan.

"The Persian Sultan invited David Alroy to meet him in Tabriz, the capital of the province of Azerbaijan. David Alroy traveled there alone. The Seljuk Sultan stroked his thick black beard, he looked across the table at Menahem ben Solomon, Alroy of Amadia, and he proposed that Alroy become a viceroy of the Persian empire. Never! responded Alroy. I am the Messiah of the Jews, he said, quoting the Scriptures from Isaiah":

> O Lord, Your mighty wrath has blazed:
> Your enemies You pursue.
> Soon Your dead shall again be raised,
> Their bodies repaired and new.
>
> They that sleep in earth will wake,
> The dead will fly and shout again.
> Your rains will heal the fatal ache,
> And green fields will bloom with once-dead men.

What was this mystical poetry? thought the Sultan. How can this Jew refuse me? The Sultan was enraged at Alroy's insolence, and he had Alroy thrown into the prison in Tabriz. Alroy was imprisoned in a citadel in the southwest of the city, built of mighty walls and with a tower rising forty meters into the sky.

"Now what should the Sultan do? Would the Jews rise up against him? While the Sultan deliberated his next move, David Alroy suddenly appeared in the royal courtroom, freed from prison. Had some traitor let loose the Jewish rabbi? Was this man a magician? In the confusion, Alroy escaped, and he made his way east across the Urmia River and back to safety in Amadia.

"In Amadia there was great rejoicing outwardly. However, many Jews were upset secretly; they had hoped that Alroy now had been deposed, once and for all. Alroy's council of religious leaders had become despots: they often pronounced summary death sentences for infractions of the religious laws. Therefore, after Alroy's return, clandestine groups of worried Jews started to meet. They began to plan and to organize, and then early one evening, David Alroy was killed by his father-in-law while Alroy was preparing for bed.

"A young cleric discovered Alroy dead on the floor. Word spread immediately. But how could this be? Was Alroy truly dead? People rushed into the streets. Then someone blew a trumpet blast. Ah, Alroy was not dead – the Messiah must have come at last, for is it not written in the Scriptures":

> On that golden jubilant day
> A trumpet blast will sound aloud:
> Abyssinia and Egypt will hear it play.
>
> The horn will waken from their shrouds
> Dead souls, who'll fly up far away
> To Zion, under God's white clouds.

"That night crowds of men, women, and children screamed and wept. With their parents' encouragement, many children jumped from rooftops. The Messiah would let them fly to Heaven – hallelujah. The spirit of the Messiah had arrived, and the little children's holy souls would be redeemed – they would be safe and sound and would soar aloft for the final time to the great golden Heaven in the clouds.

"For, when the true Messiah arrives," said Ezra, "then on that great and jubilant day the good Lord God (blessed be He) shall convert all evil hearts to good; He shall lighten our spirits, and our souls will be like the clouds that fly through the skies, amen." Then Ezra stood up, and without looking back at the Rabbi, he walked out of the little study room and he disappeared into the night, in the dark, dark streets of Cologne on the old medieval River Rhine.

es, Rabbi—please sit down here by the stove. This night fire will help you to become sleepy. The oven seems a calming holy thing to me; at least the white glow is certainly scriptural. What is that? Well, in terms of the scriptural "white the glow of an oven," I was thinking of Shadrach, Meshach, and Abed-nego. Grandmother loved those three names, so she often repeated the Bible story from the Book of Daniel:

> King Nebuchadnezzar made an image of gold. It was an idol ninety feet tall and nine feet wide, and he had it set upright in the plain of Dura in the province of Babylon. Then, the king sent out a summons to assemble the satraps, the prefects, the viceroys, the counselors, the treasurers, the judges, the chief constables, the governors, the stadholders, the lieutenants, the proconsuls, the commissars, the seneschals, the aldermen, the collectors, the princes, the lictors, the apparitors, the mayors, and the magistrates of all the regions and all the provinces.
>
> Now, when all these myriad notables arrived and had assembled, a royal herald proclaimed: "O ye peoples and nations of every creed and every language, you are commanded—whenever you hear the sound of horn,

harp, pipe, zither, triangle, lyre, dulcimer, cithara, viol, rebec, bell, tabla, or cymbals, and whenever you are nobly addressed by holy singing or chanting or cantillation of any kind—to prostrate yourselves: specifically, you must bow down and worship the golden image that the great king Nebuchadnezzar has set up. And whosoever does not pay appropriate homage will be bound and thrown into the white-hot blazing furnace—by order of his royal majesty Nebuchadnezzar, king of Babylon."

This homage-paying went on for some time. After a while, a group of Chaldaeans came to the main counselors of Nebuchadnezzar and reported that the Jews refused to bow down to the golden idol. "Most especially," they said, "certain well-known Jews—namely, Shadrach, Meshach, and Abed-nego—are setting a particularly bad example. These men have taken no notice of Nebuchadnezzar's commands, they do not serve his god, and they will not worship the golden image that has been set here in the plain of Dura."

When he heard this, Nebuchadnezzar was quite upset, and his face became distorted with anger. He immediately ordered that his huge furnace be heated up to seven times its usual heat, and he commanded three of the strongest men in his army to bind Shadrach, Meshach, and Abed-nego. Then those three Jews in their trousers and their shirts and their hats and all their clothes were tied up and were to be thrown into the white-hot blazing furnace. The king's order was urgent, and the furnace was incredibly hot, so the strong warriors who carried Shadrach, Meshach, and Abed-nego were killed by the flames that leapt out when the furnace doors were opened. And Shadrach, Meshach, and Abed-nego fell bound and helpless into the white-hot blazing furnace.

As King Nebuchadnezzar looked on in amazement, he seemed to see *four* figures in the furnace, and they were all walking about quite calmly. The king jumped up, and he said to his courtiers: "Did we not have only three men bound and thrown into the fire?" "Yes, your majesty." Then the king asked: "How is it that I now see four men walking about inside the white-hot blazing furnace, free and unharmed? And this fourth figure looks like some sort of radiant god." And the king called out:

"Shadrach, Meshach, and Abed-nego! Can you hear me? Come out of the furnace; come here and stand before me."

Then Shadrach, Meshach, and Abed-nego came out from the fire. And the satraps, the prefects, the viceroys, the counselors, the guards, the pages, the bailiffs, the bearers, and all the other courtiers and advisers and attendants and consultants of the king gathered around. To their wonder, they saw how the fire had no power to harm these Jewish men – the hair of their heads had not even been singed, and their clothes were as cool and as fresh as new. Then all those who were present knew that the one Lord God (blessed be He) of Israel had again protected the Jews, amen.

Grandmother sometimes told me this story to put me to bed. Has it made you sleepy? That is too bad, Rabbi. It is also too bad that you are not blessed like old Reb Elbaum; once again I saw him nodding off during the last prayers this evening. He has learned to sway piously even while asleep: he must have inherited some magic from the mystic Achselrad. And I suppose that you and I could use a dose of Achselrad ourselves tonight. My grandmother said that Abraham Achselrad could put men into a sleep-trance by waving a gold coin before their eyes. . . . Exactly, Rabbi, that is the same German rabbi whom I have told you about before – Rabbi Abraham ben Alexander, Achselrad of Cologne. He was a pupil of Eliazer, the mystic of Worms.

Rabbi Abraham Achselrad was always conjuring visions in the synagogue. I doubt whether he would be tolerated nowadays, but my grandmother said that Rabbi Abraham was also a scholar, and he claimed that his visions came from devout and pious study. Many an astonishing event took place in his yeshiva – or so my grandmother (blessed be her memory) was told. One day, he was called upon to revive the dead. What is that, Rabbi? No, I am not inventing this – the dead *can* be brought back to life. Do you not know the story from the Midrash *Tanchuma*? It goes:

A traveler is journeying from Palestine to Babylon. One morning, he stops to eat his breakfast, and not far off he sees two birds pecking at one another. Suddenly, one of the birds falls over mortally wounded, and the victor flies away.

A little sparrow had been watching from a bush nearby; the little bird flies off, but it soon returns carrying a green herb in its beak. The sparrow carefully places the herb in the beak of the dead bird. A few minutes pass; then, the dead bird begins to stir. Soon, it sits up and eventually it is strong enough to fly away.

The traveler is amazed, and he walks over to the place where the birds had been. There on the ground, he sees that a piece of the magic herb remains, so the man puts it in his pocket. Then, he sets off toward Babylon. Nearing the city of Tyre, the man comes across a dead lion that the local people had pushed over to the side of the road. Ah, thinks the man, here is my chance to try out this wondrous herb. He reaches into his pocket, he takes out the plant, and he places it in the gaping mouth of the dead animal. Slowly the lion begins to move; then it rises up and with a powerful sweep of its paw, it knocks the man down and it eats him.

From this we get the proverb:

> If you do not help the wicked,
> then the wicked will not "help" you.

Yes, of course, Rabbi, this is an old tale, but the story of Rabbi Achselrad is not so old, and my grandmother swore that this is exactly the way that she heard it. You see, Rabbi, Abraham Achselrad worked night and day on a set of kabbalistic tomes of mystical knowledge; the most famous of these was the *Keter Shem Tov*. (This was never published, and it only exists as a secret manuscript hidden in the old Cologne yeshiva.) Grandmother said that it was one afternoon while writing this very book that Rabbi Abraham looked up, and in the waning light of the day he saw a crowd of his congregants standing fearfully in the doorway. "Please," called one of them, "come quickly and help rescue Reb Joseph ben Meir. He has been charged with murder."

Now, Rabbi, this is what had actually happened. Two Gentile builders were working in the house of a wealthy Jew of Cologne, one Joseph ben Meir ben Johanan. Reb Joseph lived on the Jewish street of Judengasse, not far from the main synagogue building. As the men worked to repair a roof that overhung the courtyard garden, they noticed that there was a large quantity of gold coins in a chest, partly concealed by the edge of the overhang.

"Look," said one of the men, "these Jews are always hording money. I am certain that they have no good use for it. We can take at least half the coins without being caught."

Joseph and his family had gone to the synagogue that afternoon, and no one else was about, so the workmen took more than half of the gold coins. Next to the chest of coins they found another box with some jewelry. One of the men thought to himself: "I may as well take a bit of this jewelry while I am here." And he pocketed necklaces and broaches and rings and pendants.

Then the same man thought: "Why should I share even the coins with this partner of mine." So he took a hammer and he smashed his companion on the head, killing him instantly. Seeing what he had done, the man became frightened, and he wrapped up all the coins and he ran from the house.

When he returned home, Joseph ben Meir found the dead body in his house. He sent for the city guards, who came immediately, but the officers accused Reb Joseph of the murder. They dragged poor Joseph to the local court, and as word spread through the surrounding parishes, an angry crowd collected and demanded an equal punishment. "This Jew has killed one of our workmen – he himself must be put to death."

The rumor of the death spread quickly, and Gentiles came from the St. Laurence parish, which was directly to the south, and also from the St. Albans parish, which borders on St. Laurence. A small riot seemed in the making, and Jews rushed into the synagogue, where Rabbi Abraham Achselrad was writing in the back room.

Rabbi Abraham listened, and he immediately put on his hat and his coat; he left the small back study room of the yeshiva, he walked through the main prayer hall filled with wooden benches, he passed the twelve stained glass windows with their colored lions and snakes, he went by the Holy Ark made of stone, he stepped out of the front door, and he strode off to the courthouse. The Archbishop himself was there in court; this was the Archbishop Adolph of Cologne, a noble and honorable prelate. Archbishop Adolph knew the Rabbi. "Rabbi," said the Archbishop sadly, "I am afraid that one of your Jews has committed murder. We have accusers and we have the body—so, Mr. Joseph Meir must be hanged."

"I see," said Rabbi Abraham. Abraham Achselrad looked at the accusers, he looked at Joseph ben Meir, and then he looked at the Archbishop. Rabbi Abraham closed his eyes for a moment. Then he asked: "Have you a Bible here, good Archbishop?"

"Of course," replied the Archbishop, and he instructed one of the officers to pass a leather volume to Rabbi Achselrad.

"Now, let us read from the Psalms," said the Rabbi.

"I respect your religious views, Rabbi," answered Archbishop Adolph, "but is this really relevant now?"

Rabbi Abraham Achselrad was holding the Holy Scriptures. Suddenly, his eyes opened wide and then they closed tightly; he became weak, and he sat on a nearby chair. Then, the Rabbi gently set down the Bible.

"Are you all right, Rabbi?" asked the Archbishop.

"I have just had a vision," said Rabbi Abraham. "I have seen the Heavens at night."

There was silence for a moment. "Yes, I have seen the Heavens at night. I have seen the firmament of the good Lord God (blessed be He)— He Who sees all and Who demands justice for all, especially for His children, the Jews. In addition, I have seen that Psalm 21 is quite important," said Abraham Achselrad. "And, if you will be so good as to hand me that holy book, then I will read a bit of those verses":

> The good Lord reaches for His foes again.
> His fist strikes enemies of Israel:
> He fiercely thrusts that wicked clan
> Into a blazing fireball.
> In anger, God seizes hurtful men:
> Lightning strikes—fire destroys them all.
>
> The Lord will catch them by the coat;
> He decimates their sons.
> Evilly they've begun to gloat,
> They've attacked but have not won;
> For the Lord's hand is around their throat—
> They will confess and be undone.

"Of course," said the Archbishop, "that is a most serious and holy sentiment."

"It certainly is," said the Rabbi. "Now, my good Archbishop, you are a noted cleric. What would you say that this verse means?"

"Clearly it means that the Lord avenges evil."

"I would say that it means even more than that," said the Rabbi.

"You would? Then pray tell, Rabbi Achselrad: What more do you read into this Psalm?"

"I would say, Archbishop Adolph, that the good Lord God (blessed be He)—He who is the Guardian of all Israel—watches over everyone. He has seen who has caused this murder, and He will avenge it and He will protect His people Israel against false accusations," said the Rabbi.

"Exactly what are you saying, Mr. Abraham Alexander?" asked the Archbishop.

"I am saying this, Archbishop: I have had a vision. I have seen that a man who presently stands unaccused is in fact the murderer in this very case."

Then, one of the officers laughed and said: "The Psalm has told you all this, old man?"

"Yes, it has," said the Rabbi. "My good Archbishop, what are you going to do? An angry mob has collected. Will you allow innocent people to be hurt or to be killed for the sake of one man, when you know well enough that none of us Jews is guilty?"

"At the moment, Rabbi," said the Archbishop, "I must say that I know no such thing."

"Two men were working in the house," said Rabbi Achselrad, "and I can prove to you that one of them killed the other."

The Archbishop conferred with his councilors, and after an argument, Archbishop Adolph of Cologne said: "If you can prove what you say, then no harm will befall any of you Jews." And he gave orders that the people in the court and the people in the street should all remain quiet.

Then Rabbi Abraham said: "First, good Archbishop, have the gates closed, so that the murderer will not be able to escape."

The Archbishop agreed to send out word into the town; his officers were instructed to block the gates and to maintain the peace.

Rabbi Abraham Achselrad sat down again, and he closed his eyes.

He began to sway, and he shook strangely. The members of the court looked at each other. Then the pious man opened his eyes wide, and he took a small parchment scroll from his pocket. The Rabbi covered the top of his head with a handkerchief, and he wrote a charm with holy names on the the paper; the Archbishop could see that the charm began with a quotation from Exodus: "For I am Yahweh, your Restorer–I, the Lord God, am your Healer. . . ." but Archbishop Adolph could not make out the remainder of the words.

When the Rabbi finished writing in his neat and tiny script, he rolled the parchment into a tight scroll and tied it with a cotton thread. The Rabbi tied and untied the thread–he knotted and unkotted it seven times–then he placed the charm in the hands of the dead man. There was silence, and a dark cloud passed over the sun.

Suddenly, the dead man rose up. He stood, and he turned around; he looked about him, and he saw the murderer hiding behind another man. The corpse ran to his old partner and he said: "You murderer! It was you who killed me. You wanted to have all the property that we stole, both the coins and the jewelry; so you struck me on the head with a hammer, and then I fell back into the room–dead."

Everyone was stunned. The Archbishop frowned, and he motioned to the guards; the true murderer was seized and was arrested, and he was thrown into prison immediately. Then, the Archbishop said to Rabbi Abraham: "As it is written in the Holy Scriptures":

> You shall show no mercy: life for life, eye for eye, tooth for tooth, hand for hand, foot for foot.

Therefore, the murderer was condemned to death, and not long afterward, he was executed.

What happened to the charm? Well, Rabbi, my grandmother said that in the confusion of the arrest, Rabbi Abraham Achselrad quietly took the charm away from the corpse, who then fell down and lay properly dead. Later, the Archbishop asked to see the charm, but when Rabbi Achselrad opened his hands, they were completely empty–yes, Rabbi, they were completely empty, amen.

ood evening again, Rabbi. Yes, I know—it is always hard to sleep when the moon is so bright. Put your feet up on the side bench here, and I will open the stove door. Let me push this coal back. There is nothing like that white glow: it washes away the cares of a hard day. I heard your final benediction tonight, Rabbi; there is no use denying it—you are overworked. Even a nearsighted shammas like me can tell. I kept one eye on you when I cleaned the dishes, and I saw that you were watching the door, hoping that Reb Elbaum would leave early. But then Reb Anton stayed to argue about the scriptural passage:

> You Israelites shall not wear clothes woven from two kinds of yarn at once, from wool and from flax together. Moreover, I require that you make twisted tassels, like little flowers, on the four corners of your cloaks and on the other four-cornered clothes with which you wrap yourselves.

Did you ever decide whether the "other four-cornered clothes" include winter scarfs? Well, no matter—after all this hard studying, of course you are worn out. So, what is that? A story from me? Rabbi, all I know are the old-fashioned children's tales, the grandmother fables. You need something new and fresh to keep your mind keen; otherwise you will become an old man like me, and you will find yourself constantly musing and dozing and nodding off in front of the stove.

What do you mean you are already an old man, Rabbi? Do you think that sixty years is old? You are still a child. When you reach eighty, *then* you will be old. You doubt that you will live to see eighty years? If so, Rabbi, then you will never grow old. . . . All right, all right—as I said, I know no special stories, but listening to you and Reb Anton reminded me of the tale that my grandmother told of the German Rabbi Yerahmiel ha-Kohen of Cologne and the tassels on the *tallis katan*:

It was once upon a time, said my grandmother, long, long ago when there lived in the town of Rondorf a pious Jew named Joel ben Mordecai. Rondorf had no synagogue, and the Rondorf Jews often went to the prayer services in Cologne. At that time, Yerahmiel ha-Kohen was the chief rabbi of Cologne; he was the main teacher and scholar in the old yeshiva, and he was consulted on matters both of religion and of secular life by Jews from all the surrounding towns.

A few kilometers outside Rondorf, on the road toward Cologne, there was a deserted and desolate stone building; the local people called it simply "The Ruin." Years before, this building had been built as an inn, and later it was converted into a grain mill. A rough family took it over, and they let the business deteriorate until eventually the building became only their old and dirty home. The children in the family grew up and left or were taken to prison, and when the father died, no one was certain who owned the building. That was years before. Now, rumors were afoot among the country folk—rumors told by Jews as well as by Gentiles—that The Ruin was haunted by all sorts of ghosts and dybbuks and evil spirits. Black birds flew through the windows at dawn. Music was heard at night. There were always shadows in the yard, even on the brightest of days. No wildflowers were ever seen beside the old house; the jipijapa plants along the nearby road were brown and stunted. Dogs slunk in and out of the empty doorways. The Ruin and its environs became the dread of all passers-by. Even grownups hurried when they walked nearby on the road. One man claimed that he had seen a soldier standing on the roof of The Ruin late at night as he was passing by; the soldier, said the passer-by, was blowing a black trumpet.

One day, it happened that Joel ben Mordecai ben Moses was walking home to Rondorf from evening prayers in the Cologne yeshiva, and his route took him by The Ruin. Joel noticed that he was being followed by a large black dog, and his heart began to pound uncontrollably. "O Lord God," thought Reb Joel, "please let this dog stay far away." As they passed The Ruin, the large dog suddenly turned into the courtyard, and it disappeared in the bleak shadows of the old stone walls. Then, the dog let out a fierce bark. Reb Joel was terribly frightened, he began to run, and he reached home almost unconscious.

"My dear Joel," exclaimed his wife, "you look awful!"

Joel sat down a moment, and he had a drink of wine. Then he told his family about the dog and The Ruin. "The good Lord God (blessed be He) protects the Jews, amen," said his wife. "Amen," said Joel. However, that night, his wife heard poor Joel bark in his sleep. When she woke her husband, he was covered with perspiration, he was panting, and he was weak. In fact, he was so exhausted that he could barely move.

"Whatever is the matter, Joel?" asked his wife.

"My good wife," said Joel ben Mordecai, "I dreamt that I was riding alongside a group of soldiers. Instead of horses, we rode on the backs of huge black dogs. As we reached a dark and foreboding castle, the dogs began to bark, and I too was forced to bark. It was terrible – it was just terrible."

"You have had a nightmare because of your evil experience this evening," said his wife. "Do not worry, Joel – this will pass."

Joel tossed and turned all night. In the morning, he felt weighted down and unhappy. The next night, Joel feared going to sleep, and, as he expected, he could find no peace in his dreams. That night and for every night thereafter, he was tortured by the same dream. Each night, there were soldiers and black dogs and dark castles and shadowed walls, and poor Joel became more and more exhausted. Little by little he lost his strength: he ate poorly, his business suffered, and his family was very worried.

Finally, his wife said: "Joel, we need some spiritual advice." So Joel ben Mordecai went to Rabbi Yerahmiel ha-Kohen, the chief rabbi of Cologne, accompanied by his entire family. Joel was red-eyed, his face sagged, his hair was awry, and his hands shook. He told the Rabbi the whole story, from the beginning to the end. "Rabbi," said Joel, "I am in desperate need of your help."

Rabbi Yerahmiel listened carefully. "I can see that the situation is serious," said the Rabbi. "Let me pray and think." So Rabbi Yerahmiel went into the little back study room in the old Cologne yeshiva. He closed his eyes and he prayed, and then he thought about this story. Soldiers and black dogs and dark castles and shadowed walls and The Ruin – what could these things mean? Rabbi Yerahmiel picked up the Holy Scriptures, and he began to leaf through the pages. In Exodus, he suddenly saw the sentence: "But against any of the children of Israel shall not a dog whet his tongue." "Ah," thought the Rabbi. Then he came across the passage: "Moreover, I require that you make twisted tassels, like little flowers, on the four corners of your cloaks and on the other four-cornered clothes with which you wrap yourselves." "Perhaps this is it," thought Rabbi Yerahmiel.

Rabbi Yerahmiel stood up, and he walked back into the main prayer hall where Joel's family was sitting together on the wooden benches in the light of the twelve stained glass windows with their colored lions and snakes. The Rabbi said: "Reb Joel, let me see your little prayer shawl, your *tallis katan*."

Joel was puzzled, but he unbuttoned his shirt and he showed the Rabbi his prayer shawl. The Rabbi looked at it closely. "I see," said Rabbi Yerahmiel, "that one of the fringes is torn off the back corner."

"Let me see," said Joel. "Yes, you are right, Rabbi."

"Remember," said the Rabbi, "in the Holy Scriptures, the good Lord God (blessed be He) told Moses":

You must make tassels like little blue flowers on the corners of your clothes – you and your children and your children's children. Into each tassel, work blue and violet threads, colored like the Heavens above. And whenever you see these tassels, you shall remember all the Lord's Heavenly commandments and thus you will obey them, and you will not go your own wanton ways, led astray by your own mortal eyes and by your own mortal hearts. These token reminders ensure that you will always remember the holy immortal laws and that you will stay consecrated to your God.

"Yes, Rabbi," said Joel, "I remember that very well."

"Good," said the Rabbi, "and I am certain that you also remember how the Sages of the Talmud tell us":

This particular ordinance is equal to all the other precepts, laws, proscriptions, and commandments together. And why is this? It is because: seeing leads to remembering, and remembering leads to performing, and performing means following all the other precepts, laws, proscriptions, and commandments.

The color of the blue threads in the tassels resembles the color of the great seas, and the color of the seas is the color of the towering firmament, and the color of the firmament is the color of the radiant Throne of Glory. In this way, we carry around with us a bit of Heaven, and this touch of Heaven will keep our lives pure and it will make us devout and it will keep us close to the great God Almighty.

"Yes, amen," said Joel, "I remember this passage also."

"Excellent," said the Rabbi, "because now it is clear why you have been pursued by evil dreams and dogs and spirits and why the usual guardian angels could not protect you."

"It is clear?"

"Of course," said Rabbi Yerahmiel, "you must repair the threads and the tassels on your prayer shawl."

"Now?" asked Reb Joel.

"Immediately," said the Rabbi.

Reb Joel took off his prayer shawl, the Rabbi brought some thread and a needle, and Joel's wife set to work carefully repairing the tassels on the *tallis katan*. Then Reb Joel said: "Blessed are You, O Lord our God, King of the Universe, Who has sanctified us and Who has commanded us to wrap ourselves in the holy fringes." And Joel ben Mordecai put on his little prayer shawl again.

"Now," said the Rabbi, "you must take a ritual bath."

The two men left the family sitting opposite the Holy stone Ark in the main prayer hall, and they walked to the bathhouse, next to the Jewish City Hall of Cologne. In a small side room, Joel ben Mordecai removed his prayer shawl and his clothes; he set the shawl and the clothes on a green stone shelf cut into the wall, and he wrapped himself in a clean white sheet. Then he entered the main bath room, where the ceiling was supported by seven pillars. Joel stepped down the stone steps into the spring-water bath, and in accord with the old tradition, Joel immersed himself completely in the water seven times. Meanwhile, Rabbi Yerahmiel said: "Thus is it written in the Holy Scriptures: 'So he went down and he dipped himself into the Jordan River seven times, as the man of God had told him, and his flesh was thereby restored as a little child's, and he was clean once again,' amen."

When the men returned to the synagogue, Joel ben Mordecai said: "I feel better already. Thank you very much, Rabbi."

"Just a moment," said Rabbi Yerahmiel, "we are not yet finished."

"There is more?"

"Yes, there is," said the Rabbi. He went into the back study room, and he took a strip of parchment from a drawer in the rabbi's study table. On this parchment, he wrote the quotation from the Book of Exodus, in small Hebrew script: "But against any of the children of Israel shall not a dog whet his tongue." Then the Rabbi rolled the parchment into a tiny scroll, he tied it with seven ties of a white thread, and he gave this amulet to Joel ben Mordecai.

"Now, good Joel," said the Rabbi, "wrap these holy words around your forehead at night before going to bed—and do this every night for seven nights. Furthermore, do not sleep at home in Rondorf for these seven nights. Instead, you must sleep here in the yeshiva, in the second bed in the shammas's room."

"Must I stay here tonight, Rabbi?" asked Joel.

"Yes—beginning this very night."

Joel ben Mordecai sent his family home, and he sat in the main prayer hall awaiting the evening services. Meanwhile, Rabbi Yerahmiel went to his shammas. "My good shammas," said the Rabbi, "please do this important deed for Reb Joel. Collect a bundle of straw. Then after dark, take the straw and walk toward Rondorf. You know the old broken building called 'The Ruin.' Do not be afraid. Just go inside and set the straw on the floor and light it with a match. Then, come directly back here."

The shammas looked at Rabbi Yerahmiel. Then he said: "Rabbi, it is true that I am a brave man – but you are asking a lot of me. The Ruin is haunted. How can I dare to go there at night?"

"The good Lord God (blessed be He) will protect you; in addition, I will give you a holy amulet," said the Rabbi. He reached into his pocket, and he took out a tiny metal box. On the outside of the box were engraved arcane and secret names. The lid had sixteen squares in which the numbers one, four, eight, and nine were arranged so that the total count – whether horizontal, vertical, or diagonal – would always equal twenty-two. On the inside of the box was a parchment with the *Shema* written in neat black ink. "This box once belonged to Juddah he-Hasid, the mystic of Regensburg," said the Rabbi. "Take good care of it, and return it to me when you have finished your task."

So the shammas felt braver, and he went out into the back courtyard of the yeshiva and collected the straw, and he wrapped it into a bundle. Then, late at night, he walked toward Rondorf. As he approached the black Ruin, the shammas felt weak and shaky, but he did exactly as he was instructed, and then he ran back to Cologne. That night, a fire blazed in The Ruin, and the old roof of the building collapsed in a thunderous roar – and Joel ben Mordecai had a calm and a dreamless sleep.

Seven days came and seven days went, and Joel had seven peaceful nights of sleep. Finally, after the full week had passed, Rabbi Yerahmiel said: "Reb Joel, go home and live happily." And Joel walked home. He passed The Ruin, and he was unafraid and he felt at peace. Now the old structure was just three blank and meek tumble-down walls. The sun shone brightly, the jipijapa plants all had dark shiny green leaves, small birds chattered in the trees, and the old walls grew moss and they sprouted grasslets. And, said my grandmother, so it remained for the end of all days – and so it remains today, amen.

ello, Rabbi. No sleep for the weary? That is what my grandmother said, and she said it almost nightly. If you are cold, then sit down here on the bench and I will stoke up the oven. This stoker? It is one of the iron shoe scrapers from the front hall – you probably do not recognize it because it is covered with soot. (Then, I also bent it into this strange shape in order to make it fit through the oven door.) Of course there is still another scraper in the anteroom for dirty shoes. But I myself am of the old school: I think that all pious men should pray barefoot. Did you know that converts to Judaism are required to pray barefoot? Oh – well, perhaps the tradition has been lost recently.

As my grandmother said (quoting from the Book of Proverbs): "At the outset a road may seem straightforward to a man, but it may end as the way to death." What is that, Rabbi? Well, I mention this quote because of converts. You see, conversion can be a difficult road. But in the end the difficult road may lead to salvation – and as my grandmother used to say (may the good Lord bless her and keep her on the road to salvation for ever), Judaism welcomes all who are faithful to the good Lord God, blessed be He. Even a Gentile who obeys the Torah is the equal of the highest of the high Jewish priests; in Isaiah it is written:

Open the gates of Jerusalem
To let good people enter in –
Anyone who is free from sin,
Who lives Your laws and loves all men,
May come within and blessed be
With Your peace and tranquility.

Yes, Rabbi, the convert is welcome. In this regard, I remember a story that my grandmother told me of the very pious Rabbi Yerahmiel ha-Kohen and the conversion of a priest who was the Rabbi's Catholic colleague in Cologne:

Once upon a time, said my grandmother, in the town of Cologne on the River Rhine, there lived a priest named Hermann Tienrich. Priest Hermann was the provost of the great Catholic cathedral, the Dom, in which the three kings of Cologne are buried. (Those kings – Kaspar, Melchior, and Balthazar – were the three wise men who came from the East to see the infant Jesus.) Priest Hermann knew and respected his clerical colleague, Yerahmiel ha-Kohen, the chief rabbi of the Jewish community in Cologne. Both men were scholars, and both men were widely known for their piety.

One night, as Rabbi Yerahmiel was studying as usual, he heard a pitiful cry at the back of his house. Not knowing what it was, he became frightened and he began to recite the *Shema* – "Hear, O Israel, the Lord is our God; He is our one Lord, and you must love the Lord your God with all your heart. . . ." – until the cry ceased. Although the noise had stopped, the Rabbi hesitated to go and see what had caused it, so he began to study and to read the Torah again. Slowly he felt more peaceful, and eventually he fell asleep. When the cry was repeated, Rabbi Yerahmiel did not hear it.

Now, Rabbi, let me tell you what the cry was. The world is filled with a crush of spirits and dybbuks and demons, and two of these demons (may the good Lord God, blessed be He, protect us) had come into the Rabbi's garden. They looked fiercely at each other for a moment, and then one demon made his piercing demonic cry and he said: "Listen here, you malevolent thing, why are you in this yard? Do you not know that this garden belongs to a holy man? Here lives a rabbi who is known throughout Germany for his wisdom and his piety."

"Ah, maybe this man is holy – and then maybe he is not as holy as you think," said the other demon.

"You are a son of mud," said the first demon. "Look for yourself: the rabbi is poring intently over his book. He is studying as he always does, and the whole Jewish community of Cologne depends on this study."

The second demon said: "Oh, I see him studying, but I have heard that in Cologne there is a man who is even more pious. The local priest, one Hermann Tienrich, is a cleric who is so strong in his faith that no force can cause him to deviate one tiny bit from the Church."

"All these holy men are like rocks," said the first demon. "However, there are rocks and then there are *rocks* – there is sandstone and then there is granite. I am afraid that the priest is sandstone, while the rabbi is granite."

"Ah, my foul friend, you would not speak so quickly if you had to live by your words," said the second demon.

"Are you suggesting that I am mistaken?" asked the first demon.

"You can take my comments any way that you wish," replied the second demon.

"Then I will make a wager. I will bet you that I can convert the priest to Judaism, while you cannot convert the rabbi to Christianity."

"Very well, and what will you stake on this foolish wager?"

"If I win," said the first demon, "then I can slit your throat with a rusty knife."

"Fine – and if I win, then I will cut your evil neck," said the second demon.

"I accept," said the first demon, and he shrieked his demonic cry again.

These shrieks, Rabbi, were what Yerahmiel ha-Kohen had heard on that dark night in Cologne, long, long ago. The first demon shrieked his demonic shriek, but before he could depart in order to plan his evil work, the second demon caught him by the shoulder, he smiled a cruel smile, and he said: "You have been a fool, old spirit. I have successfully converted a great many Jews in my time."

In those days, Rabbi, there had been many conversions following the Crusades. Of course, the Jewish communities were very sympathetic to the poor Jews who changed faith in order to save their lives. Practically all these converts returned to Judaism; in fact, as soon as the invading crusaders would leave a city, most proselytes would immediately become Jews again.

On the other hand, the second demon was bragging about the many voluntary converts whom he had enticed from Judaism. There were always pressures for Jews to accept the Christian faith of their surroundings. The Jewish communities were forced to lead continuous missionary campaigns in order to regain lost members. Unfortunately, opinion was divided as to how to handle the re-converts. Should their charitable gifts be accepted? Was there some obligatory waiting period before a re-convert could attend the synagogue? Could a reverted *kohen* ascend the pulpit and offer the priestly benediction; in fact, could he *ever* read the Torah to the congregation again? And then how about marriage – could a Jew marry a convert? Finally, could a convert be given a proper Jewish burial? In those medieval days, most rabbis held to the policy of forgive and forget – but many of the community members felt that they may forgive but that they could never forget.

In any event, the second demon was quite confident of his ability to convert any Jew, at least temporarily. Therefore, on the next night this demon went directly to Rabbi Yerahmiel and he said: "Rabbi, I was sent by the great Lord Almighty to tell you that you should give up Judaism. Of course Judaism is a fine religion, but in the end, the Lord only loves those who accept the faith of Christ, amen. As you know, Christianity is a warm and loving faith, and you will find that it welcomes you with open arms."

The demon spoke suavely and he spoke persuasively, and he talked in a mellow voice for many many minutes. Rabbi Yerahmiel knew that this was some malevolent spirit; the Rabbi was frightened and he covered his head with a handkerchief, all the while reciting Psalm 146:

> God gives sight to the blind again;
> He cures the cripple's deformity.
> The good Lord loves the righteous man,
> He guards the poor; He protects the needy.
> God helps the widow and the orphan –
> But wicked men get sad calamity.

And the Rabbi turned away, and he begged the demon to depart.

The following night, the demon came again; this time it arrived in the shape of an old man, with the appearance of some prophet, like Elijah. "Ah, my good Rabbi," began the demon, "I find that you are studying. This is very fine; it is quite fine indeed. Study is holy, and it is good. But the Jewish books are limited, Rabbi: you should continue your studies with the remainder of the Bible, which takes up with the coming of Christ. That is a wondrous subject for endless study. . . ."

Again, the second demon spoke calmly and smoothly for many, many minutes. The Rabbi refused to look at the demon; he covered his head with a handkerchief and he recited Psalm 106:

> Their sons bowed down to foreign gods;
> Blood was shed for the demon's rite;
> Serpents sprang up like Aaron's rods—
> The Lord was angered, His mouth grew tight.

And the Rabbi turned away, and he begged the demon to depart.

When the demon saw that the Rabbi refused to listen to him, he decided to try another approach. The next night, the evil spirit returned in the shape of a beautiful woman. "Consider, my holy Rabbi," said the demon, "the joys of Christianity. . . ." But the Rabbi looked down and he covered his head with a handkerchief, and he recited Psalm 121:

> If I lift up my eyes to the tall hill
> Will I find any guidance on high?
> Salvation comes only by God's will—
> *He* made the hills and the sky.

And the Rabbi turned away, and he begged the demon to depart.

By now the second demon had become discouraged and he stayed away for many nights; nonetheless, Rabbi Yerahmiel was worried. Had he committed a sin? He had evidently transgressed, otherwise why would such evil temptation befall him? Therefore, the Rabbi fasted and he gave alms to the poor and he studied still later into the night and he did penance, and all the members of the Jewish community in Cologne wondered why an already pious man had become even more holy.

Meanwhile, the first demon had followed these events with much satisfaction. "Granite," he said to himself, "clearly, the rabbi is granite." And then he added: "Now, my ill-smelling companion, I will go out and I will show you what a true demon can do when he puts his mind to it."

Priest Hermann was sitting praying in the great Cologne cathedral, in a room filled with candles. Holy sounds rolled in the air; holy scents wafted about the man. The first demon appeared, and he hovered beside the wall and he said to the priest: "Good evening, my priest, my provost. The Lord Almighty has sent me to tell you how holy and pious you are."

Priest Hermann looked up: "Who are you, O spirit? Are you some angel?"

"You might say that," responded the demon. "Anyway, I am here to give you a message: you have fulfilled your mission in the Church. You have been a good and true Christian, and the Lord thanks you. Now it is time to become a Jew and to enter into the covenant of Abraham."

"What?!" exclaimed the priest. "How can you say such a terrible, blasphemous thing?"

"Good priest, this is no blasphemy – it is the wish of the Lord. As you well know, Christ was a Jew; therefore, all Christians should become Jews. In fact," said the demon, "if you do not convert, then I am afraid that you shall have to spend all your everlasting days in damnation in Hell."

"I cannot believe that I am hearing this," said Priest Hermann, and he put his hands over his ears.

But the demon took up the priest in his demonic arms, and he carried the provost of Cologne to a scene that looked like Hell. The demon had fabricated a place with flames and rock and horrible smells; jagged stones lay about, molten lava oozed from the walls, choking smoke hung in thick clouds – and there crying out in pain were the priest's father and the priest's mother and all the priest's Christian teachers. Each person was burning and crying; it was a piteous scene, and the priest said: "Please, spirit – take me away from here."

"Very well," said the demon.

Then, the demon took up the priest in his demonic arms, and he carried the provost of Cologne to a scene that looked like Heaven. The demon had fabricated a place of jewels and golden light and gentle breezes – and there sitting happily studying the Torah were hundreds upon hundreds of curly-haired, bearded rabbis in their Sabbath robes. At the side of each rabbi was a table filled with holiday foods, at the feet of each rabbi were satin pillows, and around the room cherubic figures played quiet, joyous, aethereal music on lutes and citharas and zithers. "This is the Heaven of the Jews," said the demon. "And look over there, Hermann. Do you see that empty seat, beyond the rabbi in the blue satin robe? That Heavenly seat is waiting for you. You are destined to become a Jew also and to partake for ever and ever in this wondrous eternal life."

The priest looked about him, and he said to the demon. "How can I be certain that you are telling me the truth?"

The demon said: "Would an angel lie to a priest?"

What could the priest answer to that, Rabbi? So the priest finally said: "Take me back to Cologne." And the demon took up the priest in his demonic arms, and he carried the provost back to the candle-lit room in the Dom, the great Catholic cathedral of the city of Cologne.

Priest Hermann Tienrich shut himself in a little back stone room of the cathedral. He prayed and he thought; he pressed his fists against his eyes, but he could not rid himself of the horrible vision of Hell. Therefore, on the following night, he took off his priestly robes, he put on a plain shirt and rough woolen trousers, and he went to the house of Rabbi Yerahmiel. The priest knocked on the door, and he asked the Rabbi to let him inside. This was late at night, and the Rabbi wondered: Is there some devilment afoot? Am I to be charged with a crime against the Christian community of Cologne? The Rabbi hesitated, but in the end he opened the door and in came his clerical colleague, Hermann Tienrich, the provost of Cologne.

"Good evening, Priest Hermann," said the Rabbi. "Why are you here so late at night?"

The priest said: "Perhaps, good Rabbi, you will close the door. . . . Thank you. Rabbi, this may sound very strange to you, but I would like to convert to Judaism."

This did indeed sound strange to Rabbi Yerahmiel, who sat down on a chair. "You wish to convert?" asked the Rabbi.

"Yes," said the priest, "I have given this much thought, and I have decided that it is the correct course of action for me; it is the road that I must now take."

"Have you not been satisfied with your own faith?" asked the Rabbi.

"Oh, yes, it has been fine up to this point," said the priest. "However, undoubtedly you know the saying from the Book of Proverbs, Rabbi":

> At the outset a road may seem straightforward to a man,
> But it may end as the way to death.

"Yes, that is true," said the Rabbi.
"Moreover, in Isaiah it says":

> Open the gates of Jerusalem
> To let good people enter in—
> Anyone who is free from sin,
> Who lives Your laws and loves all men,
> May come within and blessed be
> With Your peace and tranquility.

From this verse, Rabbi, I know that Judaism will welcome converts with open arms," said the priest.

"Yes, that is true also," said the Rabbi.

"Then, Rabbi," said Priest Hermann, "I would like to embrace Judaism, tonight."

Rabbi Yerahmiel was quiet for a moment, and then he said: "I know that you are a serious man, Mr. Tienrich, and I know that you have not taken this step lightly. It is quite true that Judaism welcomes all converts, my good priest. Our great Rabbi Hillel once said: 'All Israelites must be disciples of Aaron—love peace and create peace, love your fellow creatures, and invite all men to study and to revere the Torah.'"

So Rabbi Yerahmiel agreed to convert Hermann Tienrich to Judaism. First, the men read together certain passages from the Holy Scriptures; then, the Rabbi said the special conversion benedictions. Finally, they went to the bathhouse, next to the Jewish City Hall in

Cologne. In a small side room, the priest removed his clothes and put them on a stone shelf, he wrapped himself in a clean white sheet, and he stepped into the large, square, pillared bath room. Hermann Tienrich stepped down the three stone steps into the spring-water bath, and in accord with the old tradition, the Rabbi instructed the priest to immerse himself completely in the water seven times. Meanwhile, Rabbi Yerahmiel said: "It is written in the Holy Scriptures: 'So he went down and he dipped himself into the Jordan River seven times, just as the man of God had told him, and his flesh was thereby restored as a little child's, and he was clean once again,' amen."

Then, the two men returned to Rabbi Yerahmiel's house, where the Rabbi began to teach the Jewish understanding of the Torah to the former priest and provost of the Dom, the great cathedral of Cologne. It was late in the darkest hours of the night, and the two men were engrossed in reading Genesis. Suddenly, they heard a demonic shriek coming from the garden. The priest looked at the Rabbi and the Rabbi looked at the priest, and for safety, the Rabbi said:

> May it be Your will, O God of Heaven and of earth, O God of Abraham, Isaac, and Jacob, O God of Moses, Aaron, David, and Solomon, and by virtue of Your great and holy Name (that is, Shaddai *Sar happanim*), protect and spare us and show us mercy, amen.

Then both men went out to see what was happening. In the courtyard, they found two demons, and the first demon was about to slit the throat of the second demon with a rough and rusty knife.

"What evil is happening here?" asked Rabbi Yerahmiel.

"I am about to dispatch this foul creature," said the first demon.

"Well," said the Rabbi, "kindly do it somewhere else." And he turned and he went back into his home.

The next morning, Rabbi Yerahmiel brought Hermann Tienrich to the yeshiva, and the Rabbi assigned two scholars from the community to tutor the new proselyte. After many months, Hermann Tienrich himself became a distinguished Jewish scholar; he read and he prayed and he thought, and finally he decided to journey to the Holy Land. There, in the promised land of all our forefathers, the ex-priest lived as a very pious Jew indeed—and in the warm climate he always prayed barefoot. Eventually, he married a Jewish woman and he had three fine children. In his old age, Hermann Tienrich saw his children marry into good families, and at his death he left a devout and pious name behind him. And, of course, Rabbi Yerahmiel remained always a happy and a truly pious man in Cologne, amen.

ood evening, Rabbi. You are having difficulty sleeping again? Well, just put your feet up on the side bench here and I will open the stove door. Let me push this coal back; there is nothing like that white glow to wash away the cares of a hard day. Clearly you are overworked, Rabbi–even an old shammas like me can tell. I kept one eye on you when I was cleaning the dishes; I saw that you were watching the door, hoping that Reb Elbaum would leave early. But, then, Reb Anton stayed late to argue about the Midrash passage.

That Midrash passage reminded me of our Rabbi Jehuda ben Saul. One day, he gave a Midrash sermon to his yeshiva students. "How do we know," asked Rabbi Jehuda, "that two pieces of bread are better than one?'"

He looked sternly at the young men on the benches. This seemed a strange question, and there was silence in the study hall, so the Rabbi said: "Well my young scholars–can none of you tell me about the 'wraps' portion of the Passover service?"

Then a student named Moshe ben Samuel stood up and he said: "Good Rabbi, just before the *seder* meal is begun, the head of the table breaks the third *matzoh*, he cuts slices of horseradish, and he makes little sandwiches of *matzoh* and horseradish strips. Then, he distributes the sandwiches and he says: 'This is in memory of the Temple: we eat now as the great Rabbi Hillel did long ago. Specifically, this is what Rabbi Hillel did in the days when the Holy Temple once stood–he wrapped together pieces of Passover lamb, unleavened bread, and bitter herbs, and then he ate them in a sandwich together.' "

And Rabbi Jehuda said: "Exactly, Moshe. And what scriptural passage does this fulfill?"

Then Moshe said: "This was to fulfill the scriptural injunction from Exodus":

> On that holy night, the Israelites shall eat the meat of the paschal lamb, after it has been roasted on the fire; and they shall eat the meat with unleavened cakes and also with bitter herbs.

And Rabbi Jehuda said: "Correct, young man. Now, does the good Lord God (blessed be He) command us to do anything but the best?"

The students shook their heads.

"No, of course He does not," said Jehuda. "Therefore, two pieces of unleavened bread must be the best. And so, my studious young scholars, how do we know from the commandments for Passover that the head of the household becomes prescient for one day of the year?"

The yeshiva students were puzzled. The Rabbi looked sternly at the young men on the benches. There was silence, and so Rabbi Jehuda answered his own question: "Think, scholars, think! In Exodus it is written":

> On the tenth day of *Nisan*, let each man obtain a lamb for his family. To decide the size of the paschal lamb, let the man carefully take into account the number of persons in his household and also the amount that each of them will eat.

"But, my boys, when a man buys a lamb for Passover, the eating is yet to take place. And how could someone know in advance the full details of something that is still to happen and that has not yet come to pass? It is by *prescience*, my young friends, prescience."

Ah, Rabbi, there is nothing like prescience to help a Jew in these troubled times. I remember that my grandmother told me how prescience once helped Rabbi Yerahmiel to protect Saul ben Benjamin from a miracle. Yes, Rabbi, that was the very same Yerahmiel ha-Kohen whom I have told you about before. Rabbi Yerahmiel was a fine and pious scholar, and he was the chief rabbi of Cologne. One day, said my grandmother, Rabbi Yerahmiel was eating his dinner in the little back study room of the old Cologne yeshiva. He looked down at his plate, and the noodles looked exactly like a *mezuzah*. Now, I do not mean that they just had a general oblong shape – I mean that they also had the word *Shaddai* lettered down one side.

No, Rabbi, I am not inventing this – my grandmother swore that this is exactly what she heard had happened. But there is more: Rabbi Yerahmiel then closed his eyes, and when he opened them, Saul ben Benjamin was standing in the doorway and Saul's white shirt seemed to be glowing strangely. But this was no vision; Saul was really there. Rabbi Yerahmiel looked down at his plate – but the noodles were just plain noodles again. Then Saul said: "Excuse me for interrupting you, but I thought that I had heard you call my name. And did you not also say: 'Regensburg'?"

Rabbi Yerahmiel was taken aback. Was this some holy event? Had he spoken aloud without realizing it? The Rabbi sat in silence; finally, he said: "Please sit down for a moment, Saul." Then the Rabbi closed his eyes and he prayed. Rabbi Yerahmiel prayed and he felt better – however, the Rabbi felt no wiser, so he said: "Saul, would you be so good as to come back in an hour?"

Saul was puzzled, but he left the Rabbi. An hour later, Saul returned and the Rabbi said: "Please sit down, Saul."

There was a moment of silence; then, the Rabbi said: "Saul, I have had a vision. Now, good Saul, I cannot tell you why – you must trust me on this, my friend – please take your family and all your belongings and move to Regensburg."

"I should move to Regensburg?"

"Yes, yes – to Regensburg," said Rabbi Yerahmiel. "While you were gone just now, I wrote a letter of introduction for you to the chief rabbi of Regensburg, Rabbi Abraham ben Hiyyah. I think that it is best for you to leave Cologne this evening."

"What is this that you are telling me, Rabbi," said poor Saul.

"How can I just pick up and leave my home and my relatives and my friends and my congregation? I was born here in Cologne, you know."

"I know that this is difficult, Saul. I know that this may even seem impossible," said Rabbi Yerahmiel, "but I am convinced that it is the best course of action."

"Am I in some sort of danger? Is there no other path available?"

"Unfortunately, I know very little," said the Rabbi, "but I feel that this counsel is motivated by the good Lord God (blessed be He) – and I must give you the best and the most holy advice that I can."

"Well, Rabbi, I will think about it," said Saul.

"Please do not think too long," said the Rabbi, and worriedly Saul walked home. The Rabbi, too, was worried. Some crisis was impending. But when would it fall? The Rabbi had little information, but he felt that he must do something. He did not sleep that night. Instead, he sat and he reviewed his meager clues. There was a *mezuzah*, there was Saul ben Benjamin, there was Regensburg, and there was Saul's white shirt.

The next morning, the Rabbi asked two of the yeshiva students to help him. Saul ben Benjamin's front door was visible from the synagogue, and on the post of this door was Saul's family *mezuzah*. Would the two boys take turns standing in the main prayer hall and looking out the window that faced Saul's front door? Should anything unusual happen, they must immediately tell the Rabbi. Then, the Rabbi sent a third student to Saul's house. The student greeted Saul's wife, Rachel: "Good morning, mother Rachel. Rabbi Yerahmiel would like very much to borrow one of the white shirts that belongs to your husband."

This was a strange request, but Rabbi Yerahmiel had a reputation as being a strange (albeit holy) man. Therefore, Rachel went to Saul's room, and she returned with one of the four identical white shirts that Saul wore daily. The student thanked her, and then he gave the shirt to the Rabbi. "I have done all that I can," thought Rabbi Yerahmiel; "it is now the Lord's turn." And Rabbi Yerahmiel went back to his studying.

The Jewish community in Cologne was like that of most large medieval cities; the Jewish Quarter had its own synagogue building, and it also had a community house, a hospital, a bathhouse, a bakery, and a cemetery. Except for the cemetery, all these buildings were huddled between the Cologne streets of Portalgasse, Unter Goldschmied, Obenmarspforten, and Judengasse. Although the full-time residents of this enclave were Jews, Gentiles also owned property in the Jewish Quarter. In fact, a few Christian houses reached into the very center of the Jewish district, from the side bordering on the old common-market area. Some of these houses had been in Gentile families for generations before the Jews moved into the district; other houses had been taken over by Gentiles through court orders. In most cases, the houses were rented by Gentile landlords to Jewish tenants. Such was the case with the house next to Saul's house.

Saul ben Benjamin lived along the alleyway facing the synagogue. The synagogue and yeshiva building in Cologne had a large main prayer hall containing the Holy Ark – the *Aron ha-Kodesh* – made of stone, as well as many benches for adults and children. It also had twelve stained glass windows, with pictures of lions and snakes, and these stained glass windows had given rise to a religious dispute. Rabbi Eljakim ben Joseph, one of the greatest scholars of Mainz, considered it improper for synagogue windows to be decorated with the figures of animals; Rabbi Eljakim feared that the worshippers would seem to be praying to pagan figures. On the other hand, Ephraim ben Isaac of Regensburg, in a formal opinion directed to Rabbi Joel of Cologne, permitted these and other figures and representations; Rabbi Ephraim contended that there was no longer any reason to fear idolatry among the Jews.

At the time of our story, some Jews said that the miracle was due to these very stained glass windows; others maintained that it was a freak weather occurrence. In any case and whatever the cause, the Gentile landlord of the house that was next to the house of Saul ben Benjamin claimed that a colorful holy miracle suddenly occurred beside the synagogue of Cologne. You see, Rabbi, after a violent summer thunderstorm, a tiny rainbow seemed to glow on one of the doorposts of Saul's house across from the synagogue. Saul's house was next to one owned by the Gentile. (The Gentile's house was rented to a Jewish family.) When the Gentile landlord came out of his house, he looked at the door of Saul's house. There on the *mezuzah* of Saul's doorpost was a tiny rainbow, like a radiant holy crucifix. To the Gentile, it appeared as if a glowing image of Christ had suddenly appeared on the doorpost of the Jewish house.

Of course, Rabbi, a *mezuzah* is a magic amulet – it protects the occupants of a home against harm from profane thoughts and from evil spirits. It is also sacred, and just as Jews do today, the Jews in medieval Cologne touched their *mezuzahs* whenever entering or leaving their houses, and then they kissed their hand. As the Gentile was standing and wondering at the miraculous image of Christ on the doorpost, Saul ben Benjamin came hurrying by. He covered the *mezuzah* with his hand, he touched the spot where the name *Shaddai* appears, and he said: "May the good Lord God (blessed be He) keep and preserve my going out and my coming in from henceforth and for ever more, amen." When Saul removed his hand, the image was gone; absent-mindedly, Saul kissed his hand.

The Gentile was suddenly afraid, and he was angry. What had happened here? This evil Jew had erased the miraculous vision: the glowing radiance of Christ was gone. This Jew had, in essence, wiped away the crucifix, and he had literally swallowed it up. It was profane witchcraft; it was the Devil's own work. The Gentile struck Saul fiercely. Saul fell to the ground, and the Gentile ran off.

Although it was already beginning to get dark, the watching yeshiva student saw this entire drama. He immediately ran into the back study room and he reported to Rabbi Yerahmiel, who was sitting bent over a book. The Rabbi put on Saul's white shirt, and he rushed out of the back study room. Without a glance, he hurried past the many benches in the main prayer hall. The Rabbi did not look up at the twelve stained glass windows with their colored lions and snakes, he did not look back at the Holy Ark made of stone, and he ran out the front door. With the help of the yeshiva student, Rabbi Yerahmiel lifted Saul and carried him into the synagogue. Saul was weak but awake.

"Listen," said the Rabbi, "we do not have much time. Now, Saul, hide in the loft above the back study room. As soon as it is dark, get your family and all the belongings that you can manage to take and go to Regensburg—tonight, mind you. Also, have your son remove the *mezuzah* from your doorpost and take it with you. Here is the letter that I wrote to Rabbi Abraham ben Hiyyah. Be sure to take that with you, too. Now—go into the back study room, and do not leave until the dead of night."

Then, the Rabbi took the cap from Saul's head, and Rabbi

Yerahmiel, who was the same height as Saul and who had a black curly beard like Saul, went and lay down in front of Saul's door. Soon, two officers of the guard appeared. They saw the Rabbi lying there breathing quietly with his eyes closed, and they dragged him off to the city prison. The Rabbi kept his eyes closed and he was put into a cell to await an appearance before the magistrate the next morning.

In the morning, the Rabbi was brought before the Bishop. The charge was a religious offense and it was serious – Saul ben Benjamin was charged with defaming Church relics, with profaning Church shrines, with blasphemy against the Christian Lord, and with engaging in witchcraft. The Bishop looked at the Rabbi, whom he knew. "Rabbi, what are you doing here?" asked the Bishop. "Where is the prisoner, Mr. Saul Benjamin?"

"I am not exactly certain," said the Rabbi truthfully.

The Gentile who had brought the charge looked at the Rabbi and he looked at the Bishop. Then the man said: "Just a moment, your honor – this is some sort of Jewish trick. When I left my house after the miracle occurred (amen), Saul was lying on the ground in front of his house. I went immediately and I got the guards."

The Bishop looked to the guards. One of them said: "Your honor, it is exactly as this man has said. He came running, and he found us by our posts at the Mars Gate. After he reported blasphemous and sacrilegious behavior by a Jew (an adult male with a black beard, with a cap, and with a white shirt), we went to the house next to the Jewish synagogue building and we found this man lying on the ground. He fit the description, so we brought him to the court building. That was last night, and this is the same man that we brought in."

"That is correct, Bishop," said the Rabbi.

"Well, then," said the Gentile man to the guards, "go and fetch Saul Benjamin. He lives in that same house by the synagogue; it is the house with the little white charm box on the doorpost."

The officers looked at the Bishop. "All right," said the Bishop to the guards, "bring this Mr. Benjamin here – and also bring the doorpost amulet."

The guards were gone for more than an hour. When they returned they said that the house was empty and that there was no amulet on the door. They had even looked carefully for marks on the doorpost of the house, but there was no indication that anything had ever been affixed there on the portals of that empty house across from the Jewish synagogue.

"But, Bishop," said the Gentile, "I tell you, a miracle occurred right there yesterday afternoon. I swear before the Lord!"

The Bishop looked at the man and he looked at Rabbi Yerahmiel. "I must agree," said the Rabbi, "I think that a miracle did occur there."

The Bishop remained suspicious, and he ruled that if the house were empty, then it must be given to the Gentile; he also ruled that if this Saul Benjamin ever appeared in Cologne, then he must stand trial. My grandmother said, however, that by then Saul had long been on his way to Regensburg. In Regensburg, Saul ben Benjamin was welcomed by Rabbi Abraham ben Hiyyah. When they heard the story, the entire Jewish community contributed money, and they helped Saul to buy a house and to set up a business. As his first act, of course, Saul fastened the old *mezuzah* to his doorpost, because neglecting to fasten a *mezuzah* on your house can cause death among your children. On the other hand, attending to your *mezuzah* is like having two thousand eight hundred servants, and it ensures that all your children shall forever be blessed. As it is written:

> Then all your children's children's race
> Will be forever blessed with grace
> And gentle winds will them embrace;
> While soft rains you'll forever taste
> Upon your peaceful, sleeping face.

Later, said my grandmother, Saul ben Benjamin became the Parnas of the Regensburg congregation and he had many scholars among his children and he died happily of old age. Grandmother said that all this good fortune came from the *mezuzah* that Saul had put on the post of his front door. "Remember, my little child," said my grandmother to me, "the purpose of a *mezuzah* is to provide a Jew with a continuous reminder: even in the privacy of your own home, you live under the all-seeing eye of the good Lord God (blessed be He). The Lord loves you, and He will ensure that – no matter where you are – His warm and gentle Grace will rain soft for ever on your sleeping face, amen."

hat is that, Rabbi? I was just resting my eyes. Yes, join me here by the stove. (I think that you will be too warm on that bench: try the one nearer to the wall.) An old man like me can doze forever by a warm stove; I suppose that is because I have outlived all my masters. What do I mean? Why, Rabbi, certainly you remember the scriptural proverb:

> Like vinegar on the teeth
>   Or like smoke in the eyes
> Is the sleepy servant
>   To his master.

I can sleep now because I no longer have any masters to upset with my laziness.

True, true—the good Lord God (blessed be He) is the Master of us all. Certainly my grandmother always considered Him to be her Master, and this accounted for her amazing energy even in old age. How could you ever dare to be vinegar on the teeth of the good Lord God or to be smoke in the eyes of the Almighty One? At least, that is what my grandmother said to me. Not only did she keep active in her old age, Rabbi – my grandmother remained very courteous; she always held her tongue, and she tried to think only the best of her neighbors. She never fell into the trap of the gossips living near Mordecai ben Judah. You do not know about old Mordecai? Then let me tell you:

Once upon a time, said my grandmother, in the congregation of Rabbi Yerahmiel ha-Kohen of Cologne, there lived a devout man named Mordecai ben Judah. Mordecai studied daily and he prayed devoutly, and he felt that his most important service to the Lord, his Master, was to say the *Kiddish* in his home on Sabbath eve.

Eventually, the time came for Mordecai ben Judah to die, and the Angel of Death came to him. When seen bare and unadorned, Dumah, the Angel of Death, is covered with eyes from head to foot, and he comes with a drawn sword in hand. This time, however, Dumah appeared in the guise of a clothed human being. Reb Mordecai was praying quietly in the main room of the Cologne yeshiva. The Angel of Death was a presence that could be felt without being seen, and Mordecai felt the presence of the Angel of Death and he looked up.

"Why are you standing here?" asked Mordecai. "I do not think that I have seen you before. Who are you?"

Dumah, the Angel of Death, replied: "Mordecai ben Judah, I am the holy angel of the good Lord God, blessed be He. Your Master, the Almighty Lord, has sent me to take your soul – for your time has come to die."

Then Mordecai began to shiver and he said: "But holy angel, I am praying and I am studying. Is it not true that the good Lord God (blessed be He) will not interrupt pious study, even for death?"

"Yes," said Dumah, the Angel of Death, "that is true."

Quickly, Mordecai looked down at his book, and he began to read aloud. The most holy angel waited a moment and then he disappeared from the synagogue and he reappeared before the throne of God the Almighty; and Dumah said to the Lord: "O Lord God, King of the universe, You have sent me to take the soul of Mordecai ben Judah of Cologne. But I cannot do this – the man is studying intently. He is praying, and he is reading Your Holy Law."

Then the awesome Lord God Almighty said to the angel: "It is decreed that Mordecai shall die before tonight. Go down to Mordecai ben Judah of Cologne and wait patiently – and go as your full and naked self." And the Angel of Death did as the great Lord God commanded him.

In his full glory, Dumah, the Angel of Death, reaches from Heaven to earth, and he is covered with eyes from his head to his feet. When the Angel of Death came down to Reb Mordecai, Dumah again found him studying. However, this time Mordecai ben Judah saw the Angel of Death in his most fearsome glory, with drawn sword in hand, and Mordecai began to tremble: he knew that there was no way to avoid his fate. Nonetheless, Mordecai said: "O holy angel, I am busy studying, and it is written in the Torah: 'He who studies the Torah, purchases life.'"

Then Dumah, the Angel of Death, replied: "You are correct, Mordecai. But it is also written in Isaiah":

> Your first father sinned and your intercessors and their spokesmen have also transgressed and now you yourself have rebelled against Me.

"Do not try to rebel against the will of the Almighty Lord God, your Master."

When Mordecai heard this verse, he felt very weak indeed and he said: "All right, good angel, I am ready to die. But just wait a short while longer. I would like to tell my wife and to prepare her for the inevitable."

"Very well," said the angel, "go and tell your wife—and also take the time to leave a will for your children, instructing them on how to behave after your death."

So Reb Mordecai hurried out of the synagogue, and he went home to his wife Deborah. "Why are you home from the yeshiva in the middle of the day?" asked his wife.

"Ah, Deborah, my good and pious wife," said Reb Mordecai, "please sit down."

"What is this? What is happening?" asked Deborah. "I know you well, Mordecai: something terrible is afoot. What disaster has befallen us?"

"Deborah, you must now prepare to earn your own living, for I shall not be able to support you any longer."

When the wife heard this, she said to him: "What are you telling me, my husband. Why do you suddenly talk like this? You have never spoken this way to me before. Where are you going?"

"My beloved wife, I am forced to talk like this because I have to go away from you on a long journey."

"Oh, Mordecai, I hope that it is only that you have now taken leave of your senses. Have you a fever? Have you been struck on the head? Here, sit quietly – this delusion will pass."

"No, my wife," said Mordecai, "there is no avoiding my fate. The good Lord God (blessed be He) has decreed that I should die today – today, Deborah, on this very day, amen."

When the woman heard these words from her husband, she knew exactly what the future held; she knew it was inevitable, and she began to weep and she could not be comforted. Then, she ran from the room crying. A little later, Mordecai went into the kitchen and he found his wife sitting silently. "I am sorry to have to face you with my death so soon," he said.

"I do not accept that, Chayim," she answered.

" 'Chayim'?" asked Mordecai, "Who is Chayim?"

"*You* are Chayim."

"Ah, good wife, the shock has been too much for you. Do you not remember that I am Mordecai ben Judah?"

"Oh, perhaps you were Mordecai ben Judah before, but now I have renamed you: now you are Chayim ben Judah."

"What are you saying, Deborah?" asked Mordecai.

"Ever since the most holy biblical times, it has been known that as a last resort a Jew can change the name of his sick child. In this way, the Angel of Death is fooled: he will pass right by the poor infant," said his wife. "Somehow we will protect you yet, Chayim."

"My good wife," said Mordecai, "Mordecai I was born, Mordecai I have lived, and Mordecai I shall die, amen."

Again, Mordecai's wife Deborah began to cry, and when Reb Mordecai saw how bitterly she was lamenting and how inconsolable she was, he said to her: "My wife, it cannot be otherwise – this is what the Almighty Lord God (blessed be He) has decreed, amen. But listen, Deborah: I will do this one special thing for you after my death. On the eve of every Sabbath and on the eve of every Festival, I will come to you and I will say the *Kiddush*, just as I have done all during my life." And Mordecai gave his poor sad wife a hug.

Then, Mordecai went into the next room, and he began to write out the ethical will for his children, instructing them on how to behave when he was no longer available for counsel. Mordecai seemed in good health, but within the hour he suddenly came down with a fever. Soon after this, he developed pains throughout his body, and in a little while he died and his soul departed. So the neighbors came, and the empty body of Mordecai ben Judah was washed and it was dressed in a clean white shroud, and on the next day, he was buried in the Cologne cemetery. The Cologne cemetery was quite a distance from the Jewish Quarter; it lay to the south of the city, outside the St. Severin Gate. It was more than an hour's walk for the poor widow Deborah to visit her husband's grave, and she had no hope that even the tiniest holy remnant of Mordecai's spirit could travel the distance and would ever visit her home again on the eve of the Festival nights.

After the seven days of mourning, life resumed for Deborah. On the next Friday evening, she lit the Sabbath candles alone and she said:

> Blessed are You, O Lord our God, King of the Universe, Who has sanctified us by Your commandments and Who has commanded us to light the Sabbath lamps.

Then, she spread the table with a clean tablecloth and at the head of the table, where her husband once sat, she put two loaves of bread. As always, Deborah covered the bread with a napkin, and near the loaves of bread she set an empty cup and a pitcher of wine.

When it was time for the Sabbath *Kiddush*, Reb Mordecai ben Judah walked in the front door. Deborah became weak; she felt faint. She could not look at the spirit. But Mordecai himself was very calm. He chanted the praise of a virtuous wife, he recited the verses from Genesis describing the work of Creation on the sixth and the seventh days, and then he filled the empty wine cup, saying: "Blessed are You, O Lord our God, the King of the Universe and the Creator of the fruit of the vine . . ." and so on. After completing this benediction, Mordecai handed the wine cup to his wife. Deborah took the cup without touching the spirit. Finally, Mordecai cut one loaf of bread–he set aside a piece at his place, and he put the rest on Deborah's plate. After this, and without actually eating a morsel of food or drinking a drop of wine, Mordecai suddenly disappeared. Deborah was not certain whether she had dreamed the entire scene. But the spirit of the departed man returned each week in order to say the *Kiddush*, and soon Deborah felt that this was a natural and ordinary routine of her life.

One time on a Friday evening a few months later, as Reb Mordecai was sitting with his wife and saying the blessing, some people passed by the window, and they heard a man saying the Sabbath benedictions in Deborah's house. The neighbors stopped, and they listened. "Ah, so the widow Deborah is entertaining men so soon," they thought. One of the men from the group went immediately to Rabbi Yerahmiel ha-Kohen and he asked: "Rabbi, do you know Deborah, the widow of Mordecai ben Judah?"

"Yes, she is a fine woman," said the Rabbi.

"Well, Rabbi, this fine widow is concealing a strange man in her house. I and Reb Israel and both of our wives have heard the man saying the *Kiddush* for Deborah on this very Friday night."

The next day, the story was told all around the synagogue – so Rabbi Yerahmiel could not overlook the report. The Rabbi sent for Deborah, and he told her what people were saying about her. Then Rabbi Yerahmiel said: "I am certain that there is a simple explanation, Deborah. Let us put this matter to rest."

Deborah was upset, and she said to the Rabbi: "Of course there is a simple explanation, Rabbi. The rumors are completely untrue. No strange man has been in my house since my poor dear husband, Mordecai ben Judah, departed many months ago, may the good Lord God (blessed be He) rest his soul, amen."

Then the Rabbi said: "Ah, I knew that it was a mistake."

But the other scholars standing nearby said: "Just a minute, woman. How can you deny this report when two trustworthy men and their wives have heard a man's voice with their very own ears?"

So Deborah reluctantly told the entire story of her husband and his death and his regular return in order to pronounce the holy benedictions. "You see, Rabbi," concluded Deborah, "Mordecai's spirit continues to say the Sabbath blessings for me, just as before his death."

"That is very good of him," said the Rabbi.

But the men standing there in the yeshiva would not believe Deborah's story. "We will see what we will see," said one man. "Wait until next Friday night, and then we shall find out the truth." And all the men nodded seriously.

The next Friday night – the Sabbath eve – came, and as usual Reb Mordecai walked into his old house through the front door. His wife had not cooked anything for the Sabbath because she had been too upset by all the accusations. As soon as she saw her husband, Deborah began to talk and talk, and she told the whole story to her husband. Mordecai said to her: "Do not be sad, Deborah – I will answer for you myself. These gossip-mongers will have to believe me."

So, instead of saying his usual Sabbath blessings, Mordecai ben Judah floated down the street and into the main prayer hall of the old synagogue of Cologne. As soon as he appeared, men stopped talking, and they looked up in fear and in amazement. "Well, my good scholars," said Mordecai, "I see that you are gathered here piously in the halls of study; therefore, I think that it is time for some serious study of the holy words. Let us begin, gentlemen, with the Book of Proverbs. I am certain that you recall the proverb":

> With libels, lies, and false words,
>   The godless slander good men.
> But the wronged ones will be saved
>   By a righteous citizen:
> The defamed will soon be rescued
>   By clear-sighted truth again.

All was very quiet. Then Mordecai said: "And, old friends, let me remind you that in the Book of Proverbs the Holy Scriptures also declare":

> Plot no evil against your unsuspecting neighbor,
> Or the Almighty Lord will be angry with you.

Still there was silence. The men looked away, but Mordecai continued: "The Book of Proverbs goes on to say, gentlemen":

> Disaffection stirs up quarrels,
> Tale-bearing breaks up friendships,
> And slander divides brothers.

A scoundrel repeats evil gossip —
But it is like a scorching fire
Upon his wicked lips.

Finally, Mordecai said: "I said: 'It is like a scorching fire upon your evil lips' . . . Witnesses, stand on your feet! Declare aloud what you have seen and what you have heard. *I* am the man who said the *Kiddush* blessings for my wife on the eve of the Sabbath and on eve of the Festivals. I am Mordecai ben Judah. You wish to give my devout and pious wife a bad name? Then may the Almighty Lord God judge between you and her."

No one moved. All was very quiet in the old synagogue. "As you do not reply," said Mordecai, "I presume that you wish to remain silent. Remember: 'It is like a scorching fire upon your evil lips.' So, my neighbors, you shall forever remain silent, or you will be blessed with a scorching fire upon your lips, amen." Then a wind blew through the synagogue, and the spirit of Mordecai ben Judah disappeared. And ever after, each of the scholars could only whisper in a hoarse voice for the rest of his life, otherwise his lips began to feel as if they were being burned. A few years later, the old widow Deborah died — she died and Rabbi Yerahmiel buried her by the side of her husband, and neither her spirit nor the spirit of her husband were ever seen in Cologne again.

abbi, I am glad to see you here alone. I want to apologize for my outburst during the service this evening. It was just that Reb Anton's son, Benjamin, pointed out that Reb Anton was misreading the Scriptures. I suppose that I should not have said anything, but in the olden days – in the strict and pious days of our fathers – Benjamin would have been ordered to leave and never to return. You know how the Sages taught us that even when justly provoked, even when a father truly angers his son, the son must restrain himself. Never be disrespectful to your father, says the Talmud.

Is this not the talmudic teaching, Rabbi? I am certain that somewhere in the Talmud a Sage was once asked: "How far must one go in honoring his parents?" The Rabbi replied: "Gentlemen, suppose that your father took a purse of money and threw it into the sea. Or suppose that your father dumped a bag of fine grain into the dirt. Or suppose that your father ripped his best Sabbath clothes to shreds and cast them into the garbage heap. Even in these cases, you must never criticize openly. Never be disrespectful, and never shame your parents."

And (this is more immediately relevant, Rabbi) the Talmud also tells us:

If a man sees his father violating some precept of the Torah or if a man sees his father disobeying a teaching of the Law, the son should not say: "Father, you are violating the Torah; or Father, you are disobeying the Law."

Instead, a child should say: "Father, perhaps you have forgotten exactly how this is written in the Torah; or Father, you may have forgotten this particular aspect of the Law."

And it would even be better for the child to say: "Father, let me remind you of such and such verse in the Torah; or Father, let me remind you of such and such section of the Law."

Yes, Rabbi, Benjamin had many other courses available to him than directly criticizing his father. Undoubtedly, someone pulled Benjamin's right ear rather than his left when he was a baby.

Why, Rabbi, I am surprised at you! Have you not heard that when a baby sneezes you must immediately pull its left ear? When I sneezed, my grandmother would *always* pull my left ear—then she would remind me that the Talmud tells us that we learn best from our elders: "Some men try to learn from the young—to whom are these men like? They are like those who eat unripe grapes; they are like those who drink wine directly from the fermenting vat. But other men learn from the elderly—to whom are *these* men like? They are like those who eat ripe grapes; they are like those who drink wine that has been aged properly and that is now mellow." Of course, Rabbi, all these perspectives stem ultimately from the sacred scriptural injunction:

> Honor your father and your mother;
> in this way, you will live long
> in the land that the Lord your God
> is giving to you.

Grandmother said that we should all honor our parents in the way that the devoted Reb Isaac honored his mother. You have not heard of Isaac ben Markus, Rabbi? Then let me tell you:

Once upon a time, said my grandmother, there lived in Cologne on the River Rhine a certain Isaac ben Markus whose mother was so old that she could not walk. Therefore, Reb Isaac wheeled her about in a special cart wherever she wanted to go; furthermore, good Isaac gave his mother the first choice of all his food and drink, and he tried his best to make her comfortable and happy with all his heart and soul.

At that time, Yerahmiel ha-Kohen was the chief rabbi of Cologne. One day, Rabbi Yerahmiel came to visit the mother of Reb Isaac. "How are you doing, my good mother," asked the Rabbi.

"Oh, I am fairly well," she replied.

"I understand that your son is looking after you," said Rabbi Yerahmiel.

"Ah, Rabbi, what a fine son the Lord has blessed me with," answered Isaac's mother. "Should I even hint that there is something I want, then Isaac will immediately fetch it for me. Should I glance at a comb or a brush or a shawl or a book, my Isaac grabs it and he hands it to me. If I mention that the day is pleasant, then Isaac sets me up comfortably in a chair out of doors. If I cough, then Isaac gets me an extra robe. All mothers should be so fortunate—praise the good Lord God (blessed be He), amen."

Isaac ben Markus's mother looked up to the heavens. Then she said: "And, Rabbi, I cause him such trouble. Undoubtedly, he would be happier if he did not have such a burden—but then I will not live forever; one day, Isaac will be free of all these problems."

And the Rabbi replied: "My good woman, the Holy Scriptures say":

> Honor your father and your mother; in this way, you will live long in the land that the Lord your God is giving to you.

If Isaac did a thousand times as much as he was doing, it would not be enough. The good Lord God (blessed be He) tells us that there is no limit to the honor due one's father and one's mother: one can never do too much."

"Rabbi, Rabbi," said the mother, "how could I expect my son to do even the slightest bit more for me—although, I suppose that there is one tiny thing that he could do, if he had the time. My son is so busy, that I would never dare to ask for anything more. . . . But, Rabbi, when you see him, you might casually mention something to my fine son Isaac."

When Rabbi Yerahmiel heard this, he looked down at the floor for a moment. Isaac was a serious and worthy scholar; he was a devout and pious man. Isaac actually carried his mother about in a special cart. How could the Rabbi ask for anything more from good Isaac? The Rabbi hesitated, and then he asked: "Tell me, mother, what else you would have Isaac do?"

And the mother said: "Listen, Rabbi, Isaac comes home tired from work, and then after checking on me he goes to the yeshiva. In the evening when he finally returns again, he is exhausted. But will he eat? No, he will not—not until he has prepared a meal for me. And will he then rest a moment? No, he will not—not until he has seen that I am comfortable. But, Rabbi, when I ask him if I can wash his feet, then what do you imagine that he answers? He says: 'No.' Is that any way for a good son to behave? I would like to do some little thing for him, but he lets me do nothing at all."

Rabbi Yerahmiel listened thoughtfully, and he said: "Let me speak to Isaac." And the Rabbi left and went back to the old Cologne yeshiva. The Rabbi walked into the main prayer hall with its many wooden benches and its twelve stained glass windows filled with figures of colored lions and snakes; there, before the Holy stone Ark, sat Reb Isaac ben Markus. Rabbi Yerahmiel sat down next to Isaac. "Hello, Reb Isaac," said the Rabbi.

Isaac turned and smiled: "Hello, Rabbi."

"I have just been visiting your mother," said the Rabbi.

"Does she need any help? Perhaps I had best be getting home," said Isaac.

"She looked fine," said Rabbi Yerahmiel.

"Are you certain? She had a slight cold recently," said Isaac ben Markus. "I should probably check on her before the evening prayers."

"That would be a good idea," said the Rabbi. "But, Reb Isaac, I would like to have a quiet word with you before you leave."

"Yes, Rabbi?"

"Isaac, let me be frank: you have not been doing enough for your mother."

"I know, Rabbi—often I think the same thing. But what more can I do?" asked Isaac.

"I think, Isaac, that if you added one thing, then you would be doing your full and pious duty as a son."

"What do you suggest, Rabbi?"

"Do you know the talmudic section entitled 'Architectonics'?" asked the Rabbi.

"No, I am afraid that I do not know that part."

"That is quite understandable," said the Rabbi. " 'Architectonics' is very abstruse, and it has not often been translated into Hebrew from the old Babylonian. Anyway, in one chapter, a famous old Rabbi tells us: 'In one way can a scholar always honor his mother—he must request her to wash his feet when he returns from pious study in the yeshiva.' "

"A son must let his mother wash his feet?"

"No, Isaac—a *scholar* must let his mother wash his feet, and then this is only after he has spent much time in serious and holy study of the Torah," said the Rabbi.

"Well, Rabbi," said Isaac, "I had never heard of this before, but I am glad that you have told me. I will put this policy into effect immediately."

And Isaac ben Markus went home, and humbly he asked his mother to wash his feet. Yes, yes, Rabbi—my grandmother swore that this was a true story. And then she would usually follow the story by reciting from the Book of Proverbs:

> Strength is the glory of young men;
> While gray hairs bespeak the dignity of the old.

and she also repeated:

> Gray hair is a resplendent crown,
> For it is the outcome of a virtuous life. . . .

What is that, Rabbi? No, I was just resting—let me see, where was I? Oh yes, once upon a time, said my grandmother, Rabbi Yerahmiel ha-Kohen of Cologne had a dream about parents. Rabbi Yerahmiel dreamt that his companion in Paradise was to be a certain Ephraim ben Jacob ben Shimshon, a small man with a limp. What? Of course this has to do with parents, Rabbi—please be patient.

Now, when Rabbi Yerahmiel awoke the next morning, he thought that he had just heard a voice saying: "I am an old man, but I am a young gardener." The Rabbi turned his head and looked around, he got up from his bed and looked out the door, then he looked out the window; however, there was no one about. Suddenly, Rabbi Yerahmiel remembered his dream. "How strange," thought the Rabbi, "to dream so clearly about a man whom I have never met – and then what was this voice that I heard? Something mysterious and holy is happening here." So Rabbi Yerahmiel decided that he should try to find this man Ephraim.

That very morning, the Rabbi packed his traveling bag and he set out from Cologne. Patiently he journeyed from place to place in search of Ephraim, a little man with a limp. First, Rabbi Yerahmiel went north to Mulheim, and then he went on to Stommeln. From Stommeln, he traveled east to Kaster; he crossed the Erft River at Kaster, and then he journeyed on to Linnich on the Rur River. In Linnich, the Rabbi heard that just north, in the neighboring town of Lovenich, there lived a man named Ephraim whose father was named Jacob, and this Ephraim walked with a limp.

Eventually, Rabbi Yerahmiel arrived in Lovenich, near the place where Ephraim lived. There was only a small Jewish community in Lovenich. When the local Jews heard that the head rabbi of Cologne had arrived, all the elders of the town came out to meet him and they paid him their respects and they invited him to eat and to drink and to pray with them. Rabbi Yerahmiel replied: "I will neither eat nor drink nor pray before I have seen a certain Ephraim ben Jacob ben Shimshon who, I am told, lives in your good town of Lovenich."

The townspeople were amazed. "Ephraim ben Jacob ben Shimshon? Our Ephraim? How have you even heard of him, Rabbi? What possible concern could you have with Ephraim? Has he done some wrong? He seems a harmless fellow – although he is not too smart."

Rabbi Yerahmiel replied: "As far as I know, he has done no wrong. In fact, I suspect that he is destined to be my companion in Paradise. I dreamt that Ephraim is a fine man, and I would like to find out what virtuous deeds have made him the companion of a rabbi in the Great Hereafter. When I have learned all of his wonderful history, then I will come and eat and drink and pray with you."

But the community elders said: "Good Rabbi, you must be

thinking of some other Ephraim. Our Ephraim is not worthy even to stand beside you during your living days."

Rabbi Yerahmiel replied: "Perhaps—nevertheless, I am anxious to see your Ephraim, even though you are uncertain about his merits."

So the prominent Jews sent a delegation of young people to Ephraim; they told Ephraim ben Jacob ben Shimshon that the famous Rabbi Yerahmiel ha-Kohen of Cologne was in town and that the Rabbi was looking specifically for Ephraim. Ephraim laughed, and he said: "That is a fine joke, my friends." And Ephraim went back to his gardening.

The delegation of young people returned to the town square. "I am afraid that Ephraim refuses to come," said one man. "He thinks that we are making fun of him."

Rabbi Yerahmiel said: "Well, I can understand that." So the Rabbi went off to Ephraim's house himself, and all the worthies of the Jewish community of the town of Lovenich followed.

Ephraim was weeding around his turnip plants. When he heard the crowd approach he became frightened. "What terrible thing have I done?" he thought.

The main scholar of Lovenich went up to the fence and he said: "Ephraim, my good man, this is the great sage and rabbi of Cologne, Rabbi Yerahmiel ha-Kohen. He has come to see you."

Now Ephraim was very frightened indeed. "May the good Lord God (blessed be He) save me," thought Ephraim. "If only I come out of this alive, I shall go to the synagogue every single day—not just on the Sabbath and the Festivals." Ephraim remained silent, and he continued pulling up weeds.

Then Rabbi Yerahmiel came over to the fence; Ephraim began to tie up a vine with two black-green wrinkly squashes hanging on it. "Ephraim," said the Rabbi, "you have a fine-looking garden there. Would you take a moment to talk with me?"

Ephraim stood up, but he was unsure what to say. After a moment, the Rabbi said: "My friend, I have come to ask you to tell me about your life. I would especially like to know what good deeds you have done."

Ephraim was puzzled. "Dear Rabbi," he said slowly, "I am just a poor man. There is nothing special or holy about my life."

"Tell me anyway," said the Rabbi. "How do you spend your days?"

"Well, there is nothing to tell, Rabbi. I have a garden, and I work here every day, rain or shine. Mainly I grow these squashes – I also like the garlic plants. My old father and my old mother live with me. They cannot move about easily, so I help them walk. I make the meals, and we talk in the evenings. Other than my gardening, I think that is all."

Some of the men in the crowd nodded in agreement. The Rabbi looked again at Ephraim, who was standing beside his squash vines and his turnip plants and his bean bushes. Ephraim hesitated. Then he said: "That is my entire life, good Rabbi."

Rabbi Yerahmiel took Ephraim's hand and he smiled. "I am happy to have met you, Reb Ephraim," said the Rabbi. "I hope that I shall prove a worthy companion for you in the Great Hereafter, my fine gardener."

Yes, Rabbi, that is the end of the story – my grandmother told it to me many times. I remember hearing it when we sat together by her mother's grave, as my grandmother knit for hour after hour. And my grandmother would say to me: "Honor your father and your mother, my golden little boy." You know, Rabbi, my grandmother reminded me that a person must honor his parents both in life and in death. For example, after your father's death you should not say only: "As my father said. . . ." Instead, you might say: "This is what my father said – he was my teacher, and may I be his atonement and may any sufferings due to him for his few sins alight upon me instead, amen."

I can just picture my grandmother telling me this, as she looked down at her knitting, with her fingers busily weaving in and out. "Always remember, my little one," she said, "when you are old and grey and when you speak of your father (as you will many, many times) be sure to say: 'His memory will be my blessing in eternal life – I am his child, and I was his best love, amen.' Because," said my grandmother, "you were his first love, you know, my little golden one."

abbi, I am glad to see you here tonight: I need your advice. It is really a small matter. This afternoon one of the students, Israel ben Isaac (you know him, Rabbi; he is tall with wavy reddish hair)—anyway, Israel was bragging about the amount of Torah that he had memorized. He is a very bright boy, and learning comes easily to him. I overheard his boasting, and I said to him: "Israel, my young scholar, it is good that you know so many passages: now you will have the opportunity to learn even more verses." And he said to me: "Old shammas, you should praise me—you should not chastise me. And certainly you should not assign me more work than my colleagues. Remember, it is written in the Talmud: 'A man should never make distinctions between his children.' And I am sure that this means that a shammas should never make distinctions between the yeshiva students. Why should I suffer because I am a better scholar than my friends?"

Well, Rabbi, after all these years of sitting in the study rooms during lessons, I have learned a bit of Talmud myself. And I recall what the Sages decided about humility: it is the greatest of all virtues. Of course, the arena of scholarship is a sensitive one for the Jews, so the rabbis warn us especially not to be proud of our learning. Be careful, they say—do not brag about your knowledge.

> Whoever exalts himself by means of the words of the Torah is like a dead animal flung into the road—passers-by must hold their noses and keep away. On the other hand, whoever studies the Torah, but does so quietly (and lives on dates and locusts, and wears shabby clothes, and speaks only when he is spoken to), he is a fine man—he may seem simple, but in the end he knows the most and he is the happiest.

So says the Talmud, Rabbi.

Moreover, the Scriptures, in Isaiah, say:

> The spirit of the Lord whispered a word
> When He appointed me to speak—
> And, O humble men, I have heard:
> "God will uplift all the meek."

Therefore, the Talmud reminds us that on that wondrous day when the Messiah shall come, it will be the gentle and the humble who shall inherit the earth, it will be the man of bent form and lowly appearance who shall be king, and it will be the quiet scholar who shall be most revered, amen.

I know that you remember these sections of the Talmud, so you will recall how they continue with the tale of Rabbi Hillel, a man renowned for his patience and for his unassuming nature:

> In those long gone days, two men made a wager. The first man claimed that Rabbi Hillel was endlessly patient. The second man claimed that no man was endlessly patient—eventually, he said, Hillel would lose his temper like any other mortal. The two men made a bet and agreed that the loser would forfeit ten gold coins.
>
> Now, it was the Sabbath eve, and the great Rabbi was bathing and washing his hair. The second man went to Hillel's house, he loudly pounded on the door, and he shouted: "Hillel! Hillel, come out here!"
>
> Imagine, Rabbi, this man did not address the great Rabbi Hillel with any respect whatsoever, yet Rabbi Hillel wrapped his hair in a

towel, he put another towel about his waist, and he stepped to the front door of his house. "Mr. Hillel," said the man, "I have a question to ask you."

"Well, my good sir, feel free to ask," said the Rabbi.

"Why are the Babylonians round-headed?"

The Rabbi looked at the man, he hesitated a moment, and then he replied: "Well, this is an interesting question. Let me see – I would say that the reason is simple: the Babylonians have no skilled mid-wives." So saying, Rabbi Hillel returned to his bath.

The man waited until Rabbi Hillel had again settled into the bath, then he called out: "Hillel! Hillel, come out here!" And the man began to pound loudly on the door.

The Rabbi wrapped his hair in a towel, he put a second towel about his waist, and he stepped to the front door. "Mr. Hillel," said the man, "I have a question to ask you."

"Well, friend, feel free to ask it."

"Why are the inhabitants of Palmyra blear-eyed?"

"Blear-eyed? Ah, this is a strange question. I suspect that the reason that they are blear-eyed is that the inhabitants of Palmyra live in wind-swept sandy regions," replied the Rabbi, and then he returned to his bath.

Again, the man waited a few minutes. Rabbi Hillel removed his towels and he settled into the bath waters, which were now cool. Then the man yelled: "Hillel! Hillel, come out here!" And he banged on the door with his fist.

Patiently, Rabbi Hillel stood up and wrapped his hair in a towel; he put the other damp towel about his waist and he stepped to the door. "Mr. Hillel," said the man, "I have a question to ask you."

"I suspected that you had another question. What is it this time?"

"Why are the Africans broad-footed?"

"Ah yes – I used to wonder this myself. It is a good question, and so I will give you a good answer: the Africans are broad-footed because they live in wet marshy swamplands," said Rabbi Hillel, and he returned to the cold bath.

"Just a moment, Mr. Hillel," said the man, "I have yet another question."

Rabbi Hillel came back to the front door: "Very well, what is it that you wish to know?"

"Will you answer as many questions as I ask?" asked the man.

"I will do my best," said Hillel.

"Are you angry at being pestered with questions?"

"Is that one of your questions?"

"It is," said the man.

"Well, I would rather be taking my bath," said Hillel, "and at the moment, answering questions is not my favorite occupation – but no, I am not angry. It is my responsibility to answer questions as best I can."

"I see," said the man. "Then answer this: Do you know where I can get ten gold coins?"

"Is that another one of your questions?"

"It is," said the man.

"Why do you need ten gold coins?" asked Hillel.

"It is because I have just lost a bet: I claimed that I could make you lose your temper, and I am afraid that I cannot," said the man.


Yes, Rabbi, the great Hillel is an example to us all. As my grandmother said: "Be patient and be humble, young man, and you will grow into a scholar as great as the great Rabbi Hillel himself." She said that almost daily – did you ever hear her? You never met my grandmother? Ah, more is the pity, for she was a fine woman. And, Rabbi, my grandmother knew the Talmud as no other woman I have ever met. In relation to pride and arrogance, she would quote:

> Every arrogant man is like an idolator: he denies the basic principles of religion. The conceited scholar is immoral, he does not deserve resurrection, and the Lord laments him. The haughty notice only those other men who have made themselves larger than life. But the good Lord God (blessed be He) is the opposite: the Holy One notices the meek and the lowly and the humble. In fact, the good Lord God (blessed be He) has said in the Scriptures: "I cannot dwell in the same world with those who are arrogant, for they are dishonest at heart."

What is that, Rabbi? Certainly there is more to tell: I was just resting my eyes a moment. Now let me see, what was I saying? Yes,

yes, humility was very important to my grandmother—as it is said in the Book of Proverbs:

> Six things the good Lord hates—
> Yes, seven does He despise:
> Haughty spirits and proud eyes,
> Vile tongues that criticize,
> Hands that cause an innocent's demise,
> Hearts that cruel crimes devise,
> Feet that hurry for an evil prize,
> False witnesses telling slanderous lies,
> And those who incite fights unwise
> Between brothers, where they should ne'er arise.

And in this regard, I remember my grandmother's story about Anselm ben Joel ben Isaac, a young man who lacked humility. It is a curious tale—it concerns the chief rabbi of Cologne, Yerahmiel ha-Kohen. It seems, said my grandmother, that one day a bright young student of the Cologne yeshiva, Anselm ben Joel ben Isaac, had just finished explaining a very difficult passage in the Talmud. He had been roundly complimented by all the senior scholars in the study hall, and he was feeling proud and taller than life. Anselm strode from the back study room, he passed the Holy Ark made of stone, he walked by the twelve stained glass windows with their colored lions and snakes, and he marched on out the front door of the synagogue.

As Anselm walked happily down Judengasse Street, he passed a man who was lifting a heavy load of cloaks. Without looking, the man stepped back into Anselm's path; Anselm bumped him and said angrily: "Watch out, old man."

The man dropped the cloaks, he turned around, and he said: "You watch out yourself, you young fool."

Anselm stopped; he felt as hard as an oak and as tall as a tree, and he looked at the man who was bent over and who was dirty and ill-formed. "You are certainly ugly, you wretch," said Anselm. "Are all your family so foul-looking?" And then Anselm turned and he went on his way.

Rabbi Yerahmiel had overheard this exchange. When Anselm

came to the yeshiva on the next afternoon, the Rabbi called him into the back room. "You were quite unpleasant to that cloak-hauler yesterday," said the Rabbi.

"He did not look where he was going," responded Anselm. "Besides, Rabbi, the old man spoke very impolitely himself."

"That is no excuse, Anselm. You have been disrepectful to the Almighty Lord God (blessed be He). You called this man ugly, but, I remind you, he is one of God's sacred creations, just as we all are."

"Well, perhaps I was a bit rude."

"Yes, perhaps you were. This man is not responsible for his looks: we are all products of the Great and Holy Artisan. Who are we to question His design?" asked Rabbi Yerahmiel. "Anselm, I am afraid that you have spoken with (as it says in the Talmud) the third tongue. The third tongue speaks ill of someone, and in this way it slays three persons – it harms the speaker, it harms the spoken to, and it harms the spoken of. Remember, Anselm, the Holy One (blessed be He) says of such a person: 'I and he cannot dwell together in the same world.'"

"Rabbi, you are making a large issue out of a small incident. I was just being honest – besides, this man was equally rude," said Anselm.

"Anselm, I am concerned with *you* now. Arrogance and rudeness are sins," said the Rabbi. "Therefore, you are temporarily dismissed from the yeshiva."

"Dismissed?! That is a harsh punishment for one slightly hasty word on my part. What must I do to be reinstated?"

"Young man, in order to return here, you must go to the Artisan who made this ill-formed cloak-hauler, and you must find out why He made such a misshapen article, and you must be forgiven your arrogance."

"What do you mean?" asked Anselm.

"I mean simply this: you are dismissed from the yeshiva until you repent and get forgiveness from the good Lord God," said the Rabbi. Then, the Rabbi sent Anselm ben Joel ben Isaac away from the yeshiva.

Anselm stood a moment in the courtyard outside the synagogue. He did not know what to do with himself. Soon, word would be out that he had been dismissed from the yeshiva; he was embarrassed to be seen around the community. Perhaps he should take a small journey – a pilgrimage might set matters straight again. Yes, he would take a short pilgrimage. So, Anselm decided to set out immediately, and he began to walk, with no particular direction in mind. After a bit, he found himself crossing the River Rhine, by the town of Kalk, and then he continued walking east. Anselm had no destination, but it felt good to be walking in the open countryside.

There seemed to be no one else about, and Anselm walked and walked. Windhovers circled high in the grey skies; jipijapa plants lined the road. Eventually, it began to rain. Anselm saw a broken-down old house by the edge of a field, and he hurried over to the ruin in order to get some shelter. There, sitting under the old crumbling eaves, was a man with a white beard. At first, Anselm did not notice the man because he was partly hidden by the soft tall grasses growing along the edge of the house.

"Hello," said Anselm.

"Hello," said the old man.

"May I sit here and wait out the storm?"

"Certainly," said the man.

The two men sat in silence, as the sheets of rain fell and as the lightning flashed and as the thunder rumbled and as the wind blew. After a while, Anselm said: "Do you live near here?"

"I do."

There was more silence.

Suddenly, the old man said: "You are a Jew?"

Anselm was not certain what to say. Was it safe to admit his heritage? As Anselm hesitated, the old man went on: "Tell me, young man: Are you hungry?"

"Yes," answered Anselm.

"Then," said the old man, passing some cheese and bread to Anselm, "as it is said in Ecclesiastes":

> Set to your task—take heart and eat your food and enjoy it, and drink your wine with a cheerful spirit. For already the good Lord God (blessed be He) has accepted what you have done. Then, always be dressed in white, and never fail to anoint your head.

Anselm was puzzled, but he took the food that the old man offered. "I said," repeated the old man, "the good Lord God (blessed be He) knows and has accepted what you have done."

"He knows?" asked Anselm.

"Yes," said the old man.

"Do you mean that He knows about the ugly cloak-hauler?"

"Yes."

"And He knows that I was dismissed from the yeshiva?" asked Anselm.

"Of course," said the old man.

"And He forgives me?"

"You were not listening, young man," said the white-bearded one. "As it is said in Ecclesiastes":

Set to your task – take heart and eat your food and enjoy it, and drink your wine with a cheerful spirit. For already the good Lord God (blessed be He) has accepted what you have done. Then, always be dressed in white, and never fail to anoint your head.

"I was listening," said Anselm, "but I am not certain what this passage means."

"Why, obviously this passage means that one's shroud should always be kept clean, neat, and wrinkle-free. In other words, when the good Lord God (blessed be He) calls a man to die, then each man should be ready with repentance and with a full store of good deeds," said the old man.

"But how does this apply to me and to my problems?" asked Anselm.

"Let me tell you a story," said the old man. "Once there was a king who decided to reward some of his servants. 'At the next banquet,' declared the king, 'I will reserve twenty extra places for my servants; then twenty faithful servants can join us, and they will be treated like royalty.' Therefore, the king proclaimed a general invitation to his servants for the next great feast.

"However, this king was a somewhat capricious man: he did not fix a date for the feast, and so he could not tell the servants exactly when to expect their special reward. The wise among the servants knew the king, and they humbly accepted this state of affairs. They washed and they dressed in their best clothes every morning, and they sat at the entrance of the palace whenever they had no chores – these men knew that the king might call them to the feast at any time. On the other hand, the foolish among the servants thought that they would have some warning. A king would be well organized; he would plan far in advance. Does it not take some time to prepare a large feast? These men did not wish to waste each day waiting and waiting for nothing.

"Suddenly, one morning the king arose early. He looked outside and he smiled. It was a glorious dawn; the sky was blue, the clouds were fluffy, and right then and there he decided that his special royal feast would take place on that very day. Thus, he sent out word that there would be twenty places available for the servants for a noontime banquet. The wise servants were ready and waiting—they came at once in their beautiful clothes, they were admitted to the vast luncheon hall, and they filled the twenty available seats. Unfortunately, the foolish servants were caught in their old and dirty clothes, and none of them got ready in time to take any of the available places. None of the foolish servants was admitted to the banquet.

"And this, young man, is why Ecclesiastes says that one should always keep himself ready with his holy white garments. When the great King of kings, the good Lord God (blessed be He), finally calls us to the table of the last feast, we will be ready. Who is it among us that knows the date of his own death? Will we have time enough to repent? Will we be able to do sufficient good deeds to make our lives worthwhile? Will our shrouds be spotless and wrinkle-free, spick-and-span and white? Only if we have kept ourselves holy every single day can we ever be certain to be ready when the great Lord Almighty calls.

"Therefore, the Sages say: 'Repent one day before your death.' No man is sure of the day of his death—repent today, for you may die tomorrow. Then, you had best repent tomorrow, too, because you may die the day after. In fact, if you repent every day, then you will live a completely pious life. And when you are finally called before the fearsome Lord God on that final Judgment Day, then you will be at peace, and you will certainly be prepared to partake of the eternal feast of the Great Hereafter, amen."

By now the rain had stopped. There was silence, and the old man seemed to have fallen asleep. Anselm ben Joel ben Isaac stood up quietly, and he walked back to Kalk. There, he crossed the wide River Rhine and he went into Cologne. He went into Cologne and he walked directly back to the yeshiva, where he told his story to Rabbi

Yerahmiel, and he asked for forgiveness. Rabbi Yerahmiel was sitting at the rabbi's desk in the small back study room. "Israel," said the Rabbi, "it is not really within my power either to forgive or to condemn. If you have truly repented, then the good Lord God (blessed be He) knows, and nothing that I say can make a difference. If you have repented, then you are welcome to come back to the yeshiva." And the Rabbi looked down at his book and he went back to his studies.

And my grandmother said that it was this particular experience that Rabbi Yerahmiel cited when, in his old age, he would say to his students: "A man should always be as soft as the grass, which is very, very soft—he should not be as hard as an oak, which is very, very hard."

ello, Rabbi, I will be with you in a moment—I cannot leave until every tablecloth is folded; otherwise the day has not ended properly. There, now I am finished at last and I can sit next to you by the stove. I can only rest and sleep when my work is finished. You are not sleepy? Ah, Rabbi, as the Talmud says: "There is a time for all things in life. There is a time and a place for rest and a time and a place for joy. On the other hand, there is also a time and a place for sleeplessness and a time and a place for mourning." What is that, Rabbi? Why, of course I am thinking of the dialogue between Rabbi Huna and Rabbi Nachmani:

One day, Rabbi Huni asked of Rabbi Nachmani: "Does the good Lord God (blessed be He) foresee everything that is to happen?"

"Certainly He does. How could you imagine anything different?" replied Rabbi Nachmani.

"Ah, Rabbi Nachmani, I have a vivid imagination, and I can imagine many things. But which of my imaginings is the truth? Let me ask you this, my good friend: Why is it written in the story of Noah in Genesis—'The good Lord God was sorry and repented that He had made man on earth, and He was grieved at heart'? How could the Lord not have known of man's evil ways from the very start?" asked Rabbi Huni.

"That is a good question," said Rabbi Nachmani, "and it deserves a good question in return. So tell me, Rabbi Huni: Do you have a son?"

"A son? Is this your 'good question'?" asked Rabbi Huni.

"It is."

"Well, the answer is 'yes'–actually, Rabbi Nachmani, I have two sons."

"Were you happy when they were born?" asked Rabbi Nachmani.

"I was indeed," said Rabbi Huni. "I rejoiced, I gave parties, and I made certain that these celebrations made others happy, too."

"But, my good Rabbi," continued Nachmani, "did you not know that a time would come when those sons would have to die?"

"Of course I knew that, Reb Nachmani. But the wise Sages have reminded us that there is a time for all things in life. There is a time and a place for rest and a time and a place for joy. On the other hand, there is also a time and a place for sleeplessness and a time and a place for mourning," said Rabbi Huni.

"Ah, that is so true," said Rabbi Nachmani. "And at the time of joy let there be joy; while at the time of mourning let there be mourning–praise the good Lord God (blessed be He), amen."

"Exactly, Rabbi," said Huni. "And at the time of hunger let there be eating and at the time of tiredness let there be rest, amen."

"Amen," said Rabbi Nachmani, "and so did it come to pass with the Holy One (blessed be He for ever and ever). The good Lord God rested on the first Sabbath at the end of the creation of all the world, and He was happy. On the first Sabbath, it was the appropriate time for rest and for joy, amen. Later, my friend–much later–the Lord mourned for seven days over the fate of His universe, before bringing on the great and terrible Flood–then, it was the time for sleeplessness and for mourning.

"It had nothing to do with the good Lord God's ability to foresee the future. No, Rabbi Huni–it was only that there is an appropriate time and an appropriate place for all things, amen," said Rabbi Nachmani.

True, Rabbi, it seems now to be the time for sleeplessness for me also. Fortunately, it is not a time for mourning—just yesterday ended the seventh and last day of mourning after old Reb Israel's passing (may his name be blessed for ever and ever, amen). As my grandmother would have said: "Israel ben Moyses was a fine and friendly fellow." Did you ever hear her say that, Rabbi? You never knew her? Ah, more is the pity, for she herself was a fine and friendly woman—and in the end, she met Dumah, the Angel of Death, as a friend and not as an enemy. She even said to me once: "Dumah? Why, undoubtedly he is a fine and friendly fellow." How could she say that, Rabbi? It was because of Ecclesiastes, where it says in the Holy Scriptures:

A good name smells sweeter than even the finest of spices, and the day of death is better than the day of birth. It is better to visit the house of mourning than to visit the house of feasting—for to be mourned is the appointed lot of every man. The living should take this truth to heart, and they should understand and be glad.

Then, Rabbi, my grandmother would go on to quote the Talmud: "When a person is born, then everyone rejoices; when he dies, then all weep. But things should not be this way. On the contrary, when a person is born we should merely accept this event calmly; it is a simple fact. We cannot necessarily rejoice over a birth, because who can see the future? Will this person be good, or will he be bad? Will he be righteous, or will he be wicked? Will he have a happy life, or will he suffer? Only the good Lord God (blessed be He) knows for certain—and He will not tell.

"On the other hand, when a man dies, then it should be an occasion for rejoicing—that is, we ought to be happy if that person left behind a good name, if he left behind good deeds, if he left behind a good family, and if he passed peacefully. Our life is like a ship setting out for a great voyage. At the beginning, no one but the Omniscient Lord knows what lies in store for it. What rough seas are over the horizon? What storms lie in wait tomorrow? But when the ship finally returns home and when it reaches its harbor, then all should rejoice: the ship has arrived home safely once more." . . .

What is that, Rabbi? No, no—I was just resting my eyes. Let me see now, was I telling you about Samuel ben Simon and Rabbi Yerahmiel? No? Then let me tell you about them:

Once upon a time, said my grandmother, there lived in Cologne on the River Rhine a very pious man named Samuel ben Simon ben Joel. This was in the days when Rabbi Yerahmiel had been the head of the yeshiva in Cologne for years and years and years. Samuel ben Simon died finally, and at the end of the seven days of mourning, Rabbi Yerahmiel was sitting alone in the little back room of the synagogue. Suddenly, Dumah, the Angel of Death, appeared hovering in the doorway. As you know, Rabbi, Dumah is covered with eyes all over, and every eye is wide and unblinking. And there stood Dumah, with a drawn sword in hand, silently looking at the Rabbi.

Rabbi Yerahmiel looked up. All was quiet for a moment, and then the Rabbi said: "O most holy angel, why are you here?"

"I am passing by one last time, after having seen Samuel ben Simon ben Joel to his final resting place in the Great Hereafter."

Again the Rabbi sat quietly, and then he said: "Now that you are here, O holy angel, let me ask you a rather bold question: How long do I have to live?"

With his dry raspy breath, Dumah, the Angel of Death, answered: "I never tell this information to a human being, Yerahmiel. I have taken an oath never to reveal the time of his death to any man."

Then Rabbi Yerahmiel said: "Then at least tell me this: On what day of the week am I to die?"

"You are a righteous and devout man, Rabbi," said Dumah, the Angel of Death. "Therefore, you are destined to die on a Sabbath."

But Rabbi Yerahmiel said: "Good angel, the Sabbath is a holy day. Let me die some other time—perhaps on a Sunday."

And Dumah, the Angel of Death, responded: "I have no power to change your destiny, Yerahmiel. All is fixed by the Great and Almighty Lord God, blessed be He for ever and ever."

Then, the Angel of Death departed.

Rabbi Yerahmiel thought about this information. I had best not profane the Sabbath by dying, at least not in the near future, thought the Rabbi. However, it is not an easy matter to control one's death. What should I do?

Now the good Rabbi knew that study of the Torah was the most sacred of all duties. Clearly, thought Rabbi Yerahmiel, the great Lord God (blessed be He) would not allow such sacred studies to be interrupted even by death. So from that day forward, Rabbi Yerahmiel ha-Kohen studied the Torah for the entire day on every Sabbath; in fact, the Rabbi refused to eat or to wash or to nap or to think of anything else on the Sabbath. After a while, Dumah, the Angel of Death, began to stand in the doorway of the little back room of the Cologne yeshiva on every Sabbath—each Sabbath the most holy of angels hovered there full of his unwinking eyes and holding a drawn sword. But the Rabbi studied so completely and so piously and so intently for the whole day that the Angel of Death could not touch him.

One Friday night many months later, the Rabbi felt strange before he went to bed. Then, in the stillness of the dark and in that deep black hour of the night, the Rabbi awoke suddenly. He had distinctly heard a voice whisper his name, but when he looked about there was no one there. The Rabbi pulled the covers up tightly, and all night long he could not fall back to sleep.

On the next morning—the Sabbath morning—the sky was gray. Again, Dumah, the Angel of Death, came and stood silently in the doorway. Rabbi Yerahmiel was poring over a book. The Rabbi felt the presence of the Angel of Death, and without interrupting his study Rabbi Yerahmiel recited aloud the passage from the Book of Proverbs where it is written:

> Listen, My student,
>   Take My teachings as guide,
> Know My commandments,
>   Study Law at My side—
> And the years of your life
>   Shall be far multiplied
> As the lights in the heavens,
>   Thick with stars far and wide.

The Angel of Death remained silent, and he remained watchful.
  Like all the Rabbis of Cologne before him and like all the Rabbis

of Cologne after him, Rabbi Yerahmiel stored old books and venerable papers and crumbling manuscripts in the little loft above the back study room of the yeshiva. The loft could be reached by a narrow wooden ladder. Late in the afternoon, Dumah, the Angel of Death, suddenly flew high up among the shelves and the books and the papers and the manuscripts, and he rustled the dry and ancient pages.

The Rabbi looked up. What was that noise? He stopped studying, and he looked over toward the storage room. The ladder stood against the wall, at the edge of the loft. The Rabbi went back to his reading, but again he heard a scratching and a rustling and a creaking above. The Rabbi looked around him. The Angel of Death was nowhere to be seen, so the Rabbi stood up, he walked to the ladder, and he climbed up to the loft. It was very dark in the storage space. The Rabbi turned his head to the right and to the left, but he heard nothing and he saw nothing. Then, the Rabbi started down the ladder. Suddenly, a rung of the ladder broke under him; the old Rabbi fell to the floor, and he broke his neck and he died. Gently and quickly, Dumah, the Angel of Death, pulled the Rabbi's soul from out of the top of the Rabbi's white-haired head and whisked it away to appear before the golden throne of the great Lord God (blessed be He).

In the splendor of the Heavens, Rabbi Yerahmiel's soul was blinded by the radiant light of the Most Holy of all courts, and he cried out: "O Lord God, King of the Universe, whither am I being led?"

No one answered the Rabbi, and for a moment there was a hollow silence. Then Dumah, the Angel of Death, declared: "O Lord God, Ruler of the universe, make a place for this soul. It comes from the most righteous and holy of men, Rabbi Yerahmiel ha-Kohen. He was the chief rabbi of Cologne, he studied piously and thoughtfully, he was charitable, and he was kind: he has earned a seat in Paradise, amen."

And so it was, Rabbi; and, when my grandmother would finish telling this story, then she would recite from Psalm 11:

> The Lord is alone
> Forever omnipotent
> On His gold throne,
> The high seat of judgment.

With impartiality
God tries all souls;
He weighs men fairly
On the Judgment Poles.

Then my grandmother added: "May the great Lord God (blessed be He) convert all evil hearts to good, so that Heaven will be filled to overflowing for ever and ever, amen."

ello again, Rabbi. Of course—please sit here by the stove: when you are cool, it is hard to sleep. You and I are not blessed like old Reb Elbaum; once again I saw him nodding off during the last prayers this evening. He has learned to sway piously even while asleep: he must have acquired some magic from the mystic Achselrad. I see that you could use a dose of Achselrad yourself, Rabbi—my grandmother said that he could put men into a sleep-trance by waving a gold coin before their eyes. Yes, exactly, Rabbi, that is the same German rabbi whom I have told you about before—Rabbi Abraham ben Alexander, Achselrad of Cologne.

As you remember, Achselrad was a pupil of Eliazer the mystic of Worms. Strange visions assaulted old Rabbi Abraham in the synagogue of Cologne. I doubt whether he would be tolerated nowadays, but my grandmother said that Rabbi Abraham was also a scholar, and he always claimed that his visions came from devout and pious study. Many an astonishing event took place in his yeshiva—or so my grandmother (blessed be her memory) was told. Of course, there were also some very ordinary events. "Life is ordinary when it is not extraordinary," said my grandmother.

Rabbi Abraham spent much of his free time writing an extraordinary set of kabbalistic tomes of mystic knowledge. One day, while working on one of these books–the *Keter Shem Tov* (which was never published and which now exists only as a secret manuscript hidden in the loft of the old Cologne yeshiva), Rabbi Abraham looked up and in the light of the doorway he saw a cranky old member of his congregation; it was Gabriel ben Isaac. In the early years of Abraham Achselrad's rabbinate, Gabriel ben Isaac had arrived with a letter of reference from Rabbi Petahiah of Regensburg. (That was the famous Rabbi Petahiah ben Jacob–the brother of Rabbi Isaac "the Wise" of Prague–who undertook a tour of the entire world.) The letter said simply:

To my good friend,
*Abraham, son of Alexander*
*Rabbi of Cologne*

This is to introduce Gabriel ben Isaac,
    formerly of the congregation of Regensburg.

*Yours in holy devotion,*
*Petahiah, son of Jacob*
*Rabbi of Regensburg*

Over the years since his appearance in Cologne, Gabriel complained about everything–he was never satisfied. It was like the section in the Book of Proverbs that says: "The bottomless pits of Sheol and Abaddon are insatiable, and in just this fashion, some men too are never satisfied." But the greatest irritant to Reb Gabriel, the complaint that he voiced most frequently and most bitterly, was that he had no grandchildren. Now, Rabbi, it was not that Gabriel had no children. Gabriel had a fine and mild son. This son, Joshua, was as different from his father as day is from night; Joshua was meek and kind and quiet. Joshua had found a wife that was his equal, and Miriam and Joshua were married contentedly.

Miriam and Joshua were married for almost ten years, and they remained childless. Gabriel constantly said to his son: "Joshua, it is your duty to have children."

And Joshua always replied: "I am sorry, father. We would like children, but none seem to appear."

"Then, my obedient son," said Gabriel, "I am afraid that you must divorce your wife. . . . Now, now, son—I know that Miriam is a nice woman, but *nice* is insufficient here. We must produce children in order to perpetuate the line of our family."

"Father, divorce is rather extreme—just wait a bit longer," said Joshua.

So Gabriel waited. But he also complained; he complained to everyone, and especially he complained to Rabbi Abraham Achselrad. The Rabbi said: "My good Gabriel, Miriam is a fine young woman. Remember, the Talmud tells us":

Not money or other possessions but rather *character* is the best dowry.

"True. However, remember also, Rabbi," said Gabriel ben Isaac, "the Talmud tells us that the purpose of marriage is the raising of a family."

"Yes, that is important, Reb Gabriel."

"Oh, it is more than important, Rabbi—it is essential. Does the Talmud not say":

If a man marries and if he waits ten years and if the couple still has no children, then the man need wait no longer. He may then divorce his wife and remarry.

"Do the Sages not tell us that, Rabbi?"

"Yes," said the Rabbi.

"Of course they do. And does the Talmud not continue: 'A childless person is accounted as dead.' Do the Sages not tell us that also, Rabbi?"

"Yes—that is in the Talmud, Reb Gabriel," said Rabbi Abraham.

"Well then, Rabbi, it is clear that my son has no choice: he must divorce Miriam, and then he must remarry."

"Reb Gabriel, your son, although presently childless, looks quite lively to me; I would not account him as dead. My counsel, good Gabriel, is patience."

"Patience?!" said Gabriel, "I have been patient for almost ten years, Rabbi. Now, Rabbi, perhaps you forget the the story in the Talmud":

Isaiah the Prophet was called before King Hezekiah, when the king lay dying. "Isaiah son of Amoz," said the king weakly, "what can you foretell for me?"

Isaiah glanced up at the Heavens; then, he said: "King Hezekiah, this is the word of the Almighty Lord God (blessed be He): 'Give your last instructions to your household and all therein, Hezekiah, for you are a dying man and you will not recover. You shall be buried, and you shall not live for ever and ever more.' "

"Isaiah," said the king, "you Prophets speak in such complicated sentences. What do you mean 'you will be buried and you will not live for ever and ever more'? Why do you not merely say that I will die?"

"O king, I speak very carefully; I am only repeating the word of the Lord God. You will be buried, but unfortunately you will not see the Great Hereafter."

"I will not reside in Heaven? Why is that? Why do I deserve such a severe punishment?" asked the king.

"It is simply that you have not allowed yourself to have any children at all, when it would have been in your power to beget a long line of fine children," said Isaiah.

"Perhaps that is what *you* think, Isaiah. However, I was afraid that I would bring all manner of worthless progeny into the world. My descendants might have caused mischief, they might have been duplicitous, weak, and evil, and they might even have contested with me for my rule," said the king.

"King Hezekiah, how can you ever know this? Really now, King, you are much too presumptuous. What man can ever know the future? The good Lord God (blessed be He) has commanded us to have children. Do not question the secret future that is determined by the All-Merciful One—be humble and do whatever God has commanded you. Only then can you rest in peace."

"So, Rabbi," continued Gabriel, "with this story the Sages reaffirm that our most sacred obligation is to have children. It is a divine decree."

"Well, Reb Gabriel," replied Achselrad, "I can certainly understand how important it is to you to have grandchildren. Still, good sir, I would suggest that you wait quietly for a while longer."

"Ah, Rabbi, that is easy for you to say: you already have two grandsons. But me? Why, there is no hope. It is irreligious, I tell you; my son is not fulfilling the great scriptural commandment in Genesis":

> Be fruitful and increase and fill the earth and subdue it and rule over the fish in the sea and the birds of the heavens and every living thing that moves upon the earth.

"Rabbi, I am bringing my son and my daughter-in-law here so that you may grant us a Bill of Divorcement."

The Rabbi sighed, but what could he do? Then, Gabriel ben Isaac badgered, bothered, and browbeat his children until finally the couple agreed to come to Rabbi Abraham ben Alexander for a divorce. And one afternoon, they all appeared before the Rabbi in his study in the back room of the old Cologne yeshiva.

"Now Miriam," began Reb Gabriel, "you are a fine person. However, children are our first priority, so I am afraid that you and Joshua must be divorced."

Miriam said nothing; she only looked away.

"Very well," said Gabriel. "Rabbi, let us get on with this divorce."

Rabbi Abraham looked intently at Miriam. "I am not happy with this, Reb Gabriel."

"I am not happy either," said Gabriel. "But remember, Rabbi, the Talmud tells us: 'A woman may be divorced with or without her consent – but a man can only be divorced with his consent.' And my Joshua has consented to a divorce."

"Is this true?" asked Rabbi Achselrad to Joshua ben Gabriel.

Joshua was silent. Then he said: "I am not certain, Rabbi."

"Joshua, of course it is true," said Gabriel. "I know that this is difficult for you, son, but you must consider your responsibility to me and to the Almighty Lord (blessed be He), amen. Remember, Joshua, the great scriptural commandment in Genesis says":

> Be fruitful and increase and fill the earth and subdue it and rule over the fish in the sea and the birds of the Heavens and every living thing that moves upon the earth.

"What do you think, Rabbi?" asked Joshua.

"I am afraid, Joshua, that this decision must be your own," said Rabbi Abraham ben Alexander.

Joshua looked at the Rabbi and then he looked at Miriam, but she continued to look away. "All right, Father," said Joshua.

The Rabbi was silent for a moment. "If all parties agree, then I will grant a Bill of Divorcement," he said.

"Good," said Gabriel, the father.

The Rabbi looked at Joshua. Joshua was silent, so his father said: "Remember, my son, in the words of Psalm 127":

> Sons are gifts from the Lord:
> Children are your rewards,
> Like arrows in an archer's hoard
> Or like a foilsman's swords.

> Sons and daughters make you strong.
> You shall stand with confidence
> Facing down the enemy throng
> With your children as your defense.

"All right, Father," said Joshua, the husband, "I agree."

Then the Rabbi looked at Miriam: "How about you, Miriam?"

"No," said Miriam, the wife.

"No?" said the father-in-law.

"No," repeated Miriam.

"I am afraid that you have no choice, Miriam," said Gabriel.

"Well, then, let me ask a question of the Rabbi. Tell me, Rabbi Abraham, is it not true that a normal divorce entails a settlement to be paid by the husband to the wife?"

"Yes, that is true," said the Rabbi.

"Then, I will agree to a divorce on one condition: I want a settlement," said Miriam.

"Oh?" said Gabriel. "And how much money do you want?"

"I do not want any money," said Miriam. "Instead, as settlement, I insist that I be allowed to remove one and only one thing from our house. Moreover, I must be allowed to keep that thing forever. As to the other possessions and furniture and clothes and money, I give them all to my husband, free and clear."

The Rabbi looked at Miriam. Then he nodded and said: "I see. Well, this sounds quite satisfactory to me, but your father-in-law and your husband must agree also."

"Now Miriam, do you say 'one and only one thing'?" asked the father-in-law.

"Yes, I do," said Miriam.

"And then you will give us no problems and you will ask for no money and you will make no further demands on our family?"

"Correct," said Miriam.

"Will you have this written into the Bill of Divorcement?" asked Gabriel.

"I will," said Miriam.

"Then I agree," said the father-in-law.

"And I agree also," said Joshua.

"Very well," said the Rabbi. And he assembled ten scholars in the back room of the yeshiva. Abraham Achselrad wrote out the divorce papers, and in the presence of these ten witnesses, Joshua handed the Bill of Divorcement to Miriam. The Bill stated that Joshua son of Gabriel – by his own will and purpose and without compulsion – hereby dismissed, quit, and repudiated Miriam, who up to this time had been his lawful wife. For her part, Miriam had claim to one and only one item from their household. And now, Miriam was free to go away with any man, and no one on earth could hinder her from that day and for ever forward, according to the laws of Moses and of Israel.

Although it was not a happy time, all the parties remained courteous and even amicable, and Miriam proposed that in order to seal the agreement, she would prepare one last dinner for her husband. Joshua agreed. Gabriel shook hands with the Rabbi and with the ten scholars, and he left the synagogue. Then Joshua and Miriam went home to their house for one last meal. At the dinner that evening, Miriam got her husband very, very drunk; after a while, Joshua fell fast asleep. Then Miriam took an old blanket from a neighbor and she removed every single thing that she wore, in order that she would be carrying off nothing from her house. She draped the blanket about herself, she loaded the sleeping Joshua on her shoulder, and she carried him off into the night.

The next morning, Joshua ben Gabriel awoke next to his wife in a small shack on the outskirts of Cologne.

"Where am I? What happened?" he asked.

"Oh, there was nothing in the house that I preferred to you, Joshua. So it is you that I have taken with me," said Miriam.

My grandmother told me that Miriam and Joshua lived there happily ever after; soon, they had many fine and healthy children, and they named one of their sons Abraham and another one Alexander.

ood evening, Rabbi. Of course – please sit here by the
stove: the night fire helps me to become sleepy also. You and I are not
blessed like old Reb Elbaum; once again I saw him nodding off during
the last prayers this evening. He has learned to mumble piously even
while asleep. Has he inherited some magic from the mystic Achselrad?

I suppose that we could use a dose of Achselrad ourselves,
tonight. My grandmother said that he could put men into a sleep-
trance by waving a gold coin before their eyes. Yes, Rabbi, that is the
same German rabbi whom I have told you about before – Rabbi
Abraham ben Alexander, Achselrad of Cologne. He was a pupil of
Eliazer the mystic of Worms and he was always conjuring visions in
the synagogue. I doubt whether this would be tolerated nowadays, but
my grandmother said that Rabbi Abraham was also a scholar, and he
claimed that his visions came from devout and pious study. Many an
astonishing event took place in his yeshiva – or so my grandmother
(blessed be her memory) was told.

And this same Rabbi Abraham Achselrad was a writer, too; he
authored kabbalistic tomes of mystical knowledge, including the *Keter
Shem Tov* (which was never published and which only exists as a secret
manuscript hidden above the old Cologne yeshiva). Do you know

what words the good Rabbi used to introduce his mystical book? You have never seen the book? Ah, then I will tell you: Rabbi Achselrad quotes from the Scriptures, from the Book of Proverbs:

This is the Scholar's Doubt:
  I am weary, O Lord,
I am tired and worn out.

I am an aged creature—
  I scarcely am a man,
I've learned nothing from my teacher.

No wisdom do I retain,
  I have no true insight,
All facts seem quite profane.

I am weak; I am undone:
  We mortals can't understand
The world of the Holy One.

Has any mortal ascended
  To Heaven and then returned?
Do you know him, or where he's ended?

Has man ever held a windstorm
  In the hollow of his palm
Or carved out a mountain's form?

Has anyone dared to crowd
  The seas inside his pocket
(Or jumped from cloud to cloud)?

Has someone planted wildwood
  Filled with living things?
Is there such a mortal? Could

You tell me now his name.
  Or do you know his son?
Or the country from which he came?

Is there such a man?
  Then tell me now his name –
If, in fact, you can.


Yes, this is how the great Achselrad begins his magical treatise,
and my grandmother said that it was one night while copying this very
verse that Rabbi Abraham looked up and in the light of the candle he
saw the ghost of Rabbi Akiva standing in the doorway. What is that,
Rabbi? No, I am not inventing this – my grandmother swore that this
is exactly what she had heard:


Once upon a time, said my grandmother, long, long ago, in the
town of Cologne on the River Rhine, the great Rabbi Akiva appeared
in the yeshiva late at night. Rabbi Abraham ben Alexander looked up,
he rubbed his eyes, and he said: "Hello – are you a spirit or are you a
man?"
    "I am now a spirit," said Akiva, "and once I was a man."
    "Do I know your name?" asked Achselrad.
    "I am Akiva."
    "Akiva? Ah, Rabbi Akiva," said Abraham in wonderment, and
then he just stared at the apparition. After a moment, Rabbi Abraham
said: "Good Akiva, tell me please, you know so much, but is there any
hope for me? I hardly understand anything at all. Is the world beyond
my comprehension? Or, Rabbi, must I just redouble my efforts? Must
I study longer and harder, and must I think more deeply and pray more
fervently?"
    And Rabbi Akiva answered: 'Abraham, it is not within our
power to explain many things. At some point, we must rest content
without fully understanding this world. The world of ours is complex – in fact, the good Lord God (blessed be He) has filled our universe
with pockets of incondensable complexity; here, we shall never fully
comprehend. The prosperity of the wicked, or the afflictions of the
righteous – who can ever explain these things?
    "Do not forget, Achselrad, the old fable about me in the Talmud.
You recall the story: Moses died and was carried up to Heaven. There
he wandered about, and after a while he came across a wondrous
prodigy. It was me, Akiva, as a tiny little spirit still unborn – and I was

expounding on the Torah in a most detailed and learned manner.

"Moses said to the good Lord God (blessed be He): 'Ah, my Lord, this is a beautiful sight! This infant is the greatest of all scriptural scholars; I am overwhelmed by his memory and his insight. He can explain the meaning of every single dot and mark on every single holy word in the Torah. And he is still an unborn child. What shall he do upon the earth?'

"'Watch,' said the Lord. And then the good Lord God waved His arms and He puffed a great and holy puff of His breath, and an animated vision appeared all around them. Moses saw the future; he saw how I, Akiva ben Joseph, would become the chief Palestinian rabbi of all times, he saw how my rabbinical school in Jaffa would teach twenty-four thousand scriptural scholars, and he saw how, ever after those days, my interpretations would be quoted throughout the centuries and they would echo throughout all lands of the world.

"Moses said to the Lord: 'This is a wonderful vision indeed. Rabbi Akiva is a fountain of learning and culture for the Jews for all times, amen. Now, O Lord, show me what will be his reward.'

"'Watch,' said the Lord. And then the good Lord God (blessed be He) waved His arms and He puffed a great and holy puff of His breath, and another animated vision appeared all around them. Moses saw the future again; he saw how I, Akiva ben Joseph, would die at the ripe old age of one hundred and twenty years. Yes, Rabbi Abraham, I died when I was one hundred and twenty years old: in that year, I became the sword-bearer for Bar Kochba.

"Ah, my good Abraham, that was the last Jewish revolt against Rome. And my fair-haired Bar Kochba—what a fine, fine lad he was. You know, it was I who gave him that name; he had been born Simeon bar Kozeba, but 'bar Kozeba' reminded me so much of 'Bar Kochba,' 'the son of a star,' and of course there was the wondrous prophetic verse in Numbers":

> He comes, but not quite yet.
> He shines, but not right here:
> Down from Jacob a star at sunset,
> Out of Zion a comet shall appear,
> Blunting the enemy's threat,
> Breaking the warrior's spear.

"Anyway, in those fierce days we set our sights to the Heavens – but the end came in the battle at Bet Tar. I was taken prisoner by the Romans under Julius Severus, and terrible punishments were inflicted. In the vision, Moses saw it all: I did my best to be strong, and I recited the *Shema* over and over. I was actually flayed alive, but the words of the good Lord God were ever on my lips.

"At seeing this, Moses began to cry: 'O great Sovereign of the Universe, stop this vision. Can this really be the future? Are You playing a cruel hoax on me? How can You let this terrible thing come to pass.'

"And the good Lord God (blessed be He) said gently to Moses: 'My child, do not question the ways of My world. Although these are the thoughts that come up before Me, they and many, many others shall not ever be fully explicable to you. Have faith, Moses – and then look away.'"

But the voice of the great Akiva was fading. Rabbi Abraham ben Alexander, Achselrad of Cologne, rubbed his eyes, and the vision of Rabbi Akiva wavered and disappeared. Instead, said my grandmother, Rabbi Achselrad realized that there was a woman standing in the doorway. It was Rebeka, the wife of a strange young man from the Cologne congregation.

Rebeka's husband was named Jokshan ben Lavan. Jokshan was a very serious person and he never smiled. He read all the prayers slowly and carefully word for word, and he always read aloud. Jokshan contributed exactly one gold coin a month to the poorbox. When talking in the study hall, he looked intently at each of his companions, and he carefully said each man's full name when he addressed him. And if any woman other than his wife passed him, Jokshan quickly looked at the ground.

In spite of his very serious nature, Jokshan was a good father: he was fair and patient with his son and his two daughters. Every day, he took the time to talk with them each individually – even when they were quite small. After dinner, they would form a line, and one by one he would ask each child politely about his day; then Jokshan would listen to all of their complaints. Sometimes, a child would talk on and on and on; Jokshan listened patiently and he would pat them on their heads and he would give each one hug. And, said my grandmother, it was Rebeka, the wife of this very same methodical and serious Jokshan, who was standing in the doorway of the little back study of the Cologne yeshiva late one night long, long ago when the vision of Rabbi Akiva faded and when old Abraham Achselrad looked up from writing the introduction to his mystical treatise.

"Good evening, Rebeka," said Rabbi Abraham Achselrad. "May I help you?"

Rebeka looked around uncomfortably: "Well, Rabbi, I do not really have a serious problem. . . . But, perhaps I will come in."

"Certainly, certainly," said the Rabbi.

"I am probably interrupting something: I will come back tomorrow."

"No, no, my good woman. I was just taking a break from my writing," said Rabbi Achselrad. "It is good to see you. How is Jokshan?"

"Oh, he is fine, thank you, Rabbi," said Rebeka.

Rebeka sat down on one of the small benches by the wall. "I am certain that Jokshan is quite fine; it is just that he is acting a little strangely, Rabbi. Not too strangely, of course – just a little strangely."

"Just a little?"

"Well, you see, Rabbi, he is having disturbing dreams."

"I see," said the Rabbi. "Tell me about them."

"Well," began Rebeka, "the other night, we were asleep; suddenly, I woke up. I do not know exactly what startled me. But then I heard a strange choking sound. My husband Jokshan was laughing, but it was not a happy laugh, Rabbi – it was a low, fierce, hollow laugh. So I shook him, and he awoke with a start.

" 'What were you dreaming?' I asked.

" 'I am glad that you woke me, Rebeka,' said Jokshan. 'This was a terrible dream, and I have had it before.'

" 'Tell me about it,' I said.

" 'After some vague adventures,' began Jokshan, 'I feel that I have met a demon out in the countryside. It is nighttime, there are dark shapes about, and there is no escape. I am alone in unfamiliar territory. Where are the trees, the hills, the houses? Are there low buildings somewhere far off to the left? Why is it so difficult to see anything clearly? Why is it so hard to walk?

" 'Then there is a flash of lightning, deep from the farthest reaches of the night sky. It floods the walls and the floors on high, mystically depopulating the world, laying bare pre-Deluvian evils unfurled from bare caves and blank crags. Then thunder–and I am cornered and I am trapped. But can I give in? Shall I be killed or carried off to the unthinkable bowels of the earth. No, never! As my last and final resort, when I have nothing to lose, then I turn; I turn on the dark, foreboding hulk. I turn–and I stand fast, and I laugh. I know that it is my end. I have nothing to lose, so I laugh. A chill tightens my back. It is not a happy laugh, and I guess that it is not really a laugh at all, Rebeka: it is some final shout of defiance.

" 'Anyway, now I cannot shake the gloom from my shoulders, Rebeka–let me walk down to the kitchen and have a bit of bread and see the familiar surroundings again,' said Jokshan, and he sat up in bed. And then he slowly stood, and he walked out of the room.

"The next morning was pale and fair, Rabbi. The wind came gently out of the west. Jokshan seemed worried when he went to the synagogue, but the day passed without event.

"That night when were were asleep I awoke again. Had I heard a noise? I listened but all was quiet. Then suddenly I heard a strange choking sound. My husband Jokshan was laughing, but it was not a happy laugh–it was that same low, fierce, hollow laugh. So, I shook him, and he awoke with a start.

" 'What were you dreaming?' I asked.

" 'Ah Rebeka, I am glad that you woke me,' said Jokshan. 'This was a terrible dream, and I have had it before.'

" 'Tell me about it,' I said.

" 'Well, Rebeka, first I walk for hours and hours. I get deeper and deeper into a thick gloom, and suddenly there is a terrible demon. We are far out in the countryside. It is night, there are dark shapes about, and there is no escape; I am cornered and I am trapped. I know that it is my end–but can I give in? Do I cry or beg or plead? No, how can I go like that? As my last and final resort, when I have nothing to lose, then I turn to face the evil. I turn on the dark, foreboding hulk. I turn– and I stand fast, and I laugh. It is my end, but I laugh. A chill tightens my back. It is not a happy laugh, Rebeka, it is not happy at all; in fact, it is not really a laugh. It is only a final rattle of defiance.

" 'And now, my wife, I cannot shake this doom from my

shoulders – let me walk down to the kitchen and have a bit of bread and see the familiar surroundings again,' said Jokshan, and he sat up in bed and he stood and slowly he walked from the room.

"That was yesterday, Rabbi. Today, Jokshan went to the synagogue even earlier than usual. This evening he came home exhausted and he went to bed right after dinner, without talking with our children. Tonight I had just fallen asleep, when something woke me. Had I heard a noise? I listened but all was silent. Then I realized that Jokshan was gone. I looked through the house, Rabbi, but he was nowhere to be seen. So I dressed, and I came here to you."

The Rabbi closed his eyes: "Sit quietly a moment, Rebeka," he said. What was happening out in the dark world of the nightflood? thought the Rabbi. Was there any hope for poor Jokshan?

Out in the dark world of the late nightflood, the sky was black, the hills were large, and Jokshan found himself in unfamiliar territory. Where were the trees, the houses, and the hills? Were there low buildings somewhere far off to the left? Why was it so difficult to see anything clearly? Why was it so hard to walk? There were huge towering evil shapes, and Jokshan was filled with loneliness. The world was empty. His parents were dead. His wife and children were far behind. Or were they still ahead? Jokshan ben Lavan was like a child lying alone in bed with rain in the trees outside. Lightning deep from the farthest reaches of the night sky floods the walls and floors on high, mystically depopulating the world, laying bare pre Deluvian evils unfurled from bare caves and blank crags. Then, a thunder of towered black rock that sags and suddenly splits and falls, cracking bleak primal halls – stone monuments that lean from cloud-shrouded heights, grim falling cracking towers of ice giants angered and echoing twice – where Jokshan was alone and random grown in the nighttime swirl of an empty and a motherless world.

And then, Jokshan turned in the dark. A chill tightened his back. He opened his eyes wide, his eyebrows turned down in the center, and he laughed, but it was not a happy laugh – it was a low, fierce, hollow shout of defiance.

Rabbi Achselrad heard him laugh, and the Rabbi opened his eyes and he looked at Rebeka. She was so young and pale. Abraham ben

Alexander, Achselrad of Cologne, looked at Jokshan's young wife. "You had best go home, Rebeka," said the Rabbi quietly. "Go to your children – the Lord will provide."

hat is that, Rabbi? No, no – you did not wake me. I was just resting here happily by the stove; I was thinking of old Abraham Achselrad. I must confess that he is probably my favorite of all the old Rabbis that my grandmother would talk about. You know that he was a pupil of Eliazer the mystic of Worms, and Achselrad was forever having visions. I guess that is why I am so fond of him: now, in my old age, I seem always to be having visions also – at least I see things in the glow of the stove at night.

Now? Well, Rabbi, I see a sunny morning in those white coals. Yes, it reminds me of a sunny morning when no one is about but when the clouds are high and white and when the sun is far and bright and when the sky is blue and light. It is just like that sunny morning when good Abraham ben Alexander, Achselrad of Cologne, suddenly realized that he had been writing all night in his mystical tome the *Keter Shem Tov*. (You know, Rabbi, that this book was never published, and it exists only as a secret manuscript hidden above the old Cologne yeshiva.) Grandmother said that it was one bright and sunny morning while writing this very book that Rabbi Abraham looked up, and in the light of morning filtering in from the main prayer hall – a prayer hall filled with wooden benches – in the light that had passed through the twelve stained glass windows with their colored lions and snakes, in the light that was made holy as it rolled around the stone Ark, in the light that streamed into the door of the back study room, it was in this very light of the good and radiant Lord God Almighty (blessed be He), that Rabbi Abraham looked up and he saw no one there. Yes, the Rabbi looked up, and there was no one standing in his doorway, amen.

It was very early in the morning, one day long, long ago. The sun was out and no one was about at the old yeshiva. Rabbi Abraham stood up, he walked through the main prayer hall, and he looked out the front door. Where were all the people? He stood a moment, and then he stepped into the courtyard. Was the world empty of all mankind? How could this be? It felt so bright and so warm.

Perhaps the Rabbi was remembering Moshe ben Daniel and his wife Naomi and their four children, Saul, David, Daniel, and Deborah. When they had said the traditional prayer during their last *seder* meal – "this year we celebrate here, but next year we shall be in the Holy Land; this year we celebrate as slaves, but next year shall we be free?" – after breaking the middle *matzoh* and hiding the *afikoman* piece, even then the family knew what the answer would be. They had said the prayer with special fervor, and late last month the couple and their four children left Cologne for the Holy Land. By wagon, they had gone to Frankfort and then to Venice; then by boat they had gone to Jaffa, at the edge of the holy Promised Land. Moshe and Naomi and Saul, David, Daniel, and Deborah had joined the hundreds of other German Jews who had returned to their spiritual homeland.

Moshe was a carpenter and a craftsman of wood. Frequently, he worked for Gentiles outside the Jewish Quarter, and he was ill-treated and unhappy. He and Naomi decided on an *aliyah*: they dedicated themselves to go up to the Holy Land, to the Land of the Hebrew Prophets, the land of their forefathers and of their forefathers' fathers. Neither Moshe nor Naomi had ever been to Palestine, and they knew no one who had emigrated; nonetheless, at night they felt the pull of the old Hebrew Patriarchs. At night, Moshe and Naomi talked and talked about what the fields and trees and sands would actually look like. They had read accounts of Palestine – but what would that old dry holy land feel like to their very own hands and to their very own feet? At these times, Moshe and Naomi became happy, and soon it was their days that felt like sad dreams and it was their nighttimes that felt full real.

"We are proud of our Cologne congregation, Rabbi," said Moshe ben Daniel to Rabbi Achselrad one day. "However, we are going to Palestine. As Jews, it is where we feel that we belong. Everyone needs to rest in the warm embrace of a family, and Naomi and I are certain that the hills of the Holy Land are our true family."

And Naomi said: "Rabbi, we will help to rebuild the old land; we will work hard to recreate the old cities. Of course we can take very little with us. I am afraid that we can pack only a few pots and pans and clothes, and somehow I must find room for one old embroidery of my grandmother. And the books, Rabbi, we will certainly take our holy books. But that is all that we can manage."

Then for a while, they were a whirlwind of activity. They sold things, and they packed things. Would two shirts do instead of three? How can you live without a salt shaker? Must Uncle Samuel's carved walking stick come to Palestine? Although it seemed that they packed and planned for weeks, suddenly one day Moshe ben Daniel and his wife Naomi and their four children, Saul, David, Daniel, and Deborah, were gone. And their house was silent and the cellar door was forever shut and the yard was blank and the street was empty. And it was not long after this that Rabbi Achselrad found himself looking out the front door of the synagogue, one quiet, empty, sunny morning. It was very early; the sun was out and no one was about at the old yeshiva. Rabbi Abraham stood in the doorway. Where, he thought, were all the people? He stood a moment, and then he stepped into the courtyard. Was the world suddenly empty of mankind? How could that be? It felt so bright and so warm.

Rabbi Abraham Achselrad stepped into the courtyard, and he walked down the alleyway leading from the synagogue out to Judengasse Street. He walked down the street, and there he saw two little Jewish boys playing. One was a boy who was about seven years old, and the other boy was about three. And the Rabbi heard the littler boy say: "You know what I like best in the whole world?"

"What?" said the older boy, not looking up.

"I like my little cart and having it run around and you being the driver of it."

"Oh."

"And you know what else I like?" asked the younger boy.

"What?"

"I like when you push me on the swing. . . . And you know what else I like?"

"What?"

"Lots of stuff."

"Oh," said the older boy.

"What do you like?"

"Me?" asked the older boy. "Well, I like doing grownup things. I like fixing things in the house with Father – I am allowed to use the tools, you know."

"Oh – me too," said the younger boy.

"I like important things. And now I'm going to be going to school in the yeshiva and I'm going to study with the famous rabbis."

"Can I come, too?"

"No, you're too young."

"Then, will we play afterward?"

"Probably not – I'll be too busy."

"You will?" asked the younger boy.

"Yes, of course," said the older boy.

"But afterward, after you are busy, then can we play?"

"Oh, probably not – I will be grown up then."

"I think that I will wait for you anyway," said the younger one.

ood evening, Rabbi. Of course – please sit here by the
stove: the late night fire helps me to become sleepy also. You and I are
not blessed like old Reb Elbaum; once again I saw him nod off during
the last prayers this evening. He has learned to sway piously even
while asleep: he must have inherited some magic from the mystic
Achselrad. And I suppose that you and I could use a dose of Achselrad
ourselves tonight. My grandmother said that he could put men into a
sleep-trance by waving a gold coin before their eyes.

Yes, eyesight is a strange and magical thing – we cannot always
see even those things held directly before our eyes. My grandmother
once told me a tale about eyesight; it was the story of an old woman
who lived in medieval Cologne at the time of Rabbi Achselrad:

Once upon a time there was an old woman named Sarah. During
the past few years, her vision had become much worse. Written words
looked blurred, her utensils were indistinct, and she could not see
stitches when she knit. Everything looked as if it was under water.
Sometimes, wavering halos rimmed her household objects. Sarah
remembered that her mother had also had exactly the same problem.

Sarah went to the synagogue to consult the local sages. Old Rabbi

Abraham had stayed awake all night writing in his mystical tome of kabbalistic lore, and now he was dozing in the back room. The many scholars of the yeshiva were sitting on the wooden benches along the wall; they listened to Sarah's complaint, and then they offered their advice.

First, Reb Baruch said: "Remember, my good woman, the talmudic Sages say: 'The spittle of the first born son will heal the faltering eye.' "

Reb Lewe nodded, and then Reb Joshua said: "That is fine advice, but I myself would recommend the well-known talmudic potion for dimness of the eyes. Now listen carefully, Sarah: Take an evil scorpion of seven different colors, dry it in a shaded place, far out of the sun; then grind the dried creature into two like portions of antimony powder. Apply three brushfuls to each weak eye. (Of course, do not use more medicine or the eye may burst.)"

Reb Menahem shook his head and he said quietly: "Obviously, old woman, you have night-cecity."

"I have night-cecity?" asked Sarah.

"Obviously," said Menahem, "you have night-blindness, old woman. To reverse this ill, you take a rope of hair and tie it to your leg, then tie the other end of the rope onto a neighbor's dog. Next, tell some children to make a loud noise. (Have them drop an old clay pot.) Instruct them to yell: 'Old dog—foolish hen! Buy a hog, and see again!' After that, collect some meat from seven different homes, and place them all inside the hinge of your front door. Wait for seven hours after sunset, then remove the meat, and from each piece eat seven bites while sitting in an ash heap. At this point, untie the rope and say: 'Night-blindness—you must go and leave me now without a woe.'"

But Reb Shimshon shook his head. "That is all well and good for night-blindness, Menahem," Shimshon said. "However, this woman has day-blindess."

"I have day-blindness?" asked Sarah.

"Obviously," said Shimson, "you have day-blindness, old woman. Therefore, take seven testes glands from seven male goats. Put them in a clay pot on the floor of a room. Then sit inside the room, with a table and some bread, and have a woman friend stand outside the door. The woman at the door should call out and say: 'Blind woman, inside on a seat, open the door and let me eat.' You should answer: 'Enter through the door; step upon the floor. You shall be fed, come within and eat my bread.' The friend should now come in and take a bite of bread. Then, have her slap the table and kick and break the clay pot. (Otherwise, she will get the blindness herself.)" Reb Shimshon slapped his knee to emphasize these points.

Suddenly, Rabbi Abraham awoke with a start. Sarah looked at Achselrad. Then she asked: "And what is your opinion, good Rabbi Abraham?"

Abraham Achselrad looked a bit confused. "What is my opinion? What do I think? I think that one should always put his trust in the good Lord God (blessed be He)," said the Rabbi.

The woman looked at the bearded men sitting along the wall; she looked at these scholars, and she thanked them for their advice. Then, she left the rabbi's study and she walked into the prayer hall filled with wooden benches. Sarah walked by the Holy Ark made of stone, she passed the twelve stained glass windows with their colored lions and snakes, she walked out the front door, and she went back home. Sarah thought about these counsels, and finally she went to a local doctor and she offered him a fee to cure her weakening eyes.

Now, the doctor was younger than her son; so the old woman was a bit wary, and she said to him: "Listen young man, I would like to be certain that in the end your treatment does not leave me worse than I am now."

"Have no fear," said the young doctor. "Rest assured that nothing I do will hurt your eyes."

"I hope that you are correct," said the woman, "but in my lifetime I have heard a great many empty promises. Are you being honest? If you are, then I want you to make an agreement with me: you will pay *me* if after your treatment, I end up worse than before."

The doctor hesitated, but eventually he agreed: he signed a formal paper promising to pay Sarah seven gold coins if her vision deteriorated from the treatment that he gave. Then, to be completely safe – in order to protect the gold coins that he had pledged – the doctor treated the old woman with a harmless folk ointment made from lentils mashed in milk.

The doctor came to Sarah's house each day for a week. Each day, he made a poultice of beans mashed in milk; he patted the mix on Sarah's eyes, he wrapped a cloth around her head, and for an hour he sat with her in the cluttered kitchen, as the medicine soothed her eyes. After a few days, the doctor began to stroll around the woman's house while waiting to remove the bandage from her eyes. "My goodness," he said to himself, "what a great number of odds and ends she has! There are piles of knickknacks everywhere." A few days later, he thought: "I am here for hours every day, wasting my time. In the end, I will receive only a trifling fee. The house is so crowded with odds and ends that old Sarah will not miss a few of them." Then, the doctor reached into a cupboard, and quietly he pocketed a small silver candle-holder, one of three on the shelf.

The old woman's eyesight remained unchanged. "The treatments must continue for two weeks more," announced the doctor to Sarah, standing at her door. For two more weeks, the doctor came each day; he applied the lentil mash, he wrapped the woman's eyes, and he sat a moment with her in her small cluttered kitchen. Then, casually he stood and began to walk about, and quietly he pocketed some item from her house. This went on for weeks, but eventually the shelves looked bare and the young doctor declared the treatments at an end. The doctor reported that Sarah was as well as she could be, given her old age: the cure was now complete. Then, he demanded his final fee.

"What?!" said Sarah. "Is this all that I can expect?" She refused to pay the money, and she sent the doctor away. The doctor was angry, and he filed a complaint at the synagogue; thus, the shammas summoned the old woman to appear on a Thursday before the Rabbinical Court of Abraham ben Alexander, Achselrad of Cologne.

"Now Rabbi," began the doctor, "I have done my best. Unfortunately, the good Lord God (blessed be He) has determined in His wisdom that this woman is too old to see well ever again. I am afraid that Sarah never will be a young girl; she never will have a young woman's eyes. I am only a poor healer. But I did my best, Rabbi—that is all you can ask. Sarah promised to pay for my medical skills, but now she refuses to give me my fee."

The Rabbi looked at Sarah, who said: "Listen Rabbi—yes, I did promise to pay him. It is true that this man has come to my house for many weeks: he applied a special ointment each day for two or three weeks. However, his medicine was unhealthy: now I am worse than before."

The doctor knew the ointment to be harmless – lentils mashed in milk posed no danger at all – so he said to the Rabbi: "I swear that this is impossible."

Sarah shook her head: "I am worse than before. Now, here is a written agreement; it is signed by the doctor and by me. This paper states that if his treatment harmed my eyes, then he would pay *me* compensation – seven gold coins."

The Rabbi took the paper; he studied it carefully. He looked at the old woman, he looked at her eyes, and he said to the doctor: "My good doctor, if this woman's condition is worse, then she will owe you nothing, and you must pay her seven gold coins."

"Oh, I agree, Rabbi," said the doctor, and he smiled. "But I am absolutely certain that my treatment can have done no damage to her eyes."

Rabbi Abraham turned to Sarah. "Well, Sarah, what do you say to that?"

"Rabbi, I am clearly worse than before. Before the treatments started," said the old woman, "at least I saw the many things that decorate my house. Now, I look around me, I stare hard and intent; I search the table tops, the shelves, and cupboards. But where has everything gone? Now, I cannot see a great many things that I own. I cannot see furniture and books and pots and cutlery, jewelry and candlesticks – although, I know they should be there."

Sarah waved the written pact; the doctor looked away. Rabbi Abraham looked at the doctor. "Young man, I think that you owe seven coins to Sarah," said Achselrad. The doctor muttered dark words, but he paid the money that he owed, and soon afterward, he left Cologne in order to practice medicine somewhere else.

This was Rabbi Abraham ben Alexander, also called Achselrad of Cologne. He had been a pupil of Eliazer the mystic of Worms – and Achselrad was somewhat of a mystic himself. The Rabbi suspected what had actually happened in Sarah's house, but in this case he remained quiet. Of course, at other times he took a more active role. Rabbi Achselrad was always having mystic visions in the synagogue. For example, one night he had a visionary dream, and this caused him to levy an unusual tithe on one of the members of his congregation. Here is the story:

As you recall, the Jewish Quarter in medieval Cologne was in the eastern corner of the city, close to the ancient Roman wall. There, the main street led straight to the River Rhine through the Market Gate. Did the Jews first settle in this area in order to be near the royal citadel? Or did they hope for protection from the nearby Roman Catholic cathedral, which was the seat of the Archbishop? Perhaps the early Jewish merchants wanted to be near the marketplace, which extended all along the edge of the Jewish Quarter. In any event, most sections of the Cologne Jewish community were within the jurisdiction of the far eastern parish, the parish of St. Laurence. An occasional, wealthy Jewish house was found also in the adjacent parishes of St. Brigit and St. Mary ad Gradus. The district of St. Mary ad Gradus had many wealthy Gentiles; the few Jewish houses in that district were heavily taxed, and the Jews of St. Mary ad Gradus were subject to unannounced special fees. One of the Jews who owned houses in the parish of St. Mary ad Gradus was Avigdor ben Jacob ha-Kohen.

One night, the last night of *Rosh Hashanah*, Abraham ben Alexander opened the Mishnaic Treatise *Yoma*; the Rabbi wished to review this work before reading it formally on the Day of Atonement. The Rabbi's eyes felt heavy, and his head nodded. Did he hear wingbeats? Vaguely, he wondered if some angel was hovering in the corner of the room. But the light was dim and the Rabbi was tired, and soon he fell asleep. There, in the small back study room of the yeshiva, Rabbi Abraham fell asleep, and he dreamed that one of his congregants—Avigdor ben Jacob ha-Kohen, a very prosperous businessman—would lose seven hundred gold coins. Avigdor owned two houses in the parish of St. Mary ad Gradus, and somehow it was in connection with these properties that Avigdor would be forced to forfeit the money.

The next morning, Rabbi Abraham remembered his dream. After prayer, Rabbi Abraham went to Avigdor ben Jacob, and the Rabbi said: "My good neighbor, give me some money. There are people who are in great need of alms and charity."

"Why do you come to me, Rabbi?" asked Avigdor. "I already contribute heavily to charity."

Rabbi Abraham said: "As it is written in the Book of Proverbs":

> The righteous hate falsehood and slander,
> But the wicked will readily speak lies.

"Amen," said Avigdor.

"And," continued Achselrad, "there is another saying in the Book of Proverbs":

> A lying witness will die childless,
>   But if your words are honest and true
> Then you will leave fine children behind—
>   A noble lineage will follow you.

"Yes—how true, praise the Lord," said Avigdor.

"Of course," continued the Rabbi, "you also remember the proverb":

> The wicked witness who with a false word
>   Denounces an innocent man,
> Strikes like the club or like the sword
>   Of a blood-thirsty barbarian.

"I remember it well, Rabbi," said the businessman. "But what has this to do with charity?"

"My good Avigdor," said Rabbi Abraham, "consider Chapter 19 of the Book of Proverbs":

> He who is generous to the poor
>   Lends to the Lord Himself,
> And God will repay the charitable man
>   From the fullness of His shelf.

Reb Avigdor sighed, and then Rabbi Achselrad arranged with Avigdor ben Jacob ha-Kohen that he should contribute an extra sum regularly during the coming year. In this way, Rabbi Abraham took in a total of seven hundred gold coins over the next several months. Then, at the next year's Day of Atonement, on a cold autumn morning, there suddenly came an order from the Archbishop—Avigdor must appear in court.

This is what had happened: Avigdor came from a family of shopowners, but Avigdor himself was a moneylender. A century earlier, before the First Crusade, the Jews of Cologne had had a monopoly on the import of goods from the East. However, the Crusades brought closer ties between Europe and the East; this led to a new class of Gentile traders and importers. Ah, but the Jews were entrenched competition – Jews were already well established in foreign trade. Therefore, the Gentile burghers imposed special restrictions on the sale of goods that were imported by Jewish merchants. The rules and the extra taxes were overwhelming: Jews had to find some other economic niche. What could an enterprising Jewish businessman do? The Church forbade Christians to lend money for a profit, and this was a trade open to Jews – so many Jews took to moneylending.

(Of course, moneylending posed problems for the Jews, too. The Talmud condemns usury: excessive interest charges are denounced in scathing terms. For example, a man who practiced usury could not be a witness in a court of law. The Talmud declares:

A usurer denies the God of Israel; as the singer says in the 15th Psalm:

Lord, who shall enjoy Your Heavenly tents?
Who shall bask in Your holy light?
He who speaks honest sentiments
And tells the truth from his heart aright.

He who takes no bribes and does not steal,
Who gives out charity and helps the poor.
He who is honest shall not suffer nor feel
God's wrath beating harshly upon his door.

In any case, Avigdor managed to be both a moneylender and a pious Jew. Avigdor had lent out seven hundred gold coins to a rather unscrupulous Gentile who was living in the St. Mary ad Gradus parish. The man was unable to repay his loan. So what did he do? He prevailed on friends in the local council to impose a new tax on Jewish property owners in the St. Mary ad Gradus district. In this way, it was determined that Avigdor owed exactly seven hundred gold coins; otherwise, poor Avigdor ben Jacob ha-Kohen would have to forfeit his two fine houses and go to prison.

Avigdor, his family, his friends, and Rabbi Abraham all crowded into the Archbishop's court. When the charges were read, it was clear that everything had been done legally: there was no escape from the extra taxes. Avigdor ben Jacob ha-Kohen must pay seven hundred gold coins, or he would face the forfeiture of his properties and he would be imprisoned. Avigdor looked to the Rabbi. The Rabbi looked to Heaven. Sadly, Avigdor paid the fee, and the assembled Jews returned to the synagogue in the Jewish Quarter. Rabbi Abraham said a quiet prayer. Then he called Avigdor into the back room. Achselrad reached into a drawer in his desk and he gave Avigdor the extra seven hundred gold coins, the money that had been saved as charity during the previous year.

"What is this, Rabbi?" asked Avigdor. "Where did you get this much money?"

"This is your extra tithes; it is the money that you paid to charity over the last year," answered the Rabbi. "The money has always been yours—it has only been held temporarily in the good Lord's name."

At first, Avigdor began to hand the money back to the Rabbi, but Rabbi Abraham said: "Charity is for oneself as well as for others, Avigdor: without charity, we cannot hope to learn and to study. Without charity, we cannot hope to be blessed by the golden purity of the good Lord God's Laws and Truths. Without charity, we will never rest content in the long hours of the night, amen."

"Amen," said Avigdor.

The two men had moved to the main prayer hall of the synagogue: they stood among the worn wooden benches. Avigdor looked at the Holy Ark made of stone. Late afternoon sunlight filtered through the twelve stained glass windows with their colored lions and snakes, and Rabbi Abraham ben Alexander, Achselrad of Cologne, felt the warm sun on his back. "My good friend," he reminded Avigdor, "there is a wheel; it is a wheel of fortune, and it revolves in this mortal world. Through the unpredictable revolutions of this wheel, the rich become poor and the poor become rich. For this reason, when a beggar comes, always hand him some bread; always give him some money. I say this to you for the sake of your children. Why? Because someday the same may be done for your children, too—on some day in the future, when the wheel revolves again. And the wheel shall revolve again, Avigdor. It is as certain as tomorrow's sunrise."

h, good evening again, Rabbi. Yes, I know – it is always hard to sleep on the night of the new moon. Well, just put your feet up on the side bench here and I will open the stove door. Let me push this coal back. There is nothing like that white glow; it washes away the cares of a hard day. I heard your final benedictions tonight, Rabbi; clearly, you are overworked. Oh yes, even a shammas like me can tell. I kept one eye on you when I was cleaning the dishes, and I saw that you were watching the door, hoping that Reb Elbaum would leave early. But then, Reb Anton stayed to argue about the scriptural passage, Psalm 68:

> O Lord, from Your bounty
> You refresh the world with rain:
> Our dry and thirsty fields
> Are e'er enriched again.
> Your Goodness for ever yields
> Food for hungry men.

Thoughtful scriptural analysis always takes energy; so, of course you are still worn out. What is that? A story from me? Rabbi, all I know are

the children's tales, the grandmother fables. You need something new
and fresh to keep your mind keen. Otherwise you will become an old
man like me, and you will find yourself constantly musing and dozing
and nodding off in front of the stove.

What do you mean you are already an old man, Rabbi? Old? Do
you really think that sixty years is old? You are still a child. When you
reach eighty, *then* you will be old. You doubt that you will live to see
eighty years? If so, Rabbi, then you will never grow old. . . . All right,
all right—I know no special stories, but listening to you and Reb Anton
put me in mind of rainstorms. And I am speaking of the Great
Rainstorms; I mean those storms that come during the second half of
the year, beginning on the eighth day of the Feast of the Tabernacles,
when the benedictions have the addition:

> You, O Lord, Who revives the dead—You, O Lord, Who causes the
> wind to blow and the thick rains to descend.

and when the prayers say:

> Bless us, O our Father, in all the work of our hands. Bless our year with
> gracious, enriching, and kindly rains. Make the end of our work yield
> plentiful harvests, and also peace, as in all good years—for You, O Lord
> our God, are good and love peace. Bless our years to come as You have
> blessed our years gone by, amen.

My grandmother loved the rainy season, and each year she would look
forward to the time when the prayers had a kind word to say for
rainstorms. When I was young, my grandmother always had a story
or two to tell about rain; I remember one about gutters and rainspouts:

> Once upon a time, said my grandmother, in medieval Germany
> along the wide River Rhine, there lived a pious and somewhat mystical
> scholar named Abraham ben Alexander, Achselrad of Cologne. Rabbi
> Abraham had a yeshiva, and in his congregation, one of the poor but
> faithful members was a man named Vyvus ben Symon ben Nathan.
> Vyvus once sat under a rainspout, and that was the beginning of his
> troubles.

What is the problem with rainspouts? I used to think that it was simply water – you should not sit under a gutter because water might run down on you. You would get drenched, you would get dirty, you would be wet, unhappy, and uncomfortable. But, no, that is not the reason at all. There is a grave danger in sitting under a rainspout: evil spirits lurk there. My grandmother told me how this actually happened to poor Vyvus ben Symon ben Nathan, a man who earned his living by carrying baggage and other things on a stout pole. One day, said my grandmother, Vyvus was carrying a barrel of wine, balanced at the end of his portage pole. The barrel was heavy, and Vyvus needed a rest. Therefore, he put the barrel down on the ground right under a rain pipe.

Suddenly, Vyvus heard a laugh and a shriek and a hiss, and the barrel on the pole broke and the wine ran out onto the ground. Vyvus was frightened; he did not dare to touch the broken barrel. Could he even pick up his portage pole? He went to reach for it, but again he heard the laugh and the shriek and the hiss, and the pole shattered into sixty times sixty splinters. Vyvus ben Symon backed slowly away, and when he was out of sight of the rainspout, he jumped and he ran and he hurried off to the old synagogue building in the Jewish Quarter of Cologne.

Vyvus stepped in the front door, he went through the anteroom, and he walked into the main prayer hall filled with wooden benches; he passed the twelve stained glass windows with their colored lions and snakes, he looked up at the Holy Ark made of stone, and he walked to the door of the back study room. There, Rabbi Abraham was bent over a book, lost in his reading.

"Rabbi," said Vyvus quietly.

"Yes?"

"Rabbi, I have had an upsetting experience," said Vyvus.

The Rabbi looked at Vyvus. "Please, sit down, and tell me all about it," said Rabbi Abraham.

Vyvus was pale; he sat on one of the worn benches along the wall and he told his story. The Rabbi closed his eyes, he nodded his head, and then he opened his eyes. "Vyvus," he said, "this sounds like the work of evil spirits."

"This is terrible," said Vyvus. "What shall we do?"

"We ourselves cannot know exactly what is to come," said the Rabbi. "We must ask the spirits for the meaning of all this mischief."

Rabbi Abraham took a small bronze ring from his desk. "Here, take this holy ring," he said. "With it, you will be safe today – if you stay away from the rainspout. Come back tomorrow, on Court Day."

(Rabbi Abraham kept the old talmudic tradition: he held Rabbinical Court sessions on Mondays and on Thursdays. From the time of Ezra, the Hebrew courts in all the towns of Palestine met on Mondays and on Thursdays for civil matters. On these two weekdays, the outlying farmers came into town for business – and then they always attended the synagogue.)

Vyvus appeared in court on that Thursday. After disposing of two other cases, the Rabbi turned to Vyvus. "We had best protect ourselves first," said the Rabbi. Rabbi Abraham covered his head with a handkerchief, and he uttered an old protective charm:

> May God grant me aid,
> May the Holy One protect me
> After my speech is made,
> After my words are set free.

> O Lord, God of the Israelite,
> Shield me now, I pray:
> Keep me well throughout the night
> And bless me in the day.

> Guard me, Lord, so aches
> Cannot penetrate my heart.
> Protect me from mistakes;
> Do not let evils start.

> Keep me safe and whole.
> O Lord, keep me in Your sight
> While the sun shines gold
> And the moon glows white at night.

Then, the Rabbi uttered another spell, conjuring the demon who had done the evil deed: Rabbi Abraham recited a summons charm, requesting the malevolent spirit to appear before the Rabbinical Court.

O dark one, I exhort you:
I call on you to now report—
Appear here in this holy Court.

Your history is known,
Your upbringing has been shown,
You are lower than a stone.

Are you from the grave,
From an ancient burial cave,
A pagan foul enclave?

Have you come from geyser's steam,
Like a sodden dripping dream?
Are you damp from sweaty streams?

Were you rocked by winds and hails,
Blown here by the gales,
Dragged by black storm tails?

Wherever was your birth—
From under graveyard earth,
Or in a stump's rotten girth;

Whether from a ruined shrine
Overgrown with foul vines,
Coated with the dank woodbine—

O dark one, I exhort you:
I call on you to now report—
Appear here in this holy Court!

The Rabbi closed his eyes, the sky turned dark, the earth shook, and a wind blew. There was a laugh and a shriek and a hiss, and a hairy demon wavered, darkening the doorway.

The Rabbi stared at the evil spirit, and the evil spirit stared at the Rabbi. "Now tell me, O malign one," said the Rabbi, "why did you break this poor man's barrel of wine? He had done you no harm. And why did you break his portage pole, you unholy thing?"

"'Why,' Rabbi? Do you ask me 'Why'? Well, I will tell you why," hissed the demon. "This rude man put his barrel in my ear while I was lying asleep."

"Why did you lie down right there, in a spot where people usually walk?" asked Rabbi Abraham. "You must have realized that you would get no rest."

"Rabbi, this was a rainspout. Everyone knows that demons sleep under rainspouts—and in abandoned wells and in ruined buildings and in shaded places and in the shadows of trees," said the demon.

The demon hissed and he laughed, and then he said: "And, Rabbi, it is just as everyone also knows that we demons avoid jipijapa plants and knotroot grass. Besides," added the demon, "men should have more respect for the spirits. Do you think that we have an easy life, wandering unloved throughout the world?"

"You are certainly unloved, you foul creature," said Achselrad. "Now, demon, you must pay this man for the wine; otherwise, he will bring a holy charge against you."

The demon laughed. "Very well," it said, "but I must have three days in order to pay."

"Ah yes," sighed the Rabbi, "'three' is always the number for demons."

"Why 'three'?" asked Vyvus.

Rabbi Abraham replied: "In the Talmud, Vyvus, it is written":

In three respects, demons resemble the ministering angels and in three respects they are like humans. Like the ministering angels they have wings, like the ministering angels they fly from one end of the world to the other, and like the ministering angels they know the future.

On the other hand, like humans they eat and drink, like humans they propagate, and like humans they die.

In addition, demons have three special powers: they can alter their appearance, they can copy the shape of humans, and they can become invisible at will.

Therefore, the Rabbi agreed to the delay, and Vyvus waited three days. In three days' time, the demon did not pay and he did not reappear in the Court. So, the Rabbi said: "Vyvus, we must begin again." Rabbi Abraham covered his head with a handkerchief, he closed his eyes, and he began to conjure up the evil spirit once more.

"As usual, we had best begin with a protective charm," cautioned Achselrad:

> May God grant me aid,
> May the Holy One protect me
> After my speech is made,
> After my words are set free.
>
> O Lord, God of the Israelite,
> Shield me now, I pray:
> Keep me well throughout the night
> And bless me in the day.
>
> Guard me, Lord, so aches
> Cannot penetrate my heart.
> Protect me from mistakes;
> Do not let evils start.
>
> Keep me safe and whole.
> O Lord, keep me in Your sight
> While the sun shines gold
> And the moon glows white at night.

After this precaution, the Rabbi lit two white candles, and he recited the conjuring charm:

> O dark one, I exhort you:
> I call on you to now report—
> Appear here in this holy Court.
>
> Your history is known,
> Your upbringing has been shown,
> You are lower than a stone.

Are you from the grave,
From an ancient burial cave,
A pagan foul enclave?

Have you come from geyser's steam,
Like a sodden dripping dream?
Arc you damp from sweaty streams?

Were you rocked by winds and hails,
Blown here by the gales,
Dragged by black storm tails?

Wherever was your birth –
From under graveyard earth,
Or in a stump's rotten girth;

Whether from a ruined shrine
Overgrown with foul vines,
Coated with the dank woodbine

O dark one, I exhort you:
I call on you to now report –
Appear here in this holy Court!

The Rabbi closed his eyes, the sky turned dark, the earth shook, and a wind blew. There was a laugh and a shriek and a hiss, and the hairy evil demon stood in the doorway; it stood wavering as a dark and ill-blown shape in the doorway of the small back room of the old yeshiva in Cologne on the dark River Rhine.

"Well, demon," asked the Rabbi, "now what have you to say for yourself? Why did you not pay your fine? Why did you not even appear in the Rabbinical Court?"

"I will tell you, Rabbi," said the demon. "My money is in a sack, and no demon has a power over anything that is counted or sealed or tied up: a demon can only steal from things that are neither counted nor sealed nor tied up. And, as to tools, we carry only a runcible dibblestick and an aitchbone axe. These are the reasons that kept me from the Rabbinical Court; these are the reasons why I delayed payment."

Then the demon hissed and he laughed, and Vyvus was worried, but the Rabbi was angry.

"You are talking nonsense, evil one–and I think that we have been patient enough," said Rabbi Abraham, removing a strange amulet from his robes. The amulet was like a silver star with seven points. On the back was written the *Shema*, followed by seven mystical names and seven Divine words and seven holy charms. The Rabbi held the amulet near the white candle flame. Vyvus could see the Rabbi's hands, golden in the tiny firelight.

"Now," said Rabbi Achselrad, "I have only this to say":

> Was it in a graveyard that you've grown,
> Rising in Dumah's sacred ground?
> It matters not–I send you home.
> Return there, evil one: Sink down!
>
> Is rotting soil what you choose?
> Then return to crumbling fetid clay,
> Go back to mud and dirt and ooze:
> Sink there for ever and a day.
> Nations have vanished in graveyard clay,
> And so shall you–mud is your home.
> Or are you from the black sea spray?
> Were you born in wave and foam?
> Then, fly off to the Antipodes
> And drown beneath cold vortices
> Churned to froth by the frigid breeze
> Of vast and heartless open seas.
>
> Go back to Sheol's cruel abyss
> With thick muds for your nighttime bed.
> Fall over the dank black precipice
> Where cold winds will shriek around your head.
>
> Let us never hear your laugh afar,
> Your wicked dusty hissing cry
> As long as sun and moon and star
> Light up God's wide celestial sky.

The room began to darken as the Rabbi continued:

> Now I exorcise you far beyond
>   The cottages of the dead.
> Fly back across the bleak cold pond;
>   Fall down the caves of dread.
> Never will you see a child
>   Wide-eyed, laughing in the sun.
> Never will a newborn smile
>   And hold his fist onto your thumb.
> God will smite you blind; reviled,
>   For ever you'll be blank and dumb.
> The fierce Lord sends you far from Him —
>   He only holds the gentle near.

The room darkened to blackness, and the Rabbi held the mystical amulet directly in the flame of one of the candles. The amulet began to glow. Vyvus felt a strange wind. There was a clap of thunder. Everything seemed dim and misty. Then, in a flash of lightning, the demon disappeared. There was a hiss and a shriek, and the demon of the rainspout disappeared: the evil spirit was gone; it vanished for ever. Then, Vyvus jumped back and he winked and blinked, as the amulet itself burst into flames. And, as my grandmother said, the secret of the amulet was lost, for Vyvus ben Symon ben Nathan could never remember the exact words of any of the fearsome charms.

And why was the demon there in the first place, and how did the amulet work? We may never know. The truth is simply that the demon was gone, the evil spirit was banished, and the mystical charms worked – and that is all we ever need to know. By the holy blessings of the good Lord God, Rabbi Abraham ben Alexander protected the Jews of Cologne in those dark days of medieval Germany, in those dim times along the edge of the Rhine, the wide and dark medieval River Rhine.

ood evening, Rabbi. No sleep for the weary? That is what my grandmother said—and she said it almost nightly. If you are cold, then sit down here on the bench; I will stoke up the oven. This stoker? It is one of the iron shoe scrapers from the front hall. You probably do not recognize it because it is covered with soot. (Also, I bent it in order to make it fit through the oven door.) Of course there are still two scrapers in the anteroom for dirty shoes. But I myself am of the old school: I think that all pious men should pray barefoot. Did you know that Abulafia of Toledo prophesied that the Messiah will appear barefoot? Well, we can always hope.

As my grandmother said to me: "We must always hope, my little one. Is it a delusion to hope? It does not matter, for Hope is happiness." She said this often, and, of course, how could you question a great saying like that? Sometimes she would tell stories about Hope. In particular, I remember my grandmother's tale about the hopes of Baruch ben Hananiah, a member of the congregation of Rabbi Abraham ben Alexander, Achselrad of Cologne:

Once upon upon a time, said my grandmother, in the town of Cologne on the River Rhine, lived a pious man named Baruch ben

Hananiah. One day, the wife of Reb Baruch complained to her husband about their extreme poverty. "How long must we suffer on this earth?" she asked.

"What do you mean, my dear wife?" asked Baruch.

"I mean, Baruch, we have been poor for as long as we have been alive. We are tired every day, and we often go to bed hungry; we are cold in the winter, and we are hot in the summer. I wish that the good Lord God would help out. He could give us a taste of our final reward– I would certainly appreciate just a taste," said his wife.

"I do not know if the Almighty One gives tastes in advance," said Baruch. "I will ask Rabbi Achselrad."

So Baruch ben Hananiah went to the synagogue. Baruch stepped in the front door, he removed his shoes in the anteroom, and he padded on stocking feet into the main prayer hall filled with wooden benches. Baruch passed the twelve stained glass windows with their colored lions and snakes, he looked up at the Holy Ark made of stone, and he walked to the door of the back study room. There, Rabbi Abraham ben Alexander was bent over a book, lost in his reading.

"Rabbi," said Baruch ben Hananiah quietly.

"Yes?" said the Rabbi.

"Rabbi, I have a question. Tell me: Does the good Lord God (blessed be He) give a taste of Heaven, in advance of our final rest?" asked Baruch.

Rabbi Abraham looked intently at Baruch. "What do you mean, Baruch?"

"Rabbi," said Baruch, "my wife is tired and worn from her difficult life. She was wondering whether there is any possibility that the Almighty One might share a bit of our future reward with us today."

The Rabbi closed his eyes, and then he opened them again. "Baruch, I can only say that the Lord hears all our prayers," answered Rabbi Abraham.

"Amen," said Baruch, and he walked to the front door of the synagogue, where he put his shoes on again; then, he returned home.

When he walked into his kitchen, Reb Baruch said to his wife: "My good wife, pray to Heaven. I am certain that in the end we are destined for a fine reward. Perhaps the great Lord God (blessed be He) will share some of that goodness early."

So the wife prayed and she prayed, but nothing happened. Every day, Baruch's wife reminded him that she had been praying fervently; so after a week, Baruch returned to the synagogue. He stepped in the front door, he removed his shoes in the anteroom, and he padded in his stocking feet through the main prayer hall filled with wooden benches. Baruch passed the twelve stained glass windows with their colored lions and snakes, he looked up at the Holy Ark made of stone, and he walked to the door of the back study room. There, Rabbi Abraham was bent over a book, lost in his reading.

"Rabbi," said Baruch quietly.

"Yes?"

"Rabbi, I apologize for bothering you when you are studying. You may remember," said Baruch, "that my wife has been upset over our arduous life?"

"Yes, I remember," said Achselrad.

"Well, Rabbi, you suggested prayer," said Baruch ben Hananiah.

Rabbi Abraham looked at Baruch intently. "Reb Baruch, if I remember correctly, I said that the good Lord God hears all prayers."

"Exactly, Rabbi–now, my wife has prayed fervently for the past week, and we seem to be in exactly the same straits as we were before."

The Rabbi closed his eyes and then he opened his eyes, but he remained silent. Reb Baruch looked down at his feet. "My wife was wondering," began Baruch, "she wondered whether you might have some little thing to get the Lord's attention, Rabbi."

"Get the Lord's attention?" asked the Rabbi.

"Well–I mean, Rabbi, the Omnipotent Lord Almighty is very busy. Perhaps you have some kind of magical charm or coin or something–something that might catch His attention. Perhaps you have a mystical amulet for my wife?" said Baruch.

Achselrad said: "I would like to help, but I do not think that a charm or a coin or an amulet is the best thing in this case."

"Of course you would know best, Rabbi," said Baruch.

The Rabbi looked down at his papers.

After a moment, Baruch cleared his throat. "Rabbi, my wife is a good woman at heart; she will understand–I am certain," said Baruch.

The Rabbi began to write.

Baruch waited a bit, then he said: "You know, Rabbi, I love my wife. However, it would be easier to go home if I had some little thing to take back to her."

The Rabbi stopped writing.

"I do not mean anything sacred," said Baruch. "I was just thinking of something small and simple."

Rabbi Achselrad sighed, and he opened his desk drawer. He took out a little parchment scroll on which was written one mystical word:

ABRACADABRA

What? Yes, yes, Rabbi, I am about to continue. I was just thinking quietly here in the glow of the stove. Now, where was I? ABRACADABRA? Oh yes, Abraham ben Alexander was a kabbalist, and ABRACADABRA is a kabbalistic charm. It is built from the initials of the Hebrew phrase *Ab* (Father) ha-*Ruach ACadsch* (the Holy Spirit)—although, the Christians say that the initials are: *Ab* (Father), *Ben* (Son), and *Ruach ACadsch* (the Holy Spirit)—and when written on an amulet, it is inscribed like this:

ABRACADABRA
ABRACADABR
ABRACADAB
ABRACADA
ABRACAD
ABRACA
ABRAC
ABRA
ABR
AB
A

"All right, Baruch—here is a rather mild charm," said Rabbi Abraham. "It is especially good as an antidote for ague and toothache. In order—"

"Excuse me, Rabbi," said Baruch, "did you say 'toothache'?"

"I did."

"Do you think that this is appropriate here?" asked Baruch.

"I think," said the Rabbi, "that this charm is as appropriate as any other. Now, as I was saying: in order to use it properly, the paper must be unrolled and then refolded in the form of a star. Do this carefully and neatly, Baruch. Then suspend the star from a white linen thread and hang it around your wife's neck so that it rests on the center of her stomach. Have her wear this necklace for nine days; on the ninth day, before sunrise, throw the necklace into a stream that runs east. Finally, your wife should pray again to the good Lord God (blessed be He)."

Reb Baruch returned to his wife and he repeated Rabbi Abraham's instructions. His wife listened carefully. "Amen," she said, and she began to carry out the plan—she wore the amulet, and she prayed fervently.

Baruch and his wife had always been a fine and righteous couple, and as it is said in the Book of Proverbs of the Holy Scriptures:

> God hates the prayers of wicked men,
> But He loves seekers of righteousness.

Therefore, after nine days of wearing the charm and after another week of prayer, a deafening clap of thunder arose one day. A flash of lightning shot forth from a cloud, the earth shook, and a hand reached out from Heaven and gave a gold table leg to the wife of Baruch ben Hananiah.

What was this strange and wondrous miracle? The poor woman opened wide her eyes. Hesitantly, she reached out and touched the sparkling piece of furniture. It was real, so she carried it into her house. The next day, Baruch's wife sold the gold table leg and she became rich, and now she began to live a life of ease and she was happy.

All went well for a month. Then one night, Baruch's wife had a vivid dream.

In her dream, Baruch's wife saw Heaven and the Great Hereafter—she saw the *Gan Eden*. The *Gan Eden* had three gates of ruby, by which stood sixty ministering angels, and the face of each angel glistened like the splendor of the firmament. Spirits of the dead formed a long line at each entrance. As each pious person arrived, the angels removed the shrouds in which he arose from the grave, they clothed him in eight robes of the clouds of glory, and they set two crowns upon his head—one made of gems and pearls and the other made of gold from Parvaim. The angels placed eight myrtles in each spirit's hand, and they sang to him:

> Go now, my loved one –
> Eat your heavenly food,
> Bask in the warm sun,
> Under skies golden-hued.

The newcomers felt warm and joyous and calm, and each person was escorted by a guardian angel into an oasis. The gardens of the oasis were filled with sparkling brooks, and they were surrounded by eight hundred varieties of roses and myrtles. In the distance were field upon field of asphodel. Each person also had his own pearl-lined room. Inside each room were four fountains: one of cream, one of wine, one of nectar, and one of honey. Above each room was a lintel adorned with a golden vine, studded with thirty gleaming pearls, and each pearl shone with the brilliance of the evening star. In every chamber, there was a gold table inlaid with gems and pearls, and sixty angels attended each righteous person at all times. The angels sang to each pious soul:

> Ah, my righteous shade,
> Eat honey in celebration –
> Honey that was first made
> During the Creation:
> For you read Torah and prayed
> As sweetly as gold honey.

> Ah, my righteous shade,
> Drink wine in jubilation –
> Wine that was first made
> From grapes of the Creation –
> For you read Torah and prayed
> As gently as fine wine.

And the wife of Reb Baruch saw that everyone – all the good and pious men and women and even those innocent little children who had been called to their eternal rest early – all these people were seated at the gold tables inlaid with gems and pearls, and each table had four legs. All the righteous were sitting enthroned. All the righteous had crowns on their heads. All the righteous were eating from great dishes of delicate grain, warm bread, and the roasted meat of the Leviathan, they were drinking wine from grapes of the six days of Creation, and they had plates of honey and cakes at their right hand.

Reb Baruch's wife could see herself also. But she found that she and her husband, Baruch ben Hananiah, were sitting at a wobbly table; the table had only three legs, and it was not steady enough to hold any food or drink at all. Then she awoke, and Baruch's wife told her dream to her husband.

"I am afraid," said the wife. "What could this mean, husband?"

"Clearly, the good Lord is reminding you of the gold table leg that he gave you last month," said Baruch. "But is this dream an ill omen? Is it a warning? Let me go and question Rabbi Achselrad."

Baruch went to the synagogue. He stepped in the front door, he removed his shoes in the anteroom, and he padded in his stocking feet through the main prayer hall filled with wooden benches. Baruch passed the twelve stained glass windows with their colored lions and snakes, he looked up at the Holy Ark made of stone, and he walked to the door of the back study room. There, Rabbi Abraham ben Alexander was bent over a book, lost in his reading.

"Rabbi," said Baruch quietly.

"Yes?"

"Rabbi, I apologize for bothering you again. You may remember," said Baruch, "that earlier this year my wife had been quite upset— we were very poor, and we had a difficult life. Then, you gave us a charm, and we prayed. With the help of the Almighty Lord God (blessed be He), we have had some good fortune recently, amen. Now we live quite comfortably."

"Yes—I am glad that things have worked out well for you," said Achselrad.

"Now, Rabbi," said Baruch, "my wife has had a disquieting dream." And Baruch described the dream.

The Rabbi listened, with his eyes closed; then, he opened his eyes, and he said: "Baruch, in the Talmud, we learn that Rabbi Judah the Prince said":

Whoever accepts the delights and the comforts of this earthly world will be deprived of the delights and the comforts of the Great Hereafter.

In contrast, whoever declines the delights and the comforts of this world will certainly receive the delights and the comforts of the World to Come.

"Amen," said Baruch.

"Yes – amen," said the Rabbi.

And Baruch said: "Good Rabbi, I have certainly heard this, and it must be correct. Nonetheless, it is not easy to be patient."

"I know," said Rabbi Abraham.

"It would be a bit easier if there were some little thing in this world to carry us through, here and now," said Baruch.

"There is more than a little thing, Baruch," said Achselrad, "there is a very big thing."

"To what are you referring, Rabbi?"

"It is simply this: Hope."

"Hope?" asked Baruch ben Hananiah.

"Yes, Baruch – it is Hope," said Rabbi Abraham. The Rabbi thought silently for a moment, and then he said: "Listen, my friend, to an old fable, a story told to us by Rabbi Meir of Palestine:

"Once upon a time, a hungry crow perched in a fig tree; patiently, he was waiting for the figs to ripen to a juicy yellow. However, it was still early in the season, and the figs were hard and green and inedible.

"A fox watched the crow sit there, day after day after day. Finally, the fox asked: 'Why have you become such a fixture in this field?'

"'I am hungry,' said the bird.

"'You are hungry?' repeated the fox. 'If you are hungry, then you had best go off and find some food.'

"'I like figs: I am waiting for the figs to ripen,' said the crow.

"'Do not be a fool. Hope has overtaken your senses,' said the fox. 'A wise poet once said that hopes are but the dreams of those who are awake. Hope can only delude you, foolish bird; it will never fill your belly.'

"'Ah, my fine four-footed friend,' said the bird, 'the world has many wise men. Another wise man has said: We must always hope. Even when our dreams seem to be a delusion, Hope is happiness.'"

"Old Rabbi Meir was a storyteller, and that was his fable of Hope, Baruch. The point is: Hope is happiness," said Achselrad, and he looked off into the distance, somewhere beyond the walls of the little back study room—the Rabbi looked somewhere far beyond the dark wide River Rhine.

Baruch ben Hananiah waited politely.

"Did you know that the false Messiahs come bearing gifts?" asked Rabbi Abraham.

Baruch ben Hananiah looked puzzled. The Rabbi continued: "Oh yes—it is not only that they come walking into our lives barefoot and carrying branches of myrtle and singing sweetly the old and holy psalms. They also come with a sacred gift: they come with Hope.

"The claimants to the robes of the Messiah bring the happiness of Hope, Baruch. I remember a young man. His name was Abraham Abulafia, and he appeared in Cologne one day. Abulafia came from Tudela, an old Roman town in northern Spain. In the afternoons, young Abraham Abulafia listened quietly in the yeshiva, and at night he would sit for hours quizzing me about the Kabbalah."

Rabbi Abraham paused a moment. "Yes, Baruch—young Abulafia would sit just about where you are now. He would sit and stare and talk and listen, and he would wave his hands. . . . I can remember it all so clearly."

Achselrad sighed. "Abulafia was clever," continued the Rabbi, "but he was a very strange young man, and one day he simply disappeared. He was tall, he had a lively imagination, he had considerable knowledge, and he was blessed with a golden tongue. As he wandered about Europe, he seemed to be a prophet and a worker of miracles. He lectured on his theory of the Kabbalah, and he secured students, admirers, and devotees. Abulafia was brazen enough to attempt to convert the Pope to Judaism, a move that was not well received, and young Abulafia was lucky to escape from Rome with his life.

"From Rome, Abulafia traveled by night, and eventually he arrived on the island of Sicily. One morning, he walked barefoot into the town of Messina, loudly singing Psalm 11:

> In God, I find my refuge.
> So, do not bother to say:
> "Flee to the hilltops
> Like the swift dove today."

I stay calm when I hear:
"The wicked string their bows,
They're fitting a sharp arrow,
They're donning battle clothes.

"From their hidden lairs,
They are planning to attack;
They hope to strike you down,
To smother the righteous pack."

When we are attacked
Then what can good men do?
We simply trust in God:
The Lord will see us through.

The Lord is in His Temple;
Heaven holds His throne.
God sends His anointed king
To defend Israel alone.

"In Messina, Abulafia had a warm reception, and he announced himself as the herald of the Messiah. He wrote a long Messianic sermon, which he read over and over again; it was a flowery, poetic message, and it detailed the sterling character of the ambassador of the Messiah. In the synagogue, Abulafia declared: the Kabbalah predicts that this year is the date of the True Coming.

"Abulafia preached the coming of the Messiah, and people's eyes opened wide. Would the Messiah really appear? The Jews of Sicily hoped and prayed and rejoiced. However, the Messiah never arrived that year. But, Baruch, the people of Messina were never happier, and they have never been as happy since. Always, we must hope. Is it a delusion to hope? It does not matter, for Hope is happiness."

Then Rabbi Abraham looked down at his desk, he tapped his finger on the edge of a manuscript, and soon he went back to his writing. Reb Baruch waited a moment, but when the Rabbi had nothing further to say, Baruch walked back to the front of the synagogue. Baruch put on his shoes, and he returned to his wife and he said: "My good wife, pray to Heaven."

His wife raised her eyebrows.

"The good Lord hears all prayers," said Baruch.

"Amen," said his wife.

"Even before we were rich, we had Hope," said Baruch. "We had hope for the Great Hereafter, which we knew we would enjoy together for ever."

His wife smiled and said: "Amen, Baruch."

"My wife," said Baruch, "you are now enjoying only a part of your reward. In your dream, you have seen what glorious joys await us in the Great Hereafter. Do not spoil our eternal happiness for the sake of temporary pleasures. We can be patient, my dear. Ask the good Lord God to take back the money for now – we will wait and hope, and we will be happy together."

So the wife prayed and she prayed, but nothing happened. Therefore, a week later, Baruch returned to the synagogue. He stepped in the front door, he removed his shoes in the anteroom, and he padded in his stocking feet through the main prayer hall, which was filled with wooden benches. Baruch passed the twelve stained glass windows with their colored lions and snakes, he looked up at the Holy Ark made of stone, and he walked to the door of the back study room. There, Rabbi Abraham ben Alexander was bent over a book, lost in his reading.

"Rabbi," said Baruch quietly.

"Yes?"

"Rabbi, I apologize for bothering you. My wife has been praying again," said Baruch, "but we have had no sign from the Almighty One. Perhaps the good Lord God (blessed be He) has not heard her prayers – could you give us an amulet to help?"

Rabbi Abraham looked at Baruch intently. The Rabbi closed his eyes, and then he opened his eyes. Rabbi Achselrad opened his eyes, and he sighed and he said: "Reb Baruch, the good Lord God hears all prayers." Then, the Rabbi reached inside his desk drawer and he took out a small parchment scroll, tightly rolled and with one mystical word written on it: ABRACADABRA.

Baruch thanked the Rabbi, he walked to the front of the synagogue, and he put on his shoes; then, he returned to his wife. "Amen," said Baruch's wife when she heard her husband's report. Again, she followed all of the Rabbi's original instructions: she unrolled the paper and refolded it in the form of a star, she suspended the star on a single white thread from her neck, she wore the necklace for nine days, and then she threw the necklace into a stream that runs east – meanwhile, she prayed and prayed and prayed.

At heart, the couple were fine and righteous people. Baruch and his wife were devout and faithful, and as it is said in the Book of Proverbs in the Holy Scriptures:

> The Almighty turns His radiant head,
> Standing aloof from the wicked crowd.
> But the good Lord listens closely instead
> To the prayers of the righteously endowed.

Therefore, after nine days of wearing the holy charm and after another week of prayer, a clap of thunder arose one day. A flash of lightning shot forth from a cloud, the earth shook, and a hand reached down from Heaven. The hand swept up the money and the clothes and the furniture and the jewelry and the fancy foods that the woman had bought with the proceeds from the sale of her gold table leg. And Baruch ben Hananiah and his wife were poor once more, amen.

That evening, Baruch ben Hananiah sat in his kitchen. He sat at the wooden table, and he looked across at his wife. Reb Baruch realized that his wife was an old woman: she had wrinkles next to her eyes, and her hair was gray. Baruch smiled at his wife and she smiled at him. They held hands, and they were content.

ood evening, Rabbi. You are having difficulty sleeping again? Put your feet up on the side bench and I will open the stove door. Let me push this coal back; the white glow will wash away the cares of a hard day. I heard your final prayers tonight, and there is no use denying it—you are overworked. Even an old shammas like me can tell. I kept one eye on you when I was cleaning the dishes, and I saw that you were watching the door, hoping that Reb Elbaum would leave early; but then Reb Anton stayed late to argue about the Midrash passage.

That Midrash passage reminded me of old Rabbi Jehuda ben Saul. One day, Rabbi Jehuda was lecturing to his yeshiva students:

"Midrash!" said Rabbi Jehuda, and he looked sternly at the young men on the benches. The Rabbi stared at the boys, the boys looked at the floor, and there was silence; so, the Rabbi said: "Midrash, my fine young friends—exactly what does this mean?"

The yeshiva students hesitated. After a moment, young Moshe ben Samuel said: "Rabbi, a *midrash* is commentary."

"True," said the Rabbi, "*midrash* can be commentary."

The Rabbi was silent and he looked at his desk; then, he looked at the students.

"The word *midrash* means 'to search out,'" said Rabbi Jehuda.

"The word *midrash* means 'to inquire,'" continued the Rabbi.

"The word *midrash* means 'to explain,'" said old Jehuda.

"But," said the Rabbi, pounding a stick on his table, "is *midrash any* explanation?"

Again there was silence. Rabbi Jehuda stared and then went on: "Of course not—*midrash* is not *any* explanation: *midrash* is the discovery of the spirit lying in wait below the text. The great and glorious Talmud says":

> Midrash is a hammer—it is a hammer that awakens into shining light the sparks slumbering within the rock of the text. Midrash strikes the fire that hides inside the iron.

And is this not so?" asked the Rabbi nodding his head.

Some of the students nodded also.

"Yes, of course it is so," he said, "and, young scholars, why must the sparks be freed from the iron?"

The students looked at one another. No one spoke. The Rabbi glared at the students, and finally Moshe ben Samuel asked bravely: "Good Rabbi, what exactly do you mean?"

"What do I mean?" asked Rabbi Jehuda. "What do I mean? I mean what I say, Moshe: Why do the sparks of the hidden spirit, the holy sparks, the glorious sacred sparks, need to get separated from the iron? That is what I said, and that is what I meant."

And again he looked severely at the students. No one said anything, someone shuffled his shoe, the floors creaked, and the Rabbi cleared his throat. "My young and aspiring scholars," he began, "my tentative and untutored students, let me remind you of some holy facts: Exodus!"

"Yes," said old Jehuda, "it is in the Book of Exodus. There the great and awesome Lord God Almighty (blessed be He) clearly told us that iron in any form, and iron tools in particular, cannot be used to craft the Holy altar. Listen":

> You shall make an altar of earth for Me. And you shall make it of clay and brick and stones. But you must not build it of hewn stones; for if you use a chisel on it, then you will profane it.

"I repeat, young gentlemen, if you use a chisel on it—an *iron* chisel—then you will profane it."

Rabbi Jehuda continued: "And why does iron profane the holy?"

The Rabbi looked down at his young charges. No one responded, so the Rabbi said, staring directly at Moshe: "Does not the iron sword kill?"

"Yes, it does, Rabbi," said Moshe ben Samuel.

"Of course it does," said the Rabbi. "Iron abridges life, while the altar prolongs it. Iron causes destruction and it causes misery and suffering and sadness. But the altar? The holy altar leads to reconciliation between the Almighty Lord God and man. Therefore, the use of iron cannot be allowed in making the holy altar, amen."

The Rabbi's voice died away in the blank room, wearily he looked down at his desk, and the students began to gather up their books. Suddenly, Rabbi Jehuda shouted:

> You shall not make gods of silver to be worshipped as you worship Me—you shall not make for yourselves gods of gold!

The students looked at one another in alarm.

"Hallelujah," said Rabbi Jehuda. "Hallelujah—the good Lord God (blessed be He) wants his altar made of earth, and He wants no gods of gold!"

Again the Rabbi looked down; the students were unsure whether he was finished. But Rabbi Jehuda said: "No gods of gold? Is that correct?"

He looked at the boys, but no one answered. So Rabbi Jehuda replied: "Of course that is correct—it is so written in Exodus. But young scholars, I ask you: Is gold really bad? Is it really wicked? Is it really evil? Are gold and money the tools of those hairy demons that lurk in shadows of trees?"

Moshe looked at the other students, and then he said: "If the Holy Scriptures warn us against making gold idols, then I guess that gold must be evil, Rabbi."

"What?! Gold is evil?" asked the Rabbi. "Have I heard you correctly, Moshe? Do you really think that gold is evil? Moshe, gold is certainly *not* evil. For is it not written that charity is the highest good? Is it not written that to give alms is the finest of joys? And is gold not the best of charities and the greatest of alms? Yes, it is – hallelujah and praise the Lord, amen."

And old Rabbi Jehuda put his head down on his desk, and he seemed to fall asleep.

Ah, the great Jehuda ben Saul is a warning to us all, Rabbi: a biblical passage is a complex thing. A scriptural verse is not what it appears at first. Appearances deceive, as my grandmother used to say – that is, appearances colored by desire. I remember that my grandmother once told me a little fable about appearances; actually, it was a fable from the storyteller Rabbi Meir of Palestine:

Once upon a time, began this fable, there was a dog, a yellow, short-haired dog, and this dog loved to eat eggs more than anything else on the good Lord's earth. And did this dog know the Talmud? Who can say? It is possible, because in the Talmud is written:

Take any food of the size of an egg, and you will find that a real egg is far superior to it in nourishment.

I wonder if the dog knew this elemental fact? In any case, the dog loved the taste of eggs: it could not resist eggs.

One day, this yellow dog was padding through the chicken coop when he saw two smooth round stones, each one just the size of an egg. "Ah," thought the dog, "blessed be the Lord Almighty, these must be eggs, just waiting to be eaten." (Now, if he truly knew the Talmud, then the dog would also have known:

Whoever eats forty eggs or forty nuts or a quarter of honey, his heart will burst and be torn out.

However, two eggs are not forty, so I suppose that the Talmud does not matter here.) In any case, the dog opened wide his mouth, and in one gulp he bolted down the two smooth, round, egg-shaped stones.

Immediately, the dog regretted his haste. The leaden stones

weighed so heavily on his stomach that he felt terrible. "Stone and rock do not a gentle meal make," he thought sadly. "But I suppose that it serves me right for being in such a hurry. I am sorry that I ever thought that anything round must be an egg."

Yes, things are more complex than they first appear. No one knew this better than Rabbi Abraham ben Alexander, Achselrad of Cologne. He was always looking deep into matters, peering below the surface in his mystical magical way. Achselrad read the fables of Rabbi Meir of Palestine; he looked beneath their simple words, and he discovered much forgotten and occult knowledge. Meir's fables appear often in Achselrad's famous tome the *Keter Shem Tov*. As you know, Rabbi Abraham was in the habit of spending hours and hours studying in the back room of the old yeshiva, working on this manuscript. But one day, the good Lord God had other ideas, and Rabbi Abraham was surprised to find himself leaving the yeshiva earlier than usual.

Abraham ben Alexander stepped out the front door of the synagogue, and he looked at the darkening sky. He found that the houses had a blue-gray tint, the people were far off, and the roads were hidden. Then, the Rabbi heard two voices – the voices of demons – speaking to one another (may the good Lord God protect us from such evils).

As the Rabbi stood wondering, he heard the second demon cough and hiss and ask the first demon: "Ah, you malevolent spirit, where might you be going in this dark evening hour?"

"It is strange that you should ask, and it is strange that it should be of any concern of yours – but you are a strange and wicked creature, so I will answer," said the first demon. "I have been sent by the Lord God Almighty to put my curse and my black sign upon Judah ben Jakar ha-Levi. Then, of course, I will kill him and his wife and his children."

"Ah, this sounds interesting, you hairy dybbuk. What wrong has Judah ben Jakar ha-Levi done?"

"All men have some sins on their backs," replied the first demon. "This particular man has never given alms; he has donated no charity whatsoever."

"What?!" hissed the second demon. "How can he live in a Jewish community and avoid giving at least a little bit of money or clothes or food? Is he too poor?"

"No, he is not especially poor," said the first demon. "Of course, poverty is no excuse. It is written in talmudic Law that even the beggar who lives on charity must himself be charitable. No, this man has just said to himself: 'Judah, it is best to save your money. Someday, when you and your family are more well protected, then you will be able to help others.'"

When Rabbi Abraham heard this, he thought: "Poor Judah – he is misguided, but he is not wicked. However, now he will die an early death. I had best take a hand in this matter."

The Rabbi had no doubts about what he should do, for is it not said in the Talmud:

> Sit and relax at your meal. He who prolongs his stay at the table, also prolongs his life, because there is always the chance that a poor man will appear and that he can then be given some food as charity.

So, with this in mind, Achselrad returned to the back room of the yeshiva; he put on an old cloak, he pulled a tattered hat low over his forehead, and he rubbed some dirt onto his face. Then, Abraham ben Alexander, Achselrad of Cologne, walked to the house of Judah ben Jakar ha-Levi.

The Rabbi arrived at Judah's door, and boldly he walked right in. It was dinner time, and the family was sitting around the table. Everyone looked up, astonished. Was this some thief who brazenly barged in? No one recognized the holy man. Uninvited, Achselrad sat down on a stool at the edge of the table. Judah's daughter coughed, and Judah's son said: "Who is this old beggar who comes in here so boldly, who sits down, and who seems to expect a meal?" And Judah's wife said: "Husband, tell this presumptuous man to leave."

Judah looked at Achselrad and he tilted his head – he was not certain what to do. Rabbi Abraham pulled over a plate and said: "You people can shout all that you want. I am hungry, and I am not going to leave until I have eaten – pass me some soup."

Judah did not know what to say. He looked around. His family was taken aback. There was silence. Finally, Judah said: "We will bless Him from Whose wealth we are about to eat."

Judah's wife frowned. Judah's daughter creased her brow. Judah's son opened his mouth, but he said nothing.

Then Rabbi Abraham ben Alexander responded: "Blessed be He

from Whose wealth we have eaten and through Whose goodness we live." And the Rabbi began to eat.

The family looked at one another, and then they too ate their dinner—and all was silent. When he had finished the meal, Rabbi Abraham said to Judah: "Now, my good man, take a loaf of bread and give it to me as alms. Also, I would not mind another glass of wine."

Judah ben Jakar ha-Levi replied: "You are certainly a presumptuous person, you old scoundrel. Is it not enough that I gave you food and drink? Must I now give you a new loaf of bread and a second glass of wine besides?"

Rabbi Abraham answered: "Yes, that would be nice. And if your wife would just pass the turnips, I think that I could manage to swallow another piece."

Judah's wife sat in surprise. The children looked to their father. No one offered to pass more food. Rabbi Abraham looked at the people sitting around him, and he said: "Listen, Reb Judah, I have had some dealing with the holy words of the good Lord God (blessed be He) and with the wise thoughts of the talmudic Sages. You must know, do you not, that in the Talmud it is written":

Alms shall deliver you from death; they shall purge away all your sins. Those who give charity—those who share their good fortune unselfishly—they will be filled with life.

It was dark outside by now, and Rabbi Abraham suddenly blew out the candles on the table and his face shone like the sun. Then, the Rabbi relit the candles, and he sat back in his chair.

Judah thought: "This pious man looks like our own mystical Abraham. Is he perhaps an angel in disguise? The Lord is testing me, and I had best rise to the occasion. I have saved my charity for my family, but if I am nearing the end of my days, then finally it is time to loosen the strings on my purse and pouch."

Therefore, Judah gave Abraham Achselrad a loaf of bread for the Lord God's sake. He passed the plate of turnips, and he poured an extra glass of wine; in addition, Judah ben Jakar ha-Levi gave five gold coins to the Rabbi for the poor.

Rabbi Abraham smiled, and he said: "Ah, my good Judah, I knew that deep within you, you had compassion for the needy—thank you very much."

And Judah said: "You are quite welcome, old man."

"Now," continued Achselrad, "listen to my advice. Send your wife and your children out of the house and—"

"What?!"

"Just a moment, Reb Judah, do not interrupt. As I was saying, send your wife and your children to some relative's house or to a neighbor's house or even to the synagogue. Do not allow them to come back until tomorrow, until the third hour after sunrise. Let *no one* at all into your home until then."

"This is strange advice," said Judah, "but I will do what you say. Will you stay the night with me?"

"Yes," said Rabbi Abraham, "I think that I had better help further."

So, Judah ben Jakar ha-Levi sent his wife and his son and his daughter out of the house, and Judah and the Rabbi remained inside. "Now what do we do?" asked Judah.

"Now," answered the Rabbi, "we sit, and we wait."

The two men sat at the table as the candles slowly burned down and as the smoke slowly rose up. In the small hours of the morning, as Judah's eyes were closing, the first demon came to the door and knocked; he tapped like a small stone at the door.

Judah heard the tapping, and he was afraid.

Rabbi Abraham called out: "Who is at the door?"

"It is us, good Rabbi, Judah's family. We are cold. Let us in," said a woman's voice from outside the door.

Then Rabbi Abraham said: "Go back to the neighbor's house and wait until the morning."

"Just a moment, Rabbi," said Judah, "that sounds like my wife. Hannah—is that you?"

"Yes, my good husband, I am quite cold. Open the door."

Judah got up and began to unlatch the door, but the Rabbi put a hand on Judah's shoulder. "Hannah, what are the names of your children?" asked Achselrad.

"Ah Judah, it is cold out here, and the children are shivering. Let us in, so that we may warm ourselves in the kitchen," said a sad woman's voice.

And the Rabbi said to Judah: "Do not open the door; it is really a demon outside."

"Are you certain?" asked Judah. "This sounds exactly like my Hannah."

The men stood in the safe small halo of candlelight in the deep dark of an evil night.

"Listen," said the Rabbi to Judah. "Hannah, can you hear me?"

"Yes, although with the cold wind and with all my shivering, I find it difficult to hear you clearly, good sir," said the voice. "I could listen much better from inside the door."

"Hannah, it is the good Lord God (blessed be He) Who has given you all your possessions, including your children, is it not?" asked the Rabbi.

"Certainly," said the woman's voice.

"And it is the good Lord God (blessed be He) Who has protected you against evil spirits, is it not?" asked the Rabbi.

"Yes," said the voice from the cold.

"Then, perhaps, for safety's sake, because it is the dark and dead hours of the night, you would first repeat with me a small charm for protection against demons: O Lord our God –"

"It is cold out here. Is this really necessary?" asked the voice.

"I am afraid that it is," said Rabbi Abraham.

"Very well: O Lord our God –" repeated the voice.

"Who gives us all His blessings –" said the Rabbi.

"Who gives us all His blessings –" repeated the voice.

"Drive evil demons into the black pit forever –" said the Rabbi.

"I am shivering out here, Rabbi," said the voice outside the door.

"I do not believe you: demons do not shiver," said Rabbi Achselrad. "Now tell us really, you foul spirit: What are you doing here."

The voice changed to a dry hiss: "All right, Rabbi, it is simple: the Great and Almighty Lord has sent me to kill Judah and his wife and his children."

Judah gasped, but the Rabbi said: "For what reason?"

And then Judah cried out, too: "Oh whatever for? What have I done to deserve such a sad fate?"

"You deserve to die for this reason, Judah," hissed the demon. "You have never given any alms."

"Oh? Is that what you think?" asked Rabbi Abraham. "Judah just gave a fine loaf of bread to me, a stranger in his house, as alms. Then, Judah added five gold coins from the goodness of his heart. Recall, you evil spirit, that it is written in the Book of Proverbs in the Holy Scriptures":

> Wealth is weightless
>   On Judgment Day,
> But goodness and charity
>   Shall heavily weigh.
> Generosity, mercy,
>   Kind words with each breath –
> These will protect you
>   Against a sad death.

And the demon cursed and he hissed and he spit, and he left the house.

But Rabbi Abraham said: "Judah, the night is not yet over. Do not let anyone inside until three hours after sunrise in the morning." And Rabbi Abraham checked the bolts seven times, and he paced around the kitchen table seven times. Then Rabbi Abraham took out seven candles and lit them, and the two men sat down again at the table in the cold late hours of the dead of an evil night.

Eventually, the two men's heads began to nod, and soon they were fast asleep. Then, while the men slept, the second demon came to the door as the seven candles slowly burned down and as the smoke slowly rose up, in the small hours of the morning before sunrise. The second demon knocked at the door; it tapped and tapped like a small cold stone.

Judah heard the tapping, and he awoke and was afraid.

Rabbi Abraham called out: "Who is at the door?"

"It is us, good Rabbi," said a woman's voice. "It is Judah's family. We are cold. Let us in."

Then Rabbi Abraham said: "Go back to the neighbor's house and wait until the morning."

"Just a moment, Rabbi," said Judah. "I am certain that this really is my wife. Hannah – is that you?"

"Yes, my good husband, it is me, and I am quite cold. Open the door; my dear husband, Judah, please open the door. I am almost frozen to death out here, and the children are all crying," said the sad voice outside the door.

Judah thought that he heard a child crying; he got up and began to unlatch the door. But the Rabbi put a hand on Judah's shoulder. "Hannah, what are the names of your children?" asked Achselrad.

"Ah Judah, it is cold out here," said the voice pitifully, "and the children, Judah – the children are shivering. Let us in, so that finally we may be warm in the kitchen."

And the Rabbi said to Judah: "Do not open the door; it is really another demon outside."

"Are you certain?" asked Judah. "This sounds exactly like my Hannah."

"Judah, do not fall prey to this deception: listen again," said the Rabbi. "Hannah, can you hear me?"

"Yes, with my cold, cold ears I can hear you weakly."

"Hannah," asked Rabbi Abraham, "what are the names of your children?"

"Judah, my beloved husband, do not let that old man torture me like this. Just open the door," said the voice from the cold.

"Judah," said the Rabbi, "it is another demon."

"Hannah," said Judah, "just answer his question, and then we will let you in."

"Ah, my husband, I feel foolish telling you such a simple thing; just open the door so that the little ones can finally be warm and at peace in their own home and house," said the voice sadly.

And Rabbi Achselrad said: "Good woman – are both of your sons out there with you, or did you leave one with the neighbor?"

"Yes, yes – of course, both are with me, and both are equally cold and unhappy," said the voice from outside the door.

Judah looked at the Rabbi. "I have only one son, you wicked demon," said Judah. And the evil spirit hissed and it spit, and angrily it left the house.

By now, it was almost morning, and the two demons met in the courtyard just beyond Judah's house. "Were you a success, you foul thing?" asked the first demon.

"No, I was not, you malign miasma," said the second demon. "How about you?"

"The pious Rabbi Achselrad has meddled and interfered, may he be cursed," said the first demon.

"Yes, may he for ever be cursed and damned," responded the second demon.

At that moment, an angel of the Lord was passing by, and he heard the two demons cursing old Rabbi Abraham. The angel opened wide his bright eyes, he listened well with his softest and tiniest ears, and then he flew up directly to Heaven. "O Lord my God, two evil spirits are down below in Cologne cursing Rabbi Abraham ben Alexander," said the angel.

And the good Lord God (blessed be He) frowned a terrible frown and his brows creased and his eyes flashed and the demons were knocked to the ground. The demons shrieked and they hissed and they cried out; then, they each burst into a cloud of dust, and they were never seen again. And when, in the third hour after sunrise, Judah's wife and his son and his daughter returned home, they stepped over the two little piles of dust in the courtyard just beyond their front door, and they hardly noticed the dust at all.

hat is that, Rabbi? I was just resting my eyes – please, join me here by the stove. (I think that you will be too warm on that bench: try the one nearer to the wall.) An old man like me can doze forever by a warm stove; I suppose that is because I am not hungry.

What do I mean? I mean that hunger makes the stomach growl and growling keeps you awake. I am certain that poor Nahash never slept. . . . Why, Rabbi, certainly you know how the Almighty Lord God (blessed be He) gave a ravenous, insatiable, growling hunger and a perennial irritability and a permanent insomnia to Nahash, the prince of Moab. As the Holy Scriptures say in the Book of Proverbs:

> A righteous man shall eat his fill,
> But the wicked will go hungry.

The judgment of Nahash was long, long ago, when the Israelites were in the plains of Moab, east of Jordan. It was at the close of the Forty Years' wandering, shortly before the death of Moses and the crossing of the Jordan River. Israel had conquered two kings of eastern Palestine – Sihon, king, of the Amorites, and Og, king of Bashan. Seeing these victories, Balak, king of Moab, became alarmed. More strength was needed. Perhaps, thought Balak, he should enlist other help beyond mere mortal weapons. So Balak decided to seek out magical aid. Balak thought: There is the famous seer Balaam. He has had dealings with the ancient gods, perhaps he can call forth a terrible curse upon Israel.

Balak sent a delegation of princes of Moab, under the leadership of Nahash, to find Balaam. Nahash and his fellow emissaries traveled to Pethor on the Euphrates River. Balaam politely listened to their request, he retired to meditate, and he returned to announce that a curse would be useless. Nahash frowned: "Good Balaam," said the prince, "do not be so negative – you can never know for certain until you try." In the end, the princes of Moab (with the help of many presents, promises, and persuasions) overcame the reluctance of the famous seer, and he agreed to cast a sacred curse down upon the Israelite tribes. Balaam came to Moab with the princes and he began his damning speech, but as he spoke, Balaam was caused by Yahweh to bless Israel, not to curse them.

These holy events are, of course, recounted in the Bible. It is not well known, however, that a few years later, Prince Nahash, who was the son of Balak (who, in turn, was the son of Zippor) king of Moab, inherited the throne of his father. One day, Nahash decided to build a new dining hall, and he wanted it constructed of the best possible wood. After much investigation, his councilors discovered an amazing grove of cedars in an oasis on the slopes of Mount Nebo. The trees were thirty meters in height; they were exalted above all other trees of wood or field, amen.

This was a special stand of cedars. That very grove, in the warm and sandy soil of the Holy Land, had been consecrated by the Lord God Yahweh many years earlier. All cedar wood is light and spongy, with an aethereal fragrance, but the wood of these trees was also tinged with Heaven. Once upon a time, the wandering Israelites had built a small rock altar among these cedars, when they had passed by Mount Nebo, just north of the kingdom of the Moabites. A small holy tablet had been cut of cedar, and with its Heavenly scent, it kept the sacredness of the little Yahweh shrine.

The councilors of Prince Nahash returned, and they carried with them a few branches from the cedars of the oasis of Mount Nebo. The prince smelled the wood – a bit of Heaven entered his palace.

"Ah, my good men," said Nahash, "cut down those cedars and have them brought here, in order to make the rafters and the walls of my new dining hall."

An angel was passing through Moab. He saw the councilors return, and he smelled the holy cedar wood. The angel opened wide his shining eyes; with his tiniest and softest ears, he heard the plan. Immediately, he flew up to Heaven, and he reported to the Almighty Holy One. When the good Lord God (blessed be He) discovered that the prince intended to destroy the special cedars, He sent the angel back to earth. "Take the form of the Gentile seer, Balaam, son of Beor," said the Lord. "Nahash respects Balaam; have the seer warn Nahash against this impious action."

The angel did as he was commanded, and he appeared in the court of Nahash. "Well, Balaam, it is a long time since you have visited us here," said Nahash. "What is your errand?"

"Good Prince Nahash," began the angel speaking as Balaam, "I have a message from the Israelite God. Do not cut any of the cedar trees from Mount Nebo; that grove is sacred to the Lord Yahweh, and He will not look kindly upon one who desecrates the holy spot."

"I am sorry to hear you say this," replied the Moabite prince. "I have found no wood as fine as those cedars, and I am determined to use them for my new banquet hall."

"Nahash, I would advise against such rash and impious action."

"Our own gods will protect us," said Nahash confidently.

"Trees are special, Nahash—and they take years to grow. Can all your gods working together suddenly recreate a tree? Can even the great Lord God Almighty Himself regenerate a tree instantaneously? Leave the gentle cedars for your children and your grandchildren; then your descendants will enjoy these wonders in their natural home," said Balaam.

"Balaam, my children and my grandchildren will enjoy the fine dining hall for generations to come," said Nahash. "Buildings are as long-lived as trees, my friend."

Balaam repeated his warning, but Nahash would not listen. Therefore, Balaam said: "I can only say, prince, that at this point you had best build a very large banquet hall."

"That I will," said Nahash, and he turned to other matters.

Work began the next month. By the end of the year, a beautiful cedar banquet hall adjoined the palace. However, on the night of the first feast, Nahash felt a strange rumbling and grumbling in his stomach. My goodness, he thought, never before have I felt so hungry. He was famished, he felt absolutely starving, and from that moment, Nahash was plagued for ever with a ravenous hunger, which nothing would satisfy. Do you remember in the Holy Scriptures, in the Book of Proverbs, the list of things that are never satisfied:

> The leech remains
>   An insatiable neighbor;
> "Give more!" she complains
>   As she knocks at the door.
> There are four more banes
>   Never filled to the core:
> A barren womb, an empty tomb,
>   A parched land without a bloom,
> And fire, which must e'er consume
>   And burn for ever ever more.

Nahash became like these things. Daily, he grew thinner and thinner, although he ate continually. He was reduced to the thinnest broom-straw of a man. He could not be satisfied by any meal, he could concentrate on nothing but food; meat and bread and wine and milk and cream and oats were his perpetual desire. With no difficulty, the prime minister of Moab took control of the government and he deposed Nahash. Nahash was so hungry that he hardly noticed. Nahash had no ability to work, so he was forced to beg perpetually, as he wandered from place to place, gnawing forever on bits of food – and Nahash never slept.

My grandmother told me that for years Nahash could be seen as a wraith, walking through the marketplaces of Moab, day and night. He was so thin that he was almost invisible, and no one noticed when finally he died.

Grandmother herself made it a point to eat regularly, even if it was just a small amount of food. Was it the memory of Nahash, or was it for some other reason? I do not know. In any case, my grandmother said that small regular meals accounted for her amazingly good health when she was older than me (and I am eighty, you know). Of course, my grandmother said grace after every meal. She said a prayer after the smallest snack, blessing "Him from Whose wealth we have eaten and through Whose goodness we live." And no matter how little we had to eat, my grandmother would always smile and quote the Holy Scriptures, Deuteronomy to be exact, where Moses reports:

> For the Lord your God is bringing you to a rich land, to a land of streams, of springs, and of underground waters gushing out in hill and in valley. It will be a land of wheat and barley, of vines, fig trees, and pomegranates, a land of olives, cream, and honey. It will be a land where you will never live in poverty nor will you want for anything. It will be a land whose common stones are iron ore and gold and from whose hills you will dig copper. You will have plenty to eat, and then you will bless the Lord your God for the rich warm land that He has given you. . . .

What? No, no—do not get up on my account, Rabbi: I was just resting my eyes a moment. I was resting and musing. . . . Well, to tell you the truth, Rabbi, I was remembering Chayim ben Meir.

Chayim ben Meir? He was a shammas like me, long ago in those dark medieval days of Cologne on the wide River Rhine. Food was not always plentiful then, but holiness abounded, and the warm rich land that God promised to Moses was stored, hidden in the hearts of the Jewish community. Chayim was a lonely, religious man; often he was hungry, but he had a warm rich heart, Rabbi, even to his fateful end:

Once upon a time, said my grandmother, in the congregation of Rabbi Abraham ben Alexander, Achselrad of Cologne, there was a devout man named Chayim ben Meir. Chayim was the shammas of the congregation.

Chayim was a lonely and religious man, and he kept a lonely and religious custom. Every night, this old shammas, old Chayim ben Meir, would stand in his bedroom, he would face Jerusalem, and he would recite the midnight lamentation when the hour of twelve struck. He would begin:

> I am the poor man
> Who suffered the pain—
> I felt once again
> The wrath of His cane.

> Then, He walked away
> And He left me alone
> Deep in black stone
> Where light never shone.

Chayim knew the entire poem by heart, and he would recite it from beginning to end. "Amen, Lord," he would say when he finished, and then he would go into the synagogue opposite his house. Chayim would leave his shoes in the anteroom, and he would pad barefoot into the main prayer hall. There, he would pray and begin to speak with the dead, who, as is well known, assemble in synagogues after midnight. After a full hour spent in this mystical occupation, Shammas Chayim would return home, and he would sleep a dreamless sleep until dawn.

It was the night of the eleventh of *Elul*, near the end of the year, and Chayim followed his usual routine. But Chayim ben Meir had scarcely fallen asleep after his visit to the synagogue, when he had a terrifying dream. He dreamt that he stood before a great wide stone courtyard. Gray marble benches could be seen in the distance. The sky overhead was blank and clouded. The gate to the courtyard was opened, and the old shammas walked in. He looked to the right, and he was struck by a horrifying scene. There, he saw a carved marble altar, and on the first step stood a tall dark man. Lightning seemed to flash from his eyes, and in his hand, he held a bloody knife.

Far behind the specter wound a long line of young men; they stood pitifully, waiting to be killed. The shammas recognized many of the past pupils of his yeshiva. The shammas had no wife and no children of his own: these yeshiva students were his grandchildren. Chayim ben Meir was weak and shaky; he felt like he could not move. Then, he heard a voice intoning a passage from the Talmud:

> When there are righteous men in a generation, then these men are often punished for the sins of all the men of that generation. And if there are no righteous? If no adults are strong and honorable and true, then the children suffer: the innocent schoolchildren suffer for the sins and evils of their time.

In this dream, all the yeshiva boys stood before a terrible black giant. The students looked up to the sky. Where was their beloved Master?

They were alone and abandoned, motherless in a land of cold stone and bitter rock. The boys were sad and afraid and resigned. In an even rhythm, the terrible giant slew one youth after the other after the other, in swift succession. Shammas Chayim saw blood flow from the boys, and it ran down the rocks and it dyed the dirt a dark and awful red.

Now the shammas caught sight of his favorite pupil, Yitzchak ben Simson, in the line, and beyond him was another wonderful young man, Jacob ben Chayim Sasson ha-Levi. The immense and awesome man above them stretched out his sharp knife toward these two boys. The shammas ran and ran and tore the knife from the huge iron hand, and he called out: "Stop, stop! Clearly, you are the Angel of Death, but for the sake of the good Lord God, please stop these terrible murders!" Chayim stumbled and fell back, and as he staggered, he heard a voice reading from the Holy Scriptures in Proverbs:

> Evil men are captivating;
>> They say: "Join in our plan.
> We will hide and lie in waiting
>> For the blood of a helpless man.
>
> "We will steal his clothes and money;
>> We will take his gold and shoes.
> We will trap an innocent victim—
>> Someone easy to abuse.
>
> "Is he blameless? That's no matter—
>> We will force him to submit.
> We will strike, and he will shatter
>> And sink into the endless pit."
>
> These wicked men have been sent by Dumah;
>> These men are the dank black breath
> Of the stark archangel Dumah,
>> The most fearsome Angel of Death.

And then the old shammas, old Chayim ben Meir, awoke.

Chayim was terrified, and he sat up and looked about him. He could not forget the sight of blood, and he began to shake and tremble in every limb. Something terrible was afoot. He got out of his bed, he washed his hands, and he began walking up and down the room. He paced and he paced. Somehow, this vision was a terrible warning.

It was the dark dead hours of the night. Chayim looked out his window at the synagogue building. Was there a dim light in the main prayer hall? Or were his eyes still remembering the awful dream? The shammas pulled on his clothes, and he walked across the street to the synagogue building. He unlocked the front door, and he stepped into the anteroom. There was silence throughout the building.

As always, Chayim removed his shoes, and then he walked into the main prayer hall. The building was thick with old silence, but a dog whined outside somewhere far, far away. Chayim peered into the dark hall; there, past the worn wooden benches, beyond the twelve stained glass windows with their colored lions and snakes, stood a dark figure at the Holy stone Ark. The figure turned – it turned, and Chayim saw that it was the same giant from his dream. The figure was Dumah, the Angel of Death, and this black angel stood covered from head to foot with unwinking eyes and he held a drawn and bloody sword, and his breathing was like the sound of dry leaves rustling and rustling in the blank autumn wind.

Dumah, the Angel of Death, turned slowly. He turned slowly and silently and smoothly and darkly. Was he speaking? Chayim ben Meir thought that he heard the words of the Holy One from the Book of Exodus:

> When a man has sinned against Me,
> I shall frown and blot his name
> From My holy Book of the Living
> And inscribe his name instead
> On the dusty List of the Dead.

The Angel of Death stood with his unwinking eyes and his drawn bloody sword, and in the oldest and dustiest voice of all, he began to call out names, one after the other. Like a deep dusty bell from the black abyss, Dumah named the names of men. Chayim was stunned: these were the names of the members of his congregation, and Dumah was slowly reading them aloud from a yellow parchment in his hand. The shammas felt cold and he felt weak, he began to shake, but a shiver ran through his back and he sprang to the Holy stone Ark and he tore the parchment from the hands of the Angel of Death and he ran back through the anteroom and into his own house and he sat on the edge of the bed in his stocking feet and he did not dare to look up.

Silence filled his house, and silence lay heavily on the dead streets outside. After minutes and minutes, the trembling Chayim looked at the captured scroll of parchment. He had pressed it to his chest, and the paper was wrinkled. He smoothed it out. He read through the names; it listed man after man from the congregation. Have I saved these poor souls? Will their families have a reprieve? Chayim did not know.

Then the shammas noticed that one corner of the scroll was torn away. The iron grip of Dumah, the Angel of Death, had held firm on the last name of the list. Whose name could it be? Chayim read through the list, but it seemed that all the men of the congregation were safe. The scroll had contained the names of every single member of his congregation: not one name was missing. Not one of the men, young or old, strong or weak, devout and pious or secular and worldly, no one was missing. The old shammas burned the parchment in his stove, but he could not fall asleep again that night.

A week came and a week went, and then the next passed, and then two more. The new year was welcomed, and the congregation seemed intact. All the yeshiva students remained well: these students came happily to the college every day, unaware of their near disaster. After five weeks, after six weeks, after seven cycles of seven days, Shammas Chayim finally felt safe. And one day, Chayim confided the experience to Rabbi Abraham.

The Rabbi closed his eyes. "I am not happy about this," said Abraham ben Alexander, Achselrad of Cologne.

But Chayim was content. One week passed and then another. Seven more weeks came, and seven more weeks went. Of course, Chayim was an old man, and he was sensitive to changes in the atmospherics; the weather was cold and snowy and damp and dismal, and one day the shammas became violently ill. He was feverish, he was weak, he ached, and he shook uncontrollably. The weather was bleak and hopeless for two long dark days, and the shammas remained in his bed. Late on the night of the second day, Chayim thought that he heard a noise. He tried to turn his head toward the door, but his neck was stiff and his eyes hurt when he moved. It seemed to him that a piece of paper had fallen onto the floor.

The next morning, when Rabbi Achselrad arrived for the early prayers, he found that the synagogue was still locked. Where was Shammas Chayim? The Rabbi was worried. He went across the alleyway to the shammas's room, and he found that the old man had died during the night. The Rabbi bowed his head; then he saw that on the floor was a corner torn from a parchment scroll, and on the bottom of the paper was written the name "Chayim ben Meir."

Rabbi Abraham picked up the paper, he looked at it carefully, and he took it to his study room in the old yeshiva. On the back of the parchment, the Rabbi wrote the *Shema* in neat and tiny Hebrew letters, he rolled the parchment into a tight scroll, and he tied seven white linen threads around it; in each thread, he put seven knots. "May the Almighty Lord God (blessed be He) convert all evil hearts to good, amen," said the Rabbi. Then, the Rabbi returned to Chayim's room, and gently he slipped the parchment scroll into the wrinkled hand of the old shammas of Cologne. . . .

What, Rabbi? Yes, that is the whole story; there is no more.

abbi, I am glad to see you here alone. I want to apologize for my outburst during the service this evening. It was due to Reb Anton; he was beating the rhythm of the prayers on the floor with his cane. Yes, yes – I know what Rashi wrote about the Bible readers from Palestine: they accompanied their chants by waving their arms; they beat on a desk with both of their hands. But Reb Anton was much too distracting. In the olden days, in the strict and pious days of our fathers, he would have been ordered to leave and never to return.

My grandmother said that noise during services is encouraged by sitting. Nowadays, we always sit when we pray; this leaves us with excess energy. We stand only to recite the *Amidah* or the *Kaddish* or when the Ark is open. Today, only the most pious ascetics stand continuously in the synagogue. And did you ever see an ascetic "stander" disrupt the service? Oh, you did? Well, that must have been an exception: my grandmother claimed that standing for hours of prayer takes all your strength, so you cannot also beat time or chant loudly.

What is that, Rabbi? Well, of course one can pray aloud and one can read aloud. But in the synagogue each person must be courteous; you cannot disturb the others. I tell the men: always speak prayers in the softest possible tones. Even the quietest prayer is heard clearly by the good Lord God. We learn this in the First Book of Samuel:

> For a long time, Hannah went on praying to the Lord, while Eli watched her lips. Hannah was praying silently; but, although her voice could not be heard, her lips were moving.

> And the good Lord God (blessed be He) heard her clearly, and He answered her prayers.

Soft thoughtful tones will always succeed, Rabbi – it is not the loudest speaker who prevails in the end. For instance, I remember a story my grandmother told me. This tale took place in the Rhenish city of Wesel, not far from Cologne. Wesel is an old fortress town, and inside the walls, it is filled with a tumble of quaint wood houses. Wesel is in Westphalia at the meeting of two rivers, the Rhine and the Lippe, and originally Wesel was called Lippemunde. Once, it had been a head-quarters of King Charlemagne. Later, Wesel became a busy commer-cial town, and in the days of Rabbi Abraham ben Alexander, Achselrad of Cologne, Wesel had an independent Jewish community headed by Rabbi Elia ben Hayyim, who had been a student of Achselrad. In those medieval days, in the Jewish community of Wesel, there lived a loud man, a self-centered man, a quick-speaking man, whose name was Jakar; he was Jakar Kunz ben Ephraim of Wesel.

Now, I am certain that you have heard the proverb:

> You will be left behind as Jakar Kunz
> Was left to look after the flocks of goats.

You never heard that saying, Rabbi? Well, if you ask how it was that Jakar came to be left behind to look after the goats, then I will tell you the story:

Once upon a time, said my favorite grandmother, when Elia ben Hayyim was the chief rabbi of Wesel, the elder scholars of the yeshiva formed an informal council that advised the Rabbi. Among these men was one Jakar Kunz ben Ephraim. Whenever Rabbi Elia needed some advice, and the counselors met and came to their best decision, Jakar

Kunz ben Ephraim would present himself as the council's spokesman. Jakar would always be the one to go to the Rabbi; he would walk in to the Rabbi's room and would say loudly: "This is our decision." After a while, Jakar began to say instead: "This is the decision." Sometimes, he would even say: "This is my decision" – and soon it began to look as if the other men were merely confirming Jakar's opinion. The other scholars did not wish to assert themselves individually, and the good Rabbi believed what Jakar told him. Eventually, the Rabbi began to feel that Jakar Kunz ben Ephraim might be somewhat wiser than the other men in his congregation.

The elder scholars of Wesel saw that Rabbi Elia always turned to Jakar. The Rabbi seemed to value Jakar's opinions more highly than their own, and the other men felt badly. "Humility," said one of them, "is not one of Jakar's virtues." One day, these sages met together in the prayer hall; they met after the morning benedictions and without Jakar Kunz ben Ephraim, and they decided that they should speak to Rabbi Elia. In a neat line, the council of men walked back to the little office of Rabbi Elia ben Hayyim of Wesel.

Menachem ben Simon spoke up first. "Good Rabbi," said Reb Menachem, "forgive our intrusion. What we ask is that you give us more respect. We put much effort into each of our decisions, yet Jakar Kunz ben Ephraim presents this advice as his own. Do you think better of him than you think of us? Jakar tends to speak without reflecting deeply. Jakar is a good reporter; but by itself, his counsel is not worth very much."

The other scholars, standing in a line behind old Menachem, all nodded solemnly. Then David ben Mordecai, the second sage in line, said to the Rabbi: "For example, Rabbi Elia, do you remember the case of Aleydis?"

"The case of Aleydis?" asked the Rabbi.

"Aleydis ben Anselm was convicted of fraud: he sold fake gold jewelry to Reb Heinricus," said David.

"Oh, yes," said Rabbi Elia.

"Perhaps," continued David, "you remember that at that time, one of the yeshiva students, Simon ha-Levi, asked how a Jew could possibly defraud a fellow Israelite."

"Yes," said the Rabbi, "and I also remember Jakar's apt response.

He replied: 'Wickedness has its place in every community; as it is written in the holy Book of Proverbs'":

> There is a special purpose
>   For everything God made.
> He even made the wicked
>   So that other men could say:
> "These evil men are destined
>   For the final Destruction Day."

"Exactly," said Reb David, "but, Rabbi, we scholars had been conferring together just moments before. In fact, we were discussing this scriptural passage in our council meeting. Old Reb Jehuda reminded us that the good Lord God (blessed be He) intended for some wickedness to creep about the world. Evil has its place, said Jehuda. Then, he quoted the exact proverb that Jakar later repeated."

"Amen," said the line of sages, and each of them nodded.

Rabbi Elia listened to this carefully. "I see," he said. The Rabbi thought a moment, and then he added: "I guess that you are correct. My friends, I have never held you in disrespect. However, I must admit that recently I have begun to feel that Jakar's opinion might be sufficient by itself. Whenever I request advice, it is Jakar who reports to me – and usually it seems that the ideas originated with him."

The elder sages of medieval Wesel murmured among themselves.

"It is good to hear, Rabbi, that you value our advice," said Reb Jehuda. "Nonetheless, we do not always feel that we are appreciated properly."

Rabbi Elia thought again, and then he said: "Gentlemen, let us step back: this matter needs perspective. You should not feel badly. It is the good Lord God who is the ultimate Judge – and He values humbleness, as the Talmud says":

> If you run after greatness, then greatness will flee from you; but if you flee from greatness, then greatness will chase you.

The men murmured and they nodded, and the line of elders softened. Then the men of the council of Wesel said good-bye to the

Rabbi, and they wandered back in to the main prayer hall. The scholars felt better, and the afternoon prayers were fervent and warm. Nonetheless, in the evening when the men went home and in the late hours of the night in their beds, they began to remember Jakar's loud pronouncements, his strong brash statements, and his creased brow. The elders felt like schoolboys. Had they not finally graduated from their youthful yeshiva days? Jakar treated the scholars like he was their teacher.

The next morning came, and the men talked seriously again. Jakar arrived late, and immediately he said: "Good morning, gentlemen – I must report to the Rabbi first thing this afternoon. I am afraid that I will not be able to attend your council meeting. Save any important business until tomorrow."

Reb Baruch muttered to his neighbor David ben Mordecai: "We must depose this self-exalted prime minister of ours."

After the morning services, the men stood together talking in the prayer hall, without Jakar Kunz ben Ephraim. The sages decided that they must speak to the Rabbi again. In a neat line, they walked in to the back study room, where Rabbi Elia was reading a book. "Good Rabbi," said Reb Menachem, "forgive our intrusion. What we ask of you now is a test of Jakar Kunz. Is he, by himself, really of any value? Is Jakar a good counselor? That is what we would like you to determine."

Rabbi Elia looked down at his desk. "I see that this man is really bothering you. Very well, my scholars, I will find out his true worth soon enough."

Rabbi Elia sat for an hour thinking by himself, he prayed and he tapped his fingers on the table. Then he sent for Jakar Kunz. "My good advisor," began the Rabbi, "I know that you try to be loyal and wise. I have decided to depend more on individual counsel, and frankly, I would like to test your advice. Now, Jakar, I have something in my mind – some questions that I do not wish to reveal to anyone else. I want to see whether you, alone, can find the true answers."

Jakar Kunz ben Ephraim listened, and he thought: "Well, well – the Rabbi comes first to me. He turns to me before consulting anyone else in Wesel."

Then Jakar said aloud: "Rabbi Elia, ask me whatever is on your mind, and I will give you my best answers."

So the Rabbi replied: "All right, Jakar, I will ask you three questions. The first question is: From whence did the sun arise? The second question is: How far is the sky from the earth? And the third question is: Of what am I thinking?"

"These are strange questions," thought Jakar Kunz ben Ephraim, and so he said aloud: "Well, Rabbi, these are difficult matters. I cannot give casual answers: I must take time to think. Perhaps you will allow me a few days to meditate. Then I will return with the best possible answers."

"Certainly," said Rabbi Elia, "please come back in three days." And Jakar Kunz ben Ephraim nodded, and he went away.

Jakar was not in the habit of thinking deeply. "Dare I ask the other Wesel sages for the best replies?" he wondered. "No – word may get back to old Rabbi Elia, he would learn that I shared his secrets, and he will feel betrayed."

Jakar paced back and forth: "I think that I should leave the city and walk through country. The fresh air will stimulate my mind. I am certain that when I am alone the correct answers will come to me."

Therefore, Jakar Kunz ben Ephraim set out to walk through the countryside beyond the town of Wesel and along the Lippe river. It was a fine clear day, and Jakar walked quite happily. He looked up and the sky was far, far off. "What long legs the great Lord Almighty must have in order to step from cloud to cloud," thought Jakar Kunz as he walked along.

Soon, he passed a goatherd who was tending his flock. Walking through the goat fields, Jakar talked to himself just as he would have talked in the council back home: "Now, gentlemen, who can tell me this – from whence did the sun arise? Do any of you know how far is the sky from the earth? And – here is a most difficult question – of what is the Rabbi himself thinking?" He repeated these questions aloud a great many times, but no clear answers seemed forthcoming.

Jakar walked about the goat field, he rambled back and forth, and his mind wandered too. He thought of trees and grasses. Words rolled randomly around through his head, but his only sensible thoughts seemed to be a passage from the Scriptures, in the Second Book of Samuel:

> Delightful and dearly beloved
> Were Saul and Jonathan stouthearted.

> In bright life and in dark death
> Never were the two parted.
>
> They were swifter than eagles,
> They were stronger than lions,
> They were wiser than owls
> And more faithful than brothers.

He had memorized this verse as a child, and now he absently chanted it over and over. "Curiouser and curiouser," thought Jakar Kunz, but somehow he could not get this passage from sounding in his ears.

Jakar paced back and forth through the goat field, and the goatherd watched Jakar and he heard Jakar's questions. "Excuse me, sir," mumbled the goatherd, "I could not help but hear you—"

Jakar bent toward the goatherd: "Are you talking to me? If so, speak louder."

"I am sorry, good rabbi," said the goatherd slowly and more loudly. "I was saying that I could not help but overhear your speech. You seem troubled by some deep religious problem."

"Indeed I am," said Jakar ben Ephraim. "Talk a bit more loudly please, young man."

"Certainly," replied the goatherd, speaking still more loudly. "I was wondering whether perhaps I could help you here—as the proverb says":

> You can often advise another
> More easily than counseling yourself.

"Frankly, my good man, I do not know if a goatherd can help me with these matters: they are philosophical and deep," said Jakar as he looked up at the sky.

The goatherd hesitated. Then he answered: "Well, you know what the Holy Scriptures say about goatherds":

> Make herding your profession:
>   Attend to your goat flock.
> Any other possession
>   Is a quickly emptied stock.

Money will not last,
   Wealth will not endure
For ever to be passed
   To children, full and secure.

Green shoots die in winter's cold,
   Flowers are ephemeral,
Summer grain, lush and gold,
   Is harvested in the fall.

But flocks have an endless supply
   Of goats, worth more than gold.
Their young ever multiply:
   Your goats are wealth untold.

Goatskins can be shirts and pants.
   Goat milk can be food—
Rich and healthful sustenance
   For the multitude.

Jakar looked at the goatherd. "I see. My literate friend, I am not exactly certain what those verses mean—but it sounds like a fine sentiment to me." And then Jakar Kunz ben Ephraim raised his eyebrows, he pursed his lips, and he thought to himself: "I am making no progress on my own. It cannot hurt to tell the goatherd about the questions; the Rabbi will never know that I consulted someone in the fields, far outside the town."

So Jakar said out loud: "Perhaps you can help. This is the situation: I am head of the council that advises the Rabbi of Wesel. The Rabbi—Elia ben Hayyim—depends upon me for decisions. Now he has asked me three very difficult questions, and I am using all my wisdom to decide the best answers. I must think carefully about such serious matters."

"What are the questions?" asked the goatherd.

"Simply, they are these: From whence did the sun arise? How far is the sky from the earth? And of what is Rabbi Elia thinking?"

The goatherd looked down at the earth and then up at the sky. "These are difficult questions," he said softly.

"Indeed they are," said Jakar Kunz ben Ephraim.

"Is it important to have the correct answers?"

"Absolutely," said Jakar, "it is essential that I respond to them exactly as the Rabbi would wish."

"Do you think that you know enough to find the proper answers?"

Jakar nodded wisely. "For example," he began, "from the Talmud, I remember the dimensions of the Earth":

Egypt extends almost twelve hundred square miles. And Egypt is one sixtieth the size of Aethiopia. But what of the entire earth? Aethiopia, itself, is one sixtieth the size of the whole world.

"Oh," said the goatherd. He hesitated, and then he said: "To be honest, sir, I do not see how that helps you with your three questions."

"Of course, it is a very complex and abstruse connection," replied Jakar.

"It certainly is," said the goatherd. "But the last of the Rabbi's questions seems especially problematic. Who can ever know what someone else is thinking?"

"True, these are tricky and complex issues, and it would be a shame if I spoke too quickly and made a mistake," said Jakar. "Undoubtedly, I can discover the right answers. On the other hand, to be certain, it would help to ask the Rabbi himself – however, it is important that I demonstrate my complete independence."

The two men were silent. A light breeeze blew through the tangleberry wood.

"It would be nice to have a chance to practice my responses, to try out the answers on Rabbi Elia in advance," mused Jakar.

"Well," said the goatherd, "I have an idea. We will exchange our clothes. You put on my cloak and look after the goats for a while. I will put on your robes and go to the Rabbi. Then I will tell Rabbi Elia your best answers. If the answers are correct, he will think that you answered properly. If my answers are not the best, then tell him that I stole your clothes; in that case, you will still have another chance to present better answers."

"Ah, it is noble of you, my goatherd, to sacrifice yourself for me," said Jakar, and the two men switched their clothes.

"Now," said the goatherd, "what answers shall I try out when I see the Rabbi?"

"Listen carefully," said Jakar, "tell the Rabbi of Wesel that the sun arose in the sea, tell him that the sky is sixty times sixty miles distant from the earth, and tell him that he is thinking about accumulating much fine wealth."

"Very well," said the goatherd.

Soon, the three days of thinking, as allotted by the Rabbi, had passed; so, the goatherd walked back to the town. He was dressed in Jakar's robes and in Jakar's shoes and in Jakar's hat. He stepped into the synagogue, and he stood far at the back of the main prayer hall; he stood a moment, he hesitated, and then he said: "Your holiness, I have been thinking carefully about the three questions that you asked a few days ago."

The Rabbi looked up from the book that he was reading. "Pardon me, sir?" said the Rabbi peering into the dim hall.

The goatherd stepped a bit closer, and he said more loudly: "Rabbi Elia, I have been thinking carefully about the questions that you asked, and I have come to report the best answers that I can."

"Good," said the Rabbi, "so, tell me first: From whence arose the sun? (And please speak a little louder.)"

The goatherd cleared his throat: "As always and for ever, the sun arises in the east; it arises in the east as it has always risen—and it sets in the west as it has always set, praise the Lord now and for ever, amen."

"Ah, that is a fine answer," said Elia ben Hayyim, the Rabbi of Wesel. "It is a fine answer indeed. Now, tell me this: How far is the sky from the earth?"

The goatherd looked at his feet, he thought for a moment, and then he answered: "Your holiness, the sky is as far from the earth as the earth is from the sky. It is the distance from us to Heaven, and today it seems far—but at the edge of the next life, it is hardly a breath away."

"You are wiser than I thought, good counselor of mine," replied the Rabbi, bending forward to hear the goatherd's quiet words. "Finally, answer me this: Of what am I thinking, counselor of mine?"

The goatherd hesitated, he looked at the Rabbi and the Rabbi smiled and looked at him. "Rabbi," he began slowly, "you think that I am Jakar, Jakar Kunz ben Ephraim; yet, I seem to be different from the

Jakar that you know. This is because in truth I am a goatherd. I come from the countryside, along the Lippe River. I have come here to Wesel, in Jakar Kunz ben Ephraim's clothes in order to help him out. I have tried to protect him—"

The goatherd paused for a moment: "I have tried, perhaps, to preserve the high esteem in which you already hold him."

Rabbi Elia nodded. "Yes, my fine young goatherd, you are not Jakar Kunz ben Ephraim; I knew this from the beginning. You are timid and rather soft-spoken, and you are slow to answer," said the Rabbi, "and I must say that I am happy that you are not Jakar Kunz. You are wise, my young friend, and I hope that you will choose to remain here in our congregation and to advise me when I need your counsel."

The goatherd rubbed his hands on the side of his leg; then, he looked up at the Rabbi, and he smiled and agreed to stay. In his mild and hesitant manner, the goatherd proved thoughtful, wise, and helpful. The sages of Wesel immediately liked the goatherd—they helped him begin a business as a shopkeeper, and soon the goatherd was elected the head of the Rabbi's council: the goatherd became the main advisor to the Jews of medieval Wesel.

And suddenly his life was filled with prayer and business. Council meetings and discussion groups occupied his free time; thus, the goatherd never returned to the countryside along the Lippe River. After a week, Jakar began to wonder what had become of the goatherd, and after seven weeks, he gave up waiting. Jakar looked at the hillsides; they were covered with tiny white tangleberry flowers. Jakar looked at the skies; they were filled with windhovers and turnstones soaring high above. And Jakar looked at the flocks of goats; they were shaggy stumps dotting the fields. Jakar sighed, and he decided to become a goatherd himself.

At this point in the story, my grandmother looked up at me, Rabbi: she looked up from her embroidery—with which she busied her old fingers each day when she sat at the edge of her mother's grave— my grandmother looked up at me, she smiled, and then she said: "Jakar loved the open countryside along the Lippe River, and he became a fine and happy goatherd, to the very end of his days."

ello, Rabbi, I will be with you in a moment—I cannot leave until every tablecloth is folded, otherwise the day has not ended properly. . . . There, now I am finished at last and I can sit next to you by the stove. Tomorrow night begins the Sabbath again, praise the great Lord God.

Ah, Rabbi, the beautiful Sabbath—it separates Jews from the rest of the world. It is a seal of Jewish peculiarity; it is a reminder of the good Lord's special grace. An old man like me appreciates it more and more each year—Sabbath is absolute rest from work. The Sabbath is a time for quiet devotion. We wear our best clothes, we eat our best food, we drink our fine wines, we are with our own family, and we are calm and glad.

The holy Sabbath is a time for relaxing, a time for putting aside our worries, and a time for no activities at all. On the Sabbath, we forget the cares of the workday world. So, why has a day of rest and simplicity been collecting special customs? Why has the Sabbath acquired more and more traditional activities? Why are things added instead of being removed? To me, relaxing means simplifying.

But somehow this has not been the case. Traditions are always being piled on. For example, my grandmother told me that the mystic

391

Rabbi Achselrad introduced hosts of special customs to the Sabbath days of medieval Cologne – he had kabbalistic poetry read during the synagogue service on certain Sabbaths in spring. On the Sabbath *Zakhor*, before *Purim*, and on the Sabbath *Parah*, just thereafter, Rabbi Abraham had his congregants read the poetry of Kalir from his *Shiv'ata*. Achselrad also loved the poetry of Meir ben Isaac of Worms – for instance, Meir's little prayer for the Sabbath eve:

> With Your love, in lullaby
> You held Your people Israel
> Against Your warming breast.
>
> You gave us, God of Heavenly sky,
> This Sabbath – sacred miracle –
> This seventh day of rest.
>
> With compassion, King on high,
> You welcome us to Your citadel
> Like an honored Sabbath guest.
>
> Thank you, God. We still rely
> Upon Your radiant holy spell –
> O Lord, we Jews are truly blessed.

Are you falling asleep, Rabbi? No? I am not sleepy either. Although I am an old man, the day before the Sabbath still gives me a bit of a thrill. I feel an extra excitement, a tingle of the blood. I guess that this is one of the privileges of being an old Jew. In every synagogue, in every yeshiva hall, on the day before the Sabbath, we old men sit around and review the Sabbath endlessly – it reminds me of my grandmother's Sabbath story of the old men in medieval Cologne:

Once upon a time, said my grandmother, in old Cologne on the River Rhine, on the day before the Sabbath, the men were sitting, talking idly in the rabbi's little study room. One of the scholars, Shimshon ha-Zaken (Shimshon the Old), had said that everything he bought was sorted and shelved in honor of the Sabbath. If his wife brought home a special meat or a bag of fine flour or if she baked some honey cakes, then Shimshon would always say: "We had best put this on the Sabbath shelf."

The other sages nodded, and Lewe ben Anselm said: "Amen, Shimshon – and I, too, say the same, amen. Moreover, gentlemen, whenever I do some thing, some task – any activity whatsoever, especially if it is hard – then I say to myself: 'Lewe, do this for the Sabbath.'"

Again the men nodded and murmured: "Amen."

Then old Reb Joshua said: "Let us not forget the Scriptures –"

"Amen," said Reb Lewe quickly.

"Amen," repeated Joshua, who continued: "Of course I am thinking of Psalm 68":

> Blessed is the Lord our God.
> He carries us day by day
> From one Sabbath to the next
> Our joy increases as we pray.

Again there were further 'Amens' and murmurs and some small talk; then, a younger scholar, Elisah ben Samuel, said loudly: "On the morrow of the Sabbath all is for Your Sabbath, O Lord; we begin on the day after the Sabbath to accumulate for the next holy Sabbath."

"Yes, yes – so we must, amen," said one of the older sages.

"Of course," said Baruch ben Jacob, "we must do this in secret."

"Secretly?" asked Elisah. "What do you mean 'in secret,' old man?"

"Elisah, any scholar knows that the good Lord God gave all the Commandments to Israel generally and openly – except for the Sabbath," said Baruch. "The Lord gave Israel the Sabbath directly and specially. The Sabbath is a secret. As the Holy Scriptures say in Exodus":

> The Israelites shall keep the Sabbath, they shall keep it in every generation as a unique covenant for ever. It is a special sign for ever between Me and the Israelites; for in six days I, the Lord God, made the Heavens and the earth, but on the seventh day I ceased work, I rested, and I refreshed Myself.

"This does not sound hidden. This is no secret, Baruch," said Elisah.

"Listen to me, young man," said Baruch, "the good Lord God gave the Sabbath secretly to Israel. In Exodus, God says that the Sabbath is a special and unique sign. The Sabbath is a covenant between the Lord and His children. Of course, He means that the Sabbath is for Israel alone; God means that the Sabbath rewards are concealed from other nations."

"Well, Baruch, that is a very strange interpretation," replied Elisah ben Anselm from across the room. "For example, we all know that *anyone*–be he Jew or Gentile–who does not keep the Sabbath is certain to be punished. We also know that every soul residing in the Great Hereafter must observe the Sabbath. But, Baruch, under your reading of the Holy Scriptures this makes no sense: if, as you claim, the Gentiles do not know about Sabbaths, then why punish them for not observing it?"

"Well–" began Baruch.

"Well, Baruch," interrupted Elisah, "I will tell you why they are punished: they and the entire world know very well that the Sabbath is special. This is no secret at all. Therefore, any man who does not observe the holy Sabbath is punished–praise the Lord and amen."

Some of the other men nodded and murmured "Amen."

"Ah, my young and hasty scholar," said Baruch to Elisah ben Samuel, "it is not the *fact* of the Sabbath that is concealed from the rest of the world–it is the *reward* of the Sabbath that is hidden. The reward is held back from those who do not observe this most holy day. Is this not true, Rabbi?"

But Rabbi Abraham had fallen asleep; the Rabbi had been writing all night in his book on mystic kabbalistic lore, the manuscript entitled *Keter Shem Tov*. (As you know, Rabbi, this work has never been printed; to this day, it remains hidden in the old loft above the rabbi's little study room in the yeshiva of Cologne.) The Rabbi was breathing heavily, and his eyes were closed tightly; so, after a while, Elisah asked loudly: "And what do you think, good Rabbi? Is the Sabbath really a secret?"

Achselrad awoke with a start. "The Sabbath? The Sabbath?" he said. The Rabbi looked around him. "Ah yes, the Sabbath, the most holy day–well, of course each man gains an extra soul on the eve of the Sabbath."

The Rabbi looked around at the men sitting on the worn benches; they seemed a little puzzled, so the Rabbi continued on: "Yes, my friends, we are loaned a second soul. And how is it that we know this? For one thing, we are more carefree on the Sabbath than we are on the other six days."

Rabbi Abraham smiled. He looked at old Reb Baruch, he looked up at the ceiling, and he continued with his explanation: "As you recall, gentlemen, Rabbi Simeon ben Lakish said: 'The Holy One, blessed be He, gives man an additional soul on the eve of the day of the Sabbath. And the Holy One, blessed be He, takes the second soul back into Heaven at the end of the Sabbath holiday.'"

"Yes, yes," said Reb Elisah.

"Amen," responded the others.

Then, Rabbi Abraham said: "And why do we sniff sweet spices at the end of the Sabbath? It is to regain our strength when the second soul suddenly leaves and slips away. So, if you observe the Sabbath properly, then you will be rewarded with a second soul."

The scholars murmured and nodded.

"But," asked the Rabbi firmly, "should one keep the Sabbath holy only for rewards?"

"Certainly not," said Reb Shimshon.

"Amen," responded the others.

"Exactly," said Rabbi Abraham. "Do not act like servants, my good men."

The Rabbi looked around him. "Do not follow your holy Master only for temporary gains. No," said Rabbi Abraham. "Serve the Lord from love, faith, and belief."

"Yes," said Reb Lewe.

"Amen," responded the others.

"And now, Rabbi," said Reb Baruch quickly, "about the secret of the Sabbath—"

But Achselrad was not listening. He was looking somewhere beyond the walls of the back study room. "Remember, my friends," he said, "on Friday evening, when a man returns to his house from the synagogue, two angels accompany him home."

The Rabbi was silent a moment, and Reb Lewe said: "Yes—two angels, hallelujah."

"And," continued the Rabbi, "what happens when the angels find that the Sabbath candles are already lit and that the table is properly set?"

"What happens?" asked Reb Lewe.

"Why, the good angel smiles, and he says: 'May it be the same on the next Sabbath, amen'" said the Rabbi. "And the other, the evil angel, must say: 'Amen,' against his will."

"Amen," said Reb Lewe.

"But what if the two angels find that Sabbath candles are not already lit. What if the table is in disarray or simply not set properly? Quickly, the bad angel jumps up, he laughs, and he says: 'Ah, may it be the same on the next Sabbath eve.' And against his will, the good angel must say: 'So be it, amen.'"

"So be it, amen," said Reb Lewe.

"Therefore," said Abraham Achselrad, "honor the Sabbath, amen—praise the Lord."

"Amen," said the scholars around him, and they nodded their heads again.

Rabbi Abraham sat back in his chair. He looked at the ceiling, and he said: "My good scholars, let me tell you a story. Once long ago, I knew a young man, a very pious man, named David ben Heinricus ha-Levi. To David, the Sabbath was life—it was the entire meaning of his existence. If you asked him how he felt, he would reply: I will feel much better on the Sabbath. Or he might say: I feel as well as one could feel on the day before the Sabbath. Or else David would say: I feel holy because today is the Sabbath. And if, to be polite, you asked him what is new in his life, he would look up to Heaven and say: The Sabbath is new, good Rabbi, and the Sabbath is also old."

"It is new, and it is old," repeated Reb Lewe, "amen."

"Yes, yes—new and old, amen," said Rabbi Abraham. "Now, David would always be looking at something other than you. When he talked with the *shochet* on the subject of knives, David looked at the floor—or the table or the door—and he said: 'Never touch knives on the Sabbath.' The Sabbath, lectured David, is a day without work. In fact, the Sabbath itself is a knife, because 'Sabbath' means 'to sever' or 'to put an end to': therefore, the Sabbath cuts the end of the week."

Rabbi Abraham paused, and he looked down at his desk. Then, he went on with his story: "When he talked to the shammas before the evening prayers, David looked at the benches or the Holy Ark, and regardless of the day of the week, David always was certain to say: 'The first line of the Fourth Commandment is: Remember the Sabbath day in order to hallow and to revere it.' Every Israelite, noted David, has a sacred duty: as soon as night falls on Friday, he must name, he must think of, and he must feel the pure and simple holiness of the Sabbath. And then, he must rest."

"Amen," said Reb Lewe.

"Yes–amen," said Rabbi Abraham. "Now, gentlemen, David had no close friends, and he confided in me. Soon, I discovered that David felt strongly that no Jew truly understood the Sabbath; no other Jew honored it faithfully enough."

"What?!" said Shimshon ha-Zaken, "how can this possibly be?"

"Ah, listen, my good Reb Shimshon," said Rabbi Abraham. "David would ask: 'Consider the Talmud, Rabbi. Does it not say that if Israel repented–truly repented–for only one Day of Atonement or if Israel truly observed a single Sabbath properly, then the Messiah finally would come? But where is the Messiah? Has he come and not told me?' And, gentlemen, what could I answer when David put it like that?"

There was silence in the back study room; the scholars sat quiet on the old wooden benches.

Rabbi Abraham continued: "David said that Jews miss the truth of Sabbath day. We avoid its holy heart. Instead, we obscure its simple joy, we hide its holy purity, we encrust its sacred soul with piles of convoluted rules. 'Why do we do this?' David asked of me one day. Then he answered: 'It is Samael–Samael the evil angel has lied and has told us that Jews can only receive God's holy grace through self-punishment.'"

"'How many chains?' David would ask me," said Abraham Achselrad.

"'How many chains'?" repeated Reb Baruch.

"Yes–'chains,' Baruch," said the Rabbi. "By this David meant the many Sabbath rules and guides, such as the thirty-nine forbidden kinds of work for any Sabbath day.

"'And Rabbi,' said David, 'these thirty-nine restrictions have now been decorated with exceptions, guides, and constraints of ever increasing subtilty. Picking any plant violates the prohibition on harvesting; healing the sick violates the rule that a man should not receive medical aid on the Sabbath unless his life is in danger.

"'And can you wear an amulet on the Sabbath day? Only if the amulet is written by an expert (meaning that it has proved itself with a cure). But then how could you ever tie and untie such a magic charm, when one of the oldest restrictions allows no knotting at all?'

"David shook his head. 'Or, Rabbi,' he continued, 'normally, you cannot extinguish a light on the Sabbath – but you may put out a lamp on the Sabbath if you are afraid of attack by Gentiles or by robbers or by an evil spirit. On the other hand, if bad men or evil spirits somehow convey you beyond the walking distance on the Sabbath, then you can only walk back four cubits on your own.'

" 'What sense is there in all this?' asked David. 'What is the holy purpose of all this complexifying?' "

Elisah ben Samuel looked thoughtfully at the Rabbi. "Tell me, Rabbi Abraham," he said, "if David did not like the Sabbath rules and restrictions, then what was there about the Sabbath that he *did* like?"

"To David ben Heinricus," said Rabbi Abraham, "the ideal of the Sabbath was absolute rest. The Sabbath was a respite from every possible work. To David, the only true Sabbath tasks were these: wear your best clothes, eat calmly and contentedly, drink happily, and relax."

"What about attending the synagogue for prayer?" asked Reb Lewe.

"To David ben Heinricus," said Rabbi Abraham, "the Sabbath service is a rest. It is a meeting when we bathe in Holy Law, and thereby we are refreshed."

"And, of course," added Shimshon, "the Sabbath meal is a warm relaxation, too; it is a restful world unto itself."

"Restful, holy, and sanctified," said Rabbi Abraham, "hallowed by the old and special ceremonies – on the Sabbath, we recite":

Blessed be the Lord, our God, King of the world, Who has sanctified us by His commandments and Who was pleased with us. Blessed be the Lord, our God, King of the world, Who has given us for a heritage, in love and in kindness and in His favor, the most holy peaceful Sabbath – a day of rest as a memorial to the days of the work of Creation. This day precedes all other holy convocations, and You, O Lord, have given us Your holy Sabbath for a heritage. Blessed be the Lord, Who hallows the Sabbath for our rest.

And Baruch, Lewe, Elisah, Shimshon, and all the other men sitting in the study room nodded and murmured "Amen."

Rabbi Abraham continued: "Now one time, my scholarly friends, I had a very strange experience with David, Heinricus's only son. I was working on a manuscript, and it was late at night. I was hardly paying attention to anything around me. Suddenly, I noticed that the candlelight was flickering. I looked up, and there in the doorway stood young David. Did I tell you that he was tall and thin? No? Well, he was very tall and he was very thin, and that night he looked as tall and as thin as a spirit. He stood in the door and he said not a word. It was the day after the Sabbath, and David was worn and pale, and he seemed very, very thin.

"The silence went on for minutes. Then David looked at the floor. 'The Sabbath is over, Rabbi,' he said quietly. I had to bend forward to hear him. 'But, the Talmud tells us: The Sabbath is only one sixtieth of the joy that awaits us in the Great Hereafter.'

"I looked at him. Was he wavering in the darkened door? There was silence: I said nothing. I looked at David; he was tall and thin, he was gaunt and pale. He was like the doorpost next to which he stood. He stood silent for a moment; then, he turned and walked away. He walked through the prayer hall, and he disappeared into the night and I never saw him again," said Rabbi Abraham, as the back study room darkened in the old yeshiva in Cologne, and once again it was the evening before the Sabbath begins.

ood evening, Rabbi. Of course – please sit here by the stove: the night fire helps me to become sleepy also. I see that you and I are not blessed like old Reb Elbaum; once again, he nodded off during the last prayers this evening. He has learned to sway piously even while asleep: he must have acquired some magic from the mystic Achselrad. My grandmother said that Achselrad could put men into a sleep-trance by waving a gold coin before their eyes. We could use a dose of Achselrad ourselves tonight, Rabbi.

Ah, old Abraham Achselrad, he was always conjuring visions in the synagogue. I doubt whether he would be tolerated nowadays, but my grandmother said that Rabbi Abraham was also a scholar; he claimed that his visions came from devout and pious study. Many an astonishing event took place in his yeshiva – or so my grandmother (blessed be her memory) was told. For example, one dark and cold winter day, he was teaching a lesson on Psalm 119; the Rabbi closed his eyes, and he recited:

> Though I shrink and shrivel
>   like a wineskin in the smoke,

I shall never lose my sight of
the Heavenly Laws You spoke.

At that point, a serious young student, Isaac ben Safir, interrupted: "Excuse me, good Rabbi–what does this mean: a 'wineskin
shrinking and shriveling in the smoke'? Is it a burning wineskin? Why
does the psalmist talk only about smoke? Was there a fire, too? Exactly
what is going on?"

Abraham Achselrad opened his eyes. "Well my inquisitive young
friend, that is a good set of questions. I remember when I first heard this
particular Psalm; it was in the year that I spent studying in France, with
the famous Rashi."

"You heard Rashi preach in person?" asked Isaac.

"Well, yes I did hear him talk–but 'preaching' is not really an
accurate description of his talk. Rabbi Shelomoh was very down-to-
earth," said Rabbi Abraham.

"Excuse me, Rabbi," said Isaac, "did you say 'Rabbi Shelomoh'?"

"Yes, yes–Rashi's full name was Shelomoh ben Isaac, Shelomoh
the son of Isaac. He was born in Troyes, and he died in Troyes
sixty-five years later. Even from the very beginning, Shelomoh was a
blessed child. One day when his mother was pregnant with him, she
was in Germany walking down a narrow street, in the city of Worms.
Suddenly, two carts came rushing at her in opposite directions. She
could not escape being crushed, and she gasped and leaned back against
a brick wall. Miraculously, the wall crumbled behind her; it fell
inward, making a niche that protected her–praise the good Lord.

"As a student, Shelomoh wandered from yeshiva to yeshiva in
southern France. Eventually, he set out on a tour of the world. At one
point he was sleeping in the stable behind an inn in the Orient. One
evening, a stablehand told Shelomoh that a monk had been brought to
the inn suffering from a strange illness. The local doctor had applied
some ointments, but the monk was expected to die. Shelomoh went
into the inn, and he found the monk lying on a cot in a small back
room; the monk was weak, feverish, and unaware of his surroundings.

"Young Shelomoh had learned some Hebrew healing practices in
Spain. He sat on the floor, and on a parchment, he wrote the *Shema*
followed by seven mystical names. Shelomoh rolled the parchment
into a tiny scroll, and then he tied the roll with seven white threads. In

each thread, Shelomoh put seven neat knots. Finally, he strung the-parchment packet on a thin white rope, and he put it around the monk's neck. It was time for a benediction, but did he dare recite a Jewish prayer? He looked at the poor monk, shaking and shivering, and he decided to recite one small renewal blessing:

> Let us praise God for all the blessings that He has shined down upon us. Happy are we that He has granted us another year of life: may it be His will to inscribe us for happiness, peace, and health in the Book of Life for the coming year, also – amen.

"The monk shook and he shivered, but in a few minutes he began to breath more easily, and the next morning he opened his eyes. Later that day, he spoke and said that he was hungry, and then he ate some rice, his first food in a week. In a few days, the monk was walking around; Shelomoh had completely cured his sickness. Later, the monk returned to Germany, and he became the Bishop of Olmutz. He never forgot Rashi – the Bishop of Olmutz repeatedly protected Jews who lived in his area of Moravia.

"During his travels, Shelomoh studied with Rabbi Isaac ben Judah of Mainz, and then he studied with Rabbi Jacob ben Yaqar in Worms. Shelomoh was stunning: there was no question that he was a brilliant scholar, and soon he succeeded Rabbi Jacob as the leader of the Worms yeshiva. The yeshiva in Worms was behind the same wall that collapsed when a miracle had spared the life of Shelomoh's mother, and Shelomoh set up a small chapel in the broken niche in the wall. This enclave has three stone steps called the 'Rashi Chair,' and the whole tiny stone edifice, the Rashi Chapel, remains as a quiet place for pilgrims who stop and pray in the eastern wall of the small synagogue of Worms.

"Rashi stayed in Worms until he was twenty-five years old," said Rabbi Abraham, and he smiled and nodded his head.

"I see," said Isaac. "And, Rabbi, what is it that were you going to tell us about 'preaching'?"

"Oh yes," said Achselrad, " 'preaching' – there have always been wandering Jewish preachers, the *maggid*, decorating the basic words of the Torah and the Talmud with colorful rhetoric. After the scrolls are returned to the Holy Ark, the *maggid* can expound for hours in derashic sermons on the possible numerologies underlying the consonants of the Holy Scriptures.

"I am afraid, young Isaac, that it can be said of the *maggid*" –

> They dwell in Possibility
> A fairer house than Prose,
> More numerous of windows,
> Superior of doors.

Endlessly, they argue such questions as: Was 'Adam' really a proper name like Joseph or Isaac or Abraham? The word *adam* designated man as a species of creature – it was *adam* created from *adamah*, the earth, the ground. Later in the Holy Scriptures, the article 'the' is added, meaning 'the man' – then the full designation takes on the meaning 'the first man.' But the *alef* in 'Adam" already means 'one' and 'first' and 'singular,' so does this not mean, in itself, that the name 'Adam' is one and first and singular and special? Where in Genesis it says – "

"If I might interrupt a moment, Rabbi," said Isaac, "you were telling us about Rashi."

"Ah yes, Rashi," said Rabbi Abraham, smiling and closing his eyes, "a short man with a balding head. I always supposed that he must have had reddish hair when he was young, but of course it was gray when I knew him, in the vineyards of Troyes. He was no *maggid*, Isaac: he was soft-spoken, and often he had to be coaxed into anything that resembled preaching.

"You see, Shelomoh ben Isaac – Rashi – was a traditionalist, pure and simple. He was no intellectual philosopher. He liked common sense. I know that you think of him as a brilliant commentator (which he was), but Rashi expounded real, down-to-earth commentary, not airy mystical frippery. For example, in the Talmud it says that Wind is one of the necessities of the world and:

> Four winds blow every day, and the north wind blows with them all.
> Were it not so, then the world could not exist for even a single hour.

Now what does this difficult passage mean? Rashi explains it simply: The north wind, says he, being neither excessively hot nor excessively cold, tempers the other breezes; in this way, the north wind makes the other winds endurable. Rashi's view is clear and clean: there is no unknowable magic here; there are no hidden mystical meanings."

"But, Rabbi Abraham," said Isaac, "you told us that Rashi studied mystical knowledge in Spain and that he cured the Bishop of Olmutz using old Hebrew charms. Was Rashi not a mystic?"

"Well, my young scholar," said the Rabbi, "Shelomoh did study arcane lore in Spain, in Italy, in the Orient, and elsewhere. But it was with the pure and holy *Shema* that he finally healed the monk."

"I am still puzzled," said Isaac. "Rashi seems to have been well versed in arcane and mystical lore. Did he never use this magical knowledge?"

"Rashi used everything, Isaac. He used the Law and the Lord, and the Word and the World—and sometimes, this gave the appearance of sorcery and magic. For example, one day, the grand Duke of Lorraine (whose name was Godfrey of Bouillon) came through Worms with a large army, on his way to Jerusalem; there, he intended to fight the infidel Arabs for possession of the Holy Lands. Godfrey of Bouillon had heard a great deal about the wisdom and the insight of Rashi, and he was told that Rashi was regarded as a prophet by Gentiles as well as by Jews. So, the Duke sent for Rashi in order to ask the Rabbi's advice.

"Rashi refused to come to see the Duke, and of course, this made the nobleman angry. How could a Jew dare to disobey a formal summons? The Duke fumed and he fussed, and eventually he took a contingent of officers into the Jewish Quarter of Worms, to the very house of the Rabbi. The Duke found all the doors open. Books were lying on the tables as if many people were in the midst of studies, but no one could be seen anywhere about.

"'Solomon—Mr. Solomon Isaac!' called the Duke to Shelomoh ben Isaac, 'Where are you?'

"'Here,' replied the voice of Rashi.

"'Solomon, I do not see you. Where are you hiding?' asked the Duke of Lorraine.

"'Here I am, your honor,' said a holy voice.

"The Duke called again, and Rashi answered again. And as often as the Duke called to him, the voice of Rashi gave the same answer. But the Duke could not see a person. The Duke was mystified, and he could not think of what to do next. Then, one of Rashi's students passed by the house, and the Duke asked him: 'Tell me, young man, does Mr. Solomon Isaac (also known as Rashi) live here?'

" 'Yes, sir, he does.'

"Then the Duke said: 'Well, when you see him, tell him to come to me, the Duke of Lorraine. I need his counsel–and I pledge that no harm will come to him.' And the Duke turned away, and he and his soldiers left the house of Rashi.

"Later that day, the student reported to the Rabbi, and Rashi decided that it would be safe to visit the Duke. So, Rashi walked to the royal hall in Worms where the Duke was staying.

" 'You are a strange man, Mr. Solomon Isaac,' said the Duke, 'but I have heard of your cleverness: some say you are even magical. I need to ask your advice and your opinion about an undertaking upon which I am about to embark.'

"Rashi stood quietly, looking up at the Duke.

" 'Now,' continued Godfrey, grand Duke of Lorraine, 'I have collected a large army of infantry and cavalry. I intend to go off and to capture Jerusalem. I know that God is on my side; therefore, I have no doubts that I shall defeat the infidel Arabs. However, it is always wise to be prepared. Before I begin, I could use some fortunetelling: I would like to hear your advice. Are there some difficulties that I could avoid if I am forewarned? Speak freely, my friend–do not be afraid. Do you foresee success or trouble? And if problems lie ahead, then how can I avoid them? I need to know the future.'

"Rashi thought and he prayed, and then he said: 'My lord the Duke, I will tell you the truth. At first, you will be very successful. You will capture Jerusalem, and you will reign there for one year supreme and for two years in fear. But in the fourth year, the Arabs will gather again and they will drive you out and you will be forced to flee. I see that most of your army will be killed. Those who survive will die during your retreat, and you will return to your home city old, worn, and broken, with only three men and with one horse.'

" 'What?!' exclaimed the Duke. 'Is this the best that you can prophesy? And even if you are correct (which I doubt), then what can I do to prevent this disaster?'

" 'If you insist on undertaking this ill-fated venture, then I am

afraid that there is no avoiding your fate,' said Rashi. 'I can only add a
small blessing of help':

> May the good Lord bold
> Put none of the woes untold
> On you or on your fold
> That He rained down cold
> On the Egyptians of old.

'You will be fighting the Egyptian Arabs, good Duke, and this is the
best that I can do. I am sorry to have to give you this news, but I can
only tell you the truth as I see it.'

"The grand Duke of Lorraine did not want to hear this at all. He
was angry, and he was worried. He said to Rashi: 'What does a Jew
know about the strategies of warfare. Have you ever fought in a battle?
No, you have not. If I return from this holy crusade and if I have
suffered the troubles that you predict, then it will be your fault: you
have put a curse upon my adventures.'

"Then Rashi replied: 'Let me remind you, your honor, of a
passage from the Holy Scriptures, from Chapter 24 of the Book of
Proverbs':

> Wisdom prevails
>    over brute strength,
> Knowledge wins
>    over blind force.
> Wars are won
>    by strategy at length,
> Victories come
>    through a well-planned course.

"But the Duke turned away angrily, and he dismissed the Rabbi
and he set out on his ill-fated adventure.

"Along with his brothers, Eustace and Baldwin, Godfrey of
Bouillon, the Duke of Lorraine, led a German contingent, some forty
thousand strong, along Charlemagne's road, through Hungary, over
the Danube River, and on to Constantinople. The Duke was the first
of the crusading princes to arrive in the Lord's Holy Land, and he led
the siege on Jerusalem. His division was the first to enter the walls

when the ancient city finally was captured. Then, in the month of Tammuz, Godfrey of Bouillon, the grand Duke of Lorraine, was crowned the Ruler of Jerusalem and the Advocate of the Holy Sepulcher.

"During his short reign of a few years, Godfrey repeatedly fought the Arabs of Egypt. At first, he succeeded; for example, he repelled the Egyptian attack during a major battle at Ascalon, but he failed to capture the town itself. Soon, however, dissension among the crusaders left the Duke isolated, and at the end of the autumn, he had an army of only two thousand men. Nonetheless, Godfrey pushed on, and he captured the towns of Acre, Arsuf, Ascalon, and Caesarea during the next spring. But the bitter rivalries among the crusading princes had eroded the Duke's authority and power. Finally, the battles began to turn against him, exactly as Rashi had foretold—"

"Excuse me, good Rabbi," said Isaac, "may I interrupt?"

"Certainly."

"I am still puzzled," said Isaac. "Clearly, Rashi was some sort of prophet; he seems to have been a sorcerer."

"A sorcerer? A sorcerer, my friend, is one who practices witchcraft in an unholy way," answered Rabbi Abraham. "Rashi himself said that holy rabbis, especially those of the Rabbinical Courts, must *know* sorcery. This knowledge is necessary: clever sorcerers and wily conjurors can use their magical skills in order to deceive the judges and in order to escape the court-imposed penalties."

"And Rashi possessed such magical knowledge?" asked Isaac.

"Apparently he did, Isaac—so," continued Achselrad, "as I was saying, the battles in the Holy Land turned against the Duke, exactly as Rashi had foretold. Four years after he had set out from Germany, the Duke was forced to return to his capitol city, and he came back through Worms with but three soldiers and one horse.

"The Duke was worn out; he was frustrated and depressed and angry, and his mind was full of evil thoughts. All he could think of was punishing Rashi. As he was entering the gates of the city, his own horse, old, weak, and broken from the wars, the weathers, and the travels, collapsed and died—and Godfrey of Bouillon, the grand Duke of Lorraine, entered Worms on foot. When he returned to his court, the Duke had Rashi brought before him.

"'Well, my evil Jew,' said the Duke, 'your curse worked. I

returned defeated, with three soldiers and with one horse. And I promised that if you were correct then I would throw you in prison.'

" 'Good Duke,' said Rashi, 'I see that I was not correct. I predicted that you would return home alive with three soldiers and with one horse. Unfortunately, your horse died, and you returned home on foot. Therefore, you cannot hold me responsible – my prophecy was inaccurate.'

"The Duke was already angry, and he became furious when Rashi began to quibble over details, so Rashi was thrown into prison. However, like his horse, the Duke of Lorraine was now old, worn, and broken, and he suddenly took ill and he died the next week. The Duke's successors were afraid of the Rabbi, and Shelomoh ben Isaac was released from prison and he returned to his congregation safe and sound.

"And, Isaac, Rabbi Shelomoh's prophecy occurred in Worms – it all happened before young Rashi was twenty-five years old. At that time, Rashi returned from Worms in Germany to his hometown of Troyes in France. As you young men know, Troyes is now a center of Jewish learning, and its prominence is due to Rashi, our Shelomoh ben Isaac. Rashi became Rabbi and he became Judge for the Jews of most of western Europe. He accepted no salary, and he and his family worked with their hands in the Champagne vineyards of the rich Troyes grapelands. When I met him, many, many years later, it was only a few years before his death, and we walked and talked among the summer grape vines of Champagne.

"One day, Shelomoh ben Isaac died peacefully in Troyes. He was sixty-five years old, and my good friend Rabbi Benjamin Shalom said of him: 'Rashi's lips were the seats of wisdom, his tongue was the chair of understanding. Thanks to Rabbi Shelomoh ben Isaac, the Lord's Heavenly Laws, which Rashi examined and interpreted and set in commentary with pen, have come to earth to live among common people again, in praise of the good Lord God. Hallelujah and amen.' "

And Rabbi Abraham closed his eyes, and then he said: "Amen."

Isaac waited a moment, and then he asked: "But Rabbi Abraham, what about Psalm 119?"

> Though I shrink and shrivel
> like a wineskin in the smoke,

I shall never lose my sight of
the Heavenly Laws You spoke.

"The psalm? Oh yes," said the Rabbi, looking off far beyond the walls of the little back study room.

It was getting quite dark now, and the candles were lit alongside the study table. "Look carefully at these flames, young man," said Rabbi Abraham ben Alexander, Achselrad of Cologne.

Isaac stared at the flames; he could not move his eyes. Soon, he saw a wineskin shriveling in the smoke, and then glowing fine and white was the pure radiance of Heaven and the everlasting joys beyond, and they filled his vision with magnificent white clouds, and he felt calm and happy, amen.

h, good evening again, Rabbi. I know that it is always hard to sleep on the night of the half moon. Put your feet on the side bench here, and I will open the stove door. Let me push this coal back: there is nothing like that white glow; it washes away the cares of a hard day. I heard your final benediction tonight, Rabbi—clearly, you are overworked. Oh yes, even a shammas like me can tell. I kept one eye on you as I cleaned the dishes, and I saw that you were watching the door, hoping that Reb Elbaum would leave early. And then, Reb Anton stayed to argue about the scriptural passage from Job:

> Terror upon terror overwhelms me,
> Dissolving my strength; I am bowed.
> My hope of victory vanishes
> Like a wispy windblown cloud.
>
> My soul is in turmoil within me—
> Daily, I see misery increase.
> Will the Messiah bring resurrection?
> Will my soul ever rest in peace?

That is anguished verse: Of course it would wear you out. So what is that? A story from me? Rabbi, all I know are the children's tales, the grandmother fables. You need something new and fresh to keep your mind keen. Otherwise you will become an old man like me, and you will find yourself constantly musing and dozing and nodding off in front of the stove.

What do you mean you are already an old man, Rabbi? Old? Do you think that sixty years is old? You are still a child. When you reach eighty or ninety, *then* you will be old. You doubt that you will live to see eighty years? If so, Rabbi, then you will never grow old .... All right, all right – as I have said, I know no special stories, but listening to you and Reb Anton reminded me of souls and ants and of Solomon Amora and of the location of the soul within us. Now where shall I begin? I guess that I had best start with a tale that my grandmother told me about Rabbi Abraham ben Alexander, Achselrad of Cologne:

Once upon a time, said my grandmother, in old Cologne in the days of Rabbi Abraham ben Alexander, there lived a serious young yeshiva student named Isaac ben Safir. Isaac listened carefully to everything that he heard – and with his young and serious ears, he heard much – and although he was still a boy, Isaac thought deeply. One day, he asked Achselrad: "God lives in Heaven – does he not, Rabbi?"

"So we are told," said Rabbi Abraham, looking up from his writing.

"Tell me, Rabbi, exactly where does the Lord God live?" asked Isaac. "Where is Heaven?"

The Rabbi replied: "I do not know."

The boy looked at the Rabbi. "But you are a rabbi. You pray to the good Lord God (blessed be He) many times every single day. Do you send Him prayer after prayer without knowing where He is?"

Rabbi Achselrad looked at Isaac. Then he said: "Ah, my young scholar, it is quite true that I begin every single day with":

Blessed be the Lord our God in Heaven, my King of the world. He has formed light and created darkness, He makes peace, and He created all and everything. He is my God – Who in His infinite mercy lights up the earth and everyone and everything living thereon, and Who renews on each day and unceasingly the work of Creation, as He looks down from His great seat in Heaven, amen.

"And, young man, I admit readily that this prayer makes me content, although I cannot pinpoint the exact location to which it is addressed."

"But Rabbi," pressed Isaac, "how can you send off a prayer, aiming it vaguely somewhere – just letting it float away in the wind – when you do not know to where it must go?"

"Isaac, Isaac – the good Lord God hears me even when I am not a good archer with my prayer, even when I cannot aim it precisely."

"All right, Rabbi, I see that you cannot tell me *exactly* where Heaven is," said Isaac. "Nonetheless, you must be able to tell me something about the location of Heaven. Is it everywhere, or is it in one special place? Is Heaven in the clouds? Is it on top of some mountain? Can you not give me some details?"

"Now, my young student, I cannot pretend to more knowledge than I have," said the Rabbi. Rabbi Abraham sat quietly for a moment. "I will tell you what I have learned, Isaac. The Sages say that the good Lord God (blessed be He) lives at a distance corresponding to a journey of three thousand five hundred years. There, God dwells in the highest heaven, that is, in the seventh heaven of Heaven."

"The seventh heaven of Heaven?" asked Isaac.

"Yes," said the Rabbi. "You see, Isaac, in the beginning of Creation, the Lord made Heaven and earth; on the second day, the Almighty Lord set an unimaginably vast vault to separate the waters, and He called this vault Heaven. There was a great amount of detail and craftsmanship and holy handiwork in this wondrous vault. In fact, there were actually seven heavens within the original vault. Each heaven rose in happiness above the other, and the seventh and highest heaven is the abode of the majestic Lord God (blessed be He), amen."

"I did not know this. There are really *seven* heavens?" asked Isaac with wide eyes.

"So we are told, young man," said the Rabbi. "The first heaven is built of pure silver. In this heaven, the stars are hung like lamps on golden chains, and each star has its own individual angel warder. This heaven is now the home of Adam and Eve.

"Higher up, like a shining yellow plateau, is the second heaven. This heaven is built of pure yellow gold, and it is the domain of the holy prophets such as Ezekiel and Isaiah.

"The third heaven is carved of pearl, and it is allotted to Joseph. Here also resides Dumah, the Angel of Death. Dumah sits stationed at a vast pearl desk, and he is forever writing names in a large book and blotting out names from another book.

"The fourth heaven glistens like the nighttime moon, and it is built of pure white gold. Here lives Enoch. In addition –"

"Excuse me, good Rabbi," said Isaac. "Who is Enoch?"

"Enoch," said Rabbi Abraham, "was Methuselah's father and Noah's great-grandfather, and Enoch walked with God for three hundred years. Having walked with God, Enoch was seen no more after he died, because the good Lord God, blessed be He, took Enoch away to the fourth heaven after he died. In addition, the fourth heaven is the home of Sandalfon, the Angel of Tears. Sandalfon is taller than his fellow angels: his height is five hundred days' journey. Normally, he stands behind the celestial chariot and weaves crowns out of the prayers that are offered to the Lord God Almighty, and he sheds ceaseless tears for the sins of man."

The Rabbi paused, and he seemed to be thinking.

"That is four heavens, Rabbi," said Isaac. "What about the other heavens?"

"Ah," said Rabbi Abraham, "they are equally wondrous. Like the first heaven, the fifth heaven is also built of silver, and it is Aaron's heaven. Alongside Aaron dwells the Archangel Gabriel; he is the Avenging Angel and the Messenger of God, and he is also the angel of fire.

"Towering above the fifth heaven is a mountain, and atop the mountain is the sixth heaven. The sixth heaven is composed of ruby and garnet, and it is presided over by Moses. Here dwells the Archangel Michael, half snow and half fire, the Guardian Angel of Heaven and earth, the Guardian Angel of Israel.

"Then, like a glorious cloud floating for ever and away, above all the other heavens is the seventh heaven. It is formed of Divine light beyond the power of a mortal to describe, and there lives Abraham. The inhabitants of the seventh heaven are light and bright and vast and pure; they are each as beautiful as the summer sky in the early evening.

Each inhabitant has seventy thousand tongues and each one speaks in seventy thousand languages and each one is singing forever seventy thousand psalms, all in praise of the Most High One Himself, amen.

"These are the seven heavens, Isaac, and this is all that I can answer to your question. The good Lord God (blessed be He) sits in the seventh heaven of Heaven; as He said in the Book of Isaiah":

> My throne is in Heaven
>   From which I rule,
> And the earth beneath
>   Is My own footstool.

Isaac was silent a moment, then he said: "Rabbi, I still cannot understand *where* Heaven is located."

Rabbi Abraham looked at Isaac. "Let me try to answer you this way, young man," said the Rabbi. "May I ask *you* a question?"

"Certainly, Rabbi."

"I would like to question you about something that is with you day and night. You do imagine that you can locate something that is so close to you—do you not?"

"Yes," said Isaac, "and what thing are you thinking of?"

"I refer to your soul, Isaac," said Achselrad. "Man is akin to God in that he possesses a soul. In this way, we have a holy tie to our Maker."

"Yes," said Isaac, "just the other day you were reminding us that the Talmud says: 'Man's body is from the earth, but his soul is from Heaven.'"

"Exactly," said the Rabbi, "the good Lord God (blessed be He) has given to you a holy soul from Heaven; it is always with you—day and night. Now, tell me exactly where this familiar thing is located."

The young man said: "Well, it is somewhere inside of me—I do not know exactly where."

"Is it perhaps in your heart? In Psalm 103, the psalmist says":

> O my secret holy soul,
>   Bless the most Almighty Lord;
> O my deepest heart extoll
>   And praise Him with a holy chord.

"That sounds good," said Isaac.

"Then, how does the soul get into your heart when you are born," asked Rabbi Abraham, "and how does it get out again when you die?"

The Rabbi was silent a moment, and then he continued: "Recall, young man, that the souls of the whole human race pre-exist by themselves. They wait as baby souls in the World of Emanations, and eventually, they are all destined to inhabit human bodies. When a little baby is born, the tiny holy soul dives down from the clouds like a young eagle, and it slips into the little wet wrinkly baby body. Then, when a person dies, Dumah, the Angel of Death, pulls the holy soul out again through the head like a fine silver hair, and it glides up to the Heavens, glinting with starlight as it passes through the celestial vaults."

"I see," said Isaac. He thought for a minute. Then he said: "To be honest, Rabbi, I do not know exactly where my soul lies inside of me."

"I am like you, my young and wide-eyed friend," said Achselrad. "I do not know exactly where my soul lives either. Nonetheless, like the location of Heaven, the details of the location of the soul do not keep us from being suffused with their blessings, amen."

"Amen," repeated Isaac.

"Now," said the Rabbi, "look at your hands, Isaac."

Isaac held up his hands, and he looked at them.

"You can see your hands, and you can see the works of your hands. But your hands cannot see you. Likewise, the Holy One, blessed be He, sees the works of His hands, but they cannot see Him," said Rabbi Abraham.

Isaac looked puzzled. "I do not understand what you are saying, Rabbi," said the boy.

"Ah, my curious student, we need not understand all the ways of the Almighty One (blessed be He). As Rabbi Meir of Palestine said: 'What the good Lord God does is well done. What the good Lord God says is well said. Where the good Lord God lives is well chosen. And what the good Lord God means need not be questioned.'"

What? Of course there is more, Rabbi: I only closed my eyes for a moment—can an old man not take a little rest? Now you have interrupted my thoughts. Let me see, where was I? Yes, yes—as my grandmother said: "Some Jews are as industrious as ants." Did you ever hear her say that, Rabbi? You never knew her? That is too bad; you missed a fine woman. Ah, well–anyway, Rabbi, I first heard about Rabbi Solomon Amora from my grandmother, may her soul visit happily with the souls of her parents forever. . . . Souls? Ants? Just be patient, Rabbi.

Once upon a time, said my grandmother, in the earliest days of the Jewish communities in Germany, there lived in Ohligs on the River Rhine a pious scholar named Rabbi Solomon Amora – Solomon the Speaker. Rabbi Solomon Amora had a small yeshiva in Ohligs, the brewing and brickmaking town which is a half day's walk north of Cologne.

Solomon Amora was the son of a *hazan* named Jechina ben Menachem. When he was little, Solomon was left alone to roam the countryside. In the evenings, his father taught him the old Jewish law and then sang to him softly the old Jewish songs, and when Solomon grew up, he became a wise rabbi, the chief rabbi of Ohligs. Solomon Amora was the most pious of men; he was fair-minded and devout, and he was loved dearly by the good Lord God, blessed be He.

As the chief rabbi of Ohligs, Solomon Amora repeatedly interceded with the good Lord to repair all manner of evils that befell his community. For instance, once through prayer he ended a terrible drought. After there had been no rain for a month, Solomon Amora began the sixth workday benediction as follows:

> Bless for us, O Lord our God, this year and all its produce to be the very best. And give rain – full rain – for a blessing upon the face of the earth. Fill us from Your infinite bounty, and bless our coming days that they be as the best of the good years of the past. Blessed be You, O Lord our God, Who gives the rains and Who blesses the years.

Then Solomon refused to eat, and he drank only a sip of wine each evening, until, after thirty dry days, the drenching rains finally poured down from the Heavens. Today, a worn bench in the old Ohligs yeshiva commemorates Solomon Amora's month-long fast, the fast that convinced the good Lord God, blessed be He, to bring the lush rains, amen.

One summer, all the Jews in Ohligs began dying of a terrible plague. A pestilence entirely depopulated the Jewish Quarter. Solomon Amora was heartbroken; tearfully, he prayed to God for help. He recited:

> O Lord, God of Israel, turn from Your burning anger, restrain the evils of disease that have decimated our people. Look down now from Heaven, and see how we are disappearing. Although we are few in numbers, we do not forget You: do not forget us, either. Strangers say that there is no use in our hope, that we are foolish to call out to You. Hear our voices, few and weak though they be, and renew our numbers. Multiply the faithful again as the stars of Heaven – turn few into many once more.

Then one night, Solomon dreamed that the good Lord God began to refill the town by changing all its ants into human beings. When Solomon awoke, Jews were getting well again, new Jews were appearing from other towns, and the community was suddenly revitalized. The plague had ended, and somehow there were more Jews than ever before. Where had they all come from?

Had the Almighty One actually turned ants into people? Or was the holy Lord God resurrecting the dead? Was the Messiah coming now and finally? Perhaps, perhaps, thought Solomon – therefore, each night before he fell asleep, Rabbi Solomon Amora recited:

> May the good Lord God remember and renew the soul of my respected father Jechina ben Menachem, a quiet singer who has gone to his eternal home. On his behalf, I vow alms and charity and endless devotion, and by way of reward, may his soul be restored – may it be bound up in the bundle of life with the souls of Abraham, Isaac, and Jacob, and all other righteous men that are in the Garden of Eden – and I say: "Amen."

With hope and happiness, Solomon prayed each night – and one day, Solomon Amora ben Jechina ben Menachem died. Solomon Amora died contentedly, and he was reunited with his parents in the Great Hereafter. Then, old Solomon was young again, and he heard the beautiful voice of his father Jechina the *hazan* singing him soft songs at night.

Was Resurrection really beginning at last? If not, then where had the extra Jews in Ohligs come from? Ah, Rabbi, the truth remained a secret forever, in the town of Ohligs on the edge of the dark wide River Rhine, the medieval River Rhine.

ood evening, Rabbi. No sleep for the weary? That is what my grandmother said, and she said it almost nightly. If you are cold, then sit down here on the bench, and I will stoke up the oven. This stoker? It is one of the iron shoe scrapers from the front hall – of course there are still two scrapers in the anteroom for dirty shoes. But I myself am of the old school: I think that all pious men should pray barefoot. Did you know that Maimonides said the Messiah will appear barefoot?

Yes, Maimonides himself wrote this in a letter to the mystic Rabbi Abraham – Abraham ben Alexander, Achselrad of Cologne. Grandmother said that the good Lord God (blessed be He) had taken possession of the right hand of old Rabbi Abraham: he could not stop writing. Achselrad wrote reams of letters to other scholars (scholars such as Maimonides), and he wrote a number of lengthy kabbalistic tomes. The most famous of these works was the *Keter Shem Tov*; however, the book remains unpublished to this day and only exists as a crumbling manuscript, somewhere in the loft above the back study room of the old central yeshiva in Cologne on the dark River Rhine.

Rabbi Abraham worked on this book day and night. One afternoon when he was writing and was lost in thought, he heard a noise.

The Rabbi looked up; there in the door stood a man whom he did not recognize.

"Yes?" said the Rabbi.

"Are you Mr. Abraham Alexander?" asked the man.

"I am," replied the Rabbi.

"Good – I am Wilhelm Arnold Brunswick, and I live not far from here, in the St. Laurence parish. Next door to me lives one of your Jews, an old man named Joseph Mannus. I am certain that you know him: he walks around barefoot even in the coldest winter weather."

"Yes, Mr. Brunswick, I do know him."

"Well, Joseph seems a decent person," said Wilhelm Brunswick, "although he is rather religious."

"He is definitely very religious," said the Rabbi. "Our Joseph ben Mannus is a devout and pious man."

"Clearly, he is religious, Mr. Alexander," said Wilhelm, nodding and looking around the room. "Also, Joseph is very poor," added Wilhelm. "On the other hand, I am a successful merchant, Rabbi; I am quite comfortable, and I have sufficient wealth to live well."

Wilhelm stopped talking. After a moment, the Rabbi said: "Yes, Mr. Brunswick?"

"Well, Rabbi," continued Wilhelm, "I come to you because I have had a strange dream about my wealth, and I have had the same strange dream every night last week.

"You see, Rabbi, I dream that I am very poor and that my neighbor Joseph is rich. Moreover, Joseph Mannus lives in my house, he wears my clothes, and he has my servants and my things, while I live in his house. Naturally, this backward picture was disturbing, so I went to my parish priest. He thought that this dream might be some sort of omen. In fact, he suggested that somehow all of my wealth would pass to my neighbor, Joseph. I am certain that he is mistaken: how could this ever happen? Nonetheless, I continue to have the same dream every night – so now I would like your counsel."

Wilhelm lowered his voice. "Rabbi," he said nervously, "there is some Jewish deviltry afoot. You know the Jews better than I. Do you think that Joseph is plotting against me?"

Rabbi Abraham picked up his pen, and he twisted it in his fingers. "Mr. Brunswick," said the Rabbi, "I can assure you that Joseph ben Mannus is a mild and gentle person. He walks around barefoot out of piety. He is sixty-five years old and not in the best of health, but he is renowned in our community for honoring the Sabbath, the holiest day of the week. In fact, he lives entirely for that one day. I can set your mind at ease," said the Rabbi. "Joseph ben Mannus has neither the time nor the energy to plan intrigues against you."

"I am glad to hear you say this," said Wilhelm. He stood silent for a moment; he looked at the worn benches along the wall, and he looked at the prayer books piled on a chair.

"Now, Rabbi," said Wilhelm, "there is more. In another part of my dream, a pale woman in white robes has come. She arrives with a dignitary, perhaps a young king. They appear at the eastern gate of my courtyard; they want help and they want charity, but I push them away. Old Joseph, on the other hand, comes out barefoot. He bows to them, he brings them into his house and sits them at his table, and he gives them all the finest of his food.

"My parish priest could not make any sense of this part of my dream. What do you think it means, Rabbi?"

Abraham ben Alexander, Achselrad of Cologne, closed his eyes, his head sagged, and his breathing became heavy. Suddenly, the Rabbi opened his eyes again, and he said: "Mr. Brunswick, let us read from the Holy Scriptures."

"Ah, Mr. Alexander," said Wilhelm, "I respect your religious views, but is this really necessary now?"

"Yes," said the Rabbi, "I have had a vision from the Book of Ezekiel. Listen, Mr. Brunswick":

These are the words of the good Lord God (blessed be He): The eastern gate of the inner court shall remain closed for the six working days; open it only on the Sabbath and at the New Moon.

Now, even a prince coming through the porch shall halt at the doorpost of that gate, and on the terrace he shall bow down before he goes out— and the gate shall not be shut until the evening. On Sabbaths and at New Moons, all the commonfolk too shall bow down before the Almighty Lord their God at the entrance to that gate.

"In your dream, Mr. Brunswick, the pale woman is the Sabbath. Apparently, you have not honored the Sabbath. In contrast, Joseph ben Mannus properly respects this day, the most holy of the good Lord's days."

"But, Mr. Alexander, I am not a Jew."

"Nonetheless, anyone can celebrate the Sabbath," said the Rabbi. "God gave the Ten Commandments to all the world, and the fourth commandment is: Always remember to keep the Sabbath day holy."

"Well, Rabbi," said Wilhelm, "whatever the exact cause of my strange dream, I remain worried. What will happen to me, and what will happen to my wealth?"

"Mr. Brunswick, only the good Lord God (blessed be He) knows the future."

"Now, now, Mr. Alexander, you are a rabbi: you must have some special insight into what the Jewish God has in mind," said Wilhelm Brunswick.

"The mind of the good Lord God (blessed be He) is unknowable by man," replied Rabbi Abraham, and then the Rabbi closed his eyes for a moment. "However," continued the Rabbi, "I can offer you a useful quotation from the Holy Scriptures. In the Book of Proverbs, the Bible says":

> Do not worship wealth and ease:
>   Be sensible and give up greed.
> Before you turn, up comes a breeze—
>   Gold disappears, wealth will recede,
> Money grows fleet wings and flees
>   Like an eagle, a bird of speed.

Wilhelm Arnold Brunswick raised his eyebrows and he pursed his lips. He thanked the Rabbi and he left—but Wilhelm was not satisfied; he remained worried. His dreams continued and he fretted. His joints ached, he lost his appetite, and eventually he decided to sell most of his possessions. With the accumulated money, Wilhelm bought twenty-two perfect pearls and a gold ring, and he sewed these valuables into his old gray cap. Then Wilhelm wore the cap all day every day and all night every night. Finally, Wilhelm felt better. The dreams stopped, the days seemed sunnier, and Wilhelm was happy again.

Then, one wintery day, Wilhelm was walking out of central

Cologne–he hiked across the Deutz Bridge over the dark and choppy River Rhine. Suddenly, a fierce wind sprang up from the shore. It blew the trees and the waves and the clouds, and it whipped off Wilhelm's cap. The cap disappeared into the water and was swept away. Wilhelm cursed and he cried, but there was no one in sight to help: his wealth was gone.

Wilhelm began to sleep poorly. He developed aches in his joints, his appetite left him, and eventually Wilhelm Arnold Brunswick went away from the city of Cologne, and he set up a small business with his younger brother in Coblenz. The winter ended, spring came, and soon it was the summer.

One warm afternoon in the august month of *Elul*, Joseph ben Mannus went into the marketplace and he bought himself a large fish for the Sabbath meal. Joseph returned home, and he boiled and baked the fish. That evening, he covered the table with a clean tablecloth, and on the table he set out two loaves of bread, specially baked for the occasion. Joseph covered the warm bread with a linen napkin, and next to the bread he set a cup and a jug of wine. Sunset came, the candles were lit, and the *Kiddush* ceremony began. Joseph recited:

> Blessed be the Lord, our God, King of the world, Who distinguishes between holy and profane, between light and darkness, between Israel and the nations, between the seventh day and the six work days. Blessed be God, Who distinguishes between the holiness of the Sabbath and the holiness of the other holidays. Blessed be the Almighty Lord Who has distinguished and sanctified His people Israel in His own holiness and Who has made Israel a pearl among nations.

Then it was time to eat. Joseph cut the fish open, and there inside the fish was Wilhelm's old gray cap with twenty-two perfect pearls and with a gold ring. Joseph bowed his head and he thanked the good Lord God–then, Joseph continued with the Sabbath meal. During the next week, Joseph sold the pearls and the ring and he gave all the money to charity. When he died, three years later, at the age of sixty-eight, it was on a holy Sabbath day, and Joseph died a contented man. . . .

What is that? Maimonides and the Messiah? Yes, yes, Rabbi, I am about to continue. I was just thinking quietly, in the glow of the stove. Now, where was I? Oh yes, my grandmother told me that old Rabbi Abraham had written once to Maimonides: Achselrad had asked the famous philosopher, Moses ben Maimon, about the Messiah. The letters went back and forth in the middle epoch of Maimonides' life. As you know, Rabbi, the first epoch of Maimonides was the Cordova era, the middle epoch was during the Fez years, and the last epoch was when Maimonides lived in Cairo.

Moses ben Maimon was born in Cordova on the eve of Passover. He had a brother named David, and he had one sister. Back in those years, Cordova was Arab and it was a center of learning – Cordova was filled with science and with art and with medicine, philosophy, and literature. When Moses ben Maimon was still young, Cordova was taken from the last Fatimite caliph by the North African Almohades. These militant revivalists wanted to re-establish Islam in its primitive simplicity. Jews were not tolerated, and Moses moved to the city of Fez.

In Fez in Morocco, Moses studied with Abdul Arab ibn Muisha, the fine Moslem poet. The poet pushed Moses to write books: the written word, said Abdul ibn Muisha, is the highest form of thought. So, in Fez, Moses ben Maimon became a confirmed writer, and soon he was an authority on Jewish law. Later, Maimonides moved to Cairo. Cairo was the center of Jewish thinking, and in Cairo, the thinker Maimonides was the fount of Jewish philosophy. It was here that Maimonides propounded his famous interpretative creed, now known as the Thirteen Articles –today, every Jewish community and every Jewish sect has prayers and poems, rules and commentaries, founded on these Thirteen Articles of Faith.

Two of the Articles of Maimonides deal in the Messianic hopes. These Articles were written in Cairo, but their seeds are in the old letter that Maimonides wrote earlier, from Fez, to Rabbi Abraham ben Alexander, Achselrad of Cologne:

*"My dear friend and holy colleague,*
*Abraham, the son of Alexander–*

"I thank you for your letter, which I received last month. It is good to hear of the thoughtful scholarship that flourishes under your direction in the Jewish communities of the rich Rhine valley. I know that the holy Lord God (blessed be He) has shined down his warm smile and his loving kindness upon you and all your brothers and upon the eager young children in your yeshivas, amen.

"It is true that we hear frequent rumors of the return of the Messiah. However, in answer to your inquiry, I am afraid that the predictions of the young man Abulafia have not materialized: we still wait with patience and with hope. Of course, we wait happily for that great day—but I find that we all wait with somewhat different expectations. Some say that when the Messiah comes, all men shall be like angels. We will be immortal, of great stature, and very prolific. Then, the earth shall produce ready-made garments and baked bread and carved wagons and similar wonders. Other people look especially for resurrection of the dead, when in the company of their families and of their friends, the reborn shall enjoy the blessings of the earth and they shall never die again. Still other Jews believe that after the Messiah has come and has revived the dead, then everyone will soar off through the skies to the Garden of Eden and Paradise. There, throughout eternity, they will eat honey and drink fine wine and enjoy perfect health and happiness, amen.

"Not long ago, good Abraham, I was the guest of a nobleman who lives on a ranch in Sifru, which is a half day's journey south of Fez. My host had been here in Fez on business; he is a Moslem trader in cotton cloth and in colored dyes, and as are many of the aged gentlemen farmers, he is quite learned in science and philosophy. After his business dealings, the old man came and found me in the library. He wished to talk on all matters scientific and spiritual—and so I accompanied him home one warm afternoon. That day, our wagon rolled leisurely out from the old fortress of Fez and through the low green valleys, past mosques and orange groves and thick olive gardens, and all seemed calm and endlessly at ease. We arrived at his ranch in the early evening, and we retired to a slow and soft-spoken dinner in the night.

"Continually, our talk turned to old age and to death. This gentleman is at least seventy-five years old; he is beginning to see his own end, and he said to me: 'Mr. Maimon, you Jews believe in Resurrection, do you not?'

"I reminded him of the passage from the Book of Ezekiel in the Holy Scriptures":

These are the words of the Almighty Lord God (blessed be He): O My people, I will open your graves and bring you up from them, and I will restore you to the land of Israel. You shall know that I am the Lord when I open your graves and bring you up from them, O My people. Then I will put My breath and spirit into you and you shall live, and I will settle you on your own soil again, and you shall know that I, the Lord God, have spoken and will act.

"'I see,' said the old gentleman, nodding his head. 'Now, I wonder, Mr. Maimon: How will the dead rise? Will they still be clothed in their graveyard shrouds?'

"I answered that I myself did not know for certain. However, the Jewish Sages felt that the dead would probably be clothed when they were reborn.

"'And will there still be strong and weak, rich and poor, the healthy and the sick?' asked my host.

"I told him that the good Lord God (blessed be He) loves most the humble and the studious, the faithful and the honest, the righteous and the charitable. The Holy Scriptures tell us, I said, that the meek shall inherit the earth; in Isaiah, it is written":

> The spirit of the Lord whispered a word
> When He appointed me to speak –
> And, O humble men, I have heard:
> "God will uplift all the meek."

"'Ah, Mr. Maimon, undoubtedly that will be a magical time,' said the old man. 'Do you think that mountains will crash and that rivers will run backwards and that lightning will flash skyward from great chasms in the ground?'

"Dear Rabbi Abraham, I have heard these hopes voiced many, many times. It is a great wish, a fine wish. We all hope for wondrous and fantastic things, the magic of our dreams, especially the dreams of our childhood. But my guess is that the Great Return will not be so dramatic.

"Yes, the Messiah shall come. He will walk barefoot into our lives again some day, amen. In that great day, Israel will regain its sovereignty, Jerusalem will be revived, and we will return to the Holy Lands of Palestine once more, praise the Lord. And who will this Messiah be? He will be a great king. His name will be known among all the nations of the earth. His fame will exceed that of King Solomon. Then, all peoples finally will live in peace under his guidance, hallelujah.

"But, Abraham, there will be no change in the course of nature. The world of the Messiah will not be strange – it will be a world that we know and love already. Of course, life will be much better: it will be easier to earn a living. But there will still be rich and poor, strong and weak, foolish and wise, even healthy and sick. And all the promises of the well-meaning Rabbis about ready-made garments and fresh baked bread produced by the earth and magical wagons and tireless horses and gold for all and honey flowing from the springs of the forest – these are fables. They are fairytales. They are happy fantasies that hint at the ease of our new lives under the Messiah. The Messiah will rule with understanding and with peace, and daily life will be much happier.

"And, dear Abraham, the Messiah will die, and his son will become king in his stead. There will be no immortality – but people will live longer, because they will not be harassed by the troubles and the worries and the difficulties that beset us now. Furthermore, we will be blessed with the joy of learning, which preserves and lengthens life, amen.

"So, what will be the Great Blessing of those days of resurrection? What will be the Great Joy? It will be Peace – Peace forever, amen. In the days of the Messiah, finally man will be free from the trammels of war; man will be able to devote all his time and all his concentration and all his energy to the study of wisdom. Finally – praise the Lord Almighty – men will live only to study and to fulfill the good Lord God's holy Laws, amen.

"As the psalmist has written in the eighteenth song of the Book of Psalms":

> Lord, I praise You to all men
> Among the widespread nations
> I will tell your glory again
> And sing thankful ovations;
> I will chant blessed refrains:

"Everlasting faith the Lord maintains.
His king forever ever reigns –
It is Peace our God ordains."

"These things, my good colleague Abraham, I think now and I thought then. But that night, the old nobleman of Sifru was continuing on: 'And tell me, Rabbi Moses – will the days always be light and airy and fine? Will rains only fall gently, and then just once a day in the early evenings, in order to cool off the countryside before we fall asleep? Will the leaves be a springtime green and the flowers tiny points of blue? And will we all eat honey and drink rich cream and nectars and have warm soft breads at every single meal? And will I see my children again, and will I hug my parents, and will my first love be there just as I remember her? Is this not what we are destined for? Is this not the great Eternal Age that will be ushered in by the Almighty One's eternal Messiah?'

"And I looked into his fine old eyes and I saw the yellow candles of the nighttime table glinting back at me, and I said to him: 'Yes, good sir, I am sure that these things shall come to pass, amen.' And, Abraham, I truly hope that they shall.

*Your humble friend and colleague,*
*Moses, the son of Maimon"*

ood evening, Rabbi. You are having difficulty sleeping again? Put your feet up on the side bench here and I will open the stove door. Let me push the coal back; there is nothing like that white glow to wash away the cares of a hard day. I heard your final prayers tonight: you are overworked, Rabbi. Even an old shammas like me can tell. I kept one eye on you when I was cleaning the dishes; I saw that you were watching the door, hoping that Reb Elbaum would leave early. But then Reb Anton stayed late to argue about the famous passage in Genesis. Did you hear him talking with Reb Lavan? They were wrestling with the verses that come after the Almighty Lord God has tested Abraham's devotion and trust; there, the angel of the Lord called down to Abraham from Heaven:

> Now hear the word of the Almighty Lord: By My Own Self I swear: in as much as you have not withheld your son, your only son, from his possible death, I will bless you for ever, abundantly. I will multiply your descendants until they are as numerous as the stars in the sky and as the grains of sand on the sea- shore. And, Abraham, your descendants will oversee the cities of their enemies. Until the ends of time, all nations on earth shall aspire to be blessed as your descendants are blessed– and all

goodness shall fall to you and to your children and to your grandchildren and to all others who trust in Me and who follow My Laws and who obey My Truths.

The way that Reb Lavan attacked that scriptural passage reminded me of old Rabbi Jehuda ben Saul: Jehuda was always analyzing the details of difficult passages in the Holy Scriptures. I remember one sermon that he gave to his yeshiva students:

"Why do the Jews exalt themselves as the 'Chosen People,'" he asked, and he looked sternly at the young men on the benches.

Silence filled the study hall and an uncomfortable itchiness seemed to take hold of some of the students, but soon the good Rabbi answered his own question.

"In the Holy Scriptures," began Rabbi Jehuda, "the prophet Jeremiah relates the following words of the great Lord Almighty":

If you obey Me and do all that I tell you, then you shall become My people and I will become your God. In this way, I will make good the oath that I swore to your forefathers, and to Moses at the Burning Bush, that I would give the Israelites a land flowing with milk and honey, the land you now possess.

But if you do not obey My Laws, if you do not follow My commandments, then I will bring down on you all the penalties woven into this, Our covenant, by which I have bound you and your forefathers and your children and all your descendants for ever and ever.

Rabbi Jehuda looked up at the ceiling and down at his students. "Perhaps, my young charges," he said quietly, "you think that this means we are the Chosen People."

Some of the students nodded, but Rabbi Jehuda shook his head.

"No, boys, that is too simple a view," said the Rabbi patiently. "As the Talmud points out, the election – the choosing – of Israel depends solely upon the will to follow the teachings of the good Lord God (blessed be He), amen."

The Rabbi stared at his students, and some of the boys murmured "Amen."

"Yes – amen," said the Rabbi; " 'amen' means 'certainly,' it means 'strongly' – and certainly and strongly all men have the right and the opportunity to become 'Chosen People.' Even Gentiles can certainly be 'chosen,' hallelujah and amen."

"Amen," said one of the students, and the Rabbi stared at him severely.

"Thus, for instance," continued Jehuda ben Saul, "Rabbi Meir has taught: 'The non-Jew who occupies himself with the Law, is equal to the highest of the High Priests of Israel. For it is written: Observe My precepts and My commandments, which man should practice so that he may live. It does not say that only priests or Levites or Israelites shall live by the holy law – it says that *every* man should follow the Lord.' So wrote Rabbi Meir, amen."

Rabbi Jehuda looked up at the heavens again, and he closed his book. Some of the students murmured "amen" and began to stand. Suddenly, Rabbi Jehuda shouted: "Amen!" The students were startled, and they looked at each other and then at Rabbi Jehuda. Jehuda was still looking at the ceiling. Then, the Rabbi stared down at his students.

"Young men," said the Rabbi, "at times like this the good Lord God (blessed be He) requires a parable. So let me tell you a story."

Rabbi Jehuda stepped back from his desk, and he surveyed the small group of students. "Once upon a time," began the Rabbi, "and a long time ago it was – there lived a king, a king with much wealth and with many palaces, a king who was the overlord of vast peoples. This king was named Mesha, and he was the ruler of the ancient land of Moab. Now, Mesha decided that his royal retinue needed to be bolstered by two special regiments, so he ordered two of his finest army battalions to come to his residence city on special assignment."

The Rabbi closed his eyes, and he opened his eyes – then, he said: "And, my fine young scholars, why did this king want *two* battalions?"

None of the yeshiva students volunteered an answer. The Rabbi continued: "I will tell you why he wanted two battalions – you see, to one of the units, he gave the most difficult duties."

Rabbi Jehuda looked at the boys on the benches. "On these men, he imposed the most severe restrictions," said Jehuda.

Rabbi Jehuda hit the desk with his fist. "Of this regiment, the king demanded the most exacting tasks!"

Again there was silence. The Rabbi closed his eyes. Suddenly, he said: "And what of the other men? What of the other unit of soldiers? I will tell you *what* – King Mesha asked only that they dress crisply on holidays. King Mesha asked only that they decorate the palace court-yard with their presence and that they attend the royal banquets as escorts for single young women and that they form the honor guard for visiting dignitaries. That is why the king needed two regiments, amen!"

"Now do you see what I am saying?" asked the Rabbi.

The students looked puzzled, and the Rabbi said: "Young men, my untutored boys, it is quite clear: one regiment had a most difficult life of work, work, work and exacting work it was, drilling and marching and building and training. Meanwhile, the other regiment had a life of ease and luxury and liberty."

There was a moment of silence, and one brave young student, Moshe ben Samuel, said: "But Rabbi, that seems rather unfair."

"How true, Moshe," said the Rabbi.

Rabbi Jeuhuda nodded, he looked heavenward, and then he continued. "Indeed, so it seemed to the men themselves. In fact," said Rabbi Jehuda, "a quarrel arose between the commanders of the two regiments. Each commander claimed that his regiment was the most highly favored by King Mesha. One leader insisted that his group was preferred, and therefore it had been given the most difficult tasks. Obviously, said this commander, the members of his regiment were foremost in the service of the king: King Mesha could only entrust complex, difficult, and demanding jobs to the best men. The king had not given important duties to the other regiment because he had no confidence in it.

"'What backward reasoning,' declared the other commander. 'Clearly, *my* regiment must be preferred by the king. We have been given a more favored life. We are honored at banquets, we have individual spending allowances, we have fine uniforms, and we are free to come and to go as we please. There are few work details, we escort the finest women of Moab to royal balls, and we form the honor guard for visiting dignitaries. But as for you? Your regiment must still prove itself. You must earn the privileges that we have achieved already.'

"The commanders argued back and forth, and they nearly came to blows. They could not resolve their differences, they brought up the subject every time they met, and eventually King Mesha himself heard about the dispute. The king called the two commanders before him, and he said: 'Gentlemen, stop quarreling. Which regiment is my favorite? Both regiments serve me, both battalions play an important role in the daily life of Moab. However, each group of soldiers serves in a different capacity: there should be no question of preference.

"'Now, I have decided that one group of soldiers should set the highest standards; they must produce great things, and they must prove by example to be the best of all men. One regiment must be the strictest in discipline, the fastest in war, the greatest in athletics, the finest and sharpest in strategy. This is the cutting edge of young men.

"'But,' continued the king, 'there is more to life than the precision of the military product; there is, for example, appearance. Now, the other regiment is about appearances. These soldiers are not held to the supreme standard of performance. Instead, this second group of fine young men is the face of the royal regime – these men are the dress and the polish of our rule.

"'You have come and asked me: King, which regiment satisfies you more? Here is my public answer: Neither – we need both performance and appearance for a kingdom to run smoothly. But, friends, if you ask me not once but twice and if you ask me at night and if you listen to me in a quiet moment, then here is my private answer: I prefer the highest standards.

"'Therefore, my commanders, show me a soldier in either regiment who lives up to the strictest requirements, show me a man who sets the highest standards, show me one who never compromises – it is he of whom I am most proud. In my eyes, he is the most outstanding, and it is he who is my true favorite. Deep in my heart of hearts, it is the man and not the regiment that matters.'"

Then Rabbi Jehuda added: "Of course, you see what I mean." And the yeshiva students all nodded – but did they really see?

Certainly, Rabbi, you and I know what was behind old Jehuda ben Saul's parable, for we have heard this explanation many times. I remember, for example, my grandmother telling me the same type of story. She was relating an incident from the study hall of Achselrad of Cologne, her favorite rabbi; he was an old mystical scholar from those dim medieval days in Germany along the wide River Rhine:

Once upon a time, said my grandmother, along the wide River Rhine, in the old yeshiva headed by Abraham ben Alexander, Achselrad of Cologne, a young and serious yeshiva student hurried into the study hall. The student was named Isaac ben Safir, and this is what Isaac said: "Rabbi Abraham, listen to this beautiful passage that I have just come across. It is from the *Haggadah* of the Jews of Yemen; this is how they begin their Passover service":

The good Lord God (blessed be He) was pleased with us Jews, and He made us beautiful. As a golden holy gift, He separated us from all other nations. The Almighty One allowed us to inherit a precious land of joy. Then, He sanctified His name throughout the world for the sake of our forefathers who did His will, for our forefathers who did arduous deeds for His own sake. Blessed be the Lord, His wonders are beyond our understanding.

The good Lord God called *us* the community of the saints; He called *us* a precious vineyard, a pleasant plantation. God called *us* His own property—He took us from among all other nations of the earth. Now we are compared to the host of Heaven, and we have been set like myriad shining stars in the firmament. We are uppermost in the world, and we have been honored above all tribes. The beaming of our faces is like the radiance of the sun, and our likeness has been compared to the ministering angels.

Kings look to us, and they rise. Princes bow low, on account of the Lord of Hosts, Who has chosen us. Praise the Lord, amen.

The other students smiled and nodded, and the Rabbi listened quietly.

"What a beautiful essay," said Isaac. "Is it not inspiring?"

"Yes," said the Rabbi, "it does inflate one's picture of himself to hear that."

"But, Rabbi, does this not agree with the Holy Scriptures?"

"The Holy Scriptures? Of what passages are you thinking, Isaac?" asked the Rabbi.

"Well, I remember a verse (perhaps it is from the Book of Exodus) where the good Lord God says":

I am God over all who come into the world—but I have associated My
name only with you. I am not called the God of idolaters: I am called the
God of Israel.

"So, Rabbi," said Isaac, "are we Jews not the Chosen People?"

Achselrad looked up at the ceiling. "Actually, my young friend,
that passage is commentary on Exodus: it is from the Talmud. And
here is another bit of the Talmud, where the Sages propose that God
has said":

If I leave the Israelites as they are, then they will be swallowed up
among the heathen nations. Therefore, I had best attach My great name
to them; in this way, the Israelites will be obligated to live up to My
Laws and My precepts and My high standards.

"I see, Rabbi," said Isaac, "but what is your point?"

Rabbi Abraham looked at Isaac and he looked at the other young
men sitting around on the benches. "Now, Isaac," said the Rabbi, "you
may know that at one time, many, many years ago, our yeshiva here
in Cologne was headed by a pious and devout rabbi named Amram.
Amram was originally from Mainz, where he was born and where—
through the great blessings of the good Lord God—he was also buried
beside his parents, amen. Rabbi Amram was a quiet man, but he wrote
a number of derashic essays. These were left in the old loft above our
back room here. Let me read you one of them."

Isaac sat down on a worn side bench, and Rabbi Abraham ben
Alexander began to root around among the papers and manuscripts on
the desk behind him. Rabbi Abraham pushed aside the books and he
opened folders and he mumbled to himself; the Rabbi looked at the
ceiling, he rubbed his hands, he picked up his pen, and he put it down
again. Finally, he smiled, and he reached over and pulled a parchment
from under some old prayer books.

"Yes . . . very good—this is it," said the Rabbi, and he began to
read to Isaac:

By choosing the teachings that Jehovah provides, the Jews were
elected as mankind's guides. Jews set the example of a holy lifestyle,
but difficult tasks are demanded meanwhile—for this is the price of our

sacred assignment. And when he fails God, the Jew must humbly repent.

It began long ago, in biblical days, when Moses was a shepherd. Taking flocks out to graze, he led the sheep herds alongside the wildlands and came to Mount Horeb, a hill of God's hands. There, the angel of God appeared in a low tree; the bush was aflame, burning endlessly.

The voice of the Lord called out to the shepherd: "Moses, my child."

Moses said not a word.

"Go free My people!"

But he was afraid: "If I go to the Jews, saying God is dismayed— if I say that the good Lord has sent me this day, then they will ask me His name—and what shall I say?"

God said from the bush: "*I am*—that is Me, that is who I will be. Say that *I am* has sent me."

God answered to Moses: "Tell people this—it is Jehovah, their Father, the wicked man's nemesis. Jehovah is witness: He sees how you groan. He will bring you from bondage and for ever call you His own."

The Lord chose the Jew to be an example; thus, He asks that a Jew shoulder exacting life tasks.

"The requirements are strict, high standards to reach," said Amos, the prophet, repeating God's holy speech":

> "I have cared for you only
> Among Adam's seeds;
> Therefore, I punish you
> For serious misdeeds."

Is this holy life-task a gift or a birthright? Our parents are gifts but our God is by invite. We earn Heavenly grace by free will, with good cause, by forsaking idols, by studying God's Laws. The "Chosen" is he who keeps God in his sight to the end of his days—he is the *true* Israelite. He keeps all God's Laws, holy, righteous, and wise; he lives without flaws, without false steps or lies. To such pious good men, our God will bestow insights and Truths pure as white snow. And if you observe His Commands, He will see and will know and will shelter your lands with His holy rain bow. . . .

What? Of course there is more, Rabbi: I only closed my eyes for a moment. Can an old man not take a little rest? Now you have interrupted my thoughts. Let me see, where was I? Yes, yes—as my grandmother said: the good Lord has chosen the Jews as he has chosen all the righteous on earth. The Almighty One is open to all, and He speaks in all languages and unto all hearts. As the Talmud tells us: "Every phrase which issued from the mouth of the All-powerful, blessed be He, divided itself into seventy languages. That is why Moses expounded the Torah in seventy different languages."

My grandmother reminded me that this universal offering of grace is the rainbow, covering all men everywhere, after every great storm. As it is written in the Holy Scriptures:

Then, the Almighty Lord God (blessed be He) spoke to Noah and to his sons with him: "I now make My covenant with you and with your descendants after you and with all men and with every living creature that is with you:

My longbow I will set on a cloud after the rain.
It is a holy sign of the covenant that I ordain
And vow between Myself and all living men.

When e'er I dark the sky and thunderous storms rain,
Then My colored bow shall glow on the clouds again.
It is a sacred oath: it is a sheltering promise to *all* men."

ood evening, Rabbi. I was just resting my eyes – please, join me here by the stove. (I think that you will be too warm on that bench: try the one nearer to the wall.) An old man like me can doze forever by a warm stove; I suppose that is because I am forgetful.

What do I mean? Why, Rabbi, anxiety and cares lead to sleeplessness, and these troubles all proceed from memories. Now that I am old, I do not remember all that I once knew; so, I am more carefree. My grandmother was forgetful, and she told me that this accounted for her amazing cheerfulness. It was only when she put her mind to it and recounted our sad history that she became careworn and gray – and, Rabbi, I must say that she often looked gray when she told of those old medieval days of the Crusades.

Reminiscences cut both ways? Yes, yes, Rabbi, I recall the benediction of Remembrances for the Day of Memorial:

> O Lord, You remember all events, and You visit the creatures of the oldest past. Before You, all secrets are laid bare and the multitude of things hidden since the Creation are fully revealed.
>
> There is no forgetfulness before Your throne of glory, and nothing is hidden before Your eyes. You recall every deed, and no living thing can

*439*

conceal itself from You. Every spirit and every soul is examined and visited, and every event is recorded and all the works of the world are transcribed without end.

In this way has it been since the very beginning, since You first unveiled the Heavens and the earth. And this day again is like the commencement of Your works; it is a memorial of the first day.

Yes, Rabbi – and I also recall the proverb:

> Do not move the ancient boundary stone,
> The landmark that your forefathers set up.

Certainly that is all true: remembering is an important part of our holy heritage. But, Rabbi, there are Divine and sacred remembrances, and then there are profane remembrances. Take the Jew-badge; it was a type of remembrance, a profane reminder that my grandmother would rather forget. Of course, it is largely gone nowadays – it was most widespread late in the Crusades, the Crusades which first spilled evil into all the Jewish communities of Europe.

It was a sort of backhanded evil, this dark and malign spirit; it did not flow from the regular armies of the Catholic cross: these were inspired by noble ideas. No – the malevolence came from mobs, spontaneous and undisciplined. Hatreds grew from fearful, spiteful individuals. Such men clotted together in masses for the sake of plunder, tagging along with the genuine religious enthusiasts. Sadly, at the turn of the twelfth century, massacres of Jews occurred in many cities of Germany, along the wide dark River Rhine and throughout the Rhine valley. And terrible sad problems continued for years and years, even beyond the Second Crusade. The Pope, Innocent the Third, gave these evils a boost. Innocent the Third gave a signal and a voice to the repressions of the Jews throughout Europe: he decreed that Jews must wear an identifying marker, the Jew-badge.

Pope Innocent the Third was half Catholic prince and half Italian king: where his spiritual victories did not carry him, his political victories did. Innocent the Third spurred the Crusade that led to the Latin occupation of Constantinople; then, he set a Catholic patriarch to rule the city. Later, Innocent had a dramatic political triumph in

England when King John consented to recognize the Pope's deputy, Stephen Langton, as the Archbishop of Canterbury. And as in the politics of the world at large, so it was also in the politics within the Church, where Innocent's strong authority exceeded that of all his predecessors.

Now, Rabbi, the Catholics say that in the year before his death, Pope Innocent the Third had a visitation from an angel. Grandmother could not believe this, but I do. Grandmother only remembered good angels, but I say that it was the angel Af or Chemah or Ketzef—or maybe it was Mashchit or Mechalleh or even the wicked Samael, the chief of all the Satans. In her old age, my grandmother had tried to forget these evil spirits. In any case, some angel visited the Pope and instructed him to convene the twelfth ecumenical council. And so he did, and the councilors met in the Lateran basilica in Rome.

After the angelic visitation, the Pope wrote an encyclical letter:

By the grace of God, we hereby command and instruct each sector and segment of the great Christian Society, Family, and Brotherhood throughout the world to pray and then to send official representatives to the Church of Saint John Lateran in Rome, for the month of November in the year twelve hundred and fifteen of our Lord Jesus Christ, amen.

The duly convoked and heavenly blessed and fully sanctified congregation therein will constitute the twelfth general Ecumenical Council—the fourth Lateran Council—under the presidency of the Pope, Innocent the Third, in the name of Jesus Christ our Lord, amen.

Therefore, in November, more than twelve hundred deputies (churchmen and laymen) from all Christian states converged—and during the conference, the power of Innocent the Third swept seventy canonical decrees through the Council. Four of these canons dealt with Jews, and one canon set forth the rule that Jews in all Christian countries and at all times should wear clothes that differed from those of the Christians.

And what was the reasoning behind a distinguishing dress? The reason was that in many countries where Jews wore the ordinary clothes, intermarriages took place between Jews and Christians. Christians needed protection; thus, Jews must be distinguished. Besides, the clerics were only following the dictates of Scripture. Did not the holy Bible say that an Israelite must dress in a distinct fashion? For example, in the book of Leviticus it says:

> Moses gave Aaron a tunic, girded with a sash, robed with a mantle, and tied with a waistband. Moses put a breastpiece upon Aaron's chest, and then he put a colored turban on Aaron's head and he set a gold rosette on the front of the turban as a special symbol of holy dedication, just as the Almighty Lord God (blessed be He) had commanded for the Israelites.

So, by a twist of such scriptural passages, it was decreed that, beginning when he was twelve years old, each Jew must wear a peculiar color. The color would be a badge, an identity of the Jewish race; the men must wear it on their hats, and the women must wear it on their veils. This stigma on the Jews was an invention of Pope Innocent the Third – the European Jew-badge came from the Pope's Fourth Lateran Council at Rome.

(Actually, Rabbi, the Pope had borrowed the idea of forcing the Jews to wear a special color from the Mohammedans. The Islamic Almohade Prince of the Faithful of Africa and southern Spain, Abu-Yussuff Almansur, required Jewish converts to wear a distinct costume. The Prince said: "If I could be certain that Islamic Jews had adopted the Mohammedan belief with an upright heart, then I would allow them to intermarry with the Moslems. On the other hand, these Jews still may be skeptics secretly; in this case, I should put the men to the sword, enslave their children, and confiscate their goods. Because I am unsure, we had best have all Jews remain distinguished by their clothes.")

The papal decree left the details to each locality: provincial councils, assemblies of state, and royal cabinets set the color, form, length, and breadth of the Jew-badge. Sometimes it was saffron yellow, sometimes it was purple; sometimes it was round, sometimes it was square. Influential Jews, especially in the courts of Toledo and Saragossa and Valencia, protested vigorously in the regional councils, and in a few cases reason prevailed; for example, after Innocent the Third died, King Alfonso IX of Leon did not enforce the dress regulations for Jews. Nonetheless, most Jews suffered, and the pressures to remove the Jew-badge, to convert, to assimilate, and to become peacefully anonymous were intense.

Now, Rabbi, at this time, the Jewish communities of southern France had been protected temporarily by Raymund the Seventh of Toulouse. The repeatedly excommunicated Raymund was the Count of Provence; he was the oldest and the richest of the crusading princes, and he and his barons had defied the papal orders and had continued to give Jews offices of responsibility in local governments. Also, Raymund did not require Jews to wear badges.

Raymund fought Simon de Monfort in France, and Simon and his brother captured Toulouse. Simon's army then crossed the River Garonne and proceeded westward to Albi. After the army had advanced from the city, Simon de Montfort put his wife, Alice of Montmorency, in charge of the town of Toulouse. With a firm mouth and an iron hand, Alice swept in to the town. Perhaps it was on account of the open devotion of the Jews for Simon's rival Raymund that Alice ordered all the Jews of Toulouse to be arrested.

As soon as her husband had left, Alice set up court in the old cathedral, the Church of St. Sernin, a famous shrine that had been consecrated by Pope Urban the Second. Alice sat at the scarred oak table beneath four massive pillars; she sat in the central chamber of the cathedral, and she dictated a number of orders.

Then Alice said to her courtiers: "Now, as to these Jews – they are a problem. We cannot trust them because their religion has so many secrets. They hold themselves aloof. They may do anything in the name of their God. And I have heard that they sometimes sacrifice Christian children for their springtime rites. Our only safe course is to have them convert. Then we can give them guidance, we can hold them to a righteous course, and we can keep a close watch on them."

"Basically," said Alice of Montmorency, "we must give them the choice between conversion and death."

The courtiers looked at one another. Simon and his brother had pledged that the local Jews would remain safe: the noblemen had vowed that Jews would be free to practice their religion. But Alice tightened her mouth, she turned her back, and she ordered that all Jewish children under the age of six should be removed from their parents and given over to the priests; the children must be baptized and brought up as Christians.

Jewish merchants traveling throughout southern France spread the news, and within a few weeks, word reached Simon de Montfort. Immediately, Simon sent orders back to Toulouse with a small contingent of officers: Jewish children held as prisoners should be released, and all people who believed in one Almighty God should be allowed to practice their religion freely.

This sounds like it was a happy ending, but fine-sounding words can hide the sad truth. In Toulouse, the Jewish community remained enshrouded in sadness. Alice of Montmorency had enlisted the support of the local prelate, Cardinal-Legate Bertrand. And the Cardinal set forth a formal ruling: those children who had been baptized were now Christians forever. These children had been accepted into the Catholic fold, and they would not be allowed to return to their parents – and of course, all Jews must continue to wear their Jew-badges. . . .

What? No, no – do not get up on my account, Rabbi: I was just resting my eyes a moment. I was resting and musing. . . . Well, to tell you the truth, Rabbi, I was remembering an event from Cologne, a small happening from those dim old days of Rabbi Abraham ben Alexander, Achselrad of Cologne. Just as it was in Toulouse and throughout France, conversion also was an ever-present pressure in Germany, and the pressure came in many guises. For example, my grandmother told me about a convert in Achselrad's congregation, a young man named Ephraim ben Asher. Poor Ephraim was a sad case; he had been lame since he was a small boy, when he had fallen from a wagon and his injured leg had not healed properly.

Once upon a time, said my grandmother, in the old Jewish Quarter of Cologne, lived a young man named Ephraim ben Asher. Ephraim was a weak fellow, with hair that stuck up sideways. His mother was quiet and worn, and his father worked long hours and was never at home. One day, Ephraim heard that in Bonn there had appeared a bent old man who by means of holy flower petals enabled the lame to walk, the blind to see, and the sick and the leprous to be healed.

Therefore, Ephraim ben Asher decided that he should go to Bonn so that he might be cured. Ephraim packed a sack, and he set off, limping down the road that ran alongside the dark River Rhine. On the second day of walking, he came to the outskirts of Bonn, a beautiful old town. Ephraim looked up; across the city walls, he saw the magnificent towering Munster Cathedral with its five spires of smooth gray stone.

Ephraim felt inspired by the grandeur of the old church. With an excited sense of hope, he limped into the central marketplace, and soon he was directed to the old healer who was busily rejuvenating the myriad infirm. Now, the healer was really a demon (may the good Lord God, blessed be He, protect us from them), and this evil spirit had taken the form of a bent old man. Here, in the middle of the city of Bonn, on a gray afternoon in the shadow of the great Munster Cathedral, the demon-healer was surrounded by sick people, and the crowd was talking and jostling and pushing this way and that. Eventually, Ephraim worked his way close to the old man. The man put his arm on Ephraim; then, he drew back. "What is this?" said the healer. "Clearly you are a Jew. Why are you here?"

Ephraim said: "Yes, I am a Jew from Cologne. I have heard that you heal the sick and that you make the lame walk. Therefore, I have come to you so that you will cure my lameness too."

"Do you know who I am?" said the healer.

"No," said Ephraim.

"I am a Christian healer. You must convert to Christianity if you want to be well again."

"I cannot do that—can I?" asked Ephraim.

"Of course you can," said the demon eagerly.

Conversion was quite a coup for demons. In those days, the many malign spirits that pervaded the European towns and countrysides were very disappointed: when the persecutions of the First Crusade were over, Emperor Henry IV had allowed those who were forcibly baptized to return to Judaism. Many, many Jews reverted to their family faith immediately. The ranks of the converts were thin again, and demons were working energetically in order to repopulate the army of converts.

"I am not certain that I should do this," said Ephraim.

"You do want to be healed, do you not? You do want to walk normally and not to have women and children laugh at you?" asked the demon.

"Yes," said Ephraim.

"What is your name?" asked the evil spirit.

"I am Ephraim—Ephraim ben Asher."

"All right, Ephraim, listen, and follow my directions," said the demon-healer. "Close your eyes. . . . Yes, yes, Ephraim, I feel the power of God—and you can too. Here comes Jesus; he is coming forward. He glows. He is so beautiful! Look at him: he is wearing a burgundy cape, and see—there is an inch of gold all along the edges of his gown. Now he is moving over to the trees, he is standing above the highest tree on our right past the stalls, and he is extending his hands. Christ is reaching out. He is making the sign of the cross in the name of the father and the son and the holy ghost. And the grace and the power of conversion and cure is transferred to me and to these holy flower petals here in my pouch, as blessed by Jesus Christ himself, amen."

And the demon-healer dropped some dried flower petals on Ephraim's head. Ephraim felt a tingling sensation in the back of his neck. Was he converted? He felt very strange.

"Now," said the demon, "I can cure you as I can cure anyone. Just renounce your faith, and you will be healed, Ephraim. By the Lord Jesus Christ, you will be healed, amen!"

"If I renounce Judaism," said Ephraim, "then how do I know that you will really cure me?"

"Watch," said the demon, and he recited a pagan Healer's Charm:

> In your lame leg
> Disease has a hold.
> Was this same plague
> Sent by gods of old?
> Or was it bought
> For money and gold?
> It matters not
> When this charm is told.
>
> Rise up, I say—
> Get hence, disease.
> Be blown far away:
> Fly with the breeze.
> Sink in the seas,
> In a watery bier.

Descend, disease,
To the pit of fear.
Go away – be cast afar
To black lands, drear
With no sun, no star –
With no joy, no cheer.


Then the demon-healer struck Ephraim twice upon the legs. Ephraim tried to walk, he took a step and then two; he could walk and trot and run. There was no pain – there was no limp. He jumped and he hopped. He could not believe it. All his life, others had stared at him. He had never been able to jump and to skip and to run with his friends, he could not balance on a log, he could only carry heavy loads on his right side, and no woman would agree to be his wife. Now it would all be different.

Ephraim slapped his bad leg: it felt as good as new – so, Ephraim renounced his faith. The demon-healer tapped Ephraim upon the forehead, and he said: "Amen – under our Lord Jesus Christ, amen." So, Ephraim became a Christian, and he set out for Cologne; he began to walk home from the marketplace. Ephraim walked smoothly and evenly and briskly out from under the long shadows of the Munster Cathedral, through the walls of Bonn, and north along the edge of the wide and dark River Rhine.

Ephraim walked happily all night, under the good Lord God's glorious starry heavens. When he reached Cologne, Ephraim walked in to the city through the southern gate, and he passed by the area of the old Jewish cemetery, the *Am Toten Juden*. It was a foggy, misty morning, and Ephraim could see none of the graves.

Ephraim walked toward the Jewish Quarter, but all the streets seemed to curve away. He recognized some areas, but he could not quite identify others. The Jewish Quarter of Cologne was in the eastern corner of the old city: the Jews lived along the sunrise corner of Cologne, close to the ancient Roman wall where the main street led to the River Rhine through the principal gate, the Market Gate. But where was Judengasse Street? Where were Portalgasse, Obenmarspforten, Alter Markt, and Unter Goldschmied? Where were all the streets leading into the Jewish Quarter?

Ephraim found himself on the long Hohe-strasse Street, passing the Gentile markets. Along either side were the tortuous, dark, and narrow lanes of the inner town. He passed the Dom, the Roman Catholic cathedral. Then–what was this? He was walking out the northern Eigelstein Gate. How could he have missed his home? He looked back; it was a foreign city, a fortress on the Rhine, a vast semicircle on the broad and dark River Rhine, the wide medieval River Rhine.

Although it was the morning, all was dismal and the sky was cloudy and thick and low. Ephraim had walked all night, and now he was tired. He sat on a stone; soon the wind arose, and Ephraim seemed to hear a voice. Or was he just remembering something? There was a passage in the Holy Scriptures, in Jeremiah, where the good Lord God (blessed be He) said:

> Is Ephraim still My dear young son,
> A child with whom I smiled once when,
> And even as I turn My back
> I think of him now fondly, again.
>
> My heart still yearns
> To hold him close and glad.
> A gentle tear now wets My eye:
> Ephraim, child, I too am sad.

Ephraim looked at Cologne, and he knew that it was no longer his home; there would be no one who knew him in Cologne, there would be no one to remember him in Cologne–and so he continued walking north.

abbi, I am glad to see you here alone. I want to apologize for my outburst during the service this evening. Reb Anton waved to Reb Jakar when he entered the prayer hall late. Now, I feel strongly that a worshipper cannot interrupt his devotions by even a single inappropriate word. Only in the natural breaks in benedictions can you return a greeting. Even then, however, interchanges should not be encouraged—we must respect the Lord, amen. What is that, Rabbi? Well, certainly man was not intended to live alone: God has put us into a family, and He has put each family in the midst of a community. As it is said in the Book of Numbers:

> We are tied together: if one man sins, then will You, O Lord, be angry with the entire congregation?

Nonetheless, there are limits, Rabbi. Comradery must give way to respect for others—especially during the devotions. Why, in the olden days, in the strict and pious days of our fathers, Reb Anton would have been ordered to leave and never to return. Remember the timeworn rule that even if the king himself should greet you when you are at prayer, then you must not answer.

I know what you are thinking: one must be practical. But no matter how liberal-minded you are, Rabbi, you must admit that talking in the synagogue is not compatible with devout worship. Even ecstatic mumbling is bad form. Is that not what you would say, too? No? Oh, well, I agree that balance is not a simple matter – on the one hand, there is the right of an individual to pray in his own manner; on the other hand, there is the right of the other congregants to silence.

How much should the rights of the individual be put before the rights of the masses? It is an old question, and it reminds me of an old story. Grandmother once told it to me – it was the tale of one Eleazer ben Salemannus of Remscheid, who was excommunicated because he would not follow the majority.

Do you know Remscheid? It is a German town about thirty-five kilometers northeast of Cologne. Remscheid has always been a manufacturing town, even in those medieval days when Nathan ben Solomon was head of its small Jewish community. Rabbi Nathan had been a student of the famed mystic Rabbi Abraham ben Alexander, Achselrad of Cologne – but in truth, Rabbi Nathan was one of Achselrad's more ordinary students. Nathan was methodical and plodding, and he followed the lead of the other scholars in his small congregation.

Now, at this time in the Jewish community of Remscheid lived a clever and sharp-tongued man named Eleazer ben Salemannus. Reb Eleazer was quick-thinking, strongly opinionated, and very intolerant of the slower reasoning of his colleagues, especially Rabbi Nathan, and there were often heated arguments. Eleazer was not well liked, and one day, he had an especially angry dispute with the other scholars. What Eleazer declared unclean they declared clean, and they would not change their minds and agree with him.

One of the Remscheid sages had said: "My good Eleazer, fruit fallen from a tree can be collected and eaten, even if animals have begun to gnaw on it."

But Reb Eleazer disagreed. Did not the good Lord God (blessed be He) command the Israelites in Exodus:

> You shall remain holy to Me: you shall not eat the flesh of anything found in the open country and killed by beasts; instead, you shall throw it to the dogs.

"This applies to animal meat only," said one of the sages.

"Have you never heard of the 'flesh of the fruit'?" asked Eleazer.

"Do not be so contrary," said Reb Benjamin: " 'flesh' clearly means 'animal meat.' "

"Perhaps that is what you think, but the good Lord God intended for man to be a vegetarian," responded Eleazer.

"What?! How can you say that?" asked Reb David.

And Reb Menachem said: "Eleazer, how can you propose that man should be a vegetarian, in the face of all the scriptural rules about meat-eating?"

"Yes – have you never read Leviticus?" asked Reb David.

"Eleazer, for centuries, we have had properly sanctified *shochets*, holy men who kosher meats," said another man.

"Certainly we have added meat to our diets, nowadays," responded Eleazer, "but that does not mean that the Almighty Lord first intended for us to be meat-eaters. As the Talmud says: 'The world grows dark for him who has to depend on the table of others; his life is not really the full life.' "

"Oh? And exactly what does this mean, Eleazer?" asked Goittheil ben Anselm.

Eleazer looked severely at Goittheil. "It means," said Eleazer, "that I know in my heart what is right, and all of your loose speech cannot change it. If you said that the moon was not in the sky, would that make the truth any different?"

"Now listen here, Eleazer," said Reb Joshua, "is it not true that 'kosher' means 'clean' and 'right' and 'fit'? And would you not admit that there is kosher meat, just as there is meat that is not kosher? (Now, do not interrupt, Eleazer!) I am certain that you cannot avoid agreeing. Therefore, we must conclude that some meat is clean and right and fit for man to eat, amen.' "

"Well, certainly, Joshua, certainly," said Eleazer, "but do not forget that the Talmud also says: 'When a man partakes of his own mind, then his soul is at rest.' "

"Of course the Talmud says this," answered Reb Joshua, "but it has nothing to do with proper eating habits. The Holy Scriptures go into great detail prescribing rules about meat. Leviticus tells us which meat can be eaten and how it should be prepared. There are regulations and rituals, Eleazer. Do you think that just any man may be a licensed *shochet*?"

"Exactly," agreed Reb Etan, "why are you arguing a ridiculous point, Eleazer? Do you deny Leviticus?"

But Eleazer answered: "Hold on gentlemen, you are changing the subject. Leviticus is an amendment–"

"An *amendment*?" gasped Reb Simon.

"Yes, yes–an amendment," continued Eleazer. "I am discussing the first and original intent. Did the good Lord God (blessed be He) not say to Adam the following (in the beginning of Genesis)":

> Now I give to you all the plants that bear seed everywhere on earth, and I have added every tree bearing fruit which yields seeds: they shall all be yours for food.

"This is Genesis, my friends. They are among the first words of the Holy Scriptures, amen. The good Lord God does not say that He has given animals to Adam to eat, He does not say that He has given birds to man to eat, He does not say that He has given fish to man to eat. Clearly, this passage means that the Almighty Omnipotent One intended for man to be a vegetarian–praise the Lord, hallelujah and amen."

The scholars looked at one another. Reb David said: "Eleazer, that decree came before everything was finally settled."

"Yes," added Reb Goittheil, "after the Great Flood, the Almighty Lord approved of selective meat eating. Is your mind so weak that you cannot recall all the detailed dietary rules in Chapter 11 of the Book of Leviticus?"

"Those rules were an afterthought on the part of the good Lord God (blessed be He)," said Eleazer.

The sages looked silently at one another, and they shook their heads.

And, Rabbi, why were the men of Remschied discussing meat and vegetables and clean and unclean? I will tell you why. The mother of Benjamin ben Jehuda had accused her daughter-in-law (Reb Benjamin's wife) of cooking an unclean, nonkosher, meal for the last Sabbath.

"Ah, may the good Lord have mercy," declared Reb Benjamin

the next day. "My mother is berating me, and my wife is not speaking to me. My mother claims that my wife served her a nonkosher meal."

Now, Reb Benjamin's wife had made *holishkes* according to this old recipe:

> Peel whole leaves from a cabbage mane.
> Boil them a minute; then, let them drain.
> Next, mix beef with a handful of grain,
> An egg and some salt and cooked rice plain.
> On each boiled leaf put a meat mix dole;
> Fold the boiled leaf into a little roll,
> Place each roll in a pan that's closed.
> Simmer for an hour in water kept low –
> With half cup of sugar, an onion chopped in rows,
> A little melted butter, and mashed tomatoes.

"What is wrong with that?" asked Reb Goittheil.

Eleazer frowned: "What is wrong? It is unclean, my friends – that is what is wrong. Listen to the voice of the good Lord God in Deuteronomy":

> You shall not boil a kid in its mother's milk.

"Now tell me, scholars of the Holy Scriptures – does that passage mean that Benjamin's wife can cover the kosher beef in the cabbage leaves with melted butter made from milk? Certainly not."

But the other men thought that this was being much too extreme. Bitter words continued: Eleazer ben Salemannus sided with the mother; the other scholars sided with the wife. "We are nine men to one," said Reb Etan finally. "You had best acknowledge the wisdom of the majority."

But Eleazer said: "All right, you sinners – if I am correct, then let a prayer book fall from the shelf."

Now was it a miracle, was it a coincidence, or was it a trick? Who can ever tell? All I know is that at that precise moment one of the books fell off Rabbi Nathan's shelf.

The many scholars looked at the book, and Eleazer looked at the book. Then he said: "Gentlemen, I remind you that the Talmud reports: 'A man takes greater delight in one measure of his own than in nine belonging to his fellowmen.' I am right, and I take pleasure in my rightness, regardless of what you say."

However, Reb David said: "This was just a coincidence. We should pay no attention to the book. Eleazer, do not be an obstructionist: have some respect for your fellow scholars—conform to your community."

But Eleazer said: "I am not going to be cowed. If I am correct, may someone sneeze." Each man looked around in silence, suddenly they heard someone sneeze in the courtyard. The men became nervous and doubtful, but Reb Joshua said: "We have thought deeply and seriously about our position, and we cannot give in to the tricks of evil spirits." The other men nodded, and one scholar declared: "Amen."

But Eleazer said: "Gentlemen, need I remind you that the Talmud reports: 'The man who needs help from his fellow creatures is as though he were sentenced to two penalties, specifically fire and water'?"

Then Eleazer frowned at the other sages, and he said again: "If my interpretation of the Law is correct, then let the candles blow out."

At these words, the candles began to flicker. Reb Joshua became angry: "If scholars dispute honestly among themselves," said Joshua ben Yehutiel, "what right have evil spirits to intervene?" And out of respect for Reb Joshua, the candles stopped flickering.

And then Reb Joshua said: "Eleazer, you have taken this too far."

And Reb Menachem said: "We must live in a family and in a community."

"We must blend gently with our friends," said Reb Simon.

"And with our neighbors," added Reb Etan.

"Remember, Eleazer," said Reb Benjamin, "the Talmud says: 'If I live and be and if I speak for my own self only, then what am I in the final analysis? I am only alone.'"

Eleazer answered: "There is a higher law, old Benjamin. I speak my mind rightly, and I speak it aloud; for I interpret the Law of the Lord properly, amen."

The sages looked at one another, and Reb Etan said: "Humility is more important than accuracy."

"So *you* say," answered Eleazer ben Salemannus.

"So we all say," said Reb Etan, and the other men of Remscheid nodded and murmured. "Moreover, the good Lord God (blessed be He) has declared in the Holy Scriptures in Exodus:

You shall not be led into wrongdoing by the majority.

This means that whenever an individual is in disagreement with many, then you are always safe with the majority decision: the Law is interpreted most properly by consensus. *Halakhah* is not decided by any one individual."

And Reb Benjamin added: "Eleazer, understanding comes from discussion and from reason and from argument among respectful scholars. We have considered these matters thoughtfully, and we men of this congregation agree together. We cannot acquiesce to your individual, dogmatic, and dictatorial opinions."

"Amen," said one of the other scholars.

"What?!" said Reb Eleazer. "This is typical of your sloppy reading of the holy words."

"Sloppy?" asked Reb Etan.

"Yes–sloppy," responded Eleazer. "The meaning of this scriptural passage is exactly the opposite. Listen again":

You shall not be led into wrongdoing by the majority.

"The good Lord God (blessed be He) means that even in the face of majority decrees, we must carry forth with our own knowledge. An individual is ultimately responsible only to himself and to his God: he must be true only to the Laws of the Almighty Lord, amen." And Eleazer ben Salemannus turned, and he stamped out of the study hall.

Soon after this, the Remscheid men met together without Eleazer. "We cannot take this constant bickering," said Reb Joshua.

"It is destroying our peace," said Reb Menachem.

"It makes everyone angry at council meetings," said Reb Simon.

"Eleazer takes stands opposite to ours just to be difficult," said Reb Etan.

"He is upsetting our orderly congregation," said Reb Benjamin.

"He has no respect for other people's ideas," said Reb Joshua.

"He is disturbing the peace," said Reb David.

"He flaunts the normal, quiet decision-making in our community," said Reb Goittheil. "Eleazer is not collegiate. Things would be much smoother without him: he must go."

So the sages voted, and they decided to put Eleazer in *herem*: the scholars of Remscheid excommunicated Eleazer ben Salemannus from their congregation. After voting, the men stood around, and finally they said to one another: "Now, who will face Eleazer with this ultimatum. Who will go and announce to him that he has been excommunicated?"

The rabbi, Nathan ben Solomon, looked at the many scholars and he said: "I will go myself and inform him; this is my job."

Perhaps it was just another coincidence, but when the men of Remscheid pronounced the excommunication, the world was smitten with troubles. One third of the world suffered a plague in its olive groves, one third had a devasted crop of barley, and one third of the world lost its full harvest of wheat. Some people say that even the dough dried and crumbled in the hands of women in towns throughout Europe on the very day when Eleazer was excommunicated. However, Rabbi, you know how people exaggerate these things.

In any case, the men of Remscheid were busy with their own affairs. They did not associate the excommunication with world events. So, on the next day, Rabbi Nathan dressed himself in black, like a man who is in mourning, and he stood in front of Reb Eleazer, at a distance of four cubits.

Eleazer said to him: "Rabbi, why are you dressed in black today?"

And Rabbi Nathan replied: "My friend, your colleagues have excommunicated you; they have cut you off from our community."

When Reb Eleazer heard this news, he said: "Rabbi, you know as well as I that there is a hierarchy among prayers, and the first priority of prayers are from those men who have been excommunicated unjustly. In fact, when all the gates to Heaven are closed, the good Lord God (blessed be He) still hears the pleas of those in *herem*." At these words, a cold wind began to blow and to shake the trees.

Sadly, Rabbi Nathan ben Solomon shook his head, and he began to pray: "Lord of the universe, You know that I have nothing to gain by this action. My colleagues have not excommunicated Eleazer for the sake of their personal honors. It is a blot on our congregation, and it does not enhance the holiness of our forefathers.

"No, O Lord our God, King of the Universe, we have done this for Your honor. Here is a contentious man who always says 'Black' when we say 'White,' who always says 'Small' when we say 'Large.' We have been forced to send him away for the sake of order and smoothness and stability in our small community. We have been forced to put him in *herem* to avoid disputes in Israel, in order that one person not be allowed to fight against the many, in order that the family of Israelites not be divided amongst itself. There are evils loose in the outside world; we must band together for preservation–we cannot be a family divided, amen." When the Rabbi had finished his prayer, the wind ceased and the trees stood tall and the sun shone forth.

At this, Eleazer looked about him. He looked at the quiet trees and the houses, he looked at the dust and the sky. In the sky was a single cloud, magnificently white. And then Eleazer ben Salemannus took off his shoes, he rent his garments, he sat down on the ground, and he mourned, just as if a corpse were lying before him, and he wept bitterly. And Eleazer mourned for seven long and sad days.

And who was correct, Rabbi? Should a man hold his tongue? Should an individual remain silent in the face of the majority? Or should one always speak out if he feels that he is right? I myself do not know. I only know what my grandmother said: "No man should stand up against the whole community." Each man, said my grandmother, should be humble and pious. He should consider what complex troubles are brought on by a strong-willed individualistic attitude. Grandmother said that a man is like a cloud: in an empty sky, he is always lonely, no matter how magnificently white he is.

Eleazer was smart and strong-willed and individualistic–in many ways he was a very worthy man, and at times his insight was approved by the Almighty Lord God. Was his learning ever magnificently white? I suppose that perhaps it was. Yet he was nonetheless excommunicated by the community. Eleazer flaunted the majority–of that there is no doubt. But is excommunication the appropriate punishment? Can strong individualistic spirits live side by side in the same synagogue?

What do you think, Rabbi? Ah yes, I do remember the passage from the Talmud:

> I, a mortal man, am a creature of the good Lord God (blessed be He), and my neighbor is also His creature. My work is in the city, his is in the

country. My mind is clever, his hands are agile. And this fine man rises early to his work, as I rise early to mine.

My neighbor takes joy in his family, as I do in mine. We are both proud creatures—and I cannot excel in his work, just as he cannot excel in mine.

O Lord, do I do great works, while he does small? I am certain that at times my neighbor must wonder the opposite. I only know, Almighty One, that my neighbor and I both thank You, the good Lord God, for our lives and our work and our family, and in Your warm arms we are both gathered together in the end, at peace forever, amen.

ello, Rabbi, I will be with you in a moment – I cannot leave until every tablecloth is folded, otherwise the day has not ended properly. . . . There, now I am finished at last, and I can sit next to you by the stove. Here is the front door key; I had the opportunity to polish it for you. Have you ever used it to see into the future. No? My grandmother would sometimes play the key and Bible game with us when we were children. Here is what you do:

First you open the Holy Scriptures to the Book of Ruth, Chapter 1 – where it says:

> Long ago, in the time of the Judges, there was a famine in the land, and a man from Bethlehem in Judah went to live in the Moabite country, with his wife and his two sons.

Or you open the Holy Scriptures to Psalm 51 – where it says:

> Be gracious and remember me,
> For Your name's sake.

With mercy please be kind to me:
Forgive my least mistake.

Then, you take a door key. Carefully set it in the Bible: lay it on the page so that one end of the key touches the words and the other end extends out beyond the top of the book. Next, close the Bible, and tie a white string around it with seven knots.

Now, Rabbi, you slip the fourth finger of your right hand under the string and ask the good Lord a question. Hold the book only by your one finger, and the Bible will swing around and it will point out a clue. For example, if you want to find out whom you will marry, then ask the good Lord God, and the book will swing and the key will point to the right person. Or if someone has stolen something, then the key will point out the guilty party. In fact, if someone is guilty of a very bad crime, then when the key points to the criminal, the Bible actually will fall to the ground.

I know that this sounds like folklore, but I have seen it work. At one time, common people regularly used this fortunetelling for serious matters such as solving crimes. Holy men always avoided the door key: I do not think that even the mystic Abraham Achselrad ever used such charms. Of course, Rabbi Abraham could foretell the future through holy visions. Oh yes, Rabbi, it is true – for example, my grandmother told me about the vision that Achselrad had for Philip von Heinsberg, the Archbishop of Cologne.

In those old medieval days, Cologne was a major trading center in the German empire. Cologne was noted for wine and herrings, for the exquisite woven Cologne cloths, for goldwork, and for armor. Businesses made money, traders moved in from the countryside, and the marketplaces grew. Soon, the central city spilled into its surroundings, and the once independent towns of Oversburg, Niederich, and St. Aposteln became suburbs. At first, Cologne was ruled solely by its Archbishop, but as commerce became complex and powerful, the city government was taken over by the *Richerzeche*; this was a council of wealthy businessmen and landowners.

Early in the tenure of Rabbi Abraham ben Alexander, Philip von Heinsberg was the Archbishop of Cologne. Even among Gentiles,

Rabbi Abraham had the reputation of a special seer and a mystical man, and sometimes the Archbishop consulted quietly with the Rabbi. One day, Ulrich, the Bishop of Halberstadt, came to Cologne to ask Archbishop Philip for military help, and in turn, the Archbishop came to Rabbi Abraham for a vision into the future.

The problem came about like this: Not long before, the army of King Henry the Lion, Duke of Saxony, had rolled north through the German Empire. King Henry marched forth and took control of lands and towns and forts belonging to the Bishops of Merseburg and Brandenburg and Halberstadt, and Henry refused to return the territory to the Church. Even the personal request of Emperor Manuel Comnenus of Constantinople was, like all other appeals, met with a stonewall negative. The Church's lands were occupied and beseiged—what was to be done? Finally, the Bishops decided that they must recapture the lands by force, and so Bishop Ulrich came to the Archbishop of Cologne in order to ask for troops and supplies.

Archbishop Philip listened to his friend the Bishop of Halberstadt. Then Philip replied: "First, Ulrich, I must go and see my Jew, Abraham Alexander. From this rabbi, I can find out whether to join with you: this holy man knows whether we shall be successful."

The Archbishop then sent for the Rabbi and told him about the request of Ulrich of Halberstadt. "Therefore," said the Archbishop, "I need your advice. Shall I join in the Bishop's adventure? Shall I go to war against King Henry of Saxony?"

The Rabbi said: "I am honored that you ask my advice." Then Rabbi Abraham sat down and he closed his eyes, his chin sunk to his chest, and soon his breathing became heavy.

After about five minutes, Philip said: "Rabbi, are you asleep?"

Rabbi Abraham opened his eyes, and he stood up as if he were about to leave. "Archbishop, I think that you should ask your councilors of war."

"Mr. Alexander," said the Archbishop, "you have been more accurate and more insightful than all my councilors in the past. I count on your advice. Are you not proud of your many successful predictions?"

Achselrad answered: "The Talmud tells us that if a prophet is proud then his vision clouds and his prophecy departs from him."

"Well, I respect your philosophical and religious views," said the Archbishop, "but in this case I have practical problems, and I need your thoughts about this war against King Henry of Saxony."

But the Rabbi replied: "Are you certain that you want my advice? I am only a religious man. I have no direct experience with wars and politics and land feuds and battles. What little I know, I only learn through meditation."

"Yes, yes, Mr. Alexander," answered the Catholic cleric, "I understand. However, you seem to have a special insight into the future. I do not care how you prophesy. I do not care where you get this special vision. I simply need to know what is to come for me. Fortunetelling is a rare gift in a mortal, and I value it, Rabbi."

Rabbi Abraham replied: "It is not fortunetelling, and my visions come from no mortal. I listen to our God. One of our prayers says":

O Lord, show the help of Your right hand to Your people. I do not trust in man, nor do I lean on any children of God: instead I trust in the Almighty Lord, God of Heaven, Whose Law is truth, Whose prophets speak His words, and Who shows the faithful His golden light. Be it Your will, O Lord my God, to open my heart to insights so that I may have happiness, long life, and peace, amen.

"It is only in this humble spirit that I can offer you my counsel."

"Fine, fine – whatever you say, Mr. Alexander," said the Archbishop. "Now, tell me what is in store for us in the wars?"

Rabbi Abraham sat down again, and he closed his eyes. He swayed back and forth; after a while, he stopped, silent and motionless. Then, the Rabbi opened his eyes, he opened his Bible, he read quietly, and he said: "All right, Archbishop – now, I must warn your lordship. Do not go. If you do, I am certain that neither you nor the Bishop will return alive."

Archbishop Philip listened quietly. "Rabbi," asked Philip, "are you certain about this?"

"I am afraid so, Archbishop," said Achselrad sadly.

So, Philip von Heinsberg went back to Bishop Ulrich and told him that he would send supplies. However, Philip himself could not go to war with the Bishop: his wise Jew had advised him against it. Rabbi Abraham ben Alexander (said Philip) had told him that if the Archbishop went to war against King Henry the Lion, then both the Bishop and the Archbishop would be killed.

"My counsel, Ulrich," said the Archbishop, "is that you do not start this battle either. I believe the rabbi, and I am certain that this is a fatal venture."

But the Bishop of Halberstadt said: "What? Do you pay attention to the words of some Jewish mystic?"

"I know that this is not easy to believe, Ulrich, but he has been right many times in the past. Moreover, he quoted me a very wise passage from the Bible, the proverb":

> Set goals with thoughtful counsel—
>   Care leads to successful campaigns:
> Wars are won through strategies;
>   Victories are designed by brains.

"Philip, anyone who reads can quote the Bible," replied the Bishop of Halberstadt. "How can this Jew know what will be our fortunes in war? Do you really refuse to go?"

"Ulrich, you are making this difficult—I cannot go."

"Very well," said the Bishop, "if you refuse to help, then I will go alone. And as for your false Jew—a troublemaker in whom you put so much faith—if I return home alive, then I will do my best to have this liar thrown in prison, so help me God." With these angry words, Ulrich, the Bishop of Halberstadt, departed; he left the Archbishop's home, and then he set out from Cologne.

Thus began a war, but the battles were brief. On the second day, Ulrich was killed. In Cologne, Rabbi Abraham was studying in the small back room in the yeshiva. Papers were piled in disarray on his desk. On that very morning, a wind arose and blew open his copy of the Holy Scriptures to the Psalms, and the Rabbi read the last verse of Psalm 20:

> Some boast of chariots
> And the archers' warcall—
> We boast of Yahweh,
> Holy Lord over all.

Other men tumble –
We stand tall:
The good Lord champions
The king of Israel.

And the Rabbi knew what was to come.

By the end of the week, word of the Bishop's defeat reached Cologne, and the next day, the Archbishop sent for the Rabbi. "Mr. Alexander," said Archbishop Philip, "we have just learned that Bishop Ulrich has been killed in his war against King Henry, and the Bishop's army was decimated."

When Rabbi Abraham heard, he shook his head. "I knew this before you told me, good Archbishop," said Achselrad. "I did not speak frivolously when I advised you: I knew in my heart that Bishop Ulrich would not return alive. Had you gone, you too would be lying dead on the battlefield."

There was a moment of silence; then, as the Rabbi turned to leave, he chanted quietly:

Blessed be
Our Lord Almighty,
Thwarting evil,
Blocking poisons,
Blunting arrows,
Cracking spears,
Breaking axes
Of the wicked.
God hates warfare;
He loves Peace.
God's Love is great –
May it never cease.

Yes, Rabbi, this prediction had come from one of the many visions of Rabbi Achselrad. And did you know that it was the battle between Ulrich and Henry that began the legend of the ghostly runaway wagon. Do you know that legend? During the fighting, a strange event had occurred. One night, a line snapped and one of the Bishop's wagons ran off and vanished. You see, a great storm had lashed the region for three days, and the wagon with its load of weapons and valuables disappeared, carrying a single soldier, a captain in Ulrich's army. Months later, the wagon reappeared running wild outside Cologne on a dark Sabbath night. The cart was in perfect shape after nearly four months of roaming the countryside, and the lone horse seemed to be sleek and healthy.

Originally, the wagon had been manned by two soldiers, Captain Richard von Falkenberg and Commander Bertholdt Steiner. Late one night, von Falkenberg had murdered his companion and had stolen Steiner's money. The sky clouded over. Lightning flashed and thunder crashed, and the angry Lord God Almighty had cursed the evil captain until the end of time. The great Lord God (blessed be He) condemned von Falkenberg to ride forever along the dark River Rhine in a wagon with a horse but with no reins. In the back of the wagon, von Falkenberg plays dice continually with the black angel Samael, and were the soldier to win then the ride would end. But, of course, he never wins. The countryfolk say that when they see the wagon dashing through the night, then it is a sign of ill-fortune, an omen of impending disaster. My grandmother claimed that the specter still haunts the Rhine valley. A ghostly wagon, Rabbi, was seen by many people in my grandmother's childhood. It appears most often in stormy weather, running wild through the vasty fields, and it bodes no good to those who see it. . . .

No, I am not inventing this, Rabbi: my grandmother swore that this is exactly what she had heard—may the good Lord God (blessed be He) protect us from Samael, and may He convert all evil hearts to good, amen.

ood evening, Rabbi. Of course—please sit here by the stove: the night fire helps me to become sleepy also. You and I are not blessed like old Reb Elbaum; once again I saw him nodding off during the last prayers this evening. He has learned to sway piously even while asleep: he must have acquired some magic from the mystic Achselrad. I suppose that you and I could use a dose of Achselrad ourselves tonight. My grandmother said that he could put men into a sleep-trance by waving a gold coin before their eyes: as you know, Rabbi Abraham ben Alexander, also called Achselrad of Cologne, was a pupil of Eliazer ben Judah, the mystic of Worms.

Rabbi Abraham Achselrad was always conjuring visions in the synagogue. I doubt whether he would be tolerated nowadays, but my grandmother said that Rabbi Abraham was also a scholar, and he claimed that his visions came from devout and pious study. Many an astonishing event took place in his yeshiva—or so my grandmother (blessed be her memory) was told; for example, one day his vision from Psalm 31 saved poor David ben Samuel ha-Kohen. Yes, I will gladly tell you about David—although he had nothing to do with Spain.

Did you not ask about Spain? Then I suppose that I was drifting off—for a moment, I was thinking of the time when Rabbi Abraham visited the Spanish King Ferdinand II in his court in Leon and when he made a young page boy disappear during dinner. Oh? You knew this already – then perhaps you have heard about Achselrad's vision from Psalm 31. You have not heard about this vision? Ah, then I will tell you exactly what I learned from my grandmother:

As you know, Rabbi Achselrad was the author of the mystical treatise the *Keter Shem Tov* which was never published and which only exists as a secret manuscript hidden in the loft of the old Cologne yeshiva. Grandmother said that it was early one cold winter morning while writing this very book that Rabbi Abraham looked up, and in the light of the candle he saw David ben Samuel ha-Kohen standing in the doorway, pale and shaken. "Rabbi," said David, "I need your help. I am about to be arrested for a serious theft."

This, in fact, is what actually had happened. The Jewish Quarter of Cologne is just north of the Christian parish called St. Laurence, and just beyond St. Laurence is the St. Albans parish. In St. Albans parish lived a very wealthy man, Aldan Hermann Kromer. Aldan Kromer was a friend of the Jews, and whenever he went away on business, which was at least once a month, he entrusted the keys of his house and his store and his warehouse to an honest Jew named David ben Samuel ha-Kohen.

David had worked for three years as a clerk and recordkeeper for Aldan Kromer. Before this, David had come to Cologne from Andernach. In those days, Cologne was a haven for Jews. The Cologne Jewish community had been relatively untouched by the destructions of the Crusades earlier in that century, and at the time of David ben Samuel, the archbishop – Archbishop Adolph – continued to protect the Jews. Therefore, Jews immigrated to Cologne from Aachen, Ahrweiler, Andernach, Bergheim, Coblenz, Dortmund, Dueren, Duisberg, Erkelenz, Frankenhausen, Frankfort, Geldenake, Iserlohn, Mainz, Monheim, Neuiss, Nideggen, Siegburg, Werden, and Wurzburg in Germany, and also from Holland and from England. David had come to Cologne from Andernach when his father died and when his mother moved to Frankfort in order to live with her only sister, Leah.

One day, Aldan Kromer called David in to him. "David," said his employer, "I will be leaving for Bonn this afternoon, and I will not return for a week. The keys are here in the cabinet; please take them home with you this evening. Tomorrow you can open the warehouses as usual." David ben Samuel assured Aldan Kromer that all the valuables would be well looked after.

That night there was no moon, and nine thieves broke into the Kromer storerooms and they took away as much as they could carry. All of the villains were from the St. Alban's parish, and they knew that Aldan Kromer would be away on business for a number of days; they also knew that were anything to go wrong, the Jew, David ben Samuel, would be blamed.

Early in the morning, David went to Aldan's house and he found everything in order—however, when he went to open the warehouse, David was horrified. The back door had been broken, and a great deal of jewelry and cutlery had been stolen. The cash boxes were gone, and valuable papers were missing. When he saw this, David trembled and felt weak; he was seized with a great fear. David stood frozen for a long time, but eventually he shook himself, he bent over and picked up a broken cash box, and then he stepped outside. There, he found an angry crowd accumulating; David dropped the cashbox, and he ran immediately to Rabbi Abraham.

Rabbi Abraham listened to the story told by young David. Then, the mystical old man closed his eyes. After a moment, Achselrad recited from Proverbs in the Holy Scriptures:

> The Lord curses the house of the evildoer,
> But He blesses the home of the righteous.

Rabbi Abraham ben Alexander opened his eyes, he stood, and he put on his hat and his coat. Without glancing backwards, he left the small study room of the yeshiva, and he walked through the main prayer hall filled with wooden benches. He passed the twelve stained glass windows with their colored lions and snakes, he went by the Holy Ark made of stone, he stepped out of the main door, and he strode off to the court house, with David hurrying behind.

The Archbishop himself was there in court; this was Archbishop Adolph of Cologne, a noble and honorable prelate. Archbishop Adolph knew Rabbi Abraham. "Rabbi," said the Archbishop sadly, "one of your Jews has committed a serious theft. The storerooms of Aldan Hermann Kromer were broken into last night. We have accusers who saw David Samuel come out of the burgled storerooms: Mr. Samuel was seen entering, and he was seen leaving, and when he left he was carrying warehouse keys and papers and valuables. Then, Mr. Samuel ran away. I see that you have brought the criminal, and I appreciate this – I am afraid, Rabbi, that Mr. David Samuel must be imprisoned."

"I see," said Rabbi Abraham. Abraham Achselrad looked at the witnesses, he looked at David, and he looked at the Archbishop. Rabbi Abraham closed his eyes a moment, and then he asked: "Have you a Bible here, Archbishop?"

"Of course," replied the Archbishop, and he instructed one of the court officers to pass a leather volume to Rabbi Achselrad.

"Now, let us read from the Book of Psalms," said the Rabbi.

"I respect your religious views, Rabbi," said Archbishop Adolph, "but is this really relevant now?"

Rabbi Abraham Achselrad was holding the Bible. Suddenly, his eyes opened wide and then they closed tightly, he became weak, and he sat on a nearby chair. Then, the Rabbi gently set down the Bible.

"Are you all right, Rabbi," asked the Archbishop.

"I have just had a vision: I have seen the Heavens at night. I have seen the good Lord God (blessed be He) Who never sleeps – and now I have seen also that Psalm 31 is quite important," said Abraham Achselrad. "If you will be so good as to hand me that Holy Book again, then I will read a bit of those verses":

> Lord, You are a rock eternally,
> Your Spirit is an endless flame;
> Therefore, lead, guide, and instruct me
> For the honor of Your name.

> Keep me, Lord, from being caught
> In nets hidden from my view.
> You are the safety that I've sought –
> I give my spirit unto You.

"And later, Archbishop, the same Psalm goes on to say":

> Blessed is the Lord on high,
> On Whose love the world relies;

He delivered me from storm-filled skies—
He heard my nighttime anguished cries.

In fear and in my black dismay,
I cried, and I began to pray:
"Good Father, have You looked away?
Did You forget Your protege?"

Then, Lord, You gave me clear insight,
You lit a sparkling holy light:
When I called out deep in the night
You opened my eyes to Truth and Right.

"It is beautiful verse," said the Archbishop. And when Rabbi Abraham remained silent, the Archbishop added: "That is certainly a noble and holy sentiment, Rabbi."

"You are a noted cleric, Archbishop Adolph. What would you say that this verse means?" asked the Rabbi.

"Clearly it means that He, Who guards us from all evil, cares for the truly faithful and that He gives the faithful insight into holy matters."

"I agree—and I would say that it means more," said the Rabbi.

"You would?" asked the Archbishop. "Then pray tell, Rabbi Achselrad: What more do you read into this Psalm?"

"First, I would say, Archbishop, that the good Lord God (blessed be He), Who is the guardian of all Israel, cares for the truly faithful. Second, I would say that the good Lord God, Who is the guardian of all Israel, gives the pious man insight into holy matters. In addition, I would also say that the Lord gives special sight and bestows remarkable visions in order to protect His people Israel against false accusations, amen," said the Rabbi.

"Exactly what are you saying, Mr. Alexander?" asked the Archbishop.

"I am saying this, Archbishop: I have had a vision. I have seen that in this city—in the St. Alban's parish—are the robbers and the stolen goods. I have seen the wealth of Aldan Kromer concealed."

Then one of the officers laughed and he said, "You have read this

Jewish mysticism in our Bible – and in German, Rabbi? The German
Psalm has told you all this, old man?"

"Yes, it has," said the Rabbi. "German is a fine and holy tongue,
young man. In the Jewish tradition, even the most sacred benedictions
such as the *Shema* may be recited in any language. Why? It is because
there can be no true devotion in words that the speaker himself does
not understand. We can learn the Laws of the Lord God Almighty in
any tongue and through any eyes – and I shall prove it to you. Archbishop, let me share my vision with you."

"What do you propose?" asked Archbishop Adolph.

"With a certain old charm, let me show you my vision. As it is
written in the Book of Proverbs":

> With libels, lies, and false words,
>    The godless slander good men.
> But the wronged ones will be saved
>    By a righteous citizen:
> The defamed will be soon be rescued
>    By clear-sighted truth again.

The Archbishop conferred with his councilors, and after a brief
argument, the Archbishop of Cologne agreed to try Rabbi Abraham's
idea.

First, the Rabbi looked around – then he said: "Archbishop, to
where do those stairs lead?"

"They run up to the north tower, Rabbi."

"Good – then follow me," said the Rabbi, and he took the Archbishop to a window high in the tower of the court building. "Look
through the window," said Achselrad. The Archbishop opened wide
his eyes and he looked, and the Rabbi asked: "Tell me, Archbishop,
what do you see?"

The window was very high, and one could see a great distance
into the countryside; windhovers and turnstones floated far and wee.
Archbishop Adolph said: "I see the sky and the trees and the brown
roofs of the entire eastern side of Cologne. I see chimneys and smoke
and people and animals, all seeming as small as can be."

Now the Rabbi wrote seven mystical names on a small piece of white parchment, and he tied the paper with seven white threads and in each thread he put seven neat knots. The Archbishop watched intently. Then the Rabbi strung the small packet on a slender white rope, and Rabbi Abraham gently placed the parchment necklace around the shoulders of the Archbishop. Then Rabbi Abraham pronounced certain mystical names of the Lord God Almighty (blessed be He), and he asked the Archbishop: "Now what do you see, sir?"

The Archbishop looked down at the parchment necklace, and then he looked out of the window. "Now I can see past some of the buildings, and down there I can see clearly into a courtyard. It is in the St. Alban's parish—I recognize the streets. There are a group of men, nine men in dark clothes. They are carrying boxes and papers and necklaces; they have broaches and candleholders and bracelets and decorated armor. It is strange, Rabbi, but it seems still to be dark outside, as if it were early in the morning."

Then Rabbi Abraham put his hand on the head of the Archbishop; Achselrad put his right hand ever so gently on the cap of the Archbishop. Again, Achselrad recited the seven mystical names of the Lord God Almighty (blessed be He), and he asked the Archbishop: "Now what do you see?"

The Archbishop peered out the window, deep and long. "I see, Mr. Alexander, that these nine men are trying to conceal money and jewels and clothes under the ground. But now it seems to me that they are taking these things out again. It looks as if they have changed their minds. Do they not know where to put it all?"

Archbishop Adolph was silent for a moment. Then he said: "Look, they are taking the stolen property to a blacksmith shop. Some of the men are talking to the smith; they are holding his attention, occupying him so that he cannot see what the others are doing. These other men are burying the valuables in the stable. I see one of the men holding a pitchfork—now the men are covering the gold and the jewelry and the other valuables with straw and manure."

"Have you seen precisely where they put the stolen property?" asked Rabbi Abraham. "Do you recognize the exact spot where the house is? Please observe this very carefully, so that you can send your soldiers to retrieve the goods."

The Archbishop noted the place very carefully. Then he and

Rabbi Abraham went back down the stairs. The Archbishop sent nine officers out into the town, and he had them collect the thieves at the same time as they retrieved the stolen goods.

When all nine thieves had been assembled in the ecclesiastical court, the Archbishop said to them: "You scoundrels, stand together. I know quite clearly who you are and what you have done."

The thieves were frightened; they did not know what to do or what to say. Then Rabbi Abraham said: "Sinners – in the Bible it is said":

> A bad man's word and deed
>    Are hated by the Lord.
> A pure man's acts succeed
>    In delighting our good Lord.

The Archbishop said: "Amen, rabbi." Then he turned to the court.

"These men have stolen merchandise and assorted valuables from Mr. Aldan Hermann Kromer," said the Archbishop.

"Moreover, these men attempted to implicate Mr. David Samuel, who is an innocent man (albeit a Jew)," continued the Archbishop.

"Therefore, we find these men guilty of theft and of deceit," declared the Catholic cleric.

After a moment of silence, the Archbishop turned back to Rabbi Abraham. "Now, my good sir," said the Archbishop, "you have helped to right a wrong and to solve a crime. What do you suggest as a punishment?"

"Your honor," said Achselrad, "if I might have your Bible again."

Archbishop Adolph nodded, and one of the officers from the court passed the leather volume to the Rabbi. "Let me read from the Book of Exodus," began Abraham ben Alexander. "In Chapter 22, we learn":

> When one man gives another man silver or gold or cloth or chattels for safekeeping and if these goods are stolen from that man's house, then the thief, if he is found, shall restore two-fold the valuables.

"So, Archbishop, as this is a religious court, I suggest that we follow the dictates of the Holy Scriptures. The thieves should give back the stolen goods; this shall be the first part of their restitution. Then, they should pay equal recompense to David ben Samuel; this shall be the second part of their restitution."

"That," agreed the Archbishop, "is a fine solution, Rabbi."

Thus, the stolen goods were returned, David ben Samuel ha-Kohen received a reward, and the thieves were imprisoned. As Rabbi Abraham reminded his congregation that evening:

> The pious man is saved from evil,
> And the wicked shall take his place.

So, said my grandmother to me when I was little and afraid to go to bed, the good Lord God (blessed be He) protects the Jews, even from thieves and from evil spirits in the dead of night, amen.

h, good evening again, Rabbi. Yes, I know – it is always
hard to sleep on the night of the full moon. Just put your feet up on the
side bench and I will open the stove door. Let me push this coal back:
there is nothing like that white glow; it washes away the cares of a
hard day. I heard your final benedictions tonight, Rabbi. There is no
use denying it – you are overworked. Oh yes, even a shammas like me
can tell. I kept one eye on you when I cleaned the dishes, and I saw that
you were watching the door, hoping that Reb Elbaum would leave
early. And then, Reb Anton stayed to argue about the scriptural
passage:

> At the time when Yahweh-Elohim (the good Lord God, blessed be He)
> made Heaven and earth, the earth was as yet without bushes. No
> herbage, no foliage, was sprouting, because Yahweh-Elohim had not
> yet caused rain to fall upon the earth; instead, a stream rose up from the
> earth, like a geyser, and it watered all the face of the ground. Moreover,
> no men were there to till the ground.

> Therefore, Yahweh-Elohim (the good Lord God, blessed be He) formed
> a man from the dust of the ground. Then, He blew into his nostrils the
> breath of life, and the man became a living being. And Yahweh- Elohim

476

planted a garden park in Eden, to the east, and there He put the man whom He had formed.

Ah Rabbi, I see that you are still worn out—so what is that? A story from me? All I know are the children's tales, the grandmother fables. You need something new and fresh to keep your mind keen. Otherwise you will become an old man like me, and you will find yourself constantly musing and dozing and nodding off in front of the stove.

What do you mean you are already an old man, Rabbi? Old? Do you think that sixty years is old? You are still a child. (Why, Adam lived to be nine hundred and thirty years, you know.) Perhaps you will feel old when you reach eighty or ninety. You doubt that you will live to see eighty years? If so, Rabbi, then you will never grow old . . . . All right, all right—as I have told you, I know no special stories, but listening to you and Reb Anton put me in mind of the time that young Isaac ben Safir asked how it was that the famous Rabbi Meir of Palestine could have been buried next to Adam.

Well, of course no one knows exactly where Adam is buried, Rabbi—if you will just be patient a moment, then I will explain. You see, in the days of Rabbi Abraham ben Alexander, Achselrad of Cologne, there was a young and serious yeshiva student named Isaac ben Safir. During a lesson one day, Rabbi Abraham had occasion to quote the great Rabbi Meir of Palestine:

Look not to the flask: look instead to its contents. Many a new vessel contains fine old wine—but there are old casks that do not contain even new wine.

and:

Remain respectfully silent and do not offer sympathy to a mourner while his dead is laid out before him.

and:

Man comes into this world with closed hands as though holding onto something, as if he owns all things; but man departs to the Great

Hereafter with his hands open and limp, for he can take nothing palpable with him.

and finally:

What the good Lord God (blessed be He) does is done well, amen.

"The white-haired Rabbi Meir told parables and fables," said Abraham ben Alexander. "With the death of Rabbi Meir, Jewish fabulists ceased to be. Old Rabbi Meir spoke with men and, like Adam, old Meir actually spoke with the animals, too, and when he was eighty he declared: 'I shall be buried alongside my forefather Adam, and I shall be happy.'"

What? Of course there is more, Rabbi: I only closed my eyes for a moment–can an old man not take a little rest? Now you have interrupted my thoughts. Let me see, where was I? Yes, yes–as my grandmother (may her soul visit happily with her parents forever) said:

Once upon a time, there lived along the wide and dark River Rhine a pious scholar named Rabbi Abraham ben Alexander, Achselrad of Cologne. (Now do not interrupt, Rabbi.) As I was saying, Rabbi Achselrad had a yeshiva, and in it was a student named Isaac ben Safir. Young Isaac listened carefully to the Rabbi, but he could not understand how the great Meir of Palestine knew that he would be buried next to Adam, when the exact location of Adam's grave was unknown.

"Good Rabbi," said Isaac, "was the location of Adam's grave known to some of the Palestinian Sages?"

"No, I do not think so," replied Rabbi Abraham.

"Was he perhaps buried in the Garden of Eden?" asked Isaac.

"No," answered Achselrad, "the Talmudists say that Adam lived in the Garden of Eden for only twelve hours."

"For only twelve hours?" asked young Isaac.

"Yes," said the Rabbi, "and the Sages account for the time as follows: During the first hour, God Almighty collected the dust and He animated it. As it is written in Genesis":

Then the Almighty Lord God (blessed be He) formed a man from the dust of the ground, and He breathed into his nostrils the holy breath of life. Thus, the man became a living creature.

"Adam was created in the image of the Almighty Holy One, Whose essence is goodness, brightness, purity, and light. Therefore, Adam had a luminous body like the angels. 'I made you of and for the light,' said the good Lord God to Adam during the first hour, 'and I have willed it that children of light will descend from you. You, My child, have a radiant beauty and a sun-like brightness.'

"Then, during the second and third hours, Adam stood upon his feet. As it is written in Genesis":

The good Lord God (blessed be He) took the man and stood him on his feet; God put the man in the garden of Eden to till it and to care for it. The Lord told the man: "You may eat from every tree in the garden – every tree except the Tree of Knowledge of Good and Evil. On the day that you eat from that tree, you will certainly die."

"During the fourth and fifth hours, Adam named the animals. Initially, Adam had an inborn ability to talk: he spoke just as newborn birds sing and as baby monkeys chatter and as calflings moo – also, the language of man was the same as the language of all creatures. Then, it was to Adam that the task of naming fell; as it is written in Genesis":

Next, the good Lord God (blessed be He) formed out of the dust of the ground all the wild animals of the earth and all the wild birds of the sky. He brought them to the man to see what man would call them, and whatever the man called each living creature, that was its name for ever after. Thus, the man gave names to all cattle of the field, to each bird of the sky, and to every wild animal of the forest.

"During the sixth hour, Adam slept, and Eve was created. As it is written in Genesis":

And so the Lord God Almighty (blessed be He) put the man Adam into a deep trance, and while he slept, the Holy Lord removed one of the man's ribs and then He closed the flesh over the place. The good Lord

God (blessed be He) then built up the rib, which he had taken out of the man, into a woman.

"During the seventh, eighth, and ninth hours, Adam married Eve, and he lived with her happily and innocently. As it is written in Genesis":

Now, the good Lord God (blessed be He) brought Eve to the man, and the man looked at the woman and he said: "Now this, at last–bone from my bones, flesh from my flesh–this shall be called woman, for from man was this taken." That is why a man leaves his father and mother and is united to his wife, and the two marry and become one whole person together.

"During the tenth and eleventh hours, Adam succumbed to temptation: he stumbled, and he fell from the Grace of the Lord. Eve discovered the Tree of Knowledge with its ripe fruit, and as it is written in Genesis":

When the woman, Eve, saw that the fruit of the Tree was good to eat and that it was pleasing to the eye and that it was tempting to contemplate, she took some and she ate it. It tasted delicious, and she gave her husband some and he ate it too. Then the eyes of both of them were opened wide.

"Finally, at the twelfth hour, Adam was sent from the Garden for ever. As it is written in Genesis":

So, in anger and in sadness, the Almighty Lord God (blessed be He) drove Adam out of the Garden of Eden, He sent him forth to till the dusty earth, the very ground from which the man had first been formed. God cast Adam out. And to the east of the Garden of Eden, God stationed the cherubim with swords whirling and flashing, in order to guard the way back to the Tree of Knowledge and Life.

"I see," said Isaac, "so Adam must be buried in some unknown spot east of Eden."

"Oh, the original spot where Adam was buried was known," said Rabbi Abraham.

"What?!" said Isaac, "but Rabbi, I thought that you said no one knows where Adam is buried."

"Exactly, my young scholar," said the Rabbi. "Listen a moment: after the Fall from Grace, Adam and Eve lived east of Eden in the valley of the Aras River. Adam lived for nine hundred and thirty years. At his death, his body was wrapped in a spice-filled shroud by the Archangel Michael and a blessing was said by the Archangel Gabriel and the body was buried in a small rock grotto in the shadow of the 'Painful Mountain,' Mount Ararat the Great.

"Now, Adam had begotten Seth, and Seth begot Enosh, and Enosh begot Kenan, and Kenan begot Mahalalel, and Mahalalel begot Jared, and Jared begot Enoch, and Enoch begot Methuselah, and Methuselah begot Lamech, and Lamech begot Noah, and Noah begot Shem and Ham and Japheth. And on the day when Noah went into the Ark, he took Adam's coffin with him; then, after the Flood finally subsided, Noah attempted to return the coffin to its original burial place.

"The original grave was a place that Noah had known quite well. But now the burial site was lost under water – a new inlet of the sea had been created by the last waters of the Flood, which the good Lord God (blessed be He) left as a remnant in order to remind man of those sad and stormy days. So, Noah found a new resting place for Adam, somewhere along this arcane inlet of the sea, and there the grave remains, hidden in a cave along an unknown stream connected to the main seas by many a tangled complex waterway."

Isaac looked puzzled. "But," said young Isaac ben Safir to Rabbi Abraham ben Alexander, "I do not understand. If Adam's burial place remains hidden, then how can Rabbi Meir be buried alongside Adam?"

"Ah," replied Achselrad, "the Almighty Lord God protects the Jews, Isaac. Rabbi Meir was indeed reunited with his parents and with his grandparents and with Adam himself in the Great Hereafter – although the true resting place of Adam remained a secret forever from all the Gentiles of the world. It is a simple matter of waterways –

"Rabbi Meir of Palestine was a descendant of the family of Nero, and he grew up to be the most notable of the disciples of Akiva. After his days with Akiva, Meir studied with Elisha ben Abuyah. Rabbi Elisha was born before the destruction of the Temple, he lived through many difficult eras, and finally, Rabbi Elisha became a Sadducee. Now, Isaac, that does not mean that Elisha was not Jewish or that he was in any way irreligious. It merely means that he was an intellectual. Strong secular currents were awash in his changing world, and Rabbi Elisha attempted to use his head and not his heart to face these challenges.

"The Sadducees were few, and they were wealthy. The masses were Pharisees, they called themselves *Haverim*, companions, and it was from the Pharisees that we have inherited our religious traditions. The Pharisees were dreamers: they hoped for everlasting life; they believed in angels, through whom the good Lord God Almighty could communicate with men; and they loved miracles and they hated demons, dybbuks, and evil spirits. On the other hand, the Sadducees said: 'Man is responsible for his own fortunes, both good and bad.' Sadducees denied the immortality of the soul and the punishments and rewards of the otherworld, and they studied and wrote about the secular aspects of the Gentile cultures that surrounded them, cultures such as the Greeks and the Mohammedans.

"Elisha took particular interest in the Moslem culture. He was fascinated by their explanation of the creation of man. Once upon a time (the Mohammedans proposed), the good Lord God sent the seven Archangels Michael, Gabriel, Uriel, Raphael, Ridya, Rahab, and Metatron, one after the other, to fetch seven handfuls of soil from Earth. The seven dusts and clays were to be taken from seven different depths and were to be of seven different colors for the creation of the first seven men. But each of the angels returned empty-handed. Why? It was because Earth herself foresaw that the creatures to be made in this way would be flawed: they would rebel against the good Lord God, they would fight amongst themselves because of their color differences, and in the end, they would draw down His bitter curse upon their heads.

"Nonetheless, God had made up His holy mind; therefore, He sent out the stern and mighty angel Dumah. Dumah came, he ignored Earth's entreaties, and forcibly he took the seven different earths, and man was created in seven different colors and in seven different varieties. Only Dumah was strong enough to wrest the seven dusts and clays from Earth, and for that reason, only Dumah is strong enough to wrest the soul from man's body and only Dumah has become the feared and fearsome Angel of Death for the Lord God Almighty, amen.

"Rabbi Meir was Elisha's disciple, and Meir listened to his teacher. He watched Elisha's fascination with the Moslem culture–but Rabbi Meir himself remained a Pharisee through and through. In the face of bitter condemnations from other Jewish scholars, Rabbi Meir held to Elisha, as a steadfast friend. But his heart was cut: Meir's soul was hurt by Elisha's acceptance of Gentile folklore, folklore such as the Mohammedan version of Creation. At Elisha's repeated recital of this story, Rabbi Meir would only shake his head. 'Listen, my teacher,' he would say over and over again, 'in the Psalm of Adam, Psalm 139, the singer asks of the Lord' ":

> Examine me, Lord–ascertain
> The thoughts and acts I make.
> I try my best to e'er refrain
> From stumbling or mistake.

> If I should wander down a lane
> Against Your holy codes,
> Then help to guide me home again
> On Your sacred roads.

"But Rabbi Elisha was unrepentant. So, Elisha ben Abuyah was excommunicated–he was denounced and he was reviled by the Pharisees. Elisha, now an old man, was called an infidel and he was called a heretic, and it was even rumored that he had sold his soul to the most evil angel, Samael. Meir knew that his old teacher was a pious and honorable man, and Elisha's death actually brought some relief to his saddened student, Rabbi Meir of Palestine.

"Later, Meir became a great teacher and a leader of the Pharisees. He refounded the Palestinian schools at Ushu, just southeast of Tyre. Eventually, he had a disagreement with the Patriarch, bitter words followed, and Meir left Palestine a few years before his death. Meir died somewhere in Asia Minor. But his love for Adam and for the Holy Land remained dominant to the end: as he said his prayers, he thought of Palestine and he smiled every morning.

"During his old age, Meir attracted a small group of devoted students. In the weeks before his death, Rabbi Meir gave them his last instructions: 'Wrap me in a white, spice-filled shroud, and bury me,' said Meir, 'by the shore of the sea. Then, the great blue waters that wash the land of my father's father will touch my bones too. Adam, the first father of us all, is buried somewhere at the edge of the sea—a hidden inlet, an arcane waterway, an unknown stream, laps along his grave. In this quiet way, my old remains will touch my first father: their edges will brush up against Adam himself. Buried alongside my parent, I shall walk hand-in-hand with all my fathers in the Great Hereafter, and I shall be happy, O Lord, amen.'"

ood evening, Rabbi. No sleep for the weary? That is what my grandmother said, and she said it almost nightly. If you are cold, then sit down here on the bench and I will stoke up the oven. This stoker? It is one of the iron shoe scrapers from the front hall—you probably do not recognize it because it is covered with soot. There are still two scrapers in the anteroom for dirty shoes; but I myself am of the old school: I think that all pious men should pray barefoot. Did you know that when he arrives the Messiah will walk into the city of Jerusalem barefoot? It will be through the third gate to Heaven; for the Talmud tells us that there are three entrances to the *Gan Eden*: the first is in the wilderness, a second is in the sea, and the third is in Jerusalem, amen.

As my grandmother said, Jerusalem is the peaceful mother of all Jews. She said this often—and of course how could you question that? Yes, Rabbi, undoubtedly, she was quoting Jehuda ben Samuel ha-Levi, the poet. Grandmother often recited verse of Rabbi Jehuda ben Samuel. Do you remember the verse:

> Jerusalem, peaceful city of dawn—
> Is that you, my holy mother redrawn?
> I thought that you were long ago gone,

Rolling beyond the graveyard lane.
Yet here you are: you still remain
To hold me in your lap again.

You do not know that poem? I heard it from my grandmother; perhaps
it is from an unpublished work. . . .

What? I was just resting my eyes, Rabbi. Let me see, where was
I? Oh yes, once upon a time in the town of Cologne on the wide River
Rhine there lived a man named Joel ben Joseph. During his entire life,
Reb Joel studied nothing but the treatise of Hagigah—and more specif-
ically, that part of the Hagigah that describes the free-will offerings of
the Feast of Passover. At that time, the chief rabbi of Cologne was
Abraham ben Alexander, and Rabbi Abraham would say: "Reb Joel,
you are a fanatic."

Reb Joel looked seriously at the Rabbi, and he replied: "Ah, Rabbi,
I take that as a compliment. Each man must devote himself to one
thing, and he must do that thing well. Otherwise, his life has not been
worth living.

"For me, Rabbi, the one thing is Hagigah, the free-will offering.
The humblest tributes to the good Lord God (blessed be He) are the
free-will offerings."

Reb Joel looked up toward Heaven, and he said: "Free-will
offerings are made without special reason."

Then, Reb Joel stroked his chin, and he said: "They are given on
no special occasion."

And Reb Joel closed his eyes, and he said: "They come directly
from the heart."

"Yes—free-will offerings," concluded Joel ben Joseph, "are based
on the most respectful and self-effacing reverence for our good Lord
God (blessed be He), amen."

"Amen," said Rabbi Achselrad.

"And," continued Reb Joel, "where is the most appropriate place
for free-will offerings? Of course, it is in Jerusalem, because it is written
in the Holy Scriptures, in Deuteronomy":

And the good Lord God (blessed be He) said: You shall resort to that
place which the Almighty Lord your God chose out of all the places of
your tribes to receive His Name, that It may dwell there in peace. To

that place, you shall come and bring your whole-offerings and sacrifices, your tithes and contributions, your vows and free-will offerings and the first born of your herds and flocks. There, you shall eat before the Almighty Lord your God. And so you shall find joy and peace in whatever you undertake, you and your families, because the Almighty Lord your God has blessed you.

But the Rabbi asked: "Joel, are you certain that Jerusalem is the place referred to in this passage? The city is not mentioned by name."

"My good Rabbi, I have studied this matter deeply," replied Joel. "The place is most definitely Jerusalem."

Reb Joel was silent, so Rabbi Abraham said encouragingly: "Jerusalem?"

"Yes, yes–Jerusalem," repeated Joel ben Joseph. "You see, initially, the worship of the good Lord Yahweh had been conducted everywhere, throughout the land. But that was not God's ultimate plan. The Lord wanted Israel to be unique: He decided to establish a sanctuary, with a special holy city for centralized worship. And the good Lord God chose Jerusalem–the place of peace. (As you know, the ancient name *Urusalim* means 'City of Peace.') That is clearly the underlying message in this scriptural passage."

So said Joel ben Joseph, and Rabbi Achselrad had no reason to doubt the old scholar.

Many years later, Reb Joel died, and the women of the burial society came to attend to the body. Old Joel ben Joseph was washed, his eyes and his mouth were closed, and he was dressed in his white Sabbath robes. Then he was covered with sweet spices and he was curled like an unborn baby, in order that one day he might roll to the Holy Lands for the Day of Resurrection. Joel was wrapped in a white shroud, and he lay in the synagogue on the day before he was to be buried. And late that night came a woman dressed in white; she walked up to the coffin on the rim of a light summer breeze, and she stood silently in front of the old man's body, praying. This was in the dead of the night, and the coffin was lying in the main prayer hall of the old synagogue of Cologne. Rabbi Achselrad had been reading in the small back study room; he saw a glow in the main prayer hall, and he arose and walked in. There, in front of the wooden coffin stood the woman, thin and pale and white and cool.

The Rabbi stood looking; finally, he asked quietly: "Who are you, my good woman?"

"I am Hagigah," she answered in the breath of a cool spring evening.

"Hagigah? And where do you come from?"

"I come from Jerusalem, of course, Rabbi," said the young woman. "I am Hagigah; I have come from the holy city of Jerusalem."

"Why have you come?" asked the Rabbi.

"I have come to pray, good Rabbi," said the white-robed Hagigah. "Jerusalem is filled with temples of prayer—as the Talmud recounts":

> There are three hundred and ninety-four Courts of Justice in Jerusalem, and there are a corresponding number of Synagogues, Yeshivas, and Houses of Prayer.

"Thus, I am praying for this man in Jerusalem at each of the three-hundred and ninety-four Houses of Prayer, and also I pray at the gateway to the golden reward of the other world. Joel ben Joseph studied nothing but the treatise Hagigah all his life; therefore, he deserves that I should plead for him at the edges of the Great Hereafter."

And Rabbi Abraham said: "Ah, my holy young woman, all good deeds that a man performs in this life plead for him. All good deeds speak on his behalf in Jerusalem, and they resound for him through the third gate leading in to the Great Hereafter, amen."

What? Yes, yes, Rabbi, I am about to continue. I was just thinking quietly here in the glow of the stove. Now, where was I? Oh yes—Jerusalem, our mother and the love of Rabbi Jehuda ben Samuel ha-Levi. Rabbi Jehuda was the greatest Hebrew poet of those old medieval days. He was born in Toledo and he died in Palestine, and he wrote love poems and odes and mystical magical lyrics, all modeled on the *Song of Songs*.

Rabbi Jehuda lived in Europe, but he dreamed in Jerusalem. He wrote:

> You shall be redeemed—
>     fear not, wait patiently.
> Your eyes will soon behold
>     My glorious eternity.

Say to him who boasts
    of conquering mighty kings:
"My King is the Lord of Hosts,
    the Ruler of all things.
We'll praise Him in Jerusalem,
    that warm and peaceful place;
In Jerusalem, we will rest again,
    happy in her embrace."

Jehuda ha-Levi believed in the eternity of the Jewish nation. He sang:

When the Red Sea's deepest waters
    stood as two walls apart,
Then Israel's redeemed daughters
    sang, with joy deep in their heart.
You overwhelmed the Egyptian,
    he and his horses drowned;
Then You set the Israeli nation
    on firm and solid ground.

Jeshurun, again awaken
    to the glorious morning skies.
Our God is like the bright sun:
    our enemies must look aside.
Children of the Israelite
    sing happily; recite
Sweet poems, fine verse and psalms
    that praise our Lord of light.

Let banners boldly wave
    under God's radiant sun
To be seen by the scattered brave
    family of Jeshurun.

Gather together, children all,
    like the wind-swept grain
Piled beside a threshing wall
    on harvest-days in golden fall.

Our lineages have kept holy
  the Lord's Laws and His Decrees
Through prayer and Torah study,
  remembering our long history.
And to remind us most,
  the sacred words we drew
On head and arm and doorpost,
  and we fringed our clothes with blue.

We will live together in peace again –
  once more the nation Israel
Under God's glorious sunshine mane,
  which sweeps dark clouds beyond the hill.

Like the sun and the moon which stand forever, like the great mountains of the earth, like God's rainbow repeatedly bridging the sky after
the storms, so will the sons of Jacob remain a nation eternally, Israel for
ever. And if, on dark days, it seems that the good Lord God repulses His
children with His left hand, then He will gather them near again with
His right hand. The children of Israel must believe: we shall be a nation
for eternity.

To Jehuda ben Samuel ha-Levi, Jerusalem was Israel – and Jehuda
loved Jerusalem. When any worshipper stands in prayer, he faces
toward Jerusalem, following King Solomon's words: "And all shall
pray towards this Holy House." Ha-Levi went farther than facing
Jerusalem: one day he began to walk to Jerusalem, and he continued
traveling east toward Jerusalem until he died.

As you know, Rabbi, Jerusalem is in the hill country of southern
Palestine. It stands on a rocky plateau, jutting southward from the
main line of hills. Jerusalem was always an important stronghold, far
earlier than when the Israelites entered. At first, its stoney height was
sufficient to provide for its strength. Later, King David also surrounded
the royal city of Jerusalem with a wall, and then he built a citadel on the
eastern hill across from the holy Mount Zion.

Forever during the summer, the heat of old Jerusalem has been
tempered by fresh sea-breezes, and then at night, the temperature
always drops. In spring and in the autumn, east winds blow through
the city from the heated depression of the dry dusty Ghor. And the

brief summer rains – they fall like a handful of echoes tossed up against the ancient hollow hills. May to October is the dry season – then come the winter rains. And it was mid winter when, after months of travel, Jehuda ha-Levi finally reached Damascus, still three hundred kilometers north of Jerusalem, his final home.

Jehuda was excited and he pushed on. A bit of snow fell in the highest regions of the hillsides. Jehuda hurried along the old southern roadway. As the poet neared Jerusalem, he could see the hill of Zion. A group of Arab horsemen were standing at the roadside. For no special reason, they began to ride toward Jehuda; they ran him down, and there he died at the side of the road, happy nonetheless in sight of Mother Jerusalem.

Ah, Jerusalem. As you know, Rabbi, the old city of Jerusalem was called *Urusalim*, the "City of Peace": it had this name from the most ancient days, many, many years before the Israelites, under Joshua, entered Canaan. Grandmother said that the great city of peace lived before the days of Joshua – it lives now, and it will live forever, the mother of peace, amen.

> Jerusalem, peaceful city of dawn –
> Is that you, my holy mother redrawn?
> I thought that you were long ago gone,
> Rolling beyond the graveyard lane.
> Yet here you are: you still remain
> To hold me in your lap again.

ood evening, Rabbi. You are having difficulty sleeping again? Just put your feet up on the side bench here and I will open the stove door. Let me push this coal back: the white glow washes away the worries of a hard day. I heard your final prayers tonight, and there is no use denying it. You are overworked; even an old shammas like me can tell. I kept one eye on you when I was cleaning the dishes. I saw that you were watching the door, hoping that Reb Elbaum would leave early. But then Reb Anton stayed late to argue about the passage in Genesis:

> There came a famine in the lands of southern Canaan, and it was so severe that Abraham went down to Egypt to live there for a while.

That passage reminded me of a discussion by old Rabbi Jehuda – Jehuda ben Saul, who was two rabbis before you.

One day, Jehuda gave a sermon of Midrash to his students:

"A famine!" said Rabbi Jehuda, "a famine, I say to you – and so said the Almighty Lord God (blessed be He). You will recall, my faithful students, Genesis says that once there was a terrible famine, so Abraham traveled from southern Canaan to Egypt, amen."

The Rabbi looked up to Heaven. "Now, how do we know that this is innate?" asked Rabbi Jehuda, and he looked sternly down at his yeshiva students, who were beginning to feel hungry.

The students were puzzled, but one brave boy spoke up. "Good Rabbi, we all must eat," said Moshe ben Samuel.

The Rabbi glared at Moshe: "Of course we all must eat, but how do we know, my young scholar, that we all must go to Egypt?"

The students looked at one another.

"Young men, I repeat my question: How do we know that youth craves Egypt?" asked Jehuda. He looked down at the boys sitting on the worn benches. At first there was silence. Then Moshe ben Samuel cleared his throat.

"Good Rabbi," said Moshe, "I am puzzled. Exactly what do you mean?"

"I mean, young Moshe," said Jehuda, "from where in the Bible do we learn that all youth has an inborn desire to go down to Egypt land."

The students looked at their desks, so the Rabbi continued: "I will tell you from whence we learn this – it is from the Book of Job."

Again, there was silence; finally, the Rabbi said: "I said, young men, it is the Book of Job!"

And Rabbi Jehuda said: "Let me remind you of the passage":

In my youthful vigor, with God Almighty watching over me, I thought: "Certainly I shall die with my powers unimpaired, and my days shall be uncounted as the days of the phoenix. I will be like an ancient tree, with my roots spreading out to the water and with the dew lying on my branches. I will be like an immortal warrior, with the bow always new and taut in my grasp and with an arrow ever ready to my hand.

And the Rabbi stood there tapping his fingers and staring at the boys. After a few moments, young Moshe gathered his courage and he asked: "But how does this teach us about Egypt?"

"Ah," said Rabbi Jehuda, "that is a good question, Moshe – so, it deserves a good answer: it is the phoenix within us."

"It is the phoenix within us?"

"Correct, Moshe – the phoenix within drives us," said Jehuda ben

Saul patiently. "You see, my untutored scholars, the phoenix is a fabulous bird; it is sacred to Egypt."

"And from *where* comes this wondrous creature?" asked the Rabbi.

And then he answered without pausing: "It comes from Arabia, deep in the dunes."

"And *when* comes this strange bird?" asked the Rabbi.

"It comes once every five hundred years," he answered himself.

The Rabbi looked up at the ceiling. Then he repeated: "Every five hundred years – this bird soars through the evening sky. It comes flying by the light of the night stars. And (this is the most holy and miraculous part) it carries its own dear father embalmed in a ball of cassia, frankincense, and myrrh. This legendary bird flies only twice in a millennium, and it flies directly to Egypt, to the Great Egyptian Temple of the Sun, where it buries its father in spices, hallelujah, and amen."

Rabbi Jehuda closed his eyes and his head sank onto his chest. The students began collecting their prayer books. Jehuda opened his eyes. "One!" he called out suddenly.

The young men looked at the Rabbi. "One!" said Jehuda again, "there is one phoenix; there is only one at a time. At the close of its five hundred year lifespan, it builds its own cremation nest. Yes, it does – praise the Lord! It builds with twigs of cassia and frankincense and myrrh. Then, it bows in prayer its tired head, and it lies in its nest and it dies.

"Now, by the Grace of the Holy One (the good Lord God, blessed be He), the corpse of this aged bird is then consumed by a magic fire, and from its charred remains arises a tiny worm, which grows into the new young bird. Finally, the new phoenix takes the body of its parent, and it flies to Egypt for burial in the Great Temple of the Sun."

The Rabbi looked at his students. "Clearly, young men of God, Job reminds us of a deep-seated wanderlust: like the phoenix, we are all born with an innate drive toward Egypt." And the Rabbi closed his eyes. Eventually, the yeshiva students quietly left the synagogue for their homes.

Yes, Egypt and not holy Palestine – now do not look at me like that, Rabbi. You think that this sounds impious. However, my grandmother, too, told me this: we all have a hidden wish to journey into Egypt. And do you doubt the word of my aged grandmother? Let me remind you, Rabbi, three generations – child, parent, and grandparent in league – make up an unbreakable triangle of wisdom, sacred to the Lord. It is a strong threefold cord; it is a rope of three thick braids, a threefold rugged cord. We learn best from our grandparents: learning passed down through three generations is special. In that regard, Rabbi, my grandmother would tell me the story of Solomon Amora of Ohligs:

Once, said my old grandmother, there lived in Ohligs on the Rhine, in the earliest days of German Jews, a pious scholar named Solomon Amora – Solomon the Speaker. In his later years, Rabbi Solomon Amora became head of the small yeshiva in Ohligs, the brewing and brickmaking town a half day's walk north of Cologne. In those medieval days, even the rabbis were traders and merchants and sellers of goods, and they traveled by sea and by land – and they traveled amazingly long distances, from France to Asia, China, and Tibet.

Like his colleagues, Rabbi Solomon was a merchant by trade, and he could be found at all the major fairs of Europe selling wool, skins, and furs. In Cologne, at the Great Fair in the fall, Solomon and his partner Judas ben Lewe represented the Spanish jewel merchants, selling pearls and gems and carved jade. (Actually, Solomon and Judas were wholesalers; middlemen would purchase their goods and resell them in Mainz and Coblenz, buying on a commission and paying back the profit in half.)

Solomon spent weeks at a time buying and selling, bartering, trading, and bargaining in European cities and beyond. One day when he had just returned to Ohligs, his partner Judas took Rabbi Solomon aside. "Solomon, my good friend," said Judas, "we have the opportunity of a lifetime. This Spanish Jew whom I know (one Ibrahim ibn Jakub) has found a new trader from the far mountains of Tibet. Through this man, we can buy an incredible amount of jade and also rare intricate jewelry inlaid with gold, copper, and silver. If one of us makes a trip to the Far East, then he can return with goods worth thousands of times what it will cost us to buy them."

After a cautious investigation, the two men had to agree: this truly was a rare offer. So, they sold all their stored assets, their wagons and their stalls and their goods, they liquidated mechandise and they pooled their money, and they prayed fervently. "Good Solomon," said his friend Judas, "the Lord has spoken to me and reminded me that you are the better bargainer. Therefore, you should travel, and I should stay here and run the remaining business."

Solomon tilted his head and he raised his eyebrows and he prayed again. Solomon listened intently deep in his heart, but he heard no holy words that contradicted Judas. So, Solomon kissed his wife good-bye, and he hugged his infant son, Natronai, and he left Cologne for Tibet. Solomon Amora traveled to the far ends of the earth, and he was gone from the city of Ohligs for twelve long years.

When he left, Solomon traveled by ship down the River Rhine, when he came back, he returned by ship, and finally, Solomon reached home again. Solomon Amora brought with him gold and silver and pearls and gems. He came back home with woolen cloaks and rose-wood and carved jade. All these he had gotten with the good Lord's help – blessed be the Lord. Solomon had passed through every country between France, Turkey, and China, he had talked and prayed with mystic men like Benjamin the Noble of Russia and Rabbi Isaac Elusha of Baghdad, and now Solomon Amora had come home at last, thick with wealth and knowledge, amen.

Solomon stored his treasures in a warehouse in Cologne, and he returned to the Jewish Quarter in the old fortress town of Ohligs. As he was walking toward his house, Solomon stopped, and he said to himself: "Now, my good man, I had best do this carefully. I will not be rash, like some other men. The proverbial Hakinai, for one, returned suddenly and without any sign after twelve long years abroad, and his poor wife fainted and nearly died when she saw him walk in the door. No, I will be more cautious." So Solomon Amora did not go directly home. Instead, he went and he sat down at the entrance of the Ohligs yeshiva. Then, he sent a message to his family, informing them that he would return home later that day.

After a little while, his son, Natronai, came along and sat beside his father. But Solomon Amora did not recognize the young man, and likewise Natronai did not know his aged father: Solomon was bearded and dusty, like a traveling sage, and Natronai had now grown into a handsome young man.

"Good afternoon, old rabbi," said Natronai to his father.

Solomon looked at the boy, and he answered: "Good afternoon to you."

"May I sit down here beside you?" asked Natronai politely. "I am waiting for someone to arrive."

"Certainly," said Solomon Amora.

The two sat side by side and did not say a word. The sun was warm; there was only a slight rustling breeze.

Finally, Solomon Amora said to his grown-up son: "Is it time to go in for prayers?"

"Yes, sir," said Natronai, "in a moment, I will go in to the synagogue—but I hope that I will be able to concentrate on my holy prayers today."

"Why is that?" asked Amora.

"Oh, I expect a special visitor soon. Nonetheless," said young Natronai, "I will try to keep my mind on holy matters. A pious and devout man must devote his full thoughts to God. Prayer to the Almighty should be direct and pure: it should be focused on the Lord. But, to be honest, I often find this difficult, especially when I am excited. So, I wonder, rabbi: What are the basic rules for prayer? How much actual attention must a worshipper devote when reciting the daily benedictions?"

"What do you mean?" asked Solomon.

"Well, rabbi, can a man really fix his mind only on the Lord during the entire service, for hours without a break?"

This is an interesting question, thought Solomon to himself. "Well, young man," said Solomon, "usually, you must concentrate fully. A person can do only one thing well at a time; so, when it is appropriate, immerse yourself completely in prayer. However the *Mishnah* does distinguish between the *Shema* and the other prayers. You can say the *Shema* while walking or even while you work. But never can you start the regular daily prayers unless your mind is clear and in a serious mood. You must give undivided attention to the usual daily prayers."

"I see," replied Natronai, and he sat silently a while. "I will try my best to concentrate today. I suppose that the lengthy hours required for the prayers will help me after all: after many pious chants, I am sure eventually to become calmer."

And Solomon replied: "That is why the prayers are long."

Natronai nodded, and Solomon thought to himself: "This boy is very clever."

Solomon Amora looked at the young man, and he thought to himself: "Ah, old man, if I had stayed and never gone away, then I too might have had a fine son like this."

And Solomon Amora closed his eyes, and he thought: "I would have taught my young boy holy reasoning. He would have been a scholar, and I would have been proud of him."

Solomon sat, musing silently for a while. Quietly, he repeated a proverb from the Holy Scriptures:

> Be bright and wise, my own dear son,
>     Then you will bring me endless joy.
> And I will laugh at all my foes
>     And smile at enemies, my boy.

Soon, Natronai arose; he stood and said good-bye. Then, Solomon Amora thought: "I suppose I too should go, enough time has passed by now. Let me finally go home to see my wife and son." So, Solomon stood up and walked back to his home.

Solomon Amora walked home, and he went in the front door. Had anything really changed? It felt different and yet the same. His wife was standing in the kitchen; she was gray, and she seemed shorter. Solomon looked at her and he smiled; she came and took his hand. Solomon's wife had been forewarned and she did not faint or fall, and she had prepared a fine full meal. They sat and talked, still shy; they ate their dinner happily—and soon Natronai came home. Solomon Amora stood up to greet the young man. "Well, well," thought Solomon, "this fine young scholar hopes to discuss some holy matters with me; he has come to ask me further questions of religious law or lore."

Solomon's old wife raised her eyebrows and looked up at him curiously. "Solomon," she said, "why do you stand like this? Why are you so formal in greeting your own son? Why not give him a hug? Is this some ritual, some politeness that you learned abroad?"

"What?!" said Solomon Amora, "this is my own young boy—this is Natronai, wife?"

"Of course it is," she smiled. "Does he not look just like you?"

Solomon looked at Natronai. Then he gave him a warm hug and he looked again once more. "Ah, wife – good wife – this young man is more handsome than me. And wise?" said Solomon. "Natronai is astute: he is thoughtful beyond his years."

"You are his father, and you see him in a golden glow, Solomon."

"Perhaps, perhaps – nonetheless, I am blessed by the good Lord God. The great Lord has given me a scholar," said Solomon. "As the Holy Scriptures say to us, in the Book of Ecclesiastes":

> If a man is all alone,
>   An assailant may subdue him.
> Sometimes two men arrayed
>   Can withstand one foeman's sword.
> But three stand unafraid:
>   Three is holy to the Lord.
> A rope of three thick braids –
>   A threefold rugged cord –
> Will not snap; it's a barricade
>   Against the evil horde.

"Father," said Natronai, "I know exactly what you mean. I learned and studied with *your* father –"

"What?" said Solomon Amora. "I knew nothing about this."

"Yes, father," replied Natronai, "I lived for quite some time with grandfather Jechina, in his little country house. Although he has been a *hazan*, he also knows Jewish law. Every day we sat in his kitchen, by the fire. He can no longer see well enough to read, so I would read to him. He would explain each passage from the Torah in depth to me. He told me complex meanings of very simple lines, and he told me stories from the great rabbis. And where did he learn these holy things? Why, his father taught him, too. Your grandfather taught your father, my grandfather taught me, and now I will be able to learn from you."

Solomon looked to Heaven, and he said to his boy: "Ah, my fine young son, you are woven into the strongest kind of learning, you are part of a mighty cord. If a young man studies with his grandfather, then the threefold rugged cord of learning remains alive and unbroken.

There is something very special about learning passed through three generations: it is magic, it is sturdy, and it is holy."

What is that, Rabbi? From the Book of Proverbs? Yes, certainly I remember what is written in Chapter 17:

> Grandchildren are the crown of old age.
>    And as to the children's view?
> Of course, they love their fathers –
>    But they're proud of grandfathers, too.

And it has been so since the very beginning. My grandmother (may her soul rest alongside the souls of her own grandparents) often reminded me that this is the meaning of that famous passage in the Book of Genesis from the Holy Scriptures:

> And the good Lord God (blessed be He) said to Abraham: You yourself shall join your grandfathers in peace, and you shall be buried beside them in a good old age. Then, dear Abraham, one day your grandchildren shall return here, and they shall prosper and study in the warm shade of the land of their beloved grandparents.

ood evening, Rabbi—I was just resting my eyes. Please, join me here by the stove. (I think that you will be too warm on that bench; try the one nearer to the wall.) An old man like me can doze forever by a warm stove; I suppose that is because of the spiders in the corners of the room.

What do I mean? Why, Rabbi, certainly you know that spiders spinning in a room make you sleepy. (That is, *live* spiders make you sleepy. This is the opposite of foxes: the Talmud reports that the tooth of a dead fox makes you sleepy, whereas the tooth of a live fox cures oversleeping.) And sleepiness is not the only power of spiders. My grandmother told me that spiders have many other effects. She said that the old mystic rabbi, Abraham Achselrad of Cologne, often used spiders when necessary. Fevers can be cured by wearing a spider in a nutshell around your neck, and jaundice or the ague will disappear if you swallow a live house-spider rolled in butter.

Do you know how spiders were first formed? In the beginning, the good Lord God (blessed be He) did not create any spiders. Just a minute, Rabbi—I know that Genesis says that on the sixth day of Creation:

God said: "Let the earth bring forth living creatures, of each specific type: cattle, reptiles, and wild animals— all according to their particular kind."

and later in the Holy Scriptures it is said:

Then God formed out of the dust and clay of the ground all the wild animals and all the birds of the skies.

But, Rabbi, at first, although there were many insects and crabs and scorpions, there were no spiders. Now, in those early days, there was a whole host of Heavenly angels; angels upon angels populated the glorious Heavens, amen. Michael and Gabriel are probably the most well known, but there were many, many more. There were Uriel and Raphael and Dumah, the Angel of Death; also, there were the other Archangels—Jurkemi, prince of hail; Ridya, prince of rain; Rahab, prince of the sea; and Lailah, prince of the night.

What is that, Rabbi? Well, my grandmother learned this from the mystical Achselrad, who often had dealings with angels. You see, as the Talmud tells us:

There are myriads of angels. Why? It is because an angel is created with every utterance that issues from the mouth of the most Holy One (blessed be He). We learn from Psalm 33 in the Holy Scriptures:

By the word of the Lord
Were the Heavens made—
All the heavenly horde
Formed from words that He said.

Thus, the angels were *malakhim*, that is, messengers: they were physical embodiments of holy commands. Rabbi Abraham wrote in great detail about angels in his hidden kabbalistic manuscript the *Keter Shem Tov*, and in this work he tells the story of the formation of spiders:

Among the many, many angels, wrote Achselrad, was a female spirit named Athaliah. Athaliah was patroness of all the arts, especially the art of spinning and weaving—and in this realm, Athaliah had a bitter contest with a mortal artist, Arachne of Egypt. Arachne, the daughter of Idmon, was the most skillful weaver in all of Egypt. Arachne was such a wonderful weaver that people told her she could make cloth like an angel. Eventually, Arachne believed this, and soon she boasted that she could outdo any other weaver, even Athaliah herself.

Inevitably, Athaliah heard of this boast, and one day, the angel appeared to Arachne in the form of an old woman. "I would not be too smug and presumptuous," said the old woman. "It is no mean feat to weave as well as an angel."

"Oh, it is not smugness," replied Arachne. "I am stating a simple fact: no one, mortal or immortal, can weave as well as I."

"What?!" said the old woman, and without thinking, Athaliah found herself transforming back into her angelic shape. "We will see what we will see. Perhaps you will weave one of your fine tapestries, my mortal friend. Perhaps you will demonstrate this great talent that you profess. In fact, perhaps I myself will do the same. Then we can compare your skill with that of the immortal angels."

Arachne was quiet a moment; then she said: "Perhaps I will — and perhaps we shall."

The two women sat at looms in the back courtyard of Arachne's house. Servants supplied them with baskets of fine yarns and threads of all colors. Into her web, Athaliah wove the stories of various people who had aroused the wrath of the angels and who had then been punished severely. Athaliah spun an intricate angelic pattern, including the enshrouding presence of Dumah, the Angel of Death, as he struck down arrogant mortals, right and left.

In contrast, Arachne's subject was a collection of scandalous fates and loves and quarrels among the angels. Arachne's work was quite detailed, and it was well woven, colorful, and subtle: in fact, it seemed almost perfect. Arachne's cloth had not even the tiniest flaws, and this frustrated the angel Athaliah. But then Athaliah recognized herself caricatured in the upper righthand corner of Arachne's tapestry, and the angel became absolutely furious.

Arachne's woven picture was too much for Athaliah's temper, a temper never of the mildest weathers even at its best. Athaliah jumped at the loom, she tore the insulting cloth to pieces, and she began to beat Arachne with her batten, a carved piece of cedar wood. The servants stood aghast. Arachne pulled back, she was hurt and sad and mortified;

quickly, she wound a length of heavy loom linen around her neck and she hung herself from a rafter.

Now all this noise and furor caught the attention of the good Lord God (blessed be He). He looked down from Heaven. Thunder crashed and lightning flashed, and angrily, the great Lord God intervened.

First, He loosed the linen from Arachne's neck, and He transformed the hanging-rope into a cobweb. Then, the Almighty One turned to Athaliah. "Such petty jealousy does not befit an angel. For ever, you are banished from Heaven," He ordered, and He sent Athaliah off, far into the countryside.

Now the good Lord God bent His radiant head toward Arachne, and He creased His brow. The Almighty One nodded His head and He waved His arm, and He changed the mortal woman into a spider, in which shape she still weaves. (It is because of Athaliah's cedar batten that spiders never spin webs near cedar trees, they stay away from cedar furniture, and they will not spin a web on a cedar roof.) The angry Lord God (blessed be He) turned and strode up to Heaven and gray clouds fell from His shoulders as He left, and for this reason spiders only spin their snares and gins in grays, weaving their webs on dark and cloudy days.

Athaliah was forced to wander the earth as a debased spirit, and she always remained distant from spiders. Therefore, my grandmother kept spiders in a little clay pot in the back of her pantry: this, she told me, repelled evil spirits. In fact, claimed my grandmother, a pot of spiders accounted for her amazing health, even in her old age. When she was older than me (I am eighty, you know), she rarely felt dizzy or sick or weak, and she could walk into town and back twice a day. "It is all due to spiders," my grandmother would say, patting her clay pots.

As I mentioned, my grandmother claimed that she learned of the efficacy of spiders from old tales of the mystic Achselrad of Cologne. For example, once upon a time, in the city of Bonn, there lived a wealthy Jew named Urshraga Anselm ben Aleydis. Reb Urshraga had inherited money, land, and houses from his father and from his grandfathers. One night, Urshraga had a troubling dream, and he could not forget about it the next day. The dream preyed on his mind every day thereafter, and finally Urshraga traveled north up the River Rhine from Bonn to Cologne. The dream had been so strange and so compelling and it had left him so uneasy that Urshraga Anselm ben Aleydis felt he must consult immediately the famed kabbalist, Rabbi Abraham ben Alexander, Achselrad of Cologne.

Urshraga came alone. He arrived in Cologne one morning, and he was directed to the Jewish Quarter. Rabbi Abraham was studying in the back room of the old Cologne yeshiva. Urshraga walked quickly through the prayer hall filled with wooden benches, he passed the twelve stained glass windows with their colored lions and snakes, he looked up at the Holy Ark made of stone, and he walked to the door of the back study room. There, the Rabbi was bent over a book. A number of scholars sat quietly around the room on the old worn benches.

"Rabbi Abraham?" asked Reb Urshraga.

The Rabbi looked up. "Yes?"

"Rabbi, my name is Urshraga Anselm ben Aleydis. I live in Bonn, and I have had a strange dream. I wonder, good Rabbi: could you tell me what it means?"

Carefully, the Rabbi closed his book, and he sat back in his chair. The other men listened quietly. "Tell me about your dream, Reb Urshraga," said Rabbi Abraham.

Urshraga sat on an empty worn bench along the wall. "Rabbi, it is like this—I dreamt that I was sitting in a small dark room." Urshraga looked around him: "It was a room somewhat like this one. A spider, weaving a web in the back corner, caught my eye. As I watched, fascinated, the spider web began to glow with Hebrew letters. In fact, I thought that I could recognize the words":

> Hear, O Israel, the Lord is our God. He is our one Lord. And you must love the Lord your God with all your heart and soul and strength.

Urshraga paused a moment, and he looked at the other men sitting near him. "Is this too strange, Rabbi?" he asked.

"It is strange," said Abraham ben Alexander, "but who is to say what is *too* strange. Only the good Lord God (blessed be He) is the final Judge."

"Amen," murmured the scholars on the benches.

"Please continue," said the Rabbi to Urshraga Anselm ben Aleydis.

Urshraga glanced at the other men in the room, who were watching him intently. Urshraga looked down at his feet, and he went on quietly: "Well, Rabbi, I looked at the web more closely, and I could also read these words":

> If you attend to the commandments that He has given you this day, and if you love the Lord your God and if you serve Him with all your heart and soul and strength, then here is what He shall do: He will send rain for your land in season, both autumn and spring rains, and you will gather corn and wheat and grapes and oil aplenty, and He will provide rich pasture in the fields for your cattle, sheep, and goats – you shall eat your fill always.

"I know that this is difficult to believe, Rabbi. I know that this is a long prayer to be written on one small web by a lowly gray spider – but I swear that this is what I dreamt."

"Yes, I believe you," said Achselrad.

Again, Urshraga glanced at the other men in the room, who were watching him without a word. Urshraga looked down at his feet, and he went on quietly: "There is more, Rabbi."

Urshraga was silent, and after a moment, Rabbi Abraham said: "Yes?"

"Then, Rabbi, a great wind came up. It blew away my house and my animals and my stores and my merchandise and my clothes; and I stood cold and naked. A great rain fell, and I was drenched and wet and shivering. But in the afterlight of the storm, I could see that the spiderweb still held, and the words were still embroidered there. In fact, now I could see":

> Teach the good Lord's words to your children, and speak of them indoors and out-of-doors, when you lie down and when you rise up. Then you will live long, you and your children and your children's children too, in the land which the good Lord God (blessed be He) swore to your forefathers to give them and to hold for them – for as long as the Heavens are above the earth.

The spiderweb had all this written upon it, wet with the rain and swaying in the breeze. And then I awoke.

"Well, Rabbi, I was back in my own bedroom, but the dream remained crystal clear and I was sweating and cold, and my wife says that I was shaking. I could not fall asleep again, and the dream has remained with me, vivid ever since. None of the sages in Bonn can tell me what it means, and I am worried, so I have come to you. What do you think?"

The Rabbi closed his eyes, his chin sunk to his chest, and he breathed heavily. Urshraga was not certain what to do. Finally, he said gently: "Rabbi?"

Achselrad opened his eyes. "Urshraga—Proverbs!"

"Proverbs, Rabbi?"

"Hallelujah, Urshraga—Proverbs! Specifically":

> When the whirlwind has passed by,
>   Then the wicked shall be gone;
> But the foundations of the righteous
>   Are for ever strong.

Then the Rabbi closed his eyes again.

"Yes? What does this mean, Rabbi," asked Urshraga.

"Reb Urshraga," said Rabbi Abraham, looking to the ceiling, "give all your money to charity."

"All my money?"

"Yes," said Achselrad, "give everything away."

"But Rabbi, my forefathers worked hard in order to accumulate money and property and to increase their wealth," said Urshraga. "How can I suddenly give it all away in one fleeting gesture, quite uselessly."

"Your parents accumulated much wealth here on earth?" asked Achselrad.

"They did," said Urshraga, "and they worked hard to do it."

"Then, as far as you are concerned, it is like the saying in the Book of Proverbs":

> Money, gold, and jewels
>   Are luxuries to spend,
> But the inheritance of such wealth
>   Gives no blessing in the end.

"To be honest, Rabbi," replied Urshraga, "I do not see what the problem is."

"Do you know Psalm 85, Urshraga?" asked Rabbi Abraham.

"To what are you referring, Rabbi? Why do you mention this Psalm?"

Rabbi Abraham opened his Holy Scriptures, and he read aloud:

> Love and Fidelity have come together;
> Justice and Peace have joined their hands.
> Hope and Trust grow from God's verdant earth;
> From Heaven, Goodness falls on all the lands.
>
> The good Lord God will ensure prosperity:
> We'll reap rich harvests without cease.
> God rains down Mercy on His children,
> And the path of His feet shall be at peace.

The scholars on the benches nodded and murmured "Amen."

The Rabbi looked up to Heaven. "In other words, Urshraga," said Rabbi Abraham Achselrad, "Hope springs out of God's rich and blessed earth."

"Amen," said the scholars.

"At the same time, Righteousness and Charity, Truth and Mercy look down from God's glorious Heaven," said Rabbi Abraham.

"Yes," agreed the scholars.

"Give charity," said the Rabbi.

"Amen," said the scholars.

"Accumulate learning," said the Rabbi.

"Hallelujah," said the scholars.

"Then, Urshraga," continued Achselrad, "pass these wonderful bequests on to your children – learning, my friend, is the best inheritance. Your parents accumulated wealth upon the earth. But you will have put your treasures in Heaven."

"Praise the Lord," said the scholars.

"Good Rabbi," said Urshraga, "my parents have already accumulated the wealth; now, I can go on from there. I do not need to get rid of the money. Instead, I can immediately devote myself to learning."

At this point, a white-bearded sage named Joshua ben Eliezer spoke up: "Urshraga, reflect a moment: your parents have stored their treasures in a spot where they could still be touched by human hands. On the other hand, you will have hidden your treasures in a place where no human hands can ever touch them. They cannot be tainted, spoiled, or ruined, because you will have stored great treasures within your heart."

"But—"

"My good man," continued Joshua, "recall the important insight from the Book of Proverbs":

> How much better than gold
>   It is to be thoughtful and wise;
> To learn keen discernment
>   Is better than any prize.

"Certainly," said Urshraga, "but—"

"Weave!" said another scholar, Reb Elisah. "Weave a web of study and of goodness."

"Help others with charity," added Elisah's neighbor.

"Yes," said the next sage, "your parents accumulated wealth that may yield no fruit. But you, Urshraga, still have time to create wealth that produces endless and deep good for you and for fellows."

And another scholar continued: "Hallelujah, my friends—praise the Lord. Urshraga will use his tangible wealth as fine charity. Then, Urshraga will generate learning and truth and wisdom, amen. This intangible wealth will continue to grow. And all of these acts will be in accord with the blessed verse from the Holy Scriptures in Isaiah":

> Happy is the righteous man!
> Good things come from piety.
> The selfless man enjoys forever
> The fruits of his charity.

"But my good rabbis," protested Urshraga, "is this really incompatible with being rich?"

Then another sage, Reb Menahem, spoke up and said: "When you say 'rich,' Urshraga, then you are speaking of physical, tangible things. But we say: 'Build a strong web of intangibles.'"

"Amen," said the other scholars.

"Your parents hoarded gold, jewels, money, and property," said Menahem. "On the other hand, you will have hoarded knowledge, the intangible golden treasures of the soul–and you will have dispensed your earthly tangibles. As the verse from the Holy Scriptures in Proverbs says":

> The sweet fruits of righteousness
>   Fill the Tree of the Lord–
> Those who serve with humility
>   Harvest a rich reward.

The men in the back room all nodded and murmured.

"Yes, yes, I understand, rabbis," said Urshraga, "but must I give away *all* my money?"

The scholars shook their heads, and Reb Moyses ben Nathan said: "Urshraga, my friend, you are saving your money in the vague hope that it will pass to your children. But think a moment, Urshraga–the world is filled with unpredictables. The wheel of fortune revolves in unknown ways. In the end, you will have no control."

"Your money may be stolen," said one scholar.

"Your money may be senselessly taxed," said the next scholar.

"Your children may spend the money foolishly," said a third scholar.

"All your wealth may go for the benefit of some unknown persons," continued Moyses ben Nathan. Then, he added quietly: "It may even end up supporting the pagan Gentile gods."

Again the men nodded, and a vague murmur rumbled through the little back study room.

"On the other hand, if you give to charity now," said Reb Menahem.

"If you return home and dispense alms tomorrow," said Reb Elisah.

"If you disperse your wealth next week," said Reb Joshua.

"If you finally empty your purse," said Reb Moyses, "you will have used the money for the benefit of people whom you know. And then, Urshraga, a most wondrous thing will happen. The goodness will bounce back – it will forever rebound, and it will benefit yourself. As it is written in the Holy Scriptures, in Deuteronomy":

> If a man is poor, then do not sleep in the cloak that he has pledged to you, even if he now owes it to you. Instead, give it back to him at sunset as charity so that he may sleep in it. Return his cloak and give him a blanket besides, and he will bless you. Then such good deeds will be counted to your credit in the sight of the good Lord God.

"Amen," said Reb Elisah, and a murmur of agreement rolled along the benches.

"This is difficult," said Urshraga. "Your message is clear – but my family is used to a life of ease."

Reb Baruch coughed and in his raspy voice he said: "Urshraga, do not blame your family. Listen to what we are telling you. Your parents stored their things in this mortal and dirty world. On the other hand, you will have set aside true wealth in the pure clean world to come. As the Holy Scriptures say, in Isaiah":

> In the end, your own light
> Will shine like the dawning sun,
> And you will grow strong and wise
> From the charity you have done.
> Your righteousness will march
> Before you like a shield,
> And the glory of the Lord
> Shall protect you far afield.

"Now, Urshraga, if you give your money away thoughtfully, if you make the world about you a happier place, if you ease the difficulties of the poor, if you make the hungry child smile, then would you still say that you will have given charity uselessly?"

And what could he answer to that, Rabbi? So, Urshraga said: "Amen, good scholars." And he went home. Urshraga went home, and he gave all his wealth to charity, and it is said that when he died, many, many years later, it was on a Sabbath during Passover. . . .

What? No, no—do not get up on my account, Rabbi: I was just resting my eyes a moment. I was resting and musing. . . . To tell you the truth, Rabbi, I was remembering a later adventure of Reb Urshraga.

After meeting with Achselrad, Urshraga Anselm ben Aleydis returned to Bonn a changed man. Much to the consternation of his relatives, he gave away every bit of his wealth. He took to wearing the same gray robe every single morning, he began to attend the small local yeshiva twice a day, and he became a devout and pious scholar. In the spring, he marveled at the green grasses, he wondered at the misty mornings, and he talked to himself aloud when he saw the tiny blue tangleberry flowers. During all these transformations, Urshraga's wife smiled, for she had always been a pious woman and she was proud of her husband.

Not far from Urshraga's house was the Jewish bakery, and in the yard behind it lived a very poor neighbor whose name was Isaac. Yes, his name was just "Isaac"—no one knew his father's name or his family. Isaac lived in a shack that was no more than an old wooden box. Every morning, whenever Urshraga went to the yeshiva, he put four pennies in the socket of the doorhinges in the poor man's shack. Urshraga went to pray early in the morning, and when Isaac opened the door to go out, he always found four lucky pennies.

One day, poor Isaac thought to himself: "Who is giving me four pennies every day? Is it a friend? Is it an angel? Or is it an evil spirit? I simply must find out." So Isaac hid early one morning, at the edge of his shack.

On the day that the poor man was on the watch, Urshraga awoke late. Hurriedly, Urshraga put on his *tallis katan*. Then his wife said to him: "Just a moment, dear, and I will go with you as far as the market." Eventually, the couple managed to leave, and soon they were passing by poor Isaac's shack. As usual, Urshraga planned to put some money in the door jamb. However, when he neared the old shack, Urshraga saw that Isaac was crouched down, hiding along the side.

"Quick," said Urshraga to his wife, "follow me." And Urshraga began to run toward the brick ovens behind the bakery.

"Why are we running?" asked his wife.

"I saw that Isaac was hiding by the door of his house," said Urshraga. "I do not want him to see me: he would feel ashamed if he knew that I was giving him money, especially since now we are poor ourselves."

Urshraga and his pious wife reached the back wall of the bakery building. They saw no place to hide; then, Urshraga thought of the ovens. The bread ovens were vaulted redbrick chambers, almost like rough cemetery mausoleums. Each oven was as long as a wagon and as wide as a person is long, and each oven was almost a meter in height. The loaves of dough were put in and the warm breads were taken out on long wooden shovels pushed through an iron door. Urshraga opened the door to the nearest oven, and he and his wife climbed right inside through the bread door. The door was warm, and it squeaked and creaked when it closed behind them.

The ovens were being heated for the day's baking, and already they were hot inside. After he had been in the oven for a few minutes, Urshraga began to try to distract himself from the heat by reciting from the Proverbs of the Holy Scriptures:

> Never rob a defenseless man,
>   Aid him selflessly;
> Never scorn a hungry wretch
>   Nor plague his family.
> God, our Heavenly Father,
>   Will shield the humble and weak;
> He will punish the wicked bully
>   And will redeem he who is meek.

This made him feel no better, and Urshraga said to his wife: "My goodness, it is terribly hot in here! My knees and my legs are baking; my shoulders are burning up."

"I feel awful, too," said his wife.

"But," asked Urshraga, "how can this be? Am I not a charitable man? Am I not pious? Did we not jump into this oven in order to do a good deed? How can the holy Lord God (blessed be He) allow us to roast to death?"

"My dear husband," said his wife, "it is true that you are doing your best—and I love you for it. Still, there is nothing strange in the fact that the ovens are hot: this is a bakery, you know. We climbed into the oven of our own free will, and I am not certain that you can hold the good Lord God accountable if we are baked into dry and lifeless *matzohs*. Remember the tale told by old Rabbi Meir of Palestine":

One day, a mosquito landed on the horn of a bull. After it had stayed there, resting for a long time, the insect felt like moving on again. The bull was a formidable beast, so the mosquito politely asked the bull: 'Would you mind if I go now?'

'Were you speaking to me?' said the bull.

'Yes,' said the mosquito, and it repeated its question.

'Listen, you tiny gnat,' answered the bull, 'I did not notice when you came, and I will not notice if you go.'

"I suspect," continued the wife, "that the Almighty Lord God is like the bull in Rabbi Meir's fable: He may not be attending to us at this moment. I suggest that we get out of this oven right now, on our own." And so they did.

And my grandmother would ask: "Why did these good people take so great a risk? Why did they hide in a heated oven?" Then she would give me a pat on the head and she would smile and answer the question herself: "They hid because they could not put poor Isaac to shame. It is better to risk your health than to embarrass someone in public. Remember, little man, never make your friend blush. The Talmud tells us that each person has his limitations and that each person is beset by troubles. Therefore, we must be tolerant; in fact, we must be more than tolerant–we must go out of our way in order to help others, if we are to share in the rewards of the Great Hereafter. Selfless good deeds will be counted to your credit in the sight of the good Lord God, amen."

abbi, I am glad to see you here alone. I want to apologize for my outburst during the service this evening. It was just that Reb Anton said to me: "Now that you are eighty years old, you are living in the shadow of your life, old man." In the shadow, indeed! Evil spirits live in shadows—they shun the light, they lurk in the darknesses. In order to avoid the glare of the sunlight, demons live in shady places, perils crouch in the shadows, dybbuks crawl and creep in the gray corners of the towns.

What is that, Rabbi? A casual comment? No, this is a serious matter. In the olden days, in the strict and pious days of our forefathers, shadows were no jesting subject. For example, my grandmother would always preface her demon tales with a talmudic warning about shadows:

Five shadows are dangerous because of their evil spirits, their demons and dybbuks. These are the shadows of: a single palm, a lotus tree, a caper tree, a service tree, and a fig tree. Also, some rabbis warn about the shadows of a willow tree and of the mast of any ship.

Remember, the general rule is this: the more branches that a tree has, the more dangerous is its shade; moreover, when its thorns are sharp, then its shade is *especially* dangerous.

Shadows were serious and they were important to my grandmother, and it was my grandmother who told me the famous story of Rabbi Petahiah and the African shadows.

Exactly, Rabbi—that was Petahiah ben Jacob (the brother of Rabbi Isaac "the Wise" of Prague), a rabbi who undertook a tour of the entire world. Eventually, Petahiah wrote about his adventures in a book *Sivuv ha-Olam* ("Around the World"). Rabbi Petahiah's travels took place in the days of Achselrad, well before Asher ben Yehiel was the chief rabbi of Cologne. Why do I mention Rabbi Asher? When he was the leading scholar in Cologne, Asher spent most of his time writing and reading, studying the Torah and the Talmud in the little back room of the yeshiva; this room was where for centuries the Cologne rabbis had passed hours and hours working and thinking and arguing with themselves. Above the back study room was a loft for storage. One day, when he was rooting around among the manuscripts in the loft, Rabbi Asher found a letter from Rabbi Petahiah of Regensburg to Rabbi Abraham ben Alexander, Achselrad of Cologne. The letter had to do with shadows, and it reminded Rabbi Asher of a problem that was brought to him once by a man named Anselm of Osnabrueck.

Once upon a time, there lived a man named Anselm of Osnabrueck. As you know, Rabbi, Osnabrueck is almost seventy-five kilometers northeast of Cologne. An ancient walled town, it is the home of a mint and it has a large marketplace that trades in hogs, hens, and horses. Also, Osnabrueck is the seat of the regional Bishop, and in the center of the town, there is a Roman Catholic cathedral with three towers. The Jewish Quarter was, as usual, at the edge of the town, and in it lived Anselm. He was a wealthy merchant, and one day Anselm purchased a large house near the synagogue in the Jewish Quarter.

Anselm's house was made of wood, but it had a stone cellar and a stone foundation. In the back, there was a courtyard with a small vegetable garden and a well for drinking water; just beyond the garden, there was a shed for goats. After a while, Anselm's wife decided that they should build another story on the top of the house, so that her sister could come and live with them. There was a large double-walled chimney on the front roof over the living room and kitchen. Therefore, Anselm decided to build a set of gabled rooms over the back half of the house, behind the chimney. Because Anselm was a wealthy man, the City Council of Osnabrueck agreed to permit him to raise his new gables as high as he wished.

Anselm's house was across an alleyway from the synagogue, and both the synagogue and Anselm's house were opposite the central community building, which was the Jewish City Hall. As the work on Anselm's house proceeded, Jews meeting in the City Hall admired the carvings along the woodwork. However, during those same weeks, Jews meeting in the synagogue began to have a dispirited feeling— apparently, the new house was casting a long shadow late in the day, and the stained glass windows of the prayer hall in the synagogue were not always lit by the afternoon sun.

Eventually, the third story on the house was completed, the workmen were paid, the furniture was moved in, and Anselm's sister-in-law came to live there. Not long afterward, the newly-arrived children began to have constant coughs and wet noses; then, Anselm's children developed aches in their arms, rashes on their chests, and pains in their backs. Anselm's wife had difficulty bending in order to pick things up, especially early in the morning, and Anselm himself was out of breath every time that he climbed the stairs. What was happening? Had an evil dybbuk taken up residence in the cellar? Was the well behind the house haunted by a demon?

Anselm talked with the scholars in Osnabrueck, and then he talked with the Rabbi. No, he had had no special warning dreams. No, he had not done an impious deed. Finally, the Osnabrueck Rabbi suggested that Anselm consult the head rabbi of Germany, Asher ben Yehiel of Cologne. So Anselm kissed his wife good-bye and he journeyed to Cologne on the River Rhine; there, he asked Rabbi Asher's advice.

Rabbi Asher listened carefully, but he was not certain what the problem was. "Let me come to Osnabrueck myself; I should see the situation with my own eyes," said the Rabbi to Anselm.

So Asher packed a small satchel, and he accompanied Anselm to Osnabrueck. First, they traveled north along the River Rhine to Wesel, then they followed the Lippe River east, and at Dulmen they took a wagon northeast along the old road to Osnabrueck. Once inside the walls of Osnabrueck, the Rabbi immediately saw what was wrong: "Look at your house, Anselm," said the Asher ben Yehiel.

"Yes, Rabbi?"

"Anselm, your house is too tall."

"Too tall, Rabbi?" said Anselm in surprise.

"It is too tall, Anselm. Your house is built higher than the synagogue: it casts a shadow over the holy building. This makes the stained glass windows of the synagogue dark, even on bright sunny days. The air has become unholy because your house is too high," said the Rabbi.

"Then this is the cause of our mysterious maladies?" asked Anselm.

"Definitely," said Rabbi Asher, "and, my friend, did you not tell me that your newborn child has a patch of skin as dark and as gray as an afternoon shadow?"

"Yes."

"That," said Asher, "is because your wife prayed in the synagogue while she was pregnant. Your wife prayed in the shadows cast by your own tall house."

Anselm raised his eyebrows and he pursed his lips. He thanked the Rabbi, he contributed two gold coins to the poorbox, and he reported to his wife what the Rabbi had said; then, the couple had the third story of their house torn down. Anselm saved the ornately carved gable-work, and he had it installed on the low roof of a new room – an extension on the first-floor level behind the house in the courtyard. Then, Anselm and his wife and his children and his sister-in-law and her children lived in the bright pious light of the good Lord God, and they all remained healthy from that day and for ever more, amen.

Petahiah? Yes, if you will just be patient, I am coming to him, Rabbi. You see, one day when he was rooting around among the manuscripts in the loft above the back study room in the Cologne yeshiva (a building that was brightly lit and gently warmed by the unimpeded late afternoon sun of the good Lord God, blessed be He), Rabbi Asher ben Yehiel found a letter from Rabbi Petahiah ben Jacob of Regensburg to one of Asher's predecessors, Rabbi Abraham ben Alexander, Achselrad of Cologne:

*"My dear Rabbi Abraham* – (began the letter)

"I have just met a fine young man, a Jew from Vienna. He has agreed to carry this letter to my good friend, Rabbi Natronai of Vienna, who I am certain will then arrange to transport it to you. I write to wish you and your family well, to convey my fondest greetings to all the Jews of your blessed community in Cologne, and to praise the good Lord God (blessed be He) and His Almighty Name for ever and ever, amen.

"I will not trouble you with the details of my many wagon rides and my subsequent sea voyages. Suffice it to say that they safely brought me here to the Oriental regions, regions that are so near to the great Holy Land where someday the Messiah shall return and deliver us and resurrect all souls and rebuild the Temple on Zion, amen. I write now in order to record for you some details of the lands and peoples that I have seen in these old and foreign regions. The bright and glorious hand of God is visible everywhere, if we only look – praise the Lord Yahweh-Elohim.

"Needless to say, my old friend, I have had many, many adventures in arriving here. I hope – with the good Lord willing – to relate these events to you in person. Let me just say that after touring the Holy Lands of Palestine, I turned west, and I ventured into Africa. Most recently, I have been in Aethiopia (which, as you know, is sometimes called Abyssinia); it is a most ancient district of northeastern Africa. I have wandered for weeks throughout this remarkable land. It is a microcosm of all the world: in one day's journey I passed from tropical heat to Alpine cold.

"And what does the country here actually look like? In the valleys and lowlands, the vegetation is dense; on the plateaus, it is barer, but there are many trees and bushes. The glens and ravines and gorges on the hillsides are thick with woods – they contrast markedly with the open downs. It is to this northern land of Aethiopia that the Lost Tribe of Israel has finally retired. Yes, Abraham, I refer to that Lost Tribe which will be the last to reassemble when the Messiah arrives and when the trumpets blow on the great Day of Resurrection; as it is said in the Book of Isaiah:

> On that golden jubilant day
> A trumpet blast will sound aloud:
> Abyssinia and Egypt will hear it play.

The horn will waken from their shrouds
Dead souls, who'll fly up far away
To Zion, under God's white clouds.

"In the south of Aethiopia, the vegetation is more luxuriant. I have seen date palms, mimosa, wild olive, and giant sycamores; there are junipers and laurels. Myrrh and other gum trees, gnarled and stunted, fill the eastern foothills. An absolutely magnificent pine grows here, called the Natal yellow pine. And fruit trees? I saw figs, oranges, limes, pomegranates, peaches, and apricots. (Oh, and let me not forget the bananas, grape vines, blackberries, and raspberries.) Fields of cotton and indigo plants carpet the valleys, and in some places there is sugar cane. It is a Garden of Eden, good Abraham.

"One of the strange and holy plants growing here is the K'hawah plant; it comes from the Kaffa country, so the plant is also called *coffea*. K'hawah is an evergreen bush, growing taller than two men; it has shiny green leaves and red berries. The natives make a drink from the dried beans that are found in the berries. I have tried the brew – it is bitter but somehow magical. Apparently, animals that browse on the beans become joyous at night: they cannot sleep. The brewed drink dissipates drowsiness and prevents sleep, and it is used by some Mohammedans to remain awake during prolonged religious services. The clergy condemn this practice as an evil drug-induced state, but young men in large cities continue secretly to drink the thick black K'hawah, sweetened with much sugar cane.

"The myriad plants are wondrous, but it is the Aethiopian animals that show the true richness of the Lord God's great sixth day of Creation. In addition to the domestic animals, there are elephants and rhinoceros – beasts like armored cattle with two horns pointing forward from the nose. There are hippopotamus and crocodiles in the large rivers. In the plains are lions, leopards, hyaenas, and jackals, and these chase the herds of zebras, antelopes, and gazelles. Of course, there are the remarkable giraffes of which we often heard when we were young – frankly, Abraham, I must confess that until a few weeks ago I had always thought them to be mythical beasts. And everywhere are thousands of varieties of butterflies and other insects: truly, the land is thick with colorful beasts.

"Early on, I spent some days in the capital city of Harrar. Harrar is built on the slopes of a hill above the countryside. The whole city is enclosed by a stone wall, with five gates and twenty-four stone towers. The streets are steep and narrow and dirty, and they are paved with rough boulders. The houses are made of unfinished stone and mud and they are flat-topped. Every possible corner of the town is noisy and filled with markets, small and large, devoted to the K'hawah trade and to durra, ghee, cattle, mules, camels, skins, hides, ivory, gums, and cotton.

"Most cityfolk of Harrar are Mohammedans, members of a sect from Persia, but every once in a while you will meet a black Jew. Aethiopian black Jews are the Tenth Tribe, the Lost Tribe, the fabled black Israelites. I have talked with them and prayed with them, and I find that they have been insulated from our Judaism for a thousand years. All of their religious practices come directly from the Torah. They know nothing of the oral tradition, nothing of the detailed understandings written into the Talmud; for example, they do not understand the rites of circumcision or the rites of purification in the *mikveh* baths. I would guess that they lost all contact with the mainstream of Judaism immediately after the destruction of Solomon's Great Temple. (May it be rebuilt speedily in our days, amen.)

"As best as I can reconstruct, the Aethiopian Lost Tribe descends from the dark-skinned Jews of the ancient kingdom of Israel – it must have been those black Israelites who fled when Shalmaneser and Sargon beseiged Samaria and then deported thousands upon thousands of Israelites. The black Jews fled to Abyssinia, and they isolated themselves in the old Hebrew religion. The Lost Tribe kept other cults at a distance; they walled themselves off from the Canaanite and Mesopotamian idol worship (against which the holy Prophets had railed out). It is remarkable now to see these people: they look so different from us, but they are our cousins. Of course, good Abraham, in the end, we all share God-given souls – it is just as the Holy Scriptures remind us in the Book of Proverbs":

> As one face answers another face
>   When reflected in the water,
> So one man's heart answers another's heart
>   All the world over.

"Before the separation of the Lost Tribe from the fold of Israel, the black Jews and the white Jews lived together: they lived together in

Palestine. Today, the black tribes live in another world, but I was able to visit this world for a time here in Aethiopia. In fact, I was the guest of a king and queen of the black Israelites; these Jews were wooly-haired and as black as carob, brown as the finest of thick stews, and beautiful to behold. They and all their people dress like the Arabs. Men wear a large white robe over close-fitting pants that extend below the knees. Women wear smocks with deep loose sleeves, fit tight at the wrist—and the women love strong pungent scents. In hot weather, no Aethiopian goes without a fan of woven reeds. And in any season, men of importance always wear a long curved knife in public.

"My host, the king, was quite agitated, and as soon as he had an opportunity, he drew me aside. Now, Abraham, let me mention that here in Aethiopia, holy men are esteemed—and pious dreams, omens, and visions are taken very seriously. For instance, dreams are used to solve problems and to interpret disquieting events. How is a crime solved? First, a holy man is summoned; if his prayers fail, then he takes a drug and whatever person he dreams of is accused as the criminal. Great attention is paid to the words and the prophecies of a holy man; therefore, when he found that I was a rabbi, the king called me aside in his royal court. 'Rabbi,' he began, 'my queen has borne a child who is white-skinned, and I am unsure how to proceed.'

"We were alone; the king looked down for a moment. 'I am wondering if I must send away my child and my wife,' said the king slowly.

"I was not certain what to say, Abraham. I closed my eyes for a moment. Fortunately, the good Lord God (blessed be He) spoke within my heart, and I recalled the Holy Scriptures. 'Ah, your majesty,' I said, 'I counsel against that rash action, whatever the cause. Remember the Book of Proverbs, in the Holy Scriptures'":

> A child delights his father and his mother:
> Parents rejoice in their child for ever.

'And recall, too':

> Home and wealth may come down from ancestors,
> But a fine wife is a gift from the Lord.

" 'Yes, yes, I understand,' said the king, 'but listen, Rabbi: I and my queen are quite black, and yet my wife has borne a child who is pale and white. I am afraid that I must send them away, for undoubtedly I am not the true father. Otherwise, there is some evil witchcraft afoot. In either case, I must rid myself and the kingdom of my queen.'

"I knew that polygamy is common in Aethiopia; I have even heard that there is a saying here: 'Brothers coming from different mothers will always be enemies'—imagine a culture that needed such aphorisms, Abraham. But I restrained myself from judgment, and I said: 'Do not be in a hurry, good king. Let me ask you a question: Are the walls of your palace and the pictures painted on them white or are they black?'

"The king answered: 'The walls are white and glittering and spotless; the pictures are light and airy and sunny.'

"Then I said: 'Ah—clearly, your child has to be white also.'

" 'Why is that?' asked the king.

" 'The white pictures,' I said, 'made an impression on your wife; therefore, your child is white. You see, your child resembles the objects that your wife looked at and thought about. We learn this from the Torah, in the story of Jacob from Genesis. Do you remember the passage' ":

> Jacob took fresh rods of white poplar, almond, and plane tree, and he peeled off strips of bark, exposing the bare rods. Then, he fixed the peeled rods upright along the troughs at the watering-places where the flocks came to drink. The multicolored rods faced the she-goats when they came to drink, and later the goats gave birth to young that were striped and spotted and brindled, just as were the wooden rods that their mothers had seen.

" 'Moreover,' I continued, 'in the town of Regensburg, in Germany, where I am the Rabbi, there was once a man who built his house too near the Catholic cathedral: he lived in the Christian shadow day and night. His wife became pregnant, but she spent all her time in the shadow of the cathedral, and when the child was born, it was as dark and as dim as the shadow of the Church of Obermunster, the Cathedral of Regensburg.'

"The black Israelite king heard all this. He listened, and he nodded. The color of his child, said the king, was not as deep as the heart within – if every woman has bright and light and pious thoughts, then she will have a bright and light and pious child.

"So, the king and the queen were reconciled, and I left happily. I must end my letter now – but, dear Abraham son of Alexander, think of me as you read this letter in your holy study in Cologne. Think of me, and remember always to have pious thoughts, to live in the light, in the bright and the magic light of the good Lord God (blessed be He). The Lord gives wondrous gifts to us as children in the light of our youth, and He redeems us again as children in the light of our old age – hallelujah and amen, good Abraham.

*Your childhood friend,*
*Petahiah, the son of Jacob"*

ello, Rabbi, I will be with you in a moment—I cannot leave until every tablecloth is folded; otherwise the day has not ended properly. . . . There, now I am finished at last and I can sit next to you by the stove.

I am not sleepy either. Everyone says that old people are always falling asleep; frankly, I sleep less now that I am old. It is the nature of old men to go into their last days awake and open-eyed. Ah, Rabbi, what have I done to deserve a long life? I doubt whether I really fulfilled any of Ada's rules. Ada? Oh, I first heard of Reb Ada from my grandmother.

My grandmother used to say that one time, long ago, the pupils of a certain scholar, Reb Ada ben Ahaba, came to the yeshiva and asked him: "Old father, what have you done in order to live so long?"

Now, Ada ben Ahaba was ninety-four years old. His hair was like thin cotton, his nose was pointed north, and his eyes squinted, winked, and blinked—also his hearing was no longer good, so he answered: "What? What are you saying, boys?"

The students said more loudly: "Reb Ada, you have reached a very advanced age. What were your special good deeds? What have you done to cause the Almighty Lord God (blessed be He) to give you such long life?"

"Long life?" said old Reb Ada. "Everyone always asks me the secret to long life. How should I know? How can I be certain?"

The students looked at one another. "But, Reb Ada," said one boy, "you are the oldest man around–if you do not know about long life, then who else could we ask?"

Reb Ada squinted and he blinked. "Ah, my young impatient scholars, who can you ask indeed! Read the Holy Scriptures–and in that regard, you might recall the Book of Proverbs":

> Like empty clouds and winds
> > That bring no enriching rain
> Is he who boasts of talents
> > That he never could sustain.

"Now, boys, I am a simple man. How have I lived my life? There is nothing that would surprise you. I can only say: Hold your tempers. I have tried never to be angry with members of my household. Also, young men, I respected all my elders, and I never spoke before the sages had their turns."

Reb Ada went on muttering, words that the students could not hear, then he continued more loudly: "I listened to the learned, I did not bother them with small points, and I avoided excess questions. As is written in the Proverbs":

> A wise man's teaching
> > Is a fountain of life
> For one who would escape
> > Dumah's cruel knife.

"Then," added old Reb Ada, "I never studied Torah in a dirty room, and I never walked four cubits without thinking a holy thought, without God's great Law in mind, or without *tefillin* strapped in place. In the prayer hall or study rooms, I never slept or dozed: I tried my best to stay awake. As is written in the Proverbs":

> Listen, My student,
> > Take My teachings as guide,

Know My commandments,
  Study Law at My side –
And the years of your life
  Shall be far multiplied
As the lights in the heavens,
  Thick with stars far and wide.

"Finally, when another man fell, I never laughed aloud, and I was never happy for long while my neighbor was sad. I always respected a man's full name, and I did not ridicule his family.

"So, boys, if there are any special good deeds that I have done (and frankly, I am not certain that there really are), then these be they, amen."

Yes, Rabbi, my grandmother said the same things for herself – just as with old Reb Ada, my grandmother could not decide what particular good deeds extended her long life. "All your years past seventy are a gift from the good Lord: every extra day is special," she would say. Seventy years, you ask? Why, that is a magic age, and my grandmother mentioned it often. Her favorite old rabbi, the mystic Achselrad of Cologne, lived to seventy years of fine old age. And in his seventieth year, he had a strange encounter:

Once upon a time, said my grandmother to me, there lived in Germany on the wide River Rhine, a very pious man named Abraham ben Alexander, Achselrad of Cologne. In his younger years, Abraham traveled far; once, he visited King Ferdinand II of Castile. (Although on that southern trip, Abraham called himself "Nathan Alexander" for some unknown reason.) Ferdinand II was king of Leon. His reign of thirty years was fairly unremarkable, although there was constant petty fighting until he beheaded some unruly local nobles. King Ferdinand was a simple man with no political talents. When he died at the age of sixty-one, Ferdinand II was thought of as a good knight and as a stalwart soldier. But I cannot help wondering: Did he die happy? As my grandmother once told me: "The truly happy man, the man with God's warm blessing, is he who ends a full life contented with himself."

What is that, Rabbi? Old Abraham ben Alexander? Well, my grandmother reported that "Nathan Alexander" had spent one holy Sabbath in the royal court of King Ferdinand II at Leon, in Northern Spain. There, surrounded by the courtiers, Achselrad dissolved an attendant page boy: he made the young man disappear, dispersed in thin air after dinner. No, Rabbi, I am not inventing this – my grandmother vowed this is exactly what she had heard.

And this same strange Rabbi Abraham was a prolific writer, too; but his most famous kabbalistic tome, the *Keter Shem Tov*, a book of mystic lore, has never been published. It lies in the Cologne yeshiva as forgotten crumbling papers above the rabbi's study room. Grandmother said that it was one night while writing in this vast book that Rabbi Abraham looked up, and in the yellow light of the candle on his desk, he saw a holy sight.

Abraham ben Alexander was seventy years of age. In his later years, he had written many books, he had thought deeply for many long hours, and he had seen many strange and wondrous things. But his favorite memories were still of early days, springtimes when he and Petahiah were small yeshiva students, when they played in the fields outside the city walls, and when they lay on dusty banks of the wide River Rhine in warm weathers with rains falling gently all around. Old Abraham suddenly thought back, and he remembered these fine times. Abraham smiled and felt a cool wind and saw a springtime light. Was it like this long ago on a warm afternoon, when the rains fell gentle upon his face? The candle flickered lightly, and Rabbi Abraham ben Alexander thought that there in the doorway of the old yeshiva of Cologne on the River Rhine stood a stooped and ancient man with a dusty beard.

"Hello?" said the Rabbi.

The figure remained silent, and the old Rabbi blinked and he winked and he rubbed his eyes. "Old man," said Rabbi Abraham, "are you really there? Old man, in the doorway, who are you?"

The figure in the doorway wavered dimly. Was it the candlelight? Were Achselrad's old eyes playing tricks?

Achselrad was an old man. He sat with an old man's slouch, and he waited with an old man's patience, watching with old man's eyes. So, eventually, the specter smiled and it spoke, and when the figure

talked, it talked in an ancient voice: "Yes, I am an old man, Abraham—
I am old, and you are old, too."

Abraham was silent. Then he said: "Yes, old and bent myself—
and I suppose not far from death. . . . But, friend, I am happy, and I
think that I still choose life."

"Life is fine," said the ancient voice from the door.

There was a light quietness, and Rabbi Abraham answered. "Yes,
life is fine, for the most part. But death, I suspect, is not. Death, I think,
is not so fine: Dumah is a fearsome foe," said Rabbi Abraham Achselrad in Cologne, long ago.

"Death is not so fine?" The spirit wavered in the door. "Dumah
is to be feared, old man?" The candlelight flickered again. "Achselrad,
I think that you misunderstand death."

The Rabbi blinked, and he raised his eyebrows up. "Misunderstand cold death? What do you mean by this?" And then Rabbi
Achselrad added: "Perhaps, my ghostly friend, I might address you by
your name—if I may ask: Who are you?"

The figure hovered in the door; a light breeze blew through the
room. "I am Simeon, son of Johai," said the old man. "My name is
Simeon."

Did the figure fade a bit beyond the candlelight? Old Achselrad
rubbed his eyes: "Simeon ben Johai—Rabbi Simeon, is it really you, the
student of Akiva, from far Palestine?"

"Yes, Abraham."

And Achselrad was silent a moment. Then he asked: "Good
Simeon tell me this: Did you write the golden *Radiance*? Are you the
author of the *Zohar*?"

"The *Radiance*? It is a fine title, Rabbi Abraham; yes, it is a fine
title indeed. Of course, that was long ago. Has it been five hundred
years—or a thousand years or more? Has it been that long since I dug
my toes in the warm and holy sands of Palestine? I wrote much in
those young days, my friend, and much that I wrote felt radiant—at
least that is what I remember."

Abraham ben Alexander sat quiet, thinking softly. Did the rain
fall gentle on your face in Palestine like it did beside the River Rhine?
"Yes, a thousand years is a long, long time," thought old Rabbi
Achselrad. Then Abraham ben Alexander looked up and he said out

loud: "Rabbi Simeon, tell me then: What do you mean when you say that I misunderstand death?"

"Achselrad, old man," said the specter in the door, "there are two possibilities, two at least—maybe three or four. On the one hand, death may be an endless, sound, and dreamless sleep; it may be bliss, the final peaceful rest. In this case, we should welcome it, embrace it with no fear."

Again, Achselrad was silent, thinking quietly; his mind mused, and there seemed to be no hurry in the rabbi's room at the edge of the wide River Rhine. After a while, Achselrad seemed to wake again, and he said: "Perhaps there would be no fear, but would we welcome such a death?"

"Rabbi Abraham—pick out that night on which you slept so soundly as not even to dream. Then compare this rest with all the other nights, with all the other nights and days of your long life. Tell me truly: Have you ever had any better or happier days or nights?"

And Achselrad was quiet, for he did not know what to say.

"Why," continued Simeon, "were death to be like this, then even the great Lord God Himself (to say nothing of us common folk) would have to admit that it would be the finest and the most gracious of ends."

Again Achselrad was quiet. Then he said: "Perhaps." He tapped his finger on his desk and he said: "Perhaps." Abraham ben Alexander looked along the benches by the study wall, he looked at the piles of prayer books, and he looked at the dim figure in the doorway. "Still, Rabbi Simeon, such a death is final and blank and empty. It seems an acquiescence. Must one merely give up? After a lifetime of struggling to live up to the good Lord's holy Laws, how can you simply close your eyes and sleep effortlessly, forever? This is not the heroic course, Rabbi Simeon—it cannot be God's wish."

The specter wavered in the doorway, beyond the light. "Ah, Abraham, a dreamless sleep is but one possibility. In contrast, the Sages say one *can* persist heroically, even after death. Perhaps one *can* continue to follow out one's pious tasks among the shades of those righteous men who passed before our time, the shades who wander now in the gentle fields of Heaven's *Gan Eden*, nestled in the rolling hills of roses, chicory, and asphodel."

Gentle fields? Rolling hills? Abraham Achselrad smiled and he remembered long ago, a springtime when he and young Petahiah basked in the sand and the sun and caught gray grasshoppers in the coarse grass outside the cemetery by the old River Rhine.

But Simeon ben Johai was talking to Achselrad again: "Abraham, are you listening? My friend, death is fated for us all. Do not fear black Dumah—fear only an unhappy end. Fear death only when it ends a worthless life. Only then is death a sad finale. The truly happy man, the man with God's warm blessing, is he who ends a full life contented with himself. To him, Dumah brings a fine and gentle end."

Again, the specter of Rabbi Simeon wavered in the door. "Good Abraham, my friend, do you know Odysseus's tale?"

Achselrad was musing. Or, had he dozed a moment? "Odysseus?" asked Achselrad. "Do you mean the ancient Greek, the warrior and the sailor, the hero of old Homer?"

"Yes," said Simeon, "Odysseus was long-suffering, a patient sea-borne warrior. He roamed far and wide, trying to get home from the great Greek war at Troy. It was Odysseus who tricked Kyklopes; it was he who strung the bow in his dining hall and slayed the two score suitors camping at his door. It was Odysseus who finally came home to his wife and son and father on the island of Ithaca, a home worn breath floating on the deep-waved sea."

Yes, a home-worn breath. And old Abraham Achselrad looked beyond the door, remembering long ago. He saw an early warm fall day, many years before, when he and young Petahiah lay on the bank of the River Rhine and rain fell gently on their faces for ever and a day.

Then Rabbi Simeon was talking again: "At one point in his trip, his long and painful journey across the ocean's deeps, Odysseus received the prophecy of his own gentle death. The vision came from Teiresias, seer and prince of Thebes; it came when Odysseus traveled down into Sheol, into the pit of endless night. Deep within the Land of the Shades, Odysseus heard of his own death. I remember well this prophecy, Abraham. Teiresias said to Odysseus:

> After weathering sore trials more
> (And after death you put
> To two score suitors at your door)
> Go overland on foot,
> And on your shoulder place an oar.

Walk to a far community
Where men still live with saltless meat,
Never having known the sea
Nor seen red bows of a golden fleet
With gleaming hulls that grace
The seas in swift and foam-sprayed flight.

You'll recognize the place,
For a passerby will soon recite:
"Ho! – what sort of winnowing fan
Is that you carry in your hand?"
Halt there, by that old sea-less man,
And plant your ship's oar deep inland
In the dirt, among the plants.

Then turn around again,
Without a backward glance
At man or oar or earthy glen;
Return home peacefully
To Ithaca, a home-worn breath
Floating on the deep-waved sea.

And then, fair friend, a sea-borne death
Awaits for you like mist –
Quiet, gentle, soft like tears,
Drifting in, to assist
When you are tired with seventy years.

Then all your children's children's race
Will be forever blessed with grace
And gentle winds will them embrace;
While soft rains you'll forever taste
Upon your peaceful, sleeping face.

"Abraham, I remember this because I was seventy when I died.
And I recount the prophecy, because now you too have seventy gentle
years upon your sleeping face," said the specter of old Simeon to Rabbi
Abraham. Abraham ben Alexander, Achselrad of Cologne, heard this

once long ago. It was when he was an old man dozing in front of the stove in the rabbi's study room of his small yeshiva, along the dark wide medieval River Rhine. It was many, many years ago, Rabbi Petahiah, it was many years ago.

*Tam Venishlam Shebah la'El Borei Olam*

Complete and done, praise be to God, Creator of the World.

# ACKNOWLEDGMENTS

Brief versions of some of these tales can be found in:

Abrahams, I. (1896). *Jewish Life in the Middle Ages*. New York: Macmillan.

_____ (1911). Halevi. In: *The Encyclopaedia Britannica*, 11th ed., vol. 12, p. 835.

_____ (1911). Meir. In: *The Encyclopaedia Britannica*, 11th ed., vol. 18, p. 83.

_____ (1911). Rashi. In: *The Encyclopaedia Britannica*, 11th ed., vol. 22, pp. 911–912.

_____ (1911). Sabbation. In: *The Encyclopaedia Britannica*, 11th ed., vol. 23, pp. 962–963.

_____ (1926). *Hebrew Ethical Wills*, Parts One and Two. Philadelphia: The Jewish Publication Society of America.

Barker, E. (1911). Godfrey of Bouillon. In: *The Encyclopaedia Britannica*, 11th ed., vol. 12, p. 172.

Bloch, C. (1925). *The Golem. Legends of the Ghetto of Prague*. Vienna: John N. Vernay.

Brewer, E. C. (1949). *Brewer's Dictionary of Phrase & Fable*. Revised & enlarged. New York: Harper & Brothers.

Cohen, A. (1949). *Everyman's Talmud*. New York: E.P. Dutton & Co.

Dickinson, E. (1950). I dwell in possibility. In: *The Oxford Book of American Verse*, ed. F. O. Matthiessen, pp. 413–414. New York: Oxford University Press.

Gaster, M. (1934). *Ma'aseh Book. Book of Jewish tales and legends translated from the Judeo-German.* Philadelphia: The Jewish Publication Society of America.

_____ (1934). Some stories about Jewish women. In: *The Jewish Library. Third Series,* ed. L. Jung, pp. 29–64. New York: The Jewish Library Publishing Company.

Graetz, H. (1894). *History of the Jews.* Vols. 3 & 4. Philadelphia: The Jewish Publication Society of America.

Greenstone, J. H. (1906). *The Messiah Idea in Jewish History.* Philadelphia: The Jewish Publication Society of America.

Handford, S. A., trans. (1954). *Fables of Aesop.* Harmondsworth, Middlesex, England: Penguin Books.

Hahn, A. (1879). *The Rabbinical Dialectics. A History of the Dialecticians and Dialectics of the Mishnah and Talmud.* Cleveland: Bloch & Co.

Jacobs, J. (1911). Jew, The Wandering. In: *The Encyclopaedia Britannica,* 11th ed., vol. 15, pp. 36–363.

Katz, M. J. (1988). *Socrates in September: The Entanglements of Complexity.* New York: Peter Lang.

Kisch, G. (1949). *The Jews in Medieval Germany. A Study of Their Legal and Social Status.* Chicago: The University of Chicago Press.

Kober, A. (1940). *Cologne:* In: The Jewish Communities Series, trans. S. Grayzel. Philadelphia: The Jewish Publication Society of America.

Krappe, A. H. (1930). An Indian tale in the Midrash Tanchuma. In: *Papers and Transactions. Jubilee Congress of The Folk-Lore Society, Sept. 19–Sept. 25, 1928,* pp. 277–283. London: William Glaisher.

Loewe, H. M. J. (1911). Maimonides. In: *The Encyclopaedia Britannica,* 11th ed., vol. 17, pp. 430–431.

Lonnrot, E. (1969). *The Old Kalevala and Certain Antecedents.* Cambridge, MA: Harvard University Press.

O'Sullivan, M. (1933). *Twenty Years A-Growing.* Trans. M. L. Davies and G. Thomson. New York: The Viking Press.

Rose, H. J. (1959). *A Handbook of Greek Mythology.* New York: E.P. Dutton & Co.

Spoer, A.M. (1930). Notes on some Hebrew amulets. In: *Papers and Transactions. Jubilee Congress of The Folk-Lore Society, Sept. 19–Sept. 25, 1928,* pp. 293–313. London: William Glaisher.

Straus, R. (1939). *Regensburg and Augsburg.* In: The Jewish Communities Series, trans. F. N. Gerson. Philadelphia: The Jewish Publication Society of America.

North Sea
England
Atlantic Ocean
Cologne
Mainz
Rhine
Paris
Worms
Germa
France
Rhone
Leon
Toledo
Cordova
Mediterranean
N. Burgard